THE TIDE WAS ALWAYS HIGH

The Tide Was Always High is part of Pacific Standard Time: LA/LA, a far-reaching and ambitious exploration of Latin American and Latino art in dialogue with Los Angeles, taking place from September 2017 through January 2018 at more than 70 cultural institutions across Southern California. Pacific Standard Time is an initiative of the Getty.

Pacific
Standard
Time: LA/LA
Latin American
& Latino Art in LA

Presenting Sponsors

 The Getty

Bank of America

THE TIDE WAS ALWAYS HIGH

The Music of Latin America in Los Angeles

EDITED BY

Josh Kun

PUBLISHED WITH THE ASSISTANCE OF THE GETTY FOUNDATION

UNIVERSITY OF CALIFORNIA PRESS

University of California Press, one of the most distinguished university presses in the United States, enriches lives around the world by advancing scholarship in the humanities, social sciences, and natural sciences. Its activities are supported by the UC Press Foundation and by philanthropic contributions from individuals and institutions. For more information, visit www.ucpress.edu.

University of California Press
Oakland, California

Chapter 3 was previously published in *From Tejano to Tango: Latin American Popular Music,* ed. Walter Aaron Clark, 252–76. Perspectives in Global Pop. Gage Averill, series editor. New York: Routledge, 2002.

Chapter 5 was printed with the permission of the Los Angeles Philharmonic and Hollywood Bowl Museum.

Chapter 6 originally appeared as "On the Trail of Yma Sumac: The Exotica Legend Came from Peru, but Her Career Was All Hollywood." Copyright © 2017. Los Angeles Times. Reprinted with Permission.

Chapter 8 first appeared in Hans Ulrich Obrist's book *Conversations in Mexico.*

Chapter 12 was reprinted by permission of the author.

Library of Congress Cataloging-in-Publication Data

Names: Kun, Josh, editor.

Title: The tide was always high : the music of Latin America in Los Angeles / edited by Josh Kun.

Description: Oakland, California : University of California Press, 2017. | Includes bibliographical references and index. | Description based on print version record and CIP data provided by publisher; resource not viewed.

Identifiers: LCCN 2017005579 (print) | LCCN 2017011577 (ebook) | ISBN 9780520967533 (ebook) | ISBN 9780520294394 (cloth : alk. paper) | ISBN 9780520294400 (pbk. : alk. paper)

Subjects: LCSH: Popular music—California—Los Angeles—Latin American influences. | Popular music—California—Los Angeles—History and criticism. | Latin Americans—California—Los Angeles—Music—History and criticism.

Classification: LCC ML3477.8.L67 (ebook) | LCC ML3477.8.L67 T53 2017 (print) | DDC 780.89/68079494—dc23

LC record available at https://lccn.loc.gov/2017005579

Manufactured in the United States of America

26 25 24 23 22 21 20 19 18 17
10 9 8 7 6 5 4 3 2 1

CONTENTS

PREFACE: THE MUSIC OF *LA/LA*

IN 2011, I CURATED an exhibition at the GRAMMY Museum for the first installment of the Getty Foundation initiative **Pacific Standard Time: Art in L.A. 1945–1980**. Titled *Trouble in Paradise: Music and Los Angeles 1945–1975,* the exhibition explored multiple post–World War II histories of civic unrest and social change through musical movements that reverberated across the city. The show mixed artifacts, ephemera, and photography with listening stations, film clips, and an interactive jukebox—and its accompanying *Pacific Standard Time* streaming playlist on Pandora.

For the second iteration of the Getty initiative, *Pacific Standard Time: LA/LA,* dedicated to artistic explorations of the relationships between Los Angeles and Latin America, we have tried something different. Instead of a fixed exhibition, I proposed to curate a series of live musical events, or "musical interventions"—concerts, installations, gallery performances—that would take place at multiple museums across the city, each in conversation with the themes and subject of various exhibitions. These musical experiences would all be historically engaged as contemporary performative interpretations of "LA/LA" musical history. They would all be committed to a focus on musical historiography and live reimagination—live archival remixes, live archival reperformances that revisit the LA musical legacies of Yma Sumac, Juan García Esquivel, João Donato, and many more. For details on these performances, as well as additional visual ephemera and historical photographs we were not able to include on these pages, please visit our project website: tidewasalwayshigh.com

In order to plan these performances, I assembled a research team of journalists, scholars, and musicians to begin thinking through the long history of Latin America's relationship to the music and sounds of Los Angeles. We began with a simple, but loaded, question: What does the relationship of LA/LA sound like? How to even begin unraveling the connections between Los Angeles and Latin America through music? This volume is our attempt to answer those questions and presents the result of much of our collective research. A blend of previously published articles, poems, and interviews with newly commissioned studies, histories, and conversations, *The Tide Was Always High* is meant to serve both as a kind of background catalog, or research dossier, for the live musical events happening throughout the fall of 2017 and as a stand-alone volume that we hope adds to the already rich legacy of Los Angeles scholarship and literature.

We realized very quickly that our ambitions would overreach what we could do in a single volume; an exhaustive study of the role of Latin America in LA music is a life's work, not a single book. So many genres and scenes, musicians and movements, do not appear in these pages—Latina/o techno, house, hip-hop, the thriving Regional Mexican industry, *rock en español* luminary turned film composer Gustavo Santaolalla, for starters—especially contemporary ones currently unfolding since the break of the twenty-first century like the latest waves of backyard punk and ska house parties, Latin alternative, and new school *cumbia*. Our focus on the impact of Latin America on Los Angeles rather than Los Angeles on Latin America meant not delving into histories like the influence of Mexican-American *pachucos* on Mexican music and film star Tin Tan. Our focus on popular music styles left little room for exploring parallel Latin American histories in the Los Angeles classical and art music scenes.[1] Thus, what follows is meant as an introductory primer to a range of issues—from the work of Latin American session musicians and Latin American composers in Hollywood to Brazilian musicians changing the sound of 1970s LA jazz and funk, contemporary hip hop and salsa dance companies, and contemporary Oaxacan brass bands—that have shaped my thinking during the launch of this project. The book openly builds off the previous scholarship of Steven Loza and Anthony Macías, both of whom have produced detailed historical accounts of Mexican and Mexican American music in Los Angeles, and off the long history of work on Chicano/a music on the greater Los Angeles Eastside and beyond.[2] But then it keeps listening for other directions and other histories that, I hope, open up a new way of thinking about the broader Latin American musical influence on Los Angeles. Ultimately, this volume adds to work that helps us to continually engage with counterhistories of Los Angeles and to passionately embrace genealogies of musical production that alter what we thought we already knew about a city so deeply made of sound.

NOTES

1. See, for example, Gerard Meraz, "Backyard Parties: 1980's East L.A. DJ Culture," *KCET.org*, August 2008; Javier Cabral, "Metralleta de Oro: Bringing the Bling to Cumbia," *KCET.org*, January

2014; Angela Boatright, *Los Punks: We Are All We Have* (Vans Off The Wall films, 2016); Sam Quinones, "Sing Now, Die Later: The Ballad of Chalino Sanchez," *LA Weekly,* July 29, 1998; Romeo Guzmán, "Mexico's Most Celebrated Pachuco: Tin Tan," *KCET.org,* February 23, 2017; Helena Simonett, *Banda: Mexican Musical Life Across Borders* (Middleton: Wesleyan University Press, 2001); George Lipsitz, *Footsteps in the Dark: The Hidden Histories of Popular Music* (Minneapolis: University of Minnesota Press, 2007), chap. 3; Sarah Bennett, "A New Kind of Latin Alternative Music Is Breaking Down Old Barriers in L.A. and Beyond," *LA Weekly,* March 22, 2017; and Tricia Tunstall, *Changing Lives: Gustavo Dudamel, El Sistema, and the Transformative Power of Music* (New York: W.W. Norton, 2013).

2. Steven Loza, *Barrio Rhythm: Mexican American Music in Los Angeles* (Champaign-Urbana: University of Illinois Press, 1993), Anthony Macías, *Mexican American Mojo: Popular Music, Dance, and Urban Culture in Los Angeles, 1935–1968* (Durham: Duke University Press, 2008); David Reyes and Tom Waldman, *Land of a Thousand Dances: Chicano Rock n' Roll From Southern California* (Albuquerque: University of New Mexico Press, 2009).

ACKNOWLEDGMENTS

THIS VOLUME ORIGINATED as part of an idea first discussed in a conversation with Joan Weinstein, Deputy Director of the Getty Foundation. I thank her immensely for all of her support and vision, and for believing in me enough to helm this project. I also thank Getty Foundation Director Deborah Marrow and the Getty Foundation for making it possible through generous grant support, and senior program officer Heather MacDonald for patiently holding my hand through the grant process. Thank you also to PST's Gloria Gerace for her enthusiasm for this project. The shape, content, arguments, and structure of this volume are the direct result of a research grant from the Getty Foundation that enabled me to think alongside an incredible team of research advisors, whom I thank for their generosity and expertise: Betto Arcos, Martha Gonzalez, Brian Cross, John Koegel, Carol A. Hess, and Cindy García. USC Annenberg's Calvin Cao and Matthew Terhune were instrumental to structuring and administering the grant award. Special thanks are also due to Nathan Masters, Giao Luong Baker, and Danica Schroeder of the USC Libraries, Ljiljana Grubisic, Katelyn Welch, and Leni Boorstin of the LA Philharmonic and the Hollywood Bowl Museum, Christina Rice, Terri Garst, and Xochitl Oliva of the Los Angeles Public Library, Pat Varriale, Andrew Morris, and Rick Baptist of the

American Federation of Musicians union, Ale Cohen and Mark McNeill of Dublab, Max Shackleton and Hans Ulrich Obrist, Loni Shibuyama at ONE Archives, Oliver Wang, Steve Kader, Julio César Morales, Gary Garay, Chris Veltri, Alberto López, Camilo Lara, Todd Simon, Rafael Figueroa, Ricardo Bracho, Adrian Rivas, and, for his cover design, the incredible Stephen Serrato. Gratitude is also due to all of the musicians who generously agreed to take the time to sit down with us for interviews (what an honor to have learned from your stories), with a special nod to Arice Da Costa, Mateo Laboriel, and Krishna Booker for working with us on the project, and to Berenice Esquer and Yatrika Shah-Rais, whose transcriptions and translations were essential. Thanks also to Courtney Cox and Samanta Helou for their final-hour help with the manuscript. Major thanks to Niels Hooper and his UC Press team for diving into this with us and getting the book, heroically, to the finish line. Lastly, this volume's incredible copilot has been my research assistant and project manager, USC Anennberg doctoral student Perry Johnson. Without her scholarly chops, her tireless coordination, and her rigorous research, this book would never be in your hands.

INTRODUCTION

The Tide Was Always High

Does L.A. Stand for Los Angeles or Latin America?

—RUBÉN ORTIZ-TORRES

Los Angeles, para ti, tengo mi cha cha cha

—TITO RODRÍGUEZ

BLONDIE WERE A TRIED and true New York City band. They were formed in New York, lived in New York, and made music about New York. Denizens of the city's fabled downtown punk and new wave scene throughout the 1970s, they ran with some of New York's finest artists—Warhol and the Velvet Underground and the Ramones—and were children of some of New York's finest clubs—CBGB and Max's Kansas City.

But in 1980, the West Coast called, and they relocated to Los Angeles for two months to record their fifth album, *Autoamerican*. They were stationed at the iconic United Western Recorders on Sunset Boulevard, the hit-making headquarters of LA-produced classics by Frank Sinatra and Ray Charles, the place where the Beach Boys made *Pet Sounds* and the Mamas and the Papas cut "California Dreamin'." In a memo he wrote for the band's fan club newsletter during their City of Angels stay, Blondie guitarist and cofounder Chris Stein suggested that the new album wouldn't just be recorded in LA but might somehow be of LA, that the city's history as a capital of sunshine and noir, good vibrations and bad vibrations, myth and antimyth, might just rub off the band's sound. He wrote,

Los Angeles, the city of lost angels, and angles. Dreamland. And, of course, Hollywood. L.A.'s not really a tough town. It has a strange feeling of fragility. Earthquakes on the brain may be part of the reason why the surface always seems about to crack with delicate tension. The fires burn the hills. The Strip still throbs dull reds and pinks, and the lights of the Valley still look beautiful in the hot, dusty nights ... Every day we get up, stagger into the blinding sun, drive past a huge Moon-mobile from some ancient sci-fi movie that lies rotting by the side of the road and into L.A. proper. The Strip. The sessions get under way.[1]

Among the songs produced during those early September sessions was "The Tide Is High," originally written by Jamaican legend John Holt and recorded by his rock steady trio The Paragons in 1966. Blondie's version replicates the original's classic Caribbean reggae strut—a sound that had vibrantly left its mark on the sound of new wave and punk scenes in New York and London—but then throws in a Latin American curveball. They nudge it closer to nearby Mexico and Cuba: the melody is played by trumpets and violins in the style of modern Mexican mariachi and the percussion section surrounds a steel drum with congas and timbales typically found on rumbas and mambos. It wasn't just the city's sunshine mythology and seismic doom that had made their way into the new album. It was the city's position as a key geographic and cultural hub within greater Latin America, the city's history as a Mecca of Mexican music and as a laboratory for experiments in Afro-Cuban dance music in East Los Angeles pasta restaurants, downtown ballrooms, Sunset Strip supper clubs, and Hollywood sound stages. The city had indeed rubbed off.

For the mariachi melodies of "The Tide Is High," Blondie hired a crew of the city's top session musicians that included Pete Candoli, Bill Peterson, and Dalton Smith on trumpets, and Sidney Sharp, Joe Lyle, and Tibor Zelig on violins.[2] Between them, they had dates with Elvis Presley, Elmer Bernstein, Frank Zappa, The Emotions, and Stan Kenton on their resumes, but because of the city where they worked—because they were of LA—they could lay down a mariachi horn swoon like they had just arrived in Guadalajara from the Mexican countryside. Mariachi music, long a musical symbol of Mexican national culture, has been part of the LA soundscape since at least the 1930s, when early mariachi recordings beamed over on local Spanish-language radio, immigrant audiences could hear mariachi in imported Mexican movies like *Santa* and *Allá en el Rancho Grande,* and the city's own network of working mariachi musicians began to take shape.[3]

The first major mariachi to take the music modern and commercial, Mariachi Vargas de Tecalitlán, played Los Angeles in 1940 and by the end of that decade LA had Jeanette's, a pioneering mariachi restaurant that showcased some of Mexico's biggest acts. Mariachis became as common a sight at birthday parties and tourist destinations like Olvera Street as they did on some of LA's biggest stages: the Million Dollar Theater, the Hollywood Bowl, and the Los Angeles Sports Arena. While LA has been home to multiple variations of mariachi style, it's where the idea of mariachi spectacle, a "show mariachi" or "restaurant mariachi," took off. Mariachi Los Camperos de Nati Cano became the featured nightly attraction at La

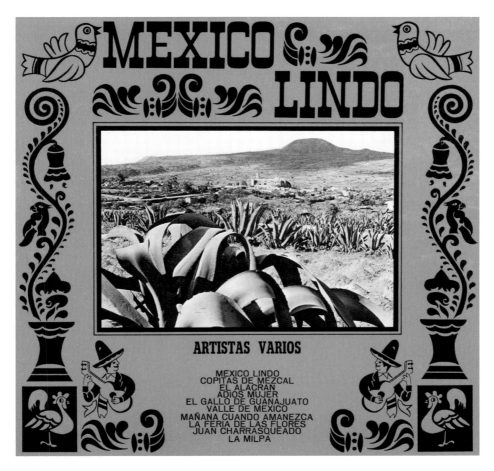

MEXICO LINDO

ARTISTAS VARIOS

MEXICO LINDO
COPITAS DE MEZCAL
EL ALACRAN
ADIOS MUJER
EL GALLO DE GUANAJUATO
VALLE DE MEXICO
MAÑANA CUANDO AMANEZCA
LA FERIA DE LAS FLORES
JUAN CHARRASQUEADO
LA MILPA

Mexico Lindo, Discos Azteca, 1960s, Idelsohn Society for Musical Preservation Archive.

Fonda restaurant in 1967, and soon the idea of a mariachi-themed evening of drinks, dinner, and dances was an LA staple. Universities, colleges, and high schools across Los Angeles have had their own mariachi ensembles since the 1960s (most famously, Uclatlán of UCLA), the same period when the city's Roman Catholic churches began slipping mariachi into mass.[4] LA was also the first city where formally "Americanizing" mariachi seemed like a good idea. In 1960, the small Beverly Hills record label CG issued *Mariachi Americana,* a collection of "great mariachi favorites sung in English." Local radio personalities Rita and Antonio De Marco handled the English, and the esteemed Mariachi Chapala, who had already relocated to Los Angeles from Jalisco and become the house band at Club Granada downtown, handled the harps, horns, *vihuela,* and *guitarrón.*[5]

So the stage was well set for a non-Mexican Los Angeleno like Herb Alpert to launch A&M Records with his Tijuana Brass version of mariachi pop that would become one of the best-selling and most ubiquitous sounds of the 1960s.[6] Or for Sunset Strip psych rockers

Mariachi Americana, CG Records, 1960, Idelsohn Society for Musical Preservation Archive.

Love in 1976 to slip mariachi horns onto "Alone Again Or" or for Jackson Browne to cut "Linda Paloma" with a traditional mariachi lineup of harp, violin, *vihuela,* and *guitarrón.* The harp came courtesy of LA mariachi Arthur Gerst, who once played with Mariachi Sol de Mexico and also added mariachi touches to songs by Warren Zevon, Lowell George, and Harry Nilsson. You can hear him on the latter two's recordings of "Cheek to Cheek," penned by George with Van Dyke Parks and Martin Kibbee about a gringo in Mexico who "came all the way from Marina del Rey / on a plane yesterday / From the gray LA air," and falls in love with a Mexican woman on Rosarito Beach. Putting mariachi front and center in a new wave reggae cover as Blondie did might have seemed new, but by 1980 it was already an established LA tradition.

As was adding Afro-Cuban percussion where you might not expect it. On "The Tide Is High" it came courtesy of the only Latin American musician on the session, Alex Acuña. Born in Peru, Acuña first came to LA in the 1960s on tour with Cuban mambo architect Pérez Prado and recorded on his Hollywood-tinged *Lights! Action! Prado!*, a Cuban dance floor makeover of popular film scores. By the time he hooked up with Blondie, Acuña had already introduced Peruvian rhythms into the jazz fusions of Weather Report's *Heavy Weather* (recorded in North Hollywood). Joni Mitchell, who frequently came down from the foothills of Laurel Canyon to let loose on the 1970s salsa dance floor at Club Virginia's, invited him to lace her *Don Juan's Reckless Daughter* with thickets of Latin American percussion (listen for him on the rhythm quest of "The Tenth World" and the tourist fantasy of "Dreamland"). He joined LA-based musicians from Costa Rica, Argentina, Brazil, and Cuba to launch the pan-American jazz fusion band Caldera, and sprayed timbales into the barrio disco-funk of Argentine composer Lalo Schifrin on the soundtrack to *Boulevard Nights*—Hollywood's first low-rider homage to East LA street life.

After Blondie, Acuña would continue to be one of LA's most in-demand session hires and one of the key links in the city's Latin American musical chain. He was part of a community of Latin American immigrant session players—many of them interviewed in chapter 10—who since the 1960s have been the invisible rhythm and horn section worker bees behind hundreds of the most commercial and influential recordings in rock, R&B and jazz. When nightclub dance floors lit up at the opening bass line of Herb Alpert's 1979 hit "Rise" (and when a generation later their kids lit up when it was sampled on Notorious B.I.G.'s "Hypnotize"), they were nodding their heads to Mexican bass player Abraham Laboriel Sr. When Roy Ayers's Ubiquity and The Commodores needed a saxophone to punctuate their vibrational LA funk, they turned to Justo Almario, the Colombian saxophonist who learned to play listening to his home country's heroes Pacho Galán and Lucho Bermúdez.

Once the *Autoamerican* recordings were done, Blondie went back to New York. For the photograph on the album's cover, they posed on a Manhattan rooftop, the Empire State Building looming behind them. Latin American Los Angeles wouldn't get the credit, but it was there in the skyline's shadows, in the grooves, a secret West Coast ingredient that forever changed an iconic East Coast sound.

THE LATIN AMERICAN CADENCE OF LOS ANGELES CULTURE

Music and musicians from Latin America are inextricable from the development of Los Angeles as a modern musical city.[7] This volume listens for the musical urbanism of Los Angeles through the ear of Latin America. It makes the argument that the musical life of this dispersed and dynamic metropolis is shaped by immigrant musicians and migrating, cross-border musical cultures that not only have determined LA's "harmonies of scenery," but have been active participants in the making of the city's modern aesthetics and modern industries.[8]

The cultural and national alchemy that went down in the "The Tide Is High" session is but one example of just how intertwined the music of Los Angeles and the music of Latin America have been since the very birth of the city in the eighteenth century. As Sidney Robertson Cowell reminded back in the 1930s, there was in fact no Anglo-Saxon music in Los Angeles until the mid-nineteenth century; before then, "Americans were numerically few and transient."[9] The original music of Los Angeles belonged to Gabrielino Indians, Mexican vaqueros, and Spanish friars and mission bands long before it began sounding like anything else. "Twenty years after the discovery of gold," Carey McWilliams wrote, "Los Angeles was still a small Mexican town."[10]

For all of the demographic and cultural shifts that were to come over the next century, to make music in Los Angeles—whether it be surf rock, bebop, gangsta rap, or cosmic canyon folk—has always borne an echo of that small Mexican town and has always meant, to some degree, engaging with the sonic traditions and experiments of Latin American music and the musical histories of immigrant Latin American musicians. This is both by virtue of its location and history (Mayor Eric Garcetti likes to call LA "the Northernmost city of Latin America") and by virtue of its multi-immigrant populations (a city that has always been a key hub for immigrants from across Latin America).

There is no music of Los Angeles without mariachi and *banda* and s*on jarocho,* without bossa nova and samba, without mambo and cha cha cha and salsa, without Latin jazz helping West Coast jazz find its sound, without R&B and rock tuning "south of the border" or "South American Way." Or to musicalize the opening question from artist Rubén Ortiz-Torres, how could we listen to LA (Los Angeles) without the music of LA (Latin America)?[11] How could we listen to Latin America without the music of Los Angeles? The city's distinctive musical urbanism is unthinkable without Latin American migrant sounds and migrant musicians. "Boom in Latin rhythms bigger than ever in L.A.," jazz magazine *Down Beat* declared in 1954, but truth is the boom was always booming, the tide was always high.[12]

Los Angeles, we might say, has a Latin American *cadence.* Inspired by Ralph Ellison's now famous aside in *Time* magazine that America is "jazz-shaped," Robert G. O'Meally has convincingly written that there is a "jazz cadence" embedded within the experiences of twentieth-century American culture—a jazz "effect" or jazz "factor" that has informed speech, style, dance, poetry, film, and politics to such a degree that jazz emerges as "the master trope of this American century: the definitive sound of America in our time."[13] There is a wider argument to be made elsewhere that the musical styles of Latin America have similarly "shaped" American culture and politics in the twentieth century—the mariachi cadence of American culture, the mambo cadence, the samba cadence—but within the history of Los Angeles, the Latin American cadence is hard to ignore: among the city's most consistent beats, its most influential set of rhythms and melodies, are those that have arrived after traveling through a century or two of cultural contact and musical creativity in the Americas and across the African Diaspora.

In John Fante's classic Los Angeles novel *Ask the Dust,* published in 1939, the Italian immigrant protagonist Arturo Bandini struggles to survive LA and its one song that never leaves him alone: "Over the Waves." Played repeatedly in the novel by a small group of musicians at the downtown Columbia Buffet restaurant, it scores his embattled relationship with the "Mayan Princess" waitress Camilla and by extension his embattled relationship with the Mexican roots of the city. It's the soundtrack to his awakening to Latin American Los Angeles and to his own position as a down-and-out writer living off oranges in his Bunker Hill apartment. The only other hint of music in the novel is also tinged with Latin America: a Central Avenue nightclub called Club Cuba.

"Over the Waves" began its life as "Sobre Las Olas," a European-style waltz written in Mexico by the composer and violinist Juventino Rosas. Rosas took the song to New Orleans for the 1884 New Orleans World Cotton Centennial Exposition sugar expo and both he and the song stayed on, introducing the latter's cross-border, cross-continental swells to both the classical and jazz repertoires of early-twentieth-century New Orleans.[14] As "Over the Waves," it became a staple for the city's working musicians, and most likely found its way to Los Angeles as New Orleans and other Southern musicians—such as Jelly Roll Morton (who went on to play in Tijuana, Mexico) and Leon René (who wrote "When It's Sleepy Time Down South" beneath the palm trees)—began to migrate west in the 1920s and 1930s. By the time Bandini couldn't escape it, "Over the Waves" was a migrant song that had become an LA staple, music from Latin America that had traveled over borders and represented, however covertly, the Black and Brown histories of all those who traveled over the waves to make Los Angeles their home. Even though Fante didn't point it out, "Over the Waves" was a musical prompt to ask the dust, to ask history for answers, to listen to what decades later the Chicano-led band Rage Against the Machine would call "the Battle of Los Angeles": the music of empires clashing.

Many scholars have asked the musical dust of Los Angeles—officially a Mexican city in 1821—about its Mexican pasts and Mexican futures. Steven Loza and Anthony Macías have both written indispensable long-form studies of the multiple facets of Mexican musical life in Los Angeles, and John Koegel and Kenneth Marcus, among others, have provided us with detailed research on the influence of Mexico on the shaping of the city's earliest musical cultures, industries, and communities.[15] Histories of regional Mexican music in LA, *banda* and *corridos* especially, also abound. And with good reason: no other Latin American music culture and no other population—spanning a century of immigration waves over the California-Mexico border—has played such a foundational role in the history, culture, and politics of the city.[16]

No wonder that of the few city statues in Los Angeles dedicated to musicians, two are from Mexico: revered composer and singer Agustín Lara and ranchera idol Antonio Aguilar. While Lara's statue in the middle of Lincoln Park hearkens back to the 1930s and 1940s when he was beloved by Mexican and Mexican American audiences in Los Angeles, the statue of Aguilar—erected in La Placita de Dolores at the El Pueblo de Los Angeles Historic Monument—is in direct dialogue with the contemporary moment. The working-class and immigrant-conscious genres that Aguilar helped popularize in his songs and feature films—*ranchera, banda, norteño*—are among the most popular and most commercially successful in twenty-first-century Los Angeles among both immigrant communities and Latina/os born and raised here.[17] In their essays for this volume, Martha Gonzalez and Xóchitl Chávez build on these histories by exploring Mexican music in Los Angeles at the turn of the twenty-first century in the *son jarocho* scene in East Los Angeles and the Oaxacan brass bands of

Koreatown and South LA—both chronicles that extend the legacy of Mexican music's role in shaping cross-border, immigrant imaginations and politics.

Beyond Mexican Los Angeles, though, the wider story of the musical interconnection between Latin America and Los Angeles has been less robustly told. That the city's rock, pop, jazz, funk, and hip-hop cultures all can trace some roots to Latin America is an open secret among musicians and fans but one that has been little documented by scholars and journalists. Much of that other history lives in the liner note essays of LPs, in band personnel credits and musicians' union session archives, in the oral histories and memoirs of label execs and musicians, and in the small print of *Billboard* magazine calendar blurbs, nightclub ads, and micro concert reviews. What they collectively reveal is that so much of the music we have come to know as belonging to Los Angeles, as being of Los Angeles—be it Ritchie Valens work-shopping "La Bamba" in a Silver Lake home studio (belonging to Del-Fi Records' Bob Keane) or Lalo Schifrin putting bongos at the foundation of the *Mission: Impossible* theme or even the Beach Boys wearing huarache sandals—has come over the waves and over the borders of the Americas.

Take, as just one example, the way that the history of West Coast jazz in Los Angeles is often told. In "A Letter from Los Angeles," a 1959 screed for *Jazz: A Quarterly of American Music,* Kenneth Hume bemoaned the lack of both legitimate jazz clubs and legitimate jazz scenes in Los Angeles, "a musically unfortunate city." He divided the city's jazz musicians into two categories: the "recording cadre" (musicians who are active in studio sessions) and the "underground people" (a mix of self-destructive creative giants and talented players stuck playing strip clubs).[18] All of the musicians he lists are either white or Black. Yet by the time he wrote about *disappearing* jazz, Latin American and Latina/o musicians mixing jazz with Afro-Cuban rhythms and instrumentation were *appearing* everywhere in the city, from the Lighthouse and the Interlude to the Zenda and Avedon Ballrooms to Ciro's and the Mocambo. The decade in which Hume was writing was the heyday of Latin jazz in Los Angeles; it was impossible to miss, yet remained socially invisible—loud and noisy and yet completely inaudible. Latin musicians and Latin bands were the hidden third category in Hume's jazz report. They were under the underground, *los de abajo* (to borrow the title of Mariano Azuela's novel of the Mexican Revolution from 1915), a brown musical underworld.

These omissions and hierarchies have been chronic in jazz history. In his detailed and influential history from 1992 of "the development of modern jazz in California," Ted Gioia notes Latin American and Latina/o musicians on the bandstands and in the album credits, but he rarely hears their contributions; they are more incidental than instrumental. Gioia categorizes "the west coast jazz movement" as breaking down into either "the black bebop-drenched sound" or the "white heavily-arranged music," a binary that leaves little room for the Latin American music and musicians that were inseparable from the music's West Coast development.[19] One of Gioia's key milestones in LA jazz is the debut recording in 1952 by the Lighthouse All-Stars, *Sunday Jazz a la Lighthouse,* which brought the crew of musicians who had been experimenting with bebop at Howard Rumsey's Lighthouse Cafe in Hermosa

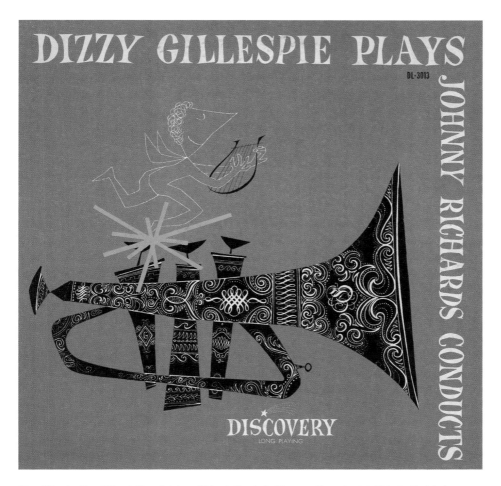

Dizzy Gillespie, *Dizzy Gillespie Plays & Johnny Richards Conducts,* Discovery Records, 1950, Idelsohn Society for Musical Preservation Archive.

Beach into the studios of Radio Recorders in Hollywood. In the center of the album is a pugilistic jazz mambo, the album's showstopper, "Viva Zapata!," written by local trumpet star Shorty Rogers. "As the name implies," Gioia writes, "the piece is more Mexican than Afro-Cuban, and Rogers sounds as though he had just served a long apprenticeship in a mariachi band."[20] It's an odd reading of a piece that has nothing mariachi and little Mexican about it, but is a jagged Afro-Cuban dance composition based around conga drums and clave patterns (my own blurb: if "Salt Peanuts" had been written in Cuba, it might sound something like "Viva Zapata!").

Carlos Vidal, a Lighthouse regular whose name is too often overshadowed by the LA bebop limelight, plays the percussion on the song. Born in Cuba, Vidal was a veteran of Machito's band and one of the first percussionists to ever commercially record Cuban rumba. He was one of the reasons the Lighthouse band frequently dipped into Latin

American styles: they recorded three mambos (including an ode to the Los Angeles neighborhood of Los Feliz) and more casual dalliances like "Mexican Passport" and "Latin for Lovers." In 1950, Vidal played congas on *Dizzy Gillespie Plays & Johnny Richards Conducts,* which featured Gillespie on arrangements by the Mexican-born composer Richards (he changed his name from Juan Manuel Cascales).[21] Recorded in Hollywood for local indie label Discovery Records, the album includes Richards leading Gillespie through a version of the African American spiritual "Swing Low Sweet Chariot" that slowly transforms into a stripped-down Cuban rumba.

Four years after his first Lighthouse sessions, Vidal released his own solo jazz album, *Congo Drums,* on LA label Tampa Records, a rhythm showcase of "jazz with a feel of Latin undercurrent." In the album's liner notes producer Robert Scherman made a push for Vidal and other Latin American musicians to receive more credit for shaping the stylistic innovations of West Coast jazz. "You cannot get good Latin jazz with musicians of the American jazz school only," he wrote, "They just don't feel it or at least, it has been my experience, they don't play it." Vidal is joined by Tony Reyes on bass, Robert Gil on piano, Tony Rizzi on guitar, and bongo player Mike Pacheco (a Pérez Prado and Peggy Lee alum), whose "love of Sunny California is a well known fact and he will stray from home shores only on rare occasions." The best-known musician on the session, though, was drummer Shelly Manne, a dominant and influential figure in West Coast jazz, who only gets a "featuring" credit on an album that is "starring" Carlos Vidal—a clear attempt to reshuffle the listener's expectations of how a jazz album from Los Angeles might be received.

The Latin American influence on the shaping of jazz in Los Angeles was not limited to the Lighthouse. The "Latin Tinge" of classic New Orleans habanera-inspired jazz had been in LA since Jelly Roll Morton showed up in the early 1920s.[22] Trumpet star Howard McGhee, usually credited as being one of the first bebop musicians to hit LA after World War II (he recorded with Charlie Parker for the Dial label in Hollywood in 1946), was also a member of Machito's legendary "Cubop" band that pioneered the melding of Afro-Cuban styles with modern jazz. Most of the biggest names in Los Angeles jazz—from Shelley Manne to Gerald Wilson—engaged with Latin American music and musicians.[23]

In the late 1950s, LA-based jazz pianist turned popular singer Nat "King" Cole didn't just do one LP of Spanish-language hits and standards, he did three: one recorded in Havana, one in Rio, and one in Mexico City. South Central–born French-Jewish saxophonist René Bloch got his start playing jazz at Roosevelt High School before joining Johnny Otis's band at the Club Alabam. But by the 1950s, he became "Mr. Latin," as one of his albums pitched him. He toured with Pérez Prado, recorded on his mambo smash "Cherry Pink and Apple Blossom White," and led his own Latin bands at the Bolero Inn in East LA and the Club Seville in Hollywood. He cut his own Latin dance albums with Juan Cheda, Willie Bobo, Mongo Santamaría, and others, and penned the first mambo dedicated explicitly to Chicano dancers, "Mambo Chicano." In the late 1960s, he was also briefly part of the progressive genre swapping of the Afro Blues Quintet— a rotating ensemble of white, Black, and Latina/o musicians—who had been merging jazz, blues, and soul with Latin music for most of the decade.[24]

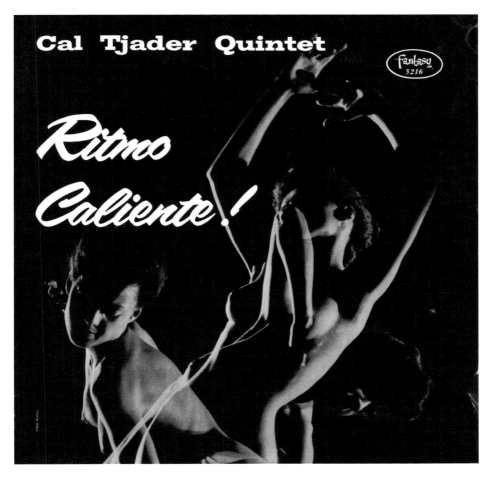

Cal Tjader Quintet, *Ritmo Caliente!,* Fantasy, 1956, Idelsohn Society for Musical Preservation Archive.

Though mostly based in San Francisco, pioneering Latin jazz hybridizer Cal Tjader was an integral part of the LA jazz and Latin scenes, which were also integral to his shaping of what would get dubbed "mambo moderno" and "progressive mambo." He was on the bill for the opening of the Los Angeles Jazz Concert Hall and recorded chunks of trailblazing 1950s albums here like *Latin Kick* and *Ritmo Caliente!* (which included his versions of two songs penned by LA Chicano pianist Eddie Cano). Cano also collaborated with Tjader's Quintet when it joined forces with East Coast Latin jazz stars Mongo Santamaría and Willie Bobo on *Latino* from 1962, a project that debuted live years earlier during a five-week run at Sunset Strip jazz club the Interlude. "His approach to contemporary jazz modernism is unmistakably unfettered," *Billboard* wrote of Tjader's Interlude engagement, a "lure for jazz hipsters." "Tjader combines his jazz numbers with an apparent penchant for the Afro-Cuban."[25]

Machito, *Afro-Cuban Jazz—the Music of Chico O'Farrill,* Clef Records, 1956 (original release), Idelsohn Society for Musical Preservation Archive.

LA-born jazz producer and activist Norman Granz premiered his first Jazz at the Philharmonic concert in 1944 as a benefit for the seventeen Mexican American defendants in the Sleepy Lagoon murder trial. After a stint in New York where he caught Dizzy Gillespie and Chano Pozo experimenting with Afro-Cuban Jazz, Granz returned to Los Angeles and cut a series of his own Afro-Cuban jazz suites, mambos, and a "Cuban Blues," with Charlie Parker and the Cuban-born, Mexico-based Chico O'Farrill for his Clef and Norgran labels.[26] By 1961, the Bell High School alum Stan Kenton, arguably the most celebrated West Coast big band jazz leader, had recorded a version of "The Peanut Vendor" with Machito, included Brazilian guitarist Laurindo Almeida in his Innovations in Modern Music Orchestra, and worked closely with Querétaro-born, San Fernando Valley–raised arranger Johnny Richards to incorporate dense Latin American rhythm and melody charts into landmark albums like *Cuban Fire* and their thrilling reimagining in 1961 of *West Side Story* on the Goldwyn Sound Stage in Hollywood.

Laurindo Almeida Quartet, *Laurindo Almeida Quartet Featuring Bud Shank,* Pacific Jazz Records, 1955 (original release), Idelsohn Society for Musical Preservation Archive.

In 1958, two stalwart LA jazzmen, Art Pepper and Conte Candoli, went into the studios of the Forum Theater (along with ubiquitous bongo ambassador Jack Costanzo and in-demand jazz pianist Russ Freeman) and recorded *Mucho Calor,* "a presentation in Latin Jazz," which included Pepper's prison ode, "Mambo de la Pinta." The heat theme would continue two years later when East LA's Eddie Cano and South LA's Buddy Collette, two of the city's leading names in Latin music and African American jazz, came together to lead *Jazz Heat Bongo Beat,* another explicit attempt by LA musicians of all backgrounds to signal the centrality of Latin American music to jazz's shifting evolutions on the West Coast.[27]

The presence of alto saxophonist Bud Shank in those early Lighthouse sessions is a reminder of one of the more meaningful shifts that shook the city's musical ground: the indirect, stylistic influence of Brazilian samba and bossa nova on how music in LA sounded and the direct influence of Brazilian musicians collaborating with LA funk, jazz, and pop

Moacir Santos, *Saudade*, Blue Note, 1974, Idelsohn Society for Musical Preservation Archive.

artists. By 1953, Shank had already recorded his genre-shifting duet album with Brazilian guitarist Laurindo Almeida for World Pacific records. Complete with session photography by jazz camera legend William Claxton, the collaboration included a composition by acclaimed Brazilian classical composer Radamés Gnattali and marked what the notes called "the interesting cohesion of native Brazilian music with American jazz forms" and "an unusual excursion into modern sounds." Shank's ongoing experiments with what he'd dub *Braziliance* and his collaboration in 1965 with Acre-born pianist and arranger João Donato on *Bud Shank & His Brazilian Friends* are part of a much larger story that connects Hollywood studio orchestras to Earth, Wind & Fire and George Duke recording sessions that both Walter Aaron Clark and Brian Cross tell in this volume.

The influence of the Lighthouse also never went away. "One night, at the Lighthouse in Hermosa Beach," Pernambuco's Moacir Santos recalled (he was playing shows there

Bud Shank, *Bud Shank & His Brazilian Friends,* Pacific Jazz Records, 1965, Idelsohn Society for Musical Preservation Archive.

with Horace Silver), "Horace introduced me to the audience; afterward he told me he was determined to really get me going here. It was through him that Blue Note became interested." Santos went on to record three LA albums in the early 1970s for the esteemed jazz label: *Maestro,* produced by LA jazz and R&B arranger Reggie Andrews; *Saudade* (which included an ode to his new home, "City of LA"); and, at the famed West Hollywood rock studio Record Plant, *Carnival of the Spirits* (which featured a couple names that will reappear on these pages—Paulinho Da Costa on percussion and Oscar Brashear on trumpet).

Once the big screen hurricane of Carmen Miranda hit Hollywood in the 1940s and LA's love affair with samba had officially begun, Brazilian music never left the city's musical identity. Famed Brazilian classical composer Heitor Villa-Lobos played the Philharmonic

Auditorium in 1944 and poet and lyricist Vinicius de Moraes, who would later pen some of modern Brazilian music's greatest verses, spent the last part of the decade in LA as a diplomatic vice consul, writing poems like "Pátria Minha" and "Rosa de Hiroshima" (the latter was turned into a hit for Secos & Molhados).[28] The Mocambo nightclub, one of the Sunset Strip's most legendary midcentury celebrity haunts, opened in 1941 with a Brazilian name (in colonial Brazil, *mocambos* were runaway slave villages) and a tropical Brazilian theme dreamed up by a Hollywood set designer that included columns wrapped in headdresses and gigantic palm fronds and an aviary full of cockatoos, macaws, and parrots. In the early 1950s, the club's house orchestra was run by Chuy Reyes, a Mexican-born pianist and society band leader, who alongside albums of mambos and rumbas would record *Samba,* a collection of Brazilian songs for Capitol Records billed to Chuy Reyes and the Brazilians (Brazilian singer and actor Nilton Paz handled vocal duties).[29]

The LA-Brazil connection went even deeper into LA's musical DNA in the 1960s and 1970s. In 1965, LA-based songwriter, producer, and Disney vet Ray Gilbert launched RioCali, an imprint with Warner Brothers Records that put out US breakthroughs by Brazilian artists like Antônio Carlos Jobim, Dorival Caymmi, Quarteto em Cy, and Marcos Valle. "Brazil used to be the place," the liner notes to Caymmi's debut began, "Where they'd get a lot of coffee in, and Carmen Miranda samba'd from, and Fred Astaire fly'd down to, and Hollywood used to put up a lot of potted palms to pretend it was. And that was about it. Well it isn't anymore." Yet for all of his claims to radical Brazilian authenticity, Gilbert was really an expert translator and internationalizer (he had written for Carmen Miranda in the 1940s). His Warner releases relied on heavy English translations and often clunky, exotic explanations. He renamed Quarteto em Cy as the Girls from Bahia and on their RioCali debut in 1967 (which he produced with Rio de Janeiro's Aloysio de Oliveira) he had them singing "teen sambas" in English, an "armada" of songs that the album promised would lead to "the pleasantest invasion in U.S. history." He called the album *Pardon My English.*

The group reverted back to their original name on their Southern California sequel, *¡Revolución con Brasilia!,* which included more Portuguese lyrics (including the LA-penned "E Nada Mais") even though the liner notes still assured listeners in "Yankeeland" that the women had "changed their address from Bahia to Burbank."[30] Gilbert's work with Jobim on *The Wonderful World of Antonio Carlos Jobim* caught the ear of Frank Sinatra, who brought the Brazilian composer back to LA for an album of duets. Jobim holed up in a suite at the Sunset Marquis—Sinatra supplied the in-room piano—and then the two recorded *Francis Albert Sinatra and Antonio Carlos Jobim* at United Recorders on the Sunset Strip, joined by a cast of musicians that included two frequent Jobim coconspirators, Brazilian percussionist Dom um Romão and German arranger Claus Ogerman.[31]

By the end of the 1960s, Brazilian pianist and bandleader Sergio Mendes was so engrained in the culture of Los Angeles that he didn't blink at turning "For What It's Worth," Buffalo Springfield's Laurel Canyon homage to the white hippie and rocker protests of the Sunset

The Sérgio Mendes Trio, *Brasil '65,* Capitol Records, 1965, Idelsohn Society for Musical Preservation Archive.

Strip riots, into slinky samba-dusted funk. Mendes, a longtime disciple of West Coast jazz, arrived in LA in 1965 and was quickly set up at Shelly's Manne-Hole jazz club. He led a trio— vocalist Wanda de Sah, guitarist Rosinha de Valenca, and Bud Shank—that put their own spin on the cool bop and postbop that Mendes loved, even enlisting cameos by local jazz lights like Chet Baker and Barney Kessel. Once Sergio Mendes and Brazil '66 were established at A&M (complete with the "Herb Alpert Presents" blessing), Mendes became LA's leading importer of Brazilian musicians. Mendes's bands throughout the 1960s became so successful, and so synonymous with the emerging Latin American tinge of California psychedelic pop, that the city became an obvious destination for Brazilian musicians looking for new studio and touring opportunities. As just one example of many, Mendes brought over Edu Lobo in 1970 to record at his LA home studio on a session with fellow Brazilians-in-LA Hermeto Pascoal, Oscar Castro-Neves, and Airto Moreira.

Stan Getz and Astrud Gilberto at Shelly's Manne-Hole in Hollywood, 1964, Photo by Steve Young, Valley Times Collection/Los Angeles Public Library.

As Moreira and Paulinho Da Costa both point out in the their interviews later in this book, it was the lure of Mendes that made them think that LA was a welcome Brazilian outpost. Da Costa first came to LA in 1973 and quickly joined Mendes's Brasil '77 band to tour and lay down percussion on the Stevie Wonder and Leon Russell covers that would end up on the group's seventeenth album, *Vintage*. Da Costa's career as a session player quickly skyrocketed, and he landed on two Dizzy Gillespie albums (including a Brazil love letter from 1976, *Bahiana*), all before cutting *Agora,* his solo debut for Granz's Pablo label, which helped him secure the visa that allowed him to stay in LA. He recorded four more for Granz, whose newfound love for Brazilian music resulted in shepherding albums from star carioca soul singer Jorge Ben Jor and drummer Dom Um Romão (who had also

Los Angeles housewives swing and sway to Latin tempos at their annual playday staged at Griffith Playground, 1941, Herald-Examiner Collection/Los Angeles Public Library.

come to LA to work with Mendes), and Brazilian albums from Sarah Vaughan and Ella Fitzgerald. Moreira was busy recording and touring with Miles Davis, Donald Byrd, and George Benson, and didn't record his first LA solo album, *Promises of the Sun,* until 1976 (there were many more to come). He and his collaborator and wife, Rio de Janeiro–born singer Flora Purim, would go on to become indispensable fixtures of the California jazz fusion and funk scene.

Purim's LA years produced one of the 1970s most singular California albums. While serving three years at Terminal Island prison (at the entrance to Los Angeles Harbor) on a cocaine charge, Purim organized a series of concerts held at the facility and broadcast over a local jazz radio station featuring an all-star LA band that included jazz legend Cannonball Adderley, funk maestro George Duke, and drummer Ndugu Chancler. The album she recorded on her release in 1976, *Open Your Eyes You Can Fly,* became the first album accidentally executive produced by Terminal Island.

By 1977, she and Moreira joined their old friend Hermeto Pascoal at Paramount Studios in Hollywood for his tripped-out fusion epic *Slaves Mass.* Purim cries, laughs, and cackles. Moreira gets a credit for playing "live pigs." When Warner Brothers put out a compilation later that year showcasing their top jazz artists, they included two tracks each from Purim and Pascoal. Neither their Brazilian roots nor the Brazilian textures of their music were mentioned anywhere. They were just like Alice Coltrane, George Benson, and Rahsaan Roland Kirk: architects of "New Music That Stays New."

LA/LA MUSICAL MODERNISMS

Latina/os are ghosts in the machine of Los Angeles modernism, ghosts of the new that stays new, of the mod, the avant-garde, and the cool.[32] As a cultural and aesthetic category "LA Modern" has relied on a mythology of whiteness that flies in the face of the historical realities of how LA culture and aesthetics have been produced and consumed since the dawn of the twentieth century. The performers, audiences, and industries of Latin American music—strongly linked to Mexico in the early 1900s, to Cuba and the Caribbean in the 1950s, to Brazil in the 1960s and 1970s—offer urgent correctives to a modern, urban story that continues to privilege Anglo Angelenos in the making of the city's modernist avant-garde and regulate Latina/os and Latin American immigrants to the narrative suburbs.[33]

At the turn of the last century, LA boosters, politicians, journalists, and industrialists all worked to create the city as a "whitewashed adobe," to borrow Bill Deverell's term, in which the Mexican past and present were managed through commodification and erasure into an invented Spanish colonial fantasy. After World War II, the city was promoted and policed as "a white spot" in which communities of color were managed through displacement, urban development, and segregation— a project that linked Hollywood films and TV series to the LAPD and freeway planners.[34] If you were under the surf-and-turf spell of most mainstream representations of post–World War II popular culture in Los Angeles, LA was the land of *Gidget, Rebel Without a Cause, Dragnet,* and the Beach Boys—a middle-class suburban wonderland of white police, white adolescence, and white beaches (until Little Stevie Wonder showed up to sing at your Muscle Beach party). Communities of color mostly entered the frames when it was time for a smoke-rings-and-whiskey night of noir jazz or a calling-all-cars visit to a boxing ring in the barrio. Listening to the city's Latin American cadences is one way to tell this history of modernization and modernism differently and more democratically, dissolving the cover-ups and uncovering the adobe, relocating the nonwhite spots of the city back into the center of urban identity.

One of the goals of this volume is to perform (and in some cases reperform) a musical "infrastructural inversion," described by communications scholar John Durham Peters as an "intentional violation of a social norm to bring the background out into the open."[35] In a sense, what I'm arguing here, and what the chapters that follow give us ample material for exploring, is that listening for Latin America in the music of Los Angeles raises the volume on the city's Latin American musical infrastructure: messages, stories, ideas, and lives that have been kept low in the urban mix, but have never been not there. In audio engineering terms, this is about masking. They are present—audible, noise-making, resonant, vibrating— but in the process of production and mastering, their presence has been masked and covered up. The attention to infrastructure involves a call to make environments audible that were already making noise but have historically gone unheard or underheard—noise on which the infrastructure's very identity in fact depends.

For example, we know about pioneering post–World War II LA R&B and rock and roll indie labels like Modern Records and its budget subsidiary Crown Records, home to Etta James, Little Richard, Joe Houston, and Hadda Brooks, among others. Yet LA music history tends to forget that Crown also released its fair share of calypso and " . . . Goes Latin" albums, and that in the 1950s Crown launched Discos Corona, an imprint dedicated to Spanish-language, predominantly Mexican music (with slight exceptions like El Caballo's *Vamos a Bailar*, an Afro-Cuban dance album put out under a pseudonym by East Los Angeles trumpet heavy Paul Lopez). Discos Corona joined a long list of LA labels dedicated to Latin music that would soon include Discos Azteca in Burbank and Anahuac Records in West Hollywood.

Among Discos Corona's dozens of mariachi, *norteño*, and *huasteco* albums was Conjunto Papaloapan de Veracruz's 1968 *Cantandole a Veracruz*. Billed as a *son jarocho* by an ensemble from Veracruz, it was actually the first exclusively *son jarocho* album recorded in Los Angeles. The Conjunto was *de Los Angeles*, led not by a Veracruzano, but by a Chicano born and raised in Boyle Heights, Roberto "Bobby" Chagoya, who was inspired to play *son jarocho* after seeing prominent Veracruz ensemble Andrés Huesca y sus Costeños perform at the Million Dollar Theater and who had his first *requinto jarocho* made at Boyle Heights's Candelas Guitars based on the one he saw on the cover of the LP *Los Tres Ases Cantan Jarocho*.[36] Conjunto Papaloapan's album cover photograph, featuring the group dressed in traditional Veracruz hats, guayaberas, and panoletas, may suggest Veracruz but it was shot in San Pedro, and its back cover was stamped with the same 5810 Normandie Avenue address as albums by Jesse Belvin and B.B. King. LA's Mexican and Latin American musical presents have always been here, right alongside the biggest names in R&B, rock and roll, and jazz—often recording in the very same studios, signing contracts in the very same offices—and yet in many cases, their contributions have been marginalized or plainly left out of dominant chronicles of modern LA musical history.

To take the lead from an album recorded in Los Angeles in 1959 by Victor Feldman, what if, instead, we understood LA as "Latinsville," a place and urban geography strongly shaped by its relationship to the musical histories, migrations, and industries of Latin American music? Feldman was born into a jazz background in London. It wasn't until he moved to Los Angeles that he heard Machito and Tito Puente play and decided to devote himself to Cuban and Caribbean styles. The Latin cadence of the city's music culture changed him too.

In calling for a "LA/LA musical modernism," I'm interested in a series of key questions that the essays in this volume explore each in their own way. What is the place of Latin American music—physically, culturally, sonically, politically, symbolically—in modern Los Angeles? How has Latin American music been a method of em-placement and place-making in a city historically defined by "place struggles" and the displacement of Latina/o populations within LA's violent "convulsive urbanism" that repeats with each new generation of urban renewals, redevelopers, and gentrifiers?[37] How is the idea of Los Angeles as a cultural center and a hub of cultural industry dependent on the musical ecologies, histories, audiences, and economies of Latin American music? How have Latin American immigrants and US Latina/os used music to broker a relationship with the mythologies and dreamscapes of Los Angeles on the one hand, and the political limits and political possibilities of Los Angeles on the other? How have Los Angeles music and culture industries used Latin American immigrants and US Latina/os as laborers in the production of the city's mythologies and as pawns in the game of the city's cultural politics?

I've been inspired by Jesse Lerner's work on what he's called "Maya Modernism," his attempt to make sense of the way the pre-Colombian civilization of the Maya has been inserted into the formation of the most mediated and popular forms of contemporary North American modernism. He sees it as a "hall of mirrors" in which US representations of Mexico get reimported to Mexico and "each reflection implies further distortions," producing a "back and forth of mutual (mis)interpretation and creative re-readings."[38] This is not the only way Latin America, Latin Americans, and Latin American music function in Los Angeles, but it's certainly one of them: a hall of echoes in which US representations of Latin America in music and on film are sold back to Latin American audiences in the city, and in which Latin American musicians and consumers themselves both participate and resist through creating echoes and reflections of their own—their own (mis)interpretations and creative re-soundings. One thing you will find on these pages is an exploration of how Los Angeles represents Latin America through musical recordings and performances, but also how Latin American musicians and audiences represent themselves within the LA/LA hall of mirrors. And once in a while, to be sure, the mirrors even break.

A Latin American revision of LA modernism might begin with the very notion of the "early moderns" themselves, who, contrary to much early scholarship on the subject, were not just European American artists, architects, writers, booksellers, designers, and printers. Mexicans were lead actors in the dramas of early LA urbanism and central to the growth of the city's music culture and industry. In many cases, they originated the roles. In the late 1800s, local Mexican musicians were featured among the very first commercial recordings and sheet music ever made and sold in Los Angeles on the racks of the city's first music shop, Tally's Phonographic Parlor. Mexican musical acts like La Banda Union, M.S. Arevalo, and the Mexican Philharmonic Band were all active as early as the 1870s. The first souvenir songbook published in Southern California, the *Golden Songster of the Land of Sunshine and Flowers,* from 1874, contained the lyrics to three Spanish-language songs. One of the city's first entrepreneurial music instructors was the Baja California–born guitarist Manuel Y. Ferrer, who learned to play from Franciscan missionaries before becoming a teacher in San Francisco.[39] In 1882, he published his own instructional book of songs and techniques, *Compositions and Arrangements for the Guitar,* among the first of its kind.

The very first noncommercial sound recordings ever made in Los Angeles—cylinders recorded as early as 1904 on a portable Edison phonograph by Charles Lummis—featured songs of Mexican and Mexican Californian origin, over a hundred of them culled from the notebooks and songbooks of local guitarist José de la Rosa and singer Manuela García. Later, with the help of composer Arthur Farwell (who had already published his own *Folk-songs of the West and South*), Lummis published select transcriptions of his recordings in the songbook *Spanish Songs of Old California,* from 1923. It was a musical snapshot—equal parts history and romance—of what Lummis called "old California, 'Before the Gringo Came'—the California of the Franciscan Missions and the vast Ranchos," a time when "they lived the happiest, the humanest, the most beautiful life that Caucasians have ever lived anywhere under the sun."[40]

The prominence of Mexican music culture began to grow as rising numbers of Mexicans arrived in the city fleeing the unrest of the Mexican Revolution. Among the city's first radio programs aired on KELA, a Spanish-language station dedicated to Mexican music and culture, and in 1920 Mexican immigrant Mauricio Calderón opened the city's first Mexican record store, Repertorio Musical Mexicana, on Main Street, just south of the original plaza, that declared itself "the only Mexican house of Mexican music for Mexicans." From the store Calderón also produced his own piano rolls through his Popocatepetl Piano Roll Company and, during the 1930s, ran his own sheet music publishing company, Editorial Los Angeles, which printed songs by Mexican artists like Chihuahua's José Perches Enriquez and Saltillo's Felipe Valdés Leal.[41] When early record companies like Columbia and Victor came to Los Angeles in the 1920s, they left with songs about undocumented dishwashers, deportees, and anti-immigrant police violence. As Koegel and Alexandra T. Vazquez discuss in their essays here (and as Steven Loza has detailed elsewhere) these early industrial footholds were part of a much larger entertainment circuit of vaudeville houses and movie theaters that continued to grow exponentially throughout the 1930s.

The Hollywood Bowl debuted in 1922 but it took a few years for Mexican and Latin American audiences to appear on its vaunted philharmonic stage nestled in the sloping hills of Bolton Canyon. As historian Kenneth H. Marcus noted in *Musical Metropolis,* his study of early Los Angeles music culture, "the progressive spirit that drove many of the Bowl's founders rarely allowed the participation of Latinos."[42] There were notable exceptions, of course: a Latin American ballet troupe did appear in 1926 and Mexican classical composer Carlos Chávez made his first of many Bowl appearances as early as 1937. "The fact that the residents of this State are the immediate neighbors of Mexico, and understand the country," the program for Chávez's debut insisted, "goes to assure Chávez of establishing for himself a permanent place in the hearts of his audience tonight."[43] It was only after the Bowl teamed up with Disney in the 1940s to launch the *Latin American Fiesta* concert—discussed in this volume by Carol A. Hess—that the popular music of both Latin America and US Latinos would start to establish its own permanent place on the Bowl stage.[44]

Hollywood itself, however, cashed in on musical Latin America from the very start. Spanish-born Xavier Cugat was a cartoonist for the *Los Angeles Times* before Rudolph Valentino convinced him to start an Argentine tango group and internationalize his way into the emergent film industry. Xavier Cugat and his Gigolos appeared in two early Vitaphone film shorts

Mexican composer and pianist Agustín Lara, 1963, Herald-Examiner Collection/Los Angeles Public Library.

in 1927 and in the feature *Cuban Love Song* a few years later. Exotic stereotype-stocked Latin-themed musicals were soon hard to avoid—you could fall in love *Under the Pampas Moon,* or take a trip *Flying Down to Rio.* Latin American musicians and actors like Dolores del Río, Lupe Vélez, Ramón Navarro, and Tito Guízar found plenty of film work north of the border and made LA their home.[45] Mexican songwriter María Grever wrote songs for Paramount and Fox and worked with Irving Ceasar and Stanley Adams, before landing "Te Quiero Dijiste" (or, as it became known in English, "Magic Is the Moonlight") in the Esther Williams spectacular *Bathing Beauty,* released in 1944.

In 1945, Grever's music was celebrated at the Hollywood Bowl as part of *Pan-American Night,* a high-meets-low, Hollywood-goes-folkloric mash-up split between classical pieces led by Chilean pianist Claudio Arrau and a grab bag of folk songs from across the Americas. The finale featured Corinna Mura doing the Grever songbook, which by then also included her "Cuando Vuelva a Tu Lado," a song originally born of her separation from her husband during the Mexican Revolution that went on to become the pop and jazz hit "What A Difference A Day Makes." As for Mura, she was no stranger to LA audiences. She had already sung at the bar of Rick's Cafe in *Casablanca* and was about to appear on screen in both *The Gay Señorita* (Columbia's "Hippy, Heppy Latin Love Show" set in Mexican California) and on Broadway in *Mexican Hayride* (Cole Porter's musical comedy about a female Mexican bullfighter).

Leading Mexican composer Agustín Lara first came to LA in 1934 on a Southern Pacific train and was headquartered downtown at the Biltmore while he did a series of local concerts at the California Theater. His visit was covered by the *Los Angeles Times,* which referred to him as the "Irving Berlin of the Southern Republic" and reviewed a private evening solo piano performance at the Biltmore sponsored by the Mexican consulate. The *Times* compared him to Mozart and Liszt, praised his modernization of the "plaintive-haunting airs of old Mexico," and celebrated him as an international sensation who had forever changed the history of Mexican music.[46] Lara came back a few years later to write songs for the hall of mirrors musical *Tropic Holiday,* a film about a Hollywood screenwriter looking for inspiration in Mexico featuring music by a Mexican who had come to Hollywood to record it. Lara's popular bolero "Solamente Una Vez" got a second LA life as "You Belong to My Heart," appearing in four different films (including two from Disney) and taken to the top of the charts by both Bing Crosby and Elvis Presley.

In the 1950s, mambo, cha cha cha, and a general taste for pan-American, pan-African, and pan-Asian exotica became part of an ethnophilia craze in American pop. TV and film studios quickly reached for the nearest bongos, timbales, and gongs to punctuate their crime dramas and detective series. The LAPD heist film *Private Hell 36* had to throw in a "Havana Interlude," and the LA private detective series *77 Sunset Strip* wasn't complete without the Warren Barker Orchestra doing "77 Sunset Strip Cha Cha."[47] Tampico-born composer Juan García Esquivel—interviewed in chapter 8—left Mexico to record in and for Hollywood in the late 1950s, placing music in *Dragnet, Kojak,* and *Markham*. He even cowrote official logo music for Universal/MCA-TV.

In the Mexican border crime saga of Orson Welles's *Touch of Evil,* Henry Mancini wrapped the last gasp of US film noir in a distinctly Latin American score of tense, jazz-orchestrated gumshoe mambo. The bongos of LA Latin scene regular Jack Costanzo seemed to follow Charlton Heston and Janet Leigh everywhere they went. "There would be a lot of music in the picture," Mancini remembers being told, "Most of it with a big band Latin sound in a Stan Kenton vein."[48] Two years later, he would slip marimbas, congas, and light mambos into his music for the CBS series *Mr. Lucky* and would then make the influence explicit with a separate release in 1961, *Mr. Lucky Goes Latin,* which included Brazilian guitarist Laurindo Almeida on songs that mixed studied elegance ("Lujon") with slinky, cartoon South of the Border exotica ("Raindrops in Rio," "Cowboys and Coffee Beans," and, of course, "Speedy Gonzalez"). In 1965, the LA-based jazz pianist Jack Wilson—an alum of

STEREO   DLP 25831

MUSIC FROM **MISSION: IMPOSSIBLE**

ARRANGED & CONDUCTED BY THE COMPOSER

LALO SCHIFRIN

"Mission Impossible" Created by BRUCE GELLER

Lalo Schifrin, *Music from Mission: Impossible,* Dot Records, 1967, Idelsohn Society for Musical Preservation Archive.

Gerald Wilson and Buddy Collette's bands—paid Mancini back by adding to the hall of mirrors with *Plays Brazilian Mancini,* a hushed and gentle jazz and bossa nova session with an all-star cast: Roy Ayers on vibes and an LA-Brazil crew of Sebastião Neto, Chico Batera, and Antonio Carlos Jobim (billed here as "Tom Brazil" to skirt contractual exclusivity).[49]

By far the most influential Latin American composer in post–World War II Hollywood was Argentine pianist, composer, and arranger Lalo Schifrin. In 1963, Schifrin took a detour from a successful solo jazz career in Latin America and the United States to record the soundtrack for the MGM film *Rhino!* The film was quickly forgotten, but Schifrin's gift for scoring wasn't. He earned a Grammy nomination for his bongo-peppered and brass-blasted theme to *The Man From U.N.C.L.E* (originally a Jerry Goldsmith theme that Schifrin transformed) and went on to slide Latin American musical touches into blues, jazz, disco, and classical scores for shows and films like *Mission: Impossible, Mannix, Cool Hand Luke, Boulevard Nights, Enter the Dragon,* and *Bullitt* (not to mention his infamous cutting-room floor score for *The Exorcist*).

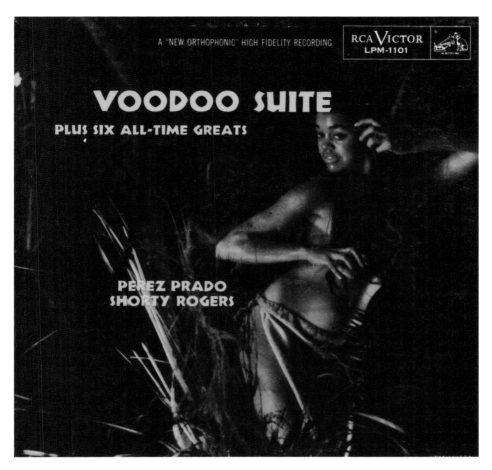

A "NEW ORTHOPHONIC" HIGH FIDELITY RECORDING RCA VICTOR LPM-1101

VOODOO SUITE

PLUS SIX ALL-TIME GREATS

PEREZ PRADO
SHORTY ROGERS

Pérez Prado, *Voodoo Suite,* RCA Victor, 1955, Idelsohn Society for Musical Preservation Archive.

Studios didn't only gravitate toward the Latin sound but in many cases toward the top Latin American performers themselves. When Elvis Presley went south to have some *Fun in Acapulco* in 1963, he took Eddie Cano's band with him. One early Hollywood adopter was Mexican trumpet player Rafael Méndez, whose first gig was playing in Pancho Villa's army and who—after a detour working the assembly line at a Buick plant in Flint, Michigan—landed in the MGM Orchestra in 1939. He became a variety show regular, playing on camera on *The Bing Crosby Show, The Red Skelton Show,* and *The Art Linkletter Show.* His light, breezy approach to "trumpet magic" was enough of a sure thing that Decca billed him as "the world's most versatile trumpeter" and signed him to a twelve-album deal. Before he died in Encino in 1981, Méndez recorded over thirty-five solo albums, including *The Singing Trumpet,* which featured him on the cover in midsolo, dressed in tux and tails, his gold watch matching his golden horn, serenading the crashing waves of the Pacific Ocean.

When Hollywood did its first major cha cha cha movie in 1956, *Cha-Cha-Cha-Boom!* Pérez Prado and Mexico City society bandleader Luis Arcaraz were brought in for on-screen performances. Multioctave Peruvian soprano Yma Sumac (Carolina A. Miranda writes about her later in the volume) was also a big screen no-brainer and appeared alongside Charlton Heston in *Secret of the Incas,* released in 1954. Before Hollywood came calling, Sumac was already beloved in Los Angeles for her theatrical live concerts—she created a sensation with her Hollywood Bowl debut—and for her magisterial exotica recordings for Capitol that mixed mambos with indigenous South American rhythms and styles.

In 1957, Puerto Rican vocalist and bandleader Tony Martinez, who took over for Chuy Reyes as the master of musical ceremonies at the Mocambo, recorded the theme song for the horror film *Pharoah's Curse,* adding Afro-Cuban percussion from his regular bandmates Carlos Vidal and Jack Costanzo in spite of it being set in Egypt. That same year, Martinez was cast in a regular role as Pepino, a Mexican farmhand in the San Fernando Valley, on the CBS series *The Real McCoys*. Martinez capitalized on it with his own LP for Del-Fi, *The Many Sides of Pepino*.

LATIN-ESQUE: DANCING ON AND OFF THE SUNSET STRIP

Latina/os may not have been living in the midcentury modern "Case Study" houses designed by Richard Neutra and Pierre Koenig, but their music mingled with Eames chairs, piped between the posts and beams over living room TV sets and hi-fi stereos. So-called bachelor pad and lounge music of the 1950s—the soundtrack to atomic age California cool—is nearly unimaginable without the work of Latin American composers and musicians working in Los Angeles. In 1954, for example, Pérez Prado went into Hollywood's Radio Recorders studios to record the ambitious and sweeping *Voodoo Suite*—a joint creation of RCA's Mexico and US offices. "The marriage of primitive rhythms to American jazz" is how the liner notes described it. "A sort of tone poem in which the African, the mambo, and the basic aspects of jazz would be united in such a way as to show their true relationship." Featuring four saxophones, six trumpets, three trombones, seven drummers, bass, and a French horn, the big band Prado put together to deliver his score was mostly made up of non-Latino jazz session players like Maynard Ferguson, Pete Candoli, and Shorty Rogers (in New York Prado would also record with future *Tonight Show* bandleader Doc Severinsen).

Perhaps no musician fits the LA modernist bill quite like Esquivel, who became synonymous with innovations in stereophonic sound recording. Following the lead of fellow Mexican big band leader Luis Arcaraz (who recorded his first LA album of lush orchestrated jazz in 1956), Esquivel arrived in Hollywood in 1958 to record *Other Worlds, Other Sounds* for RCA, one of the first full-length recordings arranged and engineered specifically for stereo recording. The album featured a twenty-six-piece orchestra, romantic sci-fi album art, and the vocals of the Van Horne Singers, veterans of sessions with Nat King Cole and Dean Martin (they were also the voices heard in the openings to *The Flintstones* and *The Jetsons*). Another of his Hollywood sessions produced *Latin-Esque,* released in 1962, a sparkling showcase of tape reverb, channel panning, and synchronized click tracks composed for "stereo-action" recording with separated channels ("sounds your eyes can follow") with half of the orchestra in one studio and the other two blocks away in another studio— "almost a city block down the long corridor of the RCA building in Hollywood," as the notes bragged. Esquivel turned well-trodden Latin American standards like "La Paloma" and "Adiós, Marquita Linda" into flashy modernist showcases.

This wink at being "Latin-esque" was a crucial cultural strategy of LA's Latin American pop modernists. RCA Victor promoted Esquivel as part of their marketing campaign "The New Sound America Loves Best," and Esquivel was keen to play along. He pushed the boundaries of what "Latin music" meant in the US recording industry and how far it went into the Hollywood imagination. Esquivel's Latin modernism didn't rely on an authentic, essential Mexicanism or Latin Americanism waiting to be revealed, but—as Edward Said wrote of Orientalism—treated it as a distributed and marketed "cultural enterprise" that moved swiftly—with stereophonic marimbas—into the heart of LA aesthetic identity.[50]

By the end of the 1950s, mambo bands and Afro-Cuban orchestras led by Latin bandleaders were as popular on the Westside as they were on the eastside and downtown. Eddie Cano, Tony Martínez, René Touzet, Machito, and George Shearing (backed by Armando Pedraza on congas and Latin session regular Al McKibbon on bass) all made albums either recorded live in or as studio tributes to world-famous Sunset Strip nightclubs and their celebrity-filled leather booths. Before the Strip became a hippie hangout and playground of rock whiteness in the 1960s, it was the main drag for Latin dance bands, the alchemical lab where Latin American rhythms were shaken and stirred into gringo-friendly cocktails.[51] When Machito recorded a set at the Crescendo in 1961, it was probably not a coincidence that he threw in "Candilejas," his Afro-Cuban makeover of Charlie Chaplin's theme to his film *Limelight*.

P.J.'s nightclub just down the road may have become, as Reprise Records once declared, "as much of a Los Angeles landmark as the Brown Derby, the Hollywood Bowl, and the footprints at Graumann's Chinese," but it did so precisely because of live recordings by two Mexican American artists—the LA-born Eddie Cano and perhaps one of the most undervalued LA musical modernists of all, Texas transplant Trini López. Though some wrote him off as a "human jukebox" who simply regurgitated chart hits, López was emblematic of the period's tendency toward nation-blurring and style-crossing pop hybrids. With an electric guitar, black suit jacket, and matching silver necktie and pocket square, he put rock-sprinkled takes on "La Bamba" and "Cielito Lindo" on the same set list as "If I Had a Hammer" and "This Land Is Your Land."

Colombian pianist Al Escobar played the Crescendo, the Seville, and the Village and then with "His Afro-Cuban Orchestra" went into Radio Recorders to cut *Al Escobar's Rhythmmagic,* an album title gifted to him in a giddy review from Walter Winchell. "He has been able to provide the variety of Latin-American dance rhythms that an increasing number of North Americans have come to demand," Nat Hentoff wrote in the album's liner notes, "And as these recordings demonstrate, he projects a flowing beat that even the neophyte in Latin-American dance steps doesn't find intimidating." Mexican American vibraphonist Bobby Montez, another Crescendo veteran, delivered "exciting latin dance rhythms" on his

Eddie Cano & Jack Costanzo with Tony Martínez and His Orchestra, *Dancing on the Sunset Strip,* GNP, 1960, Idelsohn Society for Musical Preservation Archive.

Viva! Montez album (one song was a tribute to the Hollywood nightclub the Garden of Allah) and, like so many Latin bandleaders before and after him, made sure LA audiences— and celebrities in particular—knew he was Hollywood friendly by recording a movie score album, *Hollywood Themes in Cha Cha Cha.* He did "Picnic" as a mambo, "Laura" as a bolero cha cha, and "A Place in the Sun" as a merengue.

On *Just for You,* the Downey-born "King of the Cha Cha Cha" Manny López managed to combine the Hollywood album with the Romantic Latin American Travelogue album in one place. He could cover both "Me Voy Pa'l Pueblo" and the theme from *The Apartment.* The liner notes didn't cut corners either: "Whether basking in the luxurious lounge at the El Presidente gazing out across the rugged jungle clustered cliffs of the sun swept sea at Aacapulco; or an exciting evening with hosts of film personalities in a plush Beverly Hills nitery, the consistent captivating pulse of Latin America seem always near . . . the heart

Eddie Cano, *Eddie Cano at P.J.'s,* Reprise Records, 1961, Idelsohn Society for Musical Preservation Archive.

throb . . . always with you . . . permeating your very soul . . . the chatter if maracas . . . the timed guiro scratch . . . the racing taboo of a bongo . . . the rhythmic thud of conga. This is the heart and soul of exotic Latin America . . . a call to the dance, answered by faceless millions from the ritualistic days of ancient and glorious Indian civilizations until the last cloud of dust settles quietly heralding the doom of man."

As Anthony Macías has documented in voluminous detail, the city's segregated and uneven racial geography mostly kept Latina/o audiences dancing east of Vermont at venues like the Zenda Ballroom, El Sombrero, Club La Bamba, and the Paramount Ballroom in Boyle Heights. Venues were part of a cultural hierarchy of rankings set by the Musicians Union, as David F. García writes in his chapter here (centered on a famous mid-1960s run at the Paramount by Cuban star Arsenio Rodríguez). If Latina/o audiences were typically hemmed in by the city's borders, Latin American and Latina/o musicians for hire often had more flexibility, playing on bandstands up and down the Strip, and on the Westside, as white Angelenos

Manny López, *Just for You,* Indigo Records, 1961, Idelsohn Society for Musical Preservation Archive.

crowded Arthur Murray ballroom classes to learn to mambo and cha cha cha.[52] This mix of segregation and exchange is loud and clear on the illustrated album cover of Chuy Reyes and His Orchestra's recording for Capitol from 1951, *Mambo at the Mocambo.* All of the musicians are dark-skinned. All of the clientele—the well-dressed dancers, the elegant woman emerging from her car at the valet—are all light-skinned. The cultural borders of what Macías calls the city's "sophisticated Spanish-language cosmopolitanism" began to loosen a little in 1954 when Mexican American musician, radio DJ, and promoter Chico Sesma took his Latin Holidays concert series from the Zenda downtown west to the Hollywood Palladium, an overt attempt to buck musical discrimination and slide Latina/o audiences into the Hollywood entertainment circuit.[53]

As Sesma told Steven Loza, "I had been discouraged particularly with the impresarios of that period. They don't let Mexicans in to the Hollywood Palladium." That changed quickly

How to do the Mambo? Just relax, that's all, Tony Vincent and Winifred Wakefield, 1956, Herald-Examiner Collection/Los Angeles Public Library.

once Pérez Prado headlined Sesma's Hollywood debut with Joe Loco, Tony Martínez, and Manny López. "That we had moved our community into a mainstream social area," Sesma said, "was very relevant to me."[54] The difference between Latin music being popular throughout the city and Latina/os being free to dance to Latin music throughout the city was crucial. While by the 1960s the racial and cultural transformations of the city's music spaces began to become more common, the divisions and inequalities have never vanished.

On the only album Puerto Rican singer Tito Rodríguez made in LA, *En Hollywood*, he included "Los Angeles," a valentine to the city's Latin music scene and its "tremendísimo party" that focused not on the Strip, but on the social spaces where Latino/a music fans gathered and danced. "Los Angeles, para ti mi cha cha," Rodríguez sang, name-checking the

Radio host Eddie Rodríguez (at microphone) and Lionel "Chico" Sesma onstage at the Hollywood Palladium during a Latin Holidays celebration, circa 1946, Shades of L.A. Collection/Los Angeles Public Library.

Palladium and Club Virginia's next to palm trees and sunshine. The city casts a spell on him, *un embrujo,* that inspires him to want to dream. "Yo me voy a bailar a Los Angeles." He wasn't just going to give LA another cha cha cha. He was going there for its transformations of the social. He was going there to dance.

That the cha cha cha was Rodríguez's weapon of choice was no coincidence: by the end of the 1950s, no Latin style had as thoroughly transformed the West Coast popular music scene and as thoroughly penetrated the heart of the city's popular culture. Manny López put it this way on his *Why Not Cha Cha Cha?* album: "The basic difference between Latin music and Americanized Latin music came to me. In countries such as Mexico and Cuba, people FELT the music. In our country, we THOUGHT the music. More than anything else the CHA CHA CHA has helped the American to FEEL music, and not THINK music." Lopez wrote the songs and arrangements with Eddie Cano, who had his own cha cha cha empire going. He recorded "Guara Cha Cha" and "Guajiro Cha Cha Cha," in addition to his full-length albums *Cha Cha Con Cano* for United Artists and *Time for Cha Cha Cha* for RCA

Tito Rodríguez, *From Hollywood,* United Artists Records, 1963 (original release), Idelsohn Society for Musical Preservation Archive.

Victor, which had a pair of white dancers in black-tie evening wear practicing their moves in their living room next to a potted plant before they headed out on the town.

Cuban composer and pianist René Touzet had been in LA since 1949 and, like Cano and Lopez, played on both sides of the city, popular at both the Zenda Ballroom and the Crescendo (the latter memorialized on his album for GNP in 1959, *Rene Touzet at the Crescendo*). But it was Touzet's version of Rosendo Ruiz Jr.'s "Amarren El Loco," released as a 45 rpm single and rechristened as "El Loco Cha Cha Cha" (also on the GNP label in LA), that helped spark a cha cha cha chain of influence that Ned Sublette has argued ended up changing the course of rock and R & B. As Sublette tells it, the song caught the ears of South Central LA's Richard Berry, an African American R & B and rock singer who was then fronting a dance band in Long Beach that played for Mexican Americans who liked to dance cha cha cha. Berry took Touzet's secondhand cha cha cha and turned it into "Louie, Louie,"

René Touzet, *René Touzet at the Crescendo,* GNP, 1959, Idelsohn Society for Musical Preservation Archive.

which would go on to become a nationwide hit for clean-cut white rockers the Kingsmen.[55] From Cuban cha cha cha to Hollywood cha cha cha to a rock and roll smash with a secret cha cha cha heart.

The formula would continue with other rock and R&B staples (The Rolling Stones's "I Can't Get No Satisfaction" relies on a cha cha cha/clave rhythm, for example), especially one of LA's most important recordings from the 1950s: Ritchie Valens's "La Bamba." Originally a traditional *son jarocho* folk dance song from Veracruz, Valens learned it and its Spanish lyrics in suburban Pacoima in the San Fernando Valley. Though he mostly saw himself as an R&B singer (he used to perform as "Little Richard of the Valley"), his frenetic, plugged-in electric guitar facelift of "La Bamba"—recorded with leading African American R&B and rock session players like Earl Palmer, René Hall, and Ernie Freeman—cemented his place in Chicano rock and roll history. Sublette reminds us though that his "La Bamba" wasn't just where *son jarocho* met Chicano rock and African American R&B. It too had the Cuban

Sam Cooke, *Everybody Likes to Cha-Cha-Cha!,* Famous, 1962, Idelsohn Society for Musical Preservation Archive.

clave as its primary rhythm; it too had a secret cha cha cha heart. "Without Cuban music," Sublette writes, "American music would be unrecognizable."[56] Or as LA's prince of pop gospel and R&B Sam Cooke sang at Radio Recorders studios in Hollywood just a year after Valens's hit, "Everybody likes to cha cha cha."

The Cuban and Mexican imprint on LA rock and roll didn't stop with "La Bamba." The Champs, who were named after Gene Autry's horse and led by the Huntington Beach–born Mexican American saxophonist Danny Flores (aka Chuck Rio), recorded the early rock hit "Tequila" over a mambo beat. During the surf rock craze of the 1960s, Champs guitarist Jerry Cole would go on to play lead on "El Tecolote" (Mexican slang for a cop), a typically twangy instrumental untypically penned by jazz trumpeter and Pérez Prado alum Shorty Rogers. René Bloch was already a veteran of both the Prado band and the Central Avenue jazz scene when he tried to cash in on the rock boom on his album *Mucho Rock,* released in 1958, which, save for the bump-and-grind of "Raunchy," was a standard platter of sharp mambos, cha cha cha, and pachangas. These West Coast connections between rock and Cuban music were prefigured in the film *Rock Around the Clock,* released in 1956, the first feature vehicle for Bill Haley & the Comets. Produced by the LA duo of Sam Katzman and Robert E. Kent, the film framed rock and roll's emergence as a competition with the popularity of Latin dance bands. Haley appears on screen nearly as much as LA's own mambo king Tony Martínez and his pianist Eddie Cano. Between Haley's now infamous rock numbers, we see Martínez play "Cuero," "Mambo Capri," "Solo y Triste," and "Bacalao Con Papa."

In rock and roll's first full-length movie, LA mambo was the costar.

A TASTE OF THE FUTURE

"I was looking for something that would turn my kids on." In 1972, LA City Schools teacher Arturo Preciado gave a presentation on bilingual teaching methods at a national conference on Chicano education at Pima Community College in Tucson, Arizona. He was there to speak about *A Taste of Education: Building Your Spanish Vocabulary Through Music,* a cassette and LP released by C/P Records in LA that Preciado had just finished with pianist Eddie Cano. The solution to bilingual education was getting the kids to sing along with mambos and cha cha chas. "In one year I had cut my own record," Preciado told his fellow educators, "First thing, the beat turns them on. Listen, the sound, it's our beat, it's Chicano beat."[57] Students in classrooms across LA could now virtually be part of an Eddie Cano band, singing along with him as he named the parts of the body, counted to ten, ran through the alphabet, and sang his way through pronunciation exercises. The Cuban rhythms featured on the album had become so engrained in Mexican American music culture—and so beloved and supported by the city's thriving Mexican American population—that by the 1970s Preciado hears them as the "Chicano beat."

A Taste of Education—the title was a play on the hit that Cano had a decade earlier with Herb Alpert and the Tijuana Brass's "A Taste of Honey"—was the last album Cano would record on. His fluency in 1950s-era Cuban dance music and his deep connection to a vanished Hollywood supper club scene had left him slightly out of step with the arrival of harder-edged Latin funk and salsa in the 1970s. "The salsa sound has been gaining in popularity," *Billboard* reported in the fall of 1973, even christening local singer Olga Menéndez "the Celia Cruz of Los Angeles."[58] Just as East Coast mambo, rumba, and cha cha cha found their way into the LA blender decades earlier, salsa found its way west to LA radio (KALI was an early salsa promoter) and to clubs like Virginia's, Candilejas, Chez Pico, the Mardi Gras, and Rudy's Pasta House, with a new generation of bandleaders, musicians, and singers ready for an LA relocation.

The dance scene that began to develop at these clubs (and that had its roots in the dance floors of the mambo era) would continue to grow over the next two decades, reaching an apex in the 1990s after the 1988 release of the film *Salsa* (set in a fictional LA salsa club). They were the laboratories for the evolution of LA's own salsa style, one that differed from its East Coast model by emphasizing faster tempos, theatrical choreographies, and a tendency to break on the downbeat (on the one and not the two).[59] In her chapter in this volume, salsa and dance scholar Cindy García follows the way salsa "danced latinidad" into the way latinidad is imagined by contemporary Latina-led hip-hop dance troupes.[60]

While mambo dancers were predominantly Mexican American, salsa dance floors were more noticeably Caribbean, full of a growing number of Puerto Ricans, Cubans, and other East Coast Latina/os. They were also more disco-friendly. Salsa bled into disco and disco bled into salsa; disco clubs and salsa clubs often shared the same clientele. In her study of Los Angeles salsa, Juliet McMains revisits a social dance technique book published in 1978 by LA teacher Skippy Blair, who includes disco in her chapter on salsa, which she describes as "disco dancing with a Latin flavor."[61] Discos relied on a heavily Latino/a clientele, and for queer Chicana/os and Latin American immigrants, Plush Pony and Redz, Alta Plaza and Tempo, Le Bar and Le Barcito, became after-hours sanctuaries. As Luis Alfaro writes in his poem here, clubs like the iconic Circus Disco (where disco and new wave faded in and out of Juan Gabriel and Rocío Dúrcal classics) were crucial sites for queer Latino/a performance and community making.[62]

In his interview in this collection, Cuban percussionist Luis Conte offers a detailed description of the LA salsa scene in the 1970s, from Joe Cuba at the Mardi Gras to Chocolate y Silvia (with João Donato on piano) at Chez Pico. Leading the way was Johnny Martínez's Salsa Machine big band, helming most nights at Club Virginia's, which was blessed by *Billboard* as the "best local club for Manhattan style salsa music."[63] On the nights Martínez took off, Conte was on the Virginia's stage as a member of Azuquita y Su Melao, a top Panamanian-Cuban salsa band that made LA home in the 1970s. In addition to Conte, the band was also stacked with two influential African American musicians: trumpeter Oscar Brashear (a vet of Count Basie's band who would work with Quincy Jones, Horace Silver, and Oliver Nelson) and the LA-born Munyungo Jackson who had been playing congas and timbales in Latin jazz bands since his junior high school days at Horace Mann.[64] Azuquita's band became ubiquitous in Los Angeles salsa clubs, playing everywhere from Rudy's Pasta House in East LA to Kabukis in Eagle Rock. Azuquita's album from 1974 was dedicated to his new digs, *En Hollywood,* and a year later he followed it up with the more polished *Pura Salsa,* which kicked off with a "California" ode. It was mostly Azuquita repeating "Azuquita llegó a California," making sure that everyone knew that the former East Coast staple was now a confirmed Cali boy.[65]

Willie Bobo was another new arrival. The Puerto Rican percussionist was a veteran and highly in-demand New York sideman and collaborator (working with Mongo Santamaría, Tito Puente, Herbie Hancock, and Cal Tjader) before going solo as a Latin funk pioneer. His first LA recordings were for *The Drum Session,* an all-star summit that welcomed Bobo into the West Coast jazz fold by teaming him up with Shelly Manne, Louie Bellson, and Paul Humphrey. He followed up in 1977 with *Tomorrow Is Here,* a saccharine, Latin-inflected smooth jazz cruise that's mostly worth a listen only to hear Bobo's bass-slapped and timbale-twisted funk rework of the *Kojak* theme. Bobo became a familiar face at the Sunday *tardeadas* at Kabukis, the Lighthouse, the Hollywood Palladium, the Hollywood Bowl, the Watts Jazz Festival, and, most often, Rudy's Pasta House, where he was consistently part of packed weekly calendars that also included leading California acts like Tierra, Cal Tjader, and Salsa Orchestra.[66]

Bobo and Azuquita also shared countless bills with the *orquesta* of Cuban percussionist Orlando "Mazacote" López, who moved to LA in 1964. In the 1970s, he released two important local salsa albums on the Pico-Union-based Latin Records International, *Shukandu!* and *15th Aniversario de Mazacote & Su Orquesta en el Hotel Airport Park,* the latter recorded live at Hotel Airport Park in Inglewood (the album doubled as an ad for the hotel, listing its address and phone number under its full bleed photograph on the front cover, and including a spread of advertisements for nearby businesses in the gatefold). But the venue that would sear him into the mediatized memory of Los Angeles was the Million Dollar Theater in the heart of downtown. As numerous essays in this collection allude, the Million Dollar was the city's great palace of Latin American, Spanish-language entertainment for much of the twentieth century. Mazacote was a regular seat-filler there, especially after he opened legendary singer Celia Cruz's two-week run in 1965.

Mazacote was also the headliner for a series of shows in 1981, where he shared the bill with Los Mimilocos and a screening of the film *Mamá Solita,* a Mexican immigration tear-jerker starring Pedrito Fernández and Pedro Armendáriz about a young boy who leaves his mother in Mexico to cross the Rio Grande in search of his migrant father in the United States. We know this because the Million Dollar's marquee makes an appearance in *Blade Runner,* the now-classic ur-text of dystopian global LA sci-fi that began principal photography that same year and used the Bradbury Building across the street from the Million Dollar as a primary set. Set in 2019, the film's story of disillusioned ex-cops hunting down at-risk replicants who traveled to LA illegally, live in the shadows of a crowded, internationally financed simulacra skyline of 24/7 advertisements, and speak a mashed-up global Esperanto foreshadowed a Los Angeles to come, a Los Angeles that was already in the making.

There has been much critical hand wringing about the enduring accuracy of *Blade Runner*'s futurism. Yet one thing it most certainly got right is this: Latin American music in Los Angeles is past and future at once. The accidental cameo of Mazacote and the Million Dollar Theater gave us Latin music as the time-compressed score to a time-compressed city, where history and prophecy move to migrant rhythms that have already happened, and have still yet to be heard.

NOTES

1. Barbara Schultz, "Classic Tracks: Blondie's "The Tide Was Always High," *mixonline.com,* March 1, 1999.

2. These are the personnel as listed with the AFM Local 47 union. I thank local union VP Rick Baptist and AFM's Pat Varriale and Andrew Morris for their help in sourcing this info, and to Todd Simon for his help in putting the pieces together. In his interview in this volume, Alex Acuña remembers a different set of horn players but per union records I chose to refer to the listed personnel.

3. Colin Gunckel, *Mexico on Main Street: Transnational Film Culture in Los Angeles before World War II* (New Brunswick, NJ: Rutgers University Press, 2015), 124, 132–33.

4.   Steven Loza, *Barrio Rhythm: Mexican American Music in Los Angeles* (Champaign-Urbana: University of Illinois Press, 1993), 87–93; Steven R. Pearlman, *Mariachi Music in Los Angeles* (PhD diss., UCLA, 1988).

5.   For the legacy of Mariachi Chapala in Los Angeles, see Michael Quintanilla, "From the Heart: Five Generations Carry On Tradition of Mariachi," *Los Angeles Times,* January 8, 1992.

6.   Josh Kun, "The Tijuana Sound: Brass, Blues, and the Borders of the 1960s," in *Transnational Encounters; Music and Performance at the US-Mexico Border,* ed. Alejandro Madrid (New York: Oxford University Press, 2011).

7.   While I am focusing on Latin American music and Latin American immigrants here, the vast scholarship on Chicano/a music in greater Los Angeles has been crucial to my thinking (see preface and accompanying notes). In particular, George Lipsitz's approach to peeling back the layers on the East LA music scene in his early essay "Cruising around the Historical Bloc: Postmodernism and Popular Music in East Los Angeles" (*Cultural Critique* 5 [1988]) has been instrumental to my approach here.

8.   Vaughn Cornish, "Harmonies of Scenery: An Outline of Aesthetic Geography," *Geography* 14, no. 5 (Summer 1928); Georg Simmel, "The Metropolis and Mental Life," in *The Blackwell City Reader,* ed. Gary Bridge and Sophie Watson (Hoboken, NJ, Wiley-Blackwell, 2002). There is a deep literature on musical urbanism that I am informed by in this essay. For example, Adam Krims, *Music and Urban Geography* (New York: Routledge, 2007); Marina Peterson, *Sound, Space, and the City: Civic Performance in Downtown Los Angeles* (Philadelphia: University of Pennsylvania Press, 2012); Georgina Born, ed., *Music, Sound, and Space: Transformations and Public and Private Experience* (Cambridge: Cambridge University Press, 2015); Brett Lashua, Karl Spracklen, and Stephen Wagg, eds., *Sounds and the City: Popular Music, Place, and Globalization* (New York: Palgrave, 2014).

9.   Sidney Robertson Cowell, "The Recording of Folk Music in California," *California Folklore Quarterly* 1, no. 1 (January 1942): 7.

10.   Carey McWilliams, *Southern California: An Island on the Land* (Santa Barbara: Peregrine Smith, 1973), 49–50.

11.   Rubén Ortiz-Torres, "Introduction: Does L.A. Stand for Los Angeles or Latin America?," *Mex/L.A.: "Mexican" Modernism(s) In Los Angeles, 1930–1985* (Berlin: Hatje Cantz, 2011), 15.

12.   Charles Emge, "Boom in Latin Rhythms Bigger Than Ever in L.A.," *Down Beat* 21, no. 15 (July 28, 1954): 5.

13.   Robert G. O'Meally, "Preface," in *The Jazz Cadence of American Culture,* ed. Robert G. O'Meally (New York: Columbia University Press, 1998), xi; Ralph Ellison, "What Would America Be without Blacks?," *Time,* April 6, 1970.

14.   Gaye Theresa Johnson, "Sobre Las Olas: A Mexican Genesis in Borderlands Jazz and the Legacy for Ethnic Studies," *Comparative American Studies* 6, no. 3 (2008); Raul Fernández, *Latin Jazz: The Perfect Combination/La Combinación Perfecta* (San Francisco: Chronicle, 2002), 14–17.

15.   Loza, *Barrio Rhythm;* Anthony Macías, *Mexican American Mojo: Popular Music, Dance, and Urban Culture in Los Angeles, 1935–1968* (Durham: Duke University Press, 2008); Kenneth Marcus, *Musical Metropolis: Los Angeles and the Creation of a Music Culture 1880–1940* (New York: Palgrave, 2004); John Koegel has published widely in this area. See, for example, Koegel, "Mexican

Musicians in California and the United States 1910–1950," *California History* 84, no. 1 (Fall 2006); and Koegel, "Canciones del Pais: Mexican Musical Life in California After the Gold Rush," *California History* 78, no. 3 (Fall 1999).

16. In addition to Loza and Macías, see Helena Simonett, *Banda: Mexican Musical Life Across Borders* (Middleton, CT: Wesleyan University Press, 2001); Sam Quinones, *True Tales from Another Mexico* (Albuquerque: University of New Mexico Press, 2001); Jenni Rivera, *Unbreakable: My Story, My Way* (New York: Simon & Schuster, 2013); Josh Kun, "The Twiins: Mexican Music Made in America," *New York Times,* May 14, 2006; Josh Kun, "California Sueños," *Boom* 1, no. 1 (Spring 2011); Josh Kun, "What Is an MC If He Can't Rap to Banda?: Making Music in Nuevo LA," *American Quarterly* 56, no. 3 (September 2004); Josh Kun, *Songs in the Key of Los Angeles* (Santa Monica: Angel City, 2013).

17. Alexandra Zavis, "Los Angeles Unveils Statue of Mexican Singer-Actor Antonio Aguilar," *Los Angeles Times,* September 17, 2012.

18. Kenneth Hume, "Letter from Los Angeles," *Jazz: A Quarterly of American Music* 3:211–16.

19. Ted Gioia, *West Coast Jazz: Modern Jazz in California, 1945–1960* (New York: Oxford University Press, 1992), 201.

20. Ibid., 202.

21. I thank Alberto López, percussionist and bandleader for LA bands Jungle Fire and Rumbakete, for introducing me to the story of his uncle, Johnny Richards.

22. Phil Pastras, *Dead Man Blues: Jelly Roll Morton Way Out West* (Berkeley: University of California Press, 2001).

23. Wilson was particularly immersed in Latin American music, especially Mexico and Chicano Los Angeles. See Anthony Macías, "California's Composer Laureate: Gerald Wilson, Jazz Music and Black-Mexican Connections," *Boom* 3, no. 2 (Summer 2013).

24. See my oral history with Bloch: "Rene Bloch Interview," Idelsohn Society Digital Archive, www.youtube.com/watch?v = tBhZ1KuQ1WI.

25. "Tjader Lure for Jazz Hipsters," *Billboard,* April 7, 1958. See also S. Duncan Reid, *Cal Tjader: The Life and Recordings of the Man Who Revolutionized Latin Jazz* (Jefferson, NC: McFarland, 2013).

26. For Granz's interest in Latin Jazz and Cuban music, see Tad Hershorn, *Norman Granz: The Man Who Used Jazz for Justice* (Berkeley: University of California Press, 2011), 128–31.

27. The tradition of Latin Jazz in Los Angeles has never left. In 1990, José Rizo launched his radio show *Jazz on the Latin Side* on KLON, where he interviewed leading Latin American and jazz musicians from across the Americas, and then formed his own bands dedicated to these histories: The Jazz on the Latin Side All-Stars and Mongorama. Both of them featured Colombian sax player Justo Almario, whose interview appears in this volume.

28. I thank Betto Arcos for alerting me to this. For one account of Moraes's sojourn in Los Angeles, see Joshua Ensler, "Vinicius de Moraes and 'Patria Minha': The Politics of Writing in Post-War Brazil," *Hispania* 94, no. 3 (September 2011).

29. Martin Turnbull, "Mocambo: The Nightclub's Nightclub," http://martinturnbull.com/hollywood-places/spotlight-on-mocambo/; Jim Heimann, *Out with The Stars: Hollywood Nightlife in the Golden Era* (New York: Abbeville, 2001); for more on the music of the Mocambo and other "society band" scenes, see Macías, *Mexican American Mojo.*

30. My thanks to Brian Cross for sharing this with me.

31. For more on both Gilbert and the Jobim-Sinatra Sessions, see Ruy Castro, *Bossa Nova: The Story of the Brazilian Music That Seduced the World* (Chicago: Chicago Review, 2000), 309–10, 327–28.

32. I began exploring this idea specifically focusing on Mexican immigrants and Mexican-Americans in Los Angeles in my essay "Latin-Esque: The (Mexican) Musical Modernism of L.A. 1950–1966," in *Mex/L.A.: "Mexican" Modernism(s) In Los Angeles, 1930–1985* (Berlin: Hatje Cantz, 2011).

33. An otherwise excellent book that is an example of this approach is Victoria Dailey, Natalie Shivers, and Michael Dawson, eds., *LA's Early Moderns: Art/Architecture/Photography* (South Pasadena: Balcony, 2003).

34. William Deverell, *Whitewashed Adobe: The Rise of Los Angeles and the Remaking of Its Mexican Past* (Berkeley: University of California Press, 2004); Eric Avila, *Popular Culture in the Age of White Flight: Fear and Fantasy in Suburban Los Angeles* (Berkeley: University of California Press, 2004). See also Kirse Granat May, *Golden State, Golden Youth: The California Image in Popular Culture, 1955–66* (Chapel Hill: University of North Carolina Press, 2002).

35. John Durham Peters, *The Marvelous Clouds: Toward a Philosophy of Elemental Media* (Chicago: University of Chicago Press, 2015) 35. Peters is glossing recent media and communications scholarship by Lisa Parks, Harold Garfinkel, and Geoffrey C. Bowker and Susan Leigh Star.

36. I am indebted to Rafael Figueroa, Quetzal Flores, and Martha Gonzalez for introducing me to this history. For a full account of the making of the album, including interviews with Chagoya, see Rafael Figueroa Hernández, *El son jarocho en los Estados Unidos de América: Globalizaciones, migraciones, e identitdades* (Tesis, Universidad Veracruzana, September 2014), 247–73.

37. For "place struggles," see Raúl Homero Villa, *Barrio-Logos: Space and Place in Urban Chicano Literature and Culture* (Austin: University of Texas Press, 2000); and *Urban Latino Cultures: La Vida Latina en L.A.,* ed. Raúl Homero Villa, Gustavo Leclerc, and Michael Dear (Thousand Oaks, CA: Sage, 1999); on "convulsive urbanism," see Dana Cuff, *The Provisional City: Los Angeles Stories of Architecture and Urbanism* (Cambridge, MA: MIT Press, 2000).

38. Jesse Lerner, *The Maya of Modernism: Art, Architecture, and Film* (Albuquerque: University of New Mexico Press, 2011), 4–5. I see these inquiries as being in dialogue with those of Ruben Gallo in *Mexican Modernity: The Avant-Garde and the Technological Revolution* (Cambridge, MA: MIT Press, 2005) and Julio Ramos in *Divergent Modernities: Culture and Politics in 19th Century Latin America* (Durham: Duke University Press, 2001) and a much wider pool of scholarship on African American modernism/modernity and their correctives to Eurocentric models of the modern. See, for example, Paul Gilroy, *The Black Atlantic: Modernity and Double Consciousness* (Cambridge, MA: Harvard University Press, 1995); and Richard J. Powell, *The Blues Aesthetic: Black Culture and Modernism* (Washington, DC: Washington Project for the Arts, 1989).

39. For helpful surveys of these early periods, see Michael Heisley, "Sources for the Study of Mexican Music in California," in *California's Musical Wealth,* ed. Stephen M. Fry (Southern California Chapter Music Library Association, 1988); Howard Swann, *Music in the Southwest* (Huntington Library, 1952); Owen da Silva, *Mission Music in California* (WF Lewis, 1941); and especially Robert

Stevenson's indispensable entry on Los Angeles in "Music in Southern California: A Tale of Two Cities," *Inter-American Music Review* 5, no. 1 (Fall 1988).

40. For more on the Lummis recordings and songbooks, see Marcus, *Musical Metropolis,* 120–28; John Koegel, "Mexican-American Music in Nineteenth Century California: The Lummis Wax Cylinder Collection at the Southwest Museum, Los Angeles," *Revista de Musicología* 16, no. 4 (1993).

41. I was first introduced to these histories in George J. Sanchez, *Becoming Mexican American: Ethnicity, Culture, and Identity in Chicano Los Angeles* (New York: Oxford University Press, 1995). They also appear in Loza, *Barrio Rhythm,* and Gunckel, *Mexico on Main Street.*

42. Marcus, *Musical Metropolis,* 74.

43. I thank Carol Merrill-Mirsky, former lead archivist of the Hollywood Bowl Museum, for initially sharing these materials with me as part of my contributions to the 2011 Bowl exhibition *Musica y Sabor.*

44. Josh Kun, "From South of the Border to Whittier Boulevard: Latin Music at the Bowl 1943–1967," in *Musica y Sabor,* ed. Carol Merril-Mirsky (Hollywood: Hollywood Bowl Museum, 2011).

45. For a more detailed history of these early Hollywood decades, see Loza, *Barrio Rhythm.*

46. "New Mexican Music Heard," *Los Angeles Times,* January 9, 1934. For the full discussion of Lara's Los Angeles life and work, see Andrew Grant Wood, *Agustín Lara: A Cultural Biography* (New York: Oxford University Press, 2014), 87.

47. For a more thorough list of these instances, complete with audio examples, see "Naked City Latino," an MP3 essay by Daniel Shiman for his blog *Office Naps,* January 14, 2008, http://officenaps.com/?p = 19.

48. Henry Mancini, *Did They Mention the Music?* (Chicago: Contemporary Books, 1989), 79.

49. Big thanks to Brian Cross for introducing me to this album.

50. Edward Said, *Orientalism* (New York: Vintage, 1978), xxix. For studies of Mexican cultural simulacra that follow Said's lead, see Norma Klahn, "Writing the Border: The Languages and Limits of Representation," *Travesia* 3 (1994); and William Nericcio, *Text-Mex: Seductive Hallucinations of the "Mexican" in America* (Austin: University of Texas Press, 2007).

51. Macías offers a much more detailed and complete portrait of the 1950s and 1960s "Latin Holidays" scene in *Mexican American Mojo,* 229–80.

52. Ibid., 25, 40, 92. On the popularity of mambo classes in the fifties, see Juliet McMains, *Spinning Mambo into Salsa: Caribbean Dance in Global Commerce* (New York: Oxford University Press, 2015), 216–17.

53. See Macías, *Mexican American Mojo.*

54. Steven Loza, *Tito Puente and the Making of Latin Music* (Champaign-Urbana: University of Illinois Press, 1999), 95.

55. Ned Sublette, "The Kingsmen and the Cha-Cha-Chá," in *Listen Again: A Momentary History of Pop Music,* ed. Eric Weisbard (Durham: Duke University Press, 2007).

56. Ibid., 72.

57. Rafael Chavez, ed., "National Conference: Early Childhod Education and the Chicanito," Children's Bureau (DHEW) report #OCD-CB-410(S1), 1972.

58. "Latin Music: Latin Scene," *Billboard,* September 29, 1973.

59. McMains, *Spinning Mambo into Salsa,* 198.

60. Cindy García, *Salsa Crossings: Dancing Latinidad in Los Angeles* (Durham: Duke University Press, 2013).

61. McMains, *Spinning Mambo into Salsa,* 223.

62. This is a deep and vital history that goes far beyond this brief mention and deserves far more attention than I was able to provide here. I thank Ricardo Bracho for sharing his knowledge and his memories of the music at Circus Disco with me. The ONE Archives of USC hold a treasure trove of queer Latina/o bar and club ephemera that have become indispensable to researchers on this topic. For work in this area, for example, see Horacio Roque Ramírez, "Introduction: Homoerotic, Lesbian, and Gay Ethnic and Immigrant Histories," *Journal of American Ethnic History* 29, no. 4 (Summer 2010); the club histories of queer Chicano artist and activist Joey Terrill in Lillian Faderman and Stuart Timmons, *Gay L.A.: A History of Sexual Outlaws, Power Politics, and Lipstick Lesbians* (New York: Basic, 2006); Dino Dico, "Loving and Partying at Chico: 'The Best Latino Gay Bar in Montebello,'" *KCET.org,* February 15, 2017; and James Rojas, "From the Eastside to Hollywood: Chicano Queer Trailblazers in 1970's LA," *KCET.org,* September 2, 2016.

63. "Latin Music: Latin Scene," *Billboard,* July 14, 1973.

64. Don Williams, "Jazz Artist Interviews: Darryl Munyungo Jackson," *Jazz Review,* January 29, 2011.

65. The song would get a second life in LA music history when it was sampled in 1996 by Born Jamericans on "Send My Love/Send One Your Love," for their second album for LA hip-hop label Delicious Vinyl.

66. The "Latin Scene" columns of *Billboard* magazine throughout the 1970s offer helpful context here. I also thank Adrian Rivas for sharing an advertisement for the Pasta House from 1977 with me.

1

MEXICAN MUSICAL THEATER AND MOVIE PALACES IN DOWNTOWN LOS ANGELES BEFORE 1950

WELCOME TO THE PLAZA

To begin to tell the story of Mexican music in Los Angeles, you have to start in the Plaza.[1] The first site of Spanish colonial civilian settlement in 1781, it was also the city's first entertainment district.[2] Today the Los Angeles Plaza retains its historic Roman Catholic Plaza Church, Our Lady Queen of the Angels/Nuestra Señora la Reina de los Ángeles (also known as La Placita Church), dedicated in 1822, and still an active parish serving a principally Latino congregation. The historic Pico House hotel and Merced Theater (the city's oldest surviving theater space) opened in 1870, and Masonic Hall next door was built in 1858. Los Angeles civic leaders established touristic "Mexican" Olvera Street in the late 1920s, as representative of the Spanish-heritage fantasy myth.[3] Italian Hall, built in 1908, long a multiethnic site for cultural, social, and political activities, features David Alfaro Siqueiros's restored outdoor mural *América Tropical* (Tropical America) of 1932.

The Plaza area has been reconfigured and repurposed numerous times over the centuries, and has always been in a state of adaptation and change.[4] Before the building of Union Railway Station in Los Angeles in the late 1930s, and before misguided urban redevelopment in the 1950s and the destruction of historic buildings and neighborhoods, it served as the center for the city's vibrant Mexican, Italian, and Chinese communities.[5] Civic leaders such as Christine Sterling and *Los Angeles Times* publisher Harry Chandler, instigators of the romanticized reimagining of Olvera Street, practiced what William Estrada calls "selective preservation," keeping some buildings such as those mentioned above, but almost entirely destroying the original Chinatown and gradually displacing most of the original Mexican businesses in the Plaza area.[6]

However, at different times from the mid-nineteenth century through the 1950s, Plaza-district buildings, especially along North Main Street, housed immigrant-oriented businesses, churches, restaurants and cafes, grocery stores, social clubs, billiard halls, saloons, music stores, dance halls, rooming houses, phonograph parlors, penny arcades, nickelodeons and ten-cent motion picture houses, and vaudeville theaters.[7] The development of the Plaza area over time mirrors the transition of Los Angeles from a small Spanish and Mexican pueblo to an American frontier city, and ultimately to one of the world's major cities and metropolitan areas. As the city grew outward from the Plaza, the performing arts grew with the city, in a wide diversity of genres and styles and ethnic and racial origins and audiences. New artistic and entertainment genres were introduced, created, or adapted for local use, and older traditions were both maintained and discarded.[8]

With the large-scale influx of immigrants during the Mexican Revolution of the 1910s came the strong desire to import Mexican cultural practices to what Mexican writer, politician, and philosopher José Vasconcelos (1882–1959) and other elites called a *México de Afuera,* a Mexican diaspora abroad.[9] As part of this desire to maintain strong connections to the homeland, these immigrants and exiles would establish their own popular music singing groups, *orquestas típicas* and *mariachis,* church choirs, dance and wind bands, and operatic and theater companies, creating a vitally alive and mutually supportive musical atmosphere in the Mexican community.[10] A central aspect of this essay is how musical theater directly relates to physical location, civic identity, immigration, and ethnicity. A recurring process of cultural conflict, maintenance, and accommodation played out over time on stage in Los Angeles's Latino theatrical world.[11] Music and theater thus served as conduits for communal self-expression, as powerful symbols of Mexican identity, and as signs of tradition and modernity.

LOS ANGELES'S MEXICAN MUSICAL STAGES AND MOVIE PALACES

Beginning around 1906 a group of Mexican-oriented theaters, offering mixed bills of live theatrical acts and motion pictures, was established along North Main Street adjacent to the Plaza that would continue to be active for several decades.[12] They catered especially to the Spanish-speaking, but also to Italian, Chinese, and Japanese residents of the greater Plaza district.

For a brief time in 1907, an attempt was made to establish a legitimate theater for live Spanish-language drama and musicals in the Italian Mutual Benevolent Association hall at

THE FILM SHOW BOOM IN LOS ANGELES AND SOME OF ITS MORE VIVID RESULTS.

BY HARRY C. CARR.

"The Film Show Boom in Los Angeles," *Los Angeles Times,* October 13, 1907.

730 Buena Vista Street in Sonoratown, the predominantly Mexican district immediately north of the Plaza. A Mexican company, direct from Hermosillo, Sonora, presented Ruperto Chapí's Spanish *zarzuela* (operetta) *La Tempestad* (1882), a favorite repertory piece, in February 1907. However, the enterprise failed because of lack of community support.[13] A combination of films and vaudeville acts was more successful in the community than live musical drama at that time. In May 1907, the *Los Angeles Times* commented on the makeup of the typical nickel film theater audience, and that the nickelodeon had taken over from the penny arcade in popularity: "A canvas of the nickel theaters of Los Angeles last night revealed a very large percentage of foreign patronage in the plain wooden chairs. The Mexican, especially, is an enthusiastic devotee."[14]

TABLE 1. PLAZA AREA THEATRES, 1913–14

Theater	Location	Capacity	Admission (Cents)	Music	Exits	Sanitation	Lighting	Employees
Metropolitan	513–515 N Main Street	500	5	Poor pianist	3	Fair	Excellent	Ticketman, female cashier
Plaza	421–423 N Main Street	500	5	Poor pianist	3	Fair	Excellent	Trumpeter (also ticketman?), female cashier
Hidalgo	371–373 N Main Street	700	10	Orchestra and pianist	4	Fair	Excellent	Ticketman, female cashier
New Federal	300 N Main Street	240	5	Poor pianist	2	Good	Fair	Male cashier
Electric	212 N Main Street	640	5	Pianist	3	Fair	Good	Ticketman, trumpeter, female cashier

TABLE 2. ATTENDANCE AT PLAZA THEATRES, 1913–14

Theater	Date and Hour Observed	Capacity	Attendance	Mexican	Men	Women	Boys over 12	Boys under 12	Girls over 12	Girls under 12
Metropolitan	Monday, 11/10/13, 4:45 PM	500	69	92%	80%	4%	8%	0%	4%	4%
Plaza	Saturday, 3/21/14, 2:45 PM	500	100	90%	85%	7%	0%	4%	0%	4%
Hidalgo	Thursday, 1/1/14, 2:00 PM	700	525	75%	63%	12%	5%	10%	6%	4%
New Federal	Saturday, 4/4/14, 11:20 AM	240	60	55%	85%	5%	0%	5%	0%	5%
Electric	Monday, 11/3/13, 4:30 PM	640	100	75%	85%	4%	7%	1%	1%	2%

William Wilson McEuen's thesis from 1914 on the Mexican community in Sonoratown and the Plaza area is invaluable for the data it contains, especially concerning theatrical spectatorship. He included a survey of the Plaza's Mexican-oriented theaters in the mid-1910s: their audiences, musical component, cost of admission, sanitation, and seating capacities. Tables 1 and 2, abstracted from McEuen's study, list the five theaters on North Main Street whose audience was primarily Mexican in makeup in the mid-1910s.[15] These tables show that the Teatro Hidalgo had the largest seating capacity. It offered the most elaborate music, performed by its house orchestra and pianist, and charged the highest admission—ten cents instead of the usual five. The other theaters only had a pianist to provide musical accompaniment, and, according to McEuen, three of them were "poor" musicians. Most of these theaters had "trumpeters," that is, barkers who enticed potential patrons passing by on North Main Street to enter and buy a ticket by "spieling" loudly through a megaphone. Flashy or lurid posters also enticed passersby into the theater. And cashiers sometimes doubled as ticket takers. Since the five theaters all showed films, each had a projectionist. Adult Mexican men were in the majority in the audience, and many of them were probably

PROXIMAMENTE
¡Brillante - Inauguración!
DEL

TEATRO HIDALGO

Dedicado exclusivamente a espectáculos de alta mo-
ralidad y cultura, en el bello y sonoro idioma español

Durante el año se haran temporadas de Drama,
Comedia, Opereta, Zarzuela y Variedades.

Se presentaran artistas de verdadero merito procedentes de
Madrid, Barcelona, Buenos Aires, Mexico y Habana.

Grandiosas Vistas Cinematograficas.

Gran Orquesta!   Banda Militar!

El Teatro Hidalgo

será el más amplio, elegante y cómodo lugar de cita
de las honorables Colonias de España, México y
demás naciones hispano-americanas

Pídanse Informes y Búsquense Programas.
Gerente,   Teléfono A2891.   P. O. Box 899.
S. P. LABAT.   373 N. Main St.   Los Angeles, Cal.

"¡Brillante Inauguración del Teatro Hidalgo!" (Brilliant Opening of the Hidalgo Theater), *El Heraldo de México,* February 10, 1918.

unmarried railway or agricultural workers who lived in nearby rooming houses. Compara-
tively few children attended at the times that these theaters were visited. However, later
newspaper reports indicate that Mexican children were spectators in film and live theater
presentations, although for a time city regulations required children to be accompanied by
adults.

THE TEATRO HIDALGO
The longest-lived Mexican venue in Los Angeles devoted to the presentation of live theater—musical and dramatic—and film exhibition was the seven-hundred-seat Teatro
Hidalgo, which opened at 371–373 North Main Street, probably on September 11, 1912. The
building in which it was housed was previously a livery stable, and the Portola Theater Company, which either bought or leased the property to "remodel [the] building into [a] picture
theater" sometime in the summer of 1912, reportedly spent $9,000 on the project.[16] Early
in 1913, the company advertised to lease or sell the theater for $8,000, promising that that

Teatro Hidalgo Orchestra, circa 1926, Shades of L.A. Collection/Los Angeles Public Library.

amount would buy or lease the "only strictly Spanish theater in America, featuring vaudeville and pictures, [with an] $800 monthly profit."[17]

With its core audience of the Mexican and Mexican American population residing in downtown Los Angeles near the Plaza, it was appropriate that the Teatro Hidalgo was named after the Father of Mexican Independence, Miguel Hidalgo y Costilla (1753–1811). (The president of Mexico proclaims Hidalgo's famous "Grito de Dolores" ["Cry of Dolores"] every September 15 at night from a balcony of the Palacio Nacional in Mexico City.) The Teatro Hidalgo was regularly advertised as the Teatro de la Raza (Theater of the Race), and, throughout the course of its existence from 1912 to 1936, its different owners or lessees stressed its *Mexicanidad* (Mexicaness) in their choice of theatrical repertory and personnel.[18] The repertory performed there was similar to that of all the other Mexican theaters in the Plaza district, with its mix of various live theatrical and film genres, except that the Hidalgo particularly stressed vaudeville acts, accompanied by its house orchestra, and film exhibition.

During the 1930s, the Teatro Hidalgo also reached out to the larger Latino community through radio broadcasting. In August 1934, the Hidalgo sponsored a thirty-minute program from 7:30 to 8:00 PM simultaneously on stations KGER in Long Beach and KELW in Burbank, probably through a live wire telephone feed. The Hidalgo broadcast its musical vaudeville and theatrical acts that summer, during the time slot immediately before that of the soon-to-be-famous country western music singing group the Sons of the Pioneers, with the future singing cowboy film star Roy Rogers, and also before Mexican operatic baritone Rodolfo Hoyos's local radio show.[19] Imagine hearing Rogers sing the famous song "Tumbling Tumbleweeds" and Hoyos performing the "Toreador Song" ("Votre toast, je peux vous le render") aria from Georges Bizet's popular opera *Carmen* right after listening to the Hidalgo Theater company present its favorite *actos* (acts).

ROMUALDO TIRADO AND THE *REVISTA*

In the 1920s and 1930s, a group of Los Angeles–based artists created a local Spanish-language musical theatrical repertory that reflected the life experiences of Mexican immigrants in Southern California's México de Afuera, in humorous and serious ways. Their works responded directly to the place and time in which they lived, and coexisted with a much larger number of imported Mexican, Spanish, and European musical theater pieces, including operetta and opera. This group of theater folk included impresario and librettist Romualdo Tirado; playwright-journalists Gabriel Navarro (also a composer), Adalberto Elías González, Esteban V. Escalante, Daniel Venegas, and Brígido Caro; and composer-conductors Ernesto González Jiménez and Francisco Camacho Vega. Their collaborators— the singers, actors, dancers, instrumentalists, directors, and stagehands who made up the local Mexican troupes—brought their works to life, at places such as the Teatros California, Capitol, Estella, Hidalgo, Mason, México, Novel, Principal, and Princesa, most of which were located along or near North Main Street.

The leading impresario in Los Angeles's Mexican theater scene in the 1920s and 1930s, although a Spaniard, was Mexican at heart: Romualdo Tirado (1880–1963), known affectionately as "Cachipuchi."[20] He was a multitalented man of the theater—a stage and film actor, singer, comic, director, manager, librettist, playwright, and radio performer. His career was similar to those of others in the ethnic theater in the United States. Like Boris Thomashefsky (1866–1939) in New York's Yiddish theater;[21] Swedish American Hjalmar Peterson, "Olle i Skratthult" (Olle from Laughtersville, 1886–1960), in the Upper Midwest;[22] Eduardo Migliaccio, "Farfariello" (Little Butterfly, 1892–1946) in Little Italy in New York;[23] and Adolf Philipp (1864–1936) in New York's Klein Deutschland (Little Germany),[24] Tirado had a far-reaching influence on the immigrant theater. He was the single most important figure in the history of the live Spanish-language theater in the United States in his day.

Tirado's story and the sweep of history of the Mexican musical stage in Los Angeles are told in the extensive coverage given to cultural and artistic events in the local Spanish-language press. Close study of this reportage reveals the richly varied musical and theatrical repertories offered to local Latino audiences.[25] This performing tradition was part of a vast network of theatrical connections directly linking Los Angeles and other California towns and cities to Chicago, Tucson, San Antonio, New York, and other US locations, all part of the México de Afuera, as well as to Mexico City, Madrid, Havana, Buenos Aires, and other Spanish and Latin American cities. The US Spanish-language stage ran parallel to and sometimes overlapped with the English-language theatrical world, especially vaudeville. But this web of artistic connections was not monolingual, since Spanish-speaking theater performers also moved within the larger, polyglot US entertainment world.[26]

Tirado was instrumental in bringing the Mexican and Spanish forms of the *revista* genre of the 1910s and 1920s to Los Angeles. The *revista* (musical revue) was a topical musical theater work that usually lasted about an hour. It was often paired with other theater pieces, such as Spanish *zarzuela*. Singing and dancing were integral, essential components, and these were accompanied by the theater orchestra conducted by the *maestro concertador* (concert master) or music director. Usually about eight or fewer songs were spaced throughout a *revista,* performed by the female and male principals and the chorus line. The dialogue was spoken, and not sung as in operatic recitative. Popular *revista* songs were published in Mexico City in sheet music form, often with illustrated covers prominently featuring the performers who had made the songs popular, and recordings were released of some of the biggest hits.

The Mexican *revista* was different from its American counterpart, the Broadway musical revue, such as those produced by Florenz Ziegfeld. The Spanish-language *revista* often had a substantial political, erotic, or nationalist plot or theme running through its various *cuadros* (scenes), and often began with a prologue and ended with an apotheosis.[27] The Mexican political revue often commented on developments in Mexican society, especially during the Mexican Revolution of the 1910s and its aftermath in the 1920s. Ziegfeld's revues were comic, but usually not as satirical in nature. His revues were lavishly produced and combined a variety of disparate theatrical and musical elements; they featured leading performers such as Will Rogers, Fanny Brice, and Bert Williams, and ran for much or all of an entire season. *Revistas* produced in Mexico City also centered on their stars, such as María Conesa, Celia Montalván, or Mimi Derba, and were lavish, but were not on the same scale as Ziegfeld's revues. Because of budget constraints they were even less lavish in their Los Angeles versions. Mexican *revistas* were often scrappy, catchy, and risqué; they presented a humorous, sardonic take on the news of the day that was of immediate interest to audiences. (*Revista* also means "newspaper.")

During the 1920s, Tirado wrote a series of comic musical revues and *zarzuelas* that featured him in the titles and leading roles, often as a stereotypical wise-cracking, madcap character who repeatedly finds himself in outlandish situations, highlighting tensions between modernity and tradition in the immigrant community. He was called a "Mexican Chaplin" for good reason, and his *pelado* (urchin/tramp) characters resemble certain components of Charlie Chaplin's humor. Although the scripts and music of his *revistas* are thought to be lost, their titles and the reviews of their premieres strongly suggest aspects of their plots and flavors.[28] (Many of his works are listed in Table 3.)

Tirado poked fun and cried at the trials of the recently arrived Mexican greenhorn *sastre* (tailor) in the various versions of his *revista De México a Los Ángeles* (From Mexico to Los Angeles), the most successful of his works. He may have critiqued the spread of communism, perhaps in its Mexican form, in song, comedy, and dance in *Tirado Bolsheviqui* (Tirado

TABLE 3. **ROMUALDO TIRADO'S LOS ANGELES MUSICAL THEATER WORKS**

These are most but probably not all of Tirado's works. Their composers are identified when known; the years in which they were known to have been performed in Los Angeles are given at the end of each entry.

Work	Genre	Composer (If Known)	Years Performed
El arbol milagroso (The Miraculous Tree)	*Zarzuela*		1927
Aventuras de Daniel después de una noche en la Calle New High Street (Daniel's Adventures after a Night Out on New High Street)	*Zarzuela*		1921
Aventuras de un viejo verde en Long Beach (Adventures of a Dirty Old Man in Long Beach)	*Revista*		1928
Clínica moderna (Modern Clinic)	*Revista*	Francisco Camacho Vega	1921
Dancing—México	*Zarzuela*		1927
De Los Ángeles a México (From Los Angeles to Mexico)	*Zarzuela (revista)*	Ernesto González Jiménez and Francisco Camacho Vega	1920, 1921
De México a Alaska (From Mexico to Alaska)	*Revista*		1924
De México a Los Ángeles, o aventuras de Romualdo Tirado (From Mexico to Los Angeles, or, the Adventures of Romualdo Tirado)	*Revista*	Ernesto González Jiménez	1924, 1929
De México a Los Ángeles, o aventuras de un sastre (From Mexico to Los Angeles, or, the Adventures of a Tailor)	*Revista*	Ernesto Gónzalez Jiménez and Francisco Camacho Vega	1920, 1921
De todo un poco (A Bit of Everything)	*Juguete cómico*		1922
La jaula de los leones (The Lions' Cage)	*Zarzuela*		1927
La mancha de sangre (The Blood Stain)	*A propósito lírico*		1923
Las mariposas de Hollywood (The Butterflies of Hollywood)	*Revista*		1928
Mexicanos al grito de la guerra (Mexicans, Rise to the War Cry)	*Drama lírico patriótico*	Ernesto González Jiménez	1927
Una noche en Los Ángeles (A Night in Los Angeles)	*Revista*		1921
El padrón municipal (The Municipal Census)	*Zarzuela*		1927
Los pantalones de Tirado (Tirado's Pants)	*Revista*		1921
Los pizcadores (The Fieldhands)	*Revista*		1930
Tirado Bolsheviqui/Tirado Bolshevike (Tirado the Communist)	*Revista*		1924
Tirado Bootlegger	*Humorada*		1927
Tirado dentista (Tirado the Dentist)	*Zarzuela*		1921, 1928
Tirado en el polo (Tirado on the Polo Grounds)	*Revista*	Lauro D. Uranga	1925
Tirado en la Republica del "Paramí" (Tirado in the Republic of "All for Me")	*Revista*		1924
Tirado en Long Beach	*Revista*		1927
Tirado torero (Tirado the Bullfighter)	*Revista*		1922

TEATRO MEXICO

Hoy Domingo 4 de Agosto

PRIMER CAÑONAZO

Comienza una nueva era del Teatro Mexicano en L. A.

SIGUE EL EXITO

De la Revista de Gran Espectáculo

AVENTURAS POR ROMUALDO TIRADO

MUSICA DE GONZALEZ JIMENEZ

Para poder representar esta Revista se ha tenido que aumentar el personal de Artistas, Músicos y Tramoyistas, pues es algo grandiosa su representación

Estreno de magníficas decoraciones pintadas por los afamados artistas Jane y Amador Arce, de los Teatros de Europa y México. Lujoso vestuario, primorosos efectos escénicos, magnífica Orquesta. Esta revista durará en cartel una semana para dar oportunidad de que todo el mundo vea

"De México a Los Angeles"

Romualdo Tirado's *De México a Los Ángeles* (From Mexico to Los Angeles), Teatro México; advertisement, *La Opinión,* August 4, 1929.

the Communist). He perhaps satirized the elite class in *Tirado en el polo* (Tirado on the Polo Grounds), especially since few of his audience members had the financial means with which to play this expensive sport. *Tirado Torero* (Tirado the Bullfighter) premiered on December 22, 1922, on the same bill as Oscar Straus's beloved continental operetta *El Soldado de Chocolate* (*The Chocolate Soldier/Der tapfere Soldat*) and Pola Negri's film version of *Carmen,* released in 1918, directed by Ernst Lubitsch.[29] We can imagine Tirado in his comic interpretation of the toreador Escamillo in his parody of the famous operatic tale of the gypsy Carmen, which on that day also became a parody of the Pola Negri film version of the Carmen story. In *Dancing—México* Tirado was either warning Mexican women about the dangers of the feverish dance hall craze then gripping Los Angeles society, or poking fun at it—perhaps both. In his musicals Tirado also became a dentist, a dirty old man ogling young women along the boardwalk in the nearby seaside city of Long Beach, a young man whooping it up out on the town, a lion tamer, a field hand, a bootlegger, and perhaps also a doctor and an Alaskan prospector. In writing these types of works, Tirado followed the tradition, structure, and musical style of the Mexican satirical revue, but with a distinctively Mexican American and local Los Angeles twist, even though he was a Spaniard by birth.

In addition to his long career in the live theater, from the 1890s through at least the 1940s, Tirado also had an extensive second career in Hollywood films.[30] Tirado jumped wholeheartedly into the new medium of sound film beginning in the late 1920s, in the film musical revue *Charros, gauchos, y manolos* (released in 1930), directed by bandleader Xavier Cugat, in which he served as master of ceremonies. The film included several of Tirado's colleagues from the North Main Street Mexican theaters, along with leading Spanish and Latin American performers who had recently arrived in Los Angeles seeking Hollywood gold.

THE MEXICO CITY *REVISTA* IN LOS ANGELES

Many of the musical revues popular in the 1910s and 1920s in Mexico City's theaters were also performed in Los Angeles in the 1920s. For example, the politically oriented Mexican musical *revista El país de la metralla* (The Country of Shrapnel) of 1913, written by José F. Elizondo with music by Spaniard Rafael Gascón, was produced in Los Angeles in the 1920s.[31] Tirado directed his company in it at the Teatro Novel in September and October 1920, and again in October 1924 at the Teatro Capitol.[32] *El país de la metralla* musically dramatized and satirized the bloody events of the Decena Trágica (the Ten Tragic Days) of 1913. During this terrible ten-day period in Mexico City, from February 9 through February 19, President Francisco Madero, known as the "Apostle of Democracy," was ousted from power and imprisoned. On February 21 he was assassinated under orders of the US-aligned general and war minister Victoriano Huerta (1850–1916), known as "El Chacal" (The Jackal). Huerta replaced Madero as president, and governed from February 1913 to July 1914, acting as a dictator. After his defeat by forces under Álvaro Obregón and Francisco "Pancho" Villa, Huerta was forced to resign the presidency.

Elizondo and Gascón's *El país de la metralla* premiered in Mexico City on May 10, 1913, less than three months after the Decena Trágica, and was both scandalous and very success-

Libretto, *El País de la Metralla* (The Country of Shrapnel),
1913, José F. Elizondo (Libretto) and Rafael Gascón (Music),
Collection of John Koegel.

ful. The revue commented satirically on the results of the violence and bombardment of
Mexico City perpetrated during this still-remembered period in Mexican history. It also satirized US involvement in the Mexican economy and politics, especially when a group of eight
singing Uncle Sams appeared on stage.

Because *El país de la metralla* was openly pro-Huerta, with the beginning of a new political regime under Venustiano Carranza, its librettist José Elizondo was exiled and its composer Rafael Gascón later committed suicide.[33] When it was performed in Los Angeles in
the 1920s, *El país de la metralla* had not lost its political or dramatic satire or potency, nor
had the Los Angeles community forgotten the tumultuous events of the Mexican Revolution, which had only ended recently. However, the sharp sting of the performances in 1913
may have been softened with the passage of time. And in 1927 Elizondo would be given a
hero's welcome in Los Angeles for his contributions to Mexican theater and culture.

Other Mexican musical theater trends also had a favorable reception in Los Angeles. The
invasion of Mexico City in 1925 of the famous Bataclán musical revue, named after Jacques
Offenbach's French operetta *Ba-ta-clan* of 1855 (a *chinoiserie musicale*) and the Parisian
theater of the same name, sparked a Bataclán fever on the Mexican stage that very soon
extended north to Los Angeles.[34] With its army of scantily clad, almost nude female singing
dancers, the French company scandalized and titillated Mexican audiences.[35] The ensuing
parody *Mexican Rataplán* (*Mexican Ra-ta-plán*), with saucy music by the brothers Emilio D.
and Lauro Uranga and an erotic and politically tinged satirical libretto by the stage star

Roberto "El Panzón" Soto, featured the *revista* star Celia Montalván. It was a smash hit in Mexico City in 1925 soon after the arrival of the French company and a response to exploding *Bataclanismo*.[36]

The Bataclán-Rataplán vogue was first reported in Los Angeles in February 1925,[37] and was introduced in the city by May of that year, just a few months after it first appeared in Mexico City.[38] One of its main exponents was Mexican playwright, *revista* librettist, popular songwriter, and film screenwriter Antonio Guzmán Aguilera (1894–1958), known professionally as Guz Águila. Mayer Trallis, impresario at the Teatros Hidalgo and Capitol in Los Angeles, lured him north in 1924. Trallis gave Águila a contact of which he could "never have dreamed about" in Mexico: plentiful dollars; beautiful women, costumes, and scenery; and good will and faith in his talents.[39] Águila offered his new musical revues *Los efectos del Bataclán* (The Effects of Bataclán) and *El Bataclán oriental* (The Oriental Bataclán) to local audiences at the Teatro Capitol in July 1925.[40] Los Angeles thus followed the fashion established earlier on the Parisian and Mexico City stages. Águila also wrote popularly received *revistas* set in Los Angeles, such as *Los Ángeles vacilador* (Los Angeles on a Spree) of 1924 and *Los cuatro ases de la Calle Main* (The Four Aces of Main Street) of 1925, the latter in honor of the four leading Mexican theaters in Los Angeles, located on or near North Main Street by the Plaza: the Teatros Capitol, Hidalgo, Principal, and Estella.[41]

In the mid-1920s, Los Angeles troupes also performed Águila's earlier satirical *revistas* on Mexican political and patriotic themes, such as *Alma Tricolor* (Three-Colored Soul) of 1922, with music by Manuel Rivera Baz—the title of which represented the three colors of the Mexican flag—and two works from 1920 about Mexican presidents: *El jardín de Obregón* (Obregón's Garden) and *La huerta de Don Adolfo* (The Orchard of Don Adolfo), both with music by José Palacios.

The title of Águila's *La huerta de Don Adolfo* wittily refers to Adolfo de la Huerta (1881–1955), interim president of Mexico from June through November 1920. After he was exiled from Mexico in 1924, de la Huerta settled in Los Angeles, living there until 1935. While an active politician in Mexico, he was also known as a talented tenor with an operatic-style voice, and as a pianist and violinist. (He was noted for breaking into song in Mexican cabinet meetings.) In Los Angeles he gave voice lessons to Hollywood stars and to performers from the local Mexican stage. In the late 1920s, de la Huerta taught voice to Enrico Caruso Jr., then in Los Angeles to capitalize on his famous father's name and to appear in Spanish-language Hollywood musical films. However, de la Huerta's prize pupil was tenor Roberto Guzmán Esparza, who performed frequently in the North Main Street theaters, on recordings, and in early Hollywood sound films, such as the first motion picture version of Sigmund Romberg's beloved stage operetta *The Desert Song* (1929).[42]

Many major stars of Mexico City's *revista* stage also appeared in Los Angeles's Mexican theaters in the 1920s and 1930s. The Spanish-born-but-Mexican-at-heart singer, dancer, and actress María Conesa (1890/92?–1978) was known for her voluptuous and picaresque images of *Mexicanidad*. She was the most famous Mexican representative of the *teatro sicalíptico* (erotic theater) and *teatro frívolo* (frivolous theater) traditions that emphasized the female

María Conesa as a China Poblana, 1920s, Collection of John Koegel.

body in revealing costumes, erotic situations, and the use of double entendre in song lyrics and dramatic situations, directed especially toward the male gaze.[43] Mexican poet, writer, and critic Luis G. Urbina (1868–1934) complained that Conesa could even read the *Padre Nuestro* (Our Father) prayer and make it sound salacious.[44]

During one of her visits to Los Angeles, in 1930, Conesa attempted to break into Hollywood films without luck, at the same time that she was appearing on the local Mexican stage. The *Los Angeles Times,* which barely noticed the city's Mexican theaters, published a laudatory review of her performances at the Teatro California in February 1930: "At her request, the audience spontaneously joined her in the singing of the choruses of some of her somewhat naughty songs, and again when, during her interpretations, she flirted with some of the men in the front rows."[45] Conesa surely sang her famous version of the bawdy song "El tango del morrongo" (The Song of the Tom Cat) from the Spanish *zarzuela* *Enseñanza Libre,* which was familiar to Los Angeles audiences. Recordings of the song were likely available in the city at Mauricio Calderón's Repertorio Mexicano music store on North Main Street, and its lyrics had appeared in numerous published *cancioneros* (songbooks) on both sides of the border, including in collections published or sold in Los Angeles.[46]

CHANGING TIMES

The highpoint of the live Mexican musical stage in Los Angeles occurred in the 1920s. Impresarios such as Romualdo Tirado and Ernesto González Jiménez at the Teatro México and Teatro Capitol and Mayer Trallis at the Teatro Hidalgo promoted a varied musical theater repertory—of Spanish *zarzuelas,* European operettas, and Mexican *revistas,* and some standard Italian and French operas—alternating with dramatic plays and comedies, some written by local playwrights, and regular film exhibition. These theatrical forms served as a product of both commercial consumption and artistic edification. Musical theater especially provided a means by which Latino working- and middle-class audiences could reinforce a positive sense of ethnic and racial self-identification and enjoy up-to-date popular entertainment. Since not all Mexicano/a immigrants resident in Los Angeles had had experience with theatrical and film spectatorship before their emigration, by participating in these cultural forms they received a modern artistic education in their new surroundings.

The negative financial and social effects of the Great Depression of the 1930s, along with local-, state-, and federal-government-sponsored forced repatriation of Mexican nationals and Mexican Americans with US citizenship in that decade, caused a decline in the live Mexican musical theater in Los Angeles.[47] This decline forced local performers to adapt to new circumstances, including repatriation to Mexico, giving up the stage, reduced theatrical activity and income, and more extensive and less lucrative tours to smaller US towns with Latino populations. Some sought work as extras and secondary characters in Hollywood films, and others found employment in various projects sponsored by the Works Progress Administration.

The exhibition of Mexican musical films and some Spanish-language musical films made in Hollywood, as well as *variedades* (vaudeville or variety acts), filled this gap in the 1930s. It was less expensive for impresarios to present films, periodically interspersed with live acts, since the cost of supporting a constantly changing musical and dramatic repertory performed by a full company with a stage director, stars, supporting actors, singers, dancers, orchestra, and a technical stage staff was usually greater than the cost of film exhibition. However, the live drama, spoken or sung, never entirely left the boards.

In the early 1930s, the center of Mexican theatrical activity and film exhibition was still located on or near North Main Street, close to the Plaza. After that time, however, especially from the late 1930s through the 1950s, the Mexicano theatrical center shifted to nearby

South Broadway and its environs, where many of the large and elegant English-language vaudeville theaters and movie palaces built in the 1910s and 1920s were gradually being transformed into Spanish-language film and vaudeville venues.[48] And in the 1950s, much of the original Plaza district was being destroyed in the cause of "progress" and the completion of the Hollywood/Santa Ana Freeway (Highway 101), which bisected downtown Los Angeles. The Latino population in Los Angeles grew significantly during the immediate pre– and post–World War II periods, and as the financial effects of the Great Depression lessened, the community could increasingly support an ever-more-active film and live variety show scene again, albeit with a different artistic emphasis than in the 1920s and 1930s, and in a different theater district.

Frank Fouce (1899–1962), the leading theatrical and motion picture impresario in Los Angeles's Latino community from the 1930s through the early 1960s, gradually came to control almost all the Mexican theatrical venues in downtown Los Angeles. Born in Hawaii to Spanish parents, he moved to California as a child. In the 1920s he worked in Hollywood silent film production, and had a connection to the great comic team Laurel and Hardy.[49] During his long career as an impresario, Fouce signed the best Mexican, Latino, and Latin American artistic talent for appearances at his large movie palaces—the Million Dollar, California, Roosevelt, Mason, and Mayan Theaters, among other venues, including the smaller Teatro Hidalgo. The list of the artists who appeared at his many theaters is a veritable who's who of Latin American music, theater, and film: Antonio Aguilar, Cantinflas, Celia Cruz, Dolores del Río, María Felix, Juan Gabriel, Lalo Guerrero, Rodolfo Hoyos, Pedro Infante, José Alfredo Jiménez, Libertad Lamarque, Agustín Lara, Lydia Mendoza, Jorge Negrete, Tito Puente, Trío Los Panchos, Eva Quintanar, Resortes, and many others. The Mexican government honored Fouce's contributions to Mexican culture in 1948 when it made him a member of the Orden Mexicana del Águila Azteca (Order of the Aztec Eagle), the highest award given to foreigners. Fouce was one of the most important figures in the history of live musical and motion picture presentation in Los Angeles, although his contributions have not yet been sufficiently recognized or studied. He was also a pioneer in establishing Spanish-language television stations in the United States. His son, Frank Fouce Jr. (1927–2013), followed him into these same fields.[50] Fouce's Million Dollar Theater at 307 South Broadway continued to present Mexican films and regular variety performances by leading popular musicians until at least the early 1990s, when for a time it became a church. In the late 1990s, an attempt was made to revive the variety show tradition at the Million Dollar.[51]

IMAGINING MEXICAN MUSICIANS IN LOS ANGELES'S THEATERS

The front page of the issue of *La Opinión,* Los Angeles's principal Spanish-language newspaper, from April 6, 1932, offers a good example of just how important music and the theater were to the local community. The large-type headline screamed "GUTY CARDENAS MUERTO A TIROS EN UN CABARET," forcefully announcing the tragic killing of the beloved Mexican singer-guitarist-songwriter Guty Cárdenas (b. 1905), which had occurred just a few

Million Dollar Theater, Million Dollar Show, Variedades, 1999, Photo by Gary Leonard, Gary Leonard Collection/Los Angeles Public Library.

hours earlier in the Salón Bach in Mexico City, a bar frequented by musicians and other artists.[52] Los Angeles readers lamented Cárdenas's terrible death, especially since they had loved and sung his songs, such as "Flor" (Flower), "Nunca" (Never), and "Rayito del sol" (A Little Ray of Sun). His songs had swept California and the rest of *México de Afuera* in the United States since the time the singer-songwriter had begun to record them in 1928 for the US Columbia record label.[53]

Cárdenas probably first appeared in Los Angeles in December 1928, en route to Mexico City from New York, where he had recently made a group of recordings for Columbia Records.[54] Los Angeles residents had bought his best-selling recordings and sheet music at Mauricio Calderón's Repertorio Mexicano music shop, and they probably also heard them on local Spanish-language radio programs. In the fall of 1930 Cárdenas performed his songs live on Los Angeles radio.[55] On December 11, 1930, local residents had had a chance to see and hear him perform in person, when he appeared in downtown Los Angeles at the Teatro México in a special farewell gala in his honor, accompanied by Virginia Fábregas, Mexico's first lady of the theater, the popular film and stage performer Celia Montalvan, and many leading lights of local Latino musical and theatrical society.[56] They could also have seen

Adalberto "Resortes" Martínez with two costars of the Maria Antonieta Pons Revue at the Million Dollar Theater, circa 1948, Herald-Examiner Collection/Los Angeles Public Library.

Cárdenas sing his own songs "Ojos tristes" (Sad Eyes), a Yucatecan *clave,* and "Piña madura" (Ripe Pineapple), a *huapango,* in the Warner Brothers–First National melodramatic film *La dama atrevida* (The Daring Woman). It had played one week at the Teatro California in downtown Los Angeles (May 29 through June 4, 1931), in a successful run.[57] After Cárdenas's death, Mauricio Calderón's Repertorio Mexicano released a record in his honor.

The other leading Los Angeles Spanish-language newspaper of the era besides *La Opinión* was *El Heraldo de México* (The Mexican Herald), which called itself "El Defensor de los Mexicanos en Estados Unidos" (The Defender of the Mexicans in the United States).[58] Coverage of the local Mexican musical, film, and theatrical scenes was a prominent feature of both papers. Their pages also included articles about agricultural and railroad workers who sang *corridos* (narrative ballads) to guitar accompaniment about the deeds and heroes of the Mexican Revolution. Forced repatriation of Mexicans from California and the conflicts between ethnic groups and racial discrimination were also popular *corrido* topics. The heroic deeds of prominent Mexicans such as the brave aviators Emilio Carranza (The "Lindbergh of Mexico") and Pablo Sidar, killed in tragic air crashes in 1928 and 1930, captured the attention of Los Angeles *corridistas* (corrido writers).[59] Mexican musicians also sang ballads about local disasters such as the failure on March 12, 1928, of William Mulholland's St. Francis Dam (the San Francisquito Dam), and the resulting massive flood, which killed Mexicano/a farm laborers and others in the Santa Clara Valley in Los

"Corrido de Guty Cárdenas" 1932, Released by Mauricio Calderón's Repertorio Musical Mexicano Music Store; UCLA Frontera Collection.

Angeles and Ventura counties. Esparza and Camacho's *corrido* "La inundación de Santa Paula" (The Santa Paula Flood) and the Cancioneros Acosta's "La inundación de California" (The California Flood) were released very soon after the catastrophe, showing how quickly local musicians reacted to important events.[60] Many *cancioneros* (songbooks) were published that included *corridos* such as these, along with current and older Mexican and Latin American popular songs.

The Los Angeles Spanish-language press also reported that Angelenos attended musical and dramatic films from Hollywood's own Cine Hispano, the locally produced, Spanish-language films released between 1929 and 1939 by major Hollywood studios such as Fox, MGM, Paramount, Universal, and Warner Brothers, and by some minor studios.[61] These films featured prominent Los Angeles resident performers such as actors Romualdo Tirado, Lupe Vélez, and Antonio Moreno, and the famous operatic tenor and actor José Mojica, and the popular tenor Tito Guizar (who was operatically trained). (The Cine Hispano also improbably featured Hollywood stars such as Buster Keaton and Laurel and Hardy in Spanish-language versions of their English-language talkies of the early 1930s.) A large group of other Latin American, Spanish, and Latino actors and musicians also participated in the Cine Hispano, and in Hollywood's English-language films in the 1930s and beyond.[62]

Cancionero Alma Norteña (Northern Soul Songbook), 1944, with Cover Image of Ranchera Queen Lucha Reyes, Collection of John Koegel.

Angelenos saw an even greater number of Mexican, Spanish, and Latin American films in Los Angeles's many Spanish-language motion picture houses from the 1930s through at least the 1990s.

The local Spanish-language press also featured the activities of prominent local Mexican musicians, including the three performers profiled here: conductor and composer Ernesto González Jiménez; singer and actor Rodolfo Hoyos; and pianist, songwriter, and orchestra leader Eva Quintanar. Their experiences encompass the full spectrum of musical and theatrical expression in Mexican Los Angeles, and in their careers they also engaged with the larger musical life of the city and region, and well beyond.

Composer, conductor, musical arranger, violinist, and pianist Ernesto González Jiménez (b. 1888) is one of the principal but unsung figures of Los Angeles's musical scene of the 1920s and 1930s.[63] Little is known currently about his life other than what was published in the local Spanish-language press and the information available in documentary sources such as census, immigration, border crossing, naturalization, and city directory records. A few of his musical compositions survive out of what surely was a much larger body of music, and some of his songs were recorded. Originally from Monterrey in Northern Mexico, he was residing in Los Angeles by 1920. He was Tirado's business and artistic partner in the 1920s at several North Main Street theaters. González Jiménez also ran his own private music studio, the Academía Chopin (Chopin Academy). As an *ofrecimiento* (offering) to its readers in 1921, *El Heraldo de México* published *Gracia y Alegría* (Grace and Joy), his large music collection, which includes a number of theatrically related songs, and solo piano works by local guitarist-composer Enrique Robles, arranged by González Jiménez from Robles's original guitar versions.[64] Besides *Gracia y Alegría, El Heraldo de México* also published González Jiménez's song collection *Canciones de mi tierra* (Songs of My Homeland) in 1921, which included "Yo soy pura mexicana" (I Am a True Mexican Woman), "Pensaba que tu amor" (I Thought That Your Love), and "Juchiteco."[65] As a *recuerdo* (souvenir), the collection also featured photos of three of the singing and dancing stars of Los Angeles's Mexican stage, Carmen Rodríguez, Amparito Guillot ("she of undraped legs"), and Esther Tapia.[66]

González Jiménez was the principal conductor in many of Los Angeles's Mexican theaters in the 1920s and later. He also composed musical scores to plays, *revistas,* and *zarzuelas* performed in the city in that decade, most notably the music for Tirado's popular *revista De México a Los Ángeles*. He also wrote several film scores, conducted the Orfeón Español (Spanish Choir), and gave public concerts and private recitals with his students. His Terceto Clásico (Classic Trio), a chamber music group made up of piano, violin, and cello, broadcast on Earle C. Anthony's pioneering radio station KFI in the mid-1920s.

Mexican baritone Rodolfo Hoyos (1896–1980), a longtime Los Angeles resident, was equally at home in both vernacular and cultivated performance styles, and had an important career in opera, operetta, *zarzuela,* and popular music, and as a musical impresario and director of musical stage companies on both sides of the US-Mexico border, especially in Los Angeles and New York. In Los Angeles in the 1930s and 1940s, he appeared on radio, on the city's many Spanish-language stages, and in opera at the Hollywood Bowl, the Greek Theater in Griffith Park, and Philharmonic Auditorium downtown. He also appeared in singing roles in English- and Spanish-language Hollywood films.

Recalling that his early radio programs "were a mixture of live music, poetry, drama and discussion," Hoyos described his work with "early programs as a [radio] broker" and "the subsequent change to recorded programs." He remembered that "We would present artists, I would sing and have many artists. There were groups of singers. We would put on radio dramas with recognized artists such as Romualdo Tirado and José Peña Pepén [Pepet], who were artists here in the theater. I would put dramas on the radio, first live and then using records. I began to use records and it became easier for us and less expensive."[67]

Beginning in the early 1920s, Hoyos made numerous recordings over several decades for many of the major American record companies, including the Edison, Columbia, Victor, Brunswick, Vocalion, and Okeh labels.[68] He was as talented at singing Mexican *corridos, huapangos* from the state of Veracruz, and other Latin American folk music as he was at performing recent romantic, urbane popular songs by the best Mexican songwriters, such as María Grever, Mario Talavera, or Jorge del Moral. He could sing in a crooning style à la Bing Crosby, and he recorded comic sketches, all in Spanish. Besides enthusiastically singing Mexican and American popular music in Spanish, he was a noted interpreter of the demanding title role of Verdi's opera *Rigoletto* (although he never seems to have recorded it) and other major operatic baritone roles.[69] Hoyos sang in the premiere in 1932 of California composer Mary Carr Moore's (1873–1957) Italian-language, American opera *David Rizzio* (about Mary Queen of Scots) at Los Angeles's Shrine Auditorium. Los Angeles–based journalist Gabriel Navarro praised him as "el cantante mas sensacional que se ha presentado en Los Ángeles después de Lawrence Tibbett" (the most sensational singer to appear in Los Angeles after Lawrence Tibbett).[70] Since Tibbett (1896–1960)—born in Bakersfield, California, and active in Los Angeles early in his career—was America's leading operatic baritone in the 1930s, and a major star at New York City's Metropolitan Opera, this was high praise indeed.[71]

Though men dominated the field of professional music in Mexican Los Angeles, there were key exceptions. Pianist, songwriter, and orchestra leader Eva Quintanar was once dubbed by the Mexican press as the "female Agustín Lara."[72] She was known for her fine pianistic skills, and her talent for composing well-crafted, sensitive, and sophisticated popular songs with rich harmonies, excellent orchestrations, and memorable melodies. She also wrote the lyrics for many of her songs. She especially favored the romantic bolero genre, numerous examples of which she recorded on piano with various vocal soloists and orchestras. Quintanar was noted for her ability to transpose on the spot whatever arrangement was set in front of her—a valuable talent for a pianist accompanying singers with a wide variety of voice types and ranges.[73]

Born in El Paso, Texas, in 1915, and still playing piano as of 2016, Quintanar arrived with her family in Los Angeles by 1936, settling on North Grand Avenue in the northern section of the Bunker Hill area of the city.[74] She reportedly performed as a piano soloist on Spanish-language radio in Los Angeles while still a teenager, and studied music at the Los Angeles Conservatory of Music in the late 1930s or early 1940s.[75] She began her documented compositional career in 1939 with the *canciones-boleros* "Fue" (It Was) and Déjame" (Leave Me), the *canción-fox* "Que va a ser de mí" (What Will Become of Me), and the *bambuco* "Te he vuelto a ver" (I've Returned to See You).[76] She would continue to write songs, many of which she recorded with her own orchestra and tenor Rubén Reyes for the

Eva Quintanar in the Recording Studio, Courtesy of John McGowan.

Los Angeles–based Discos Taxco, Imperial, and Tri-Color labels. Prominent Mexican and Mexican American singers such as Adelina García, Las Hermanas Águila, and Chelo Silva also recorded her songs. García made the first-known recording of a Quintanar song, the *bolero* "Tengo miedo" (I'm Afraid), in 1941, conducted by Los Angeles music composer and impresario Manuel S. Acuña.[77] It became one of her biggest hits.[78]

Quintanar was very active in the 1940s and early 1950s as a pianist and orchestra leader in the Mexican movie palaces in downtown Los Angeles, such as the Million Dollar, Mayan, and Orpheum theaters. She and her orchestra accompanied some of Mexico's greatest singers in their live performances at these theaters, such as film superstar Pedro Infante and the famous tenor Pedro Vargas. Quintanar also collaborated or alternated with African American musicians at the Million Dollar Theater, such as the great jazz vibraphone soloist and bandleader Lionel Hampton.

ENVISIONING THE PAST

Many resources exist that can help us envision and understand the musical and theatrical worlds in Mexican Los Angeles in their rich complexity. We can *study* the disparate but interrelated elements that made up these traditions: musical and theatrical repertories; recordings of those repertories; the lives of performers, composers, and playwrights; the audiences who patronized their artistic offerings; critical and popular responses to performance; changing venues; the economic aspects of performance; social and political contexts and meanings; and issues of gender and ethnicity.

Some documentary sources have long been available in physical form, and others are increasingly being made available in digital format. In order to understand this topic, one would *read* about the history of musical and theatrical performance in local newspapers and periodicals. One can *see and hear* these performers in musical and dramatic films from the Mexican cinema and Hollywood's Cine Hispano.[79] One can *read and perform* Mexican and Mexican American popular music and Mexican- and "Latin"-themed music by American popular songwriters in digital sheet music collections such as UCLA's Sheet Music Consortium and Archive of American Popular Music.[80] One can *hear* the songs and dance music popular in the Mexican community in Southern California as recorded by the major American record companies such as Edison, Victor, Brunswick, and Columbia, and by local Los Angeles labels such as Discos Taxco, Azteca, and Imperial. Many of these recordings are available online on the Library of Congress's National Jukebox, UCLA's Strachwitz Frontera Collection of Mexican and Mexican American Recordings, Syracuse University's Belfer Cylinders Digital Collection, and the University of California, Santa Barbara's Cylinder Preservation and Digitization Project.[81]

We can also *experience* this music today since it continues to live on in public memory and performance. The current Mexican, Chicano, and Latin American music scenes of Los Angeles are unthinkable without these early foundations of music and musical theater. The art and business of making Spanish-language music are as old as the city itself, and they continue to shape contemporary Los Angeles in profound ways.

NOTES

1. César López, "El Descanso: A Comparative History of the Los Angeles Plaza Area and the Shared Racialized Space of the Mexican and Chinese Communities, 1853–1933" (PhD diss., University of California, Berkeley, 2002); Jean Bruce Poole and Tevvy Ball, *El Pueblo: The Historic Heart of Los Angeles* (Los Angeles: Getty Conservation Institute and the J. Paul Getty Museum, 2002); and William Estrada, *The Los Angeles Plaza: Sacred and Contested Space* (Austin: University of Texas Press, 2008).

2. The foundational study of Hispanic theater in Los Angeles and the United States is Nicolás Kanellos, *A History of Hispanic Theater: Origins to 1940* (Austin: University of Texas Press, 1990).

3. "Olvera Street might not be authentic Old California or even authentic Mexico, but it was better than the bulldozer": Kevin Starr, *Material Dreams: Southern California through the 1920s* (New York: Oxford University Press, 1990), 205.

4. George J. Sánchez, *Becoming Mexican American: Ethnicity, Culture, and Identity in Chicano Los Angeles, 1900–1945* (New York: Oxford University Press, 1993); and William Deverell, *Whitewashed Adobe: The Rise of Los Angeles and the Remaking of Its Mexican Past* (Berkeley: University of California Press, 2004).

5. Mark Wild, *Street Meeting: Multiethnic Neighborhoods in Early Twentieth-Century Los Angeles* (Berkeley: University of California Press, 2005); and Isabela Seong Leong Quintana,

"Making Do, Making Home: Borders and the Worlds of Chinatown and Sonoratown in Early Twentieth-Century Los Angeles," *Journal of Urban History* 41, no. 1 (2015): 47–74.

6. Estrada, *The Los Angeles Plaza,* 245.

7. Colin Gunckel, *Mexico on Main Street: Transnational Film Culture in Los Angeles before World War II* (New Brunswick, NJ: Rutgers University Press, 2015); and Jan Olsson, *Los Angeles before Hollywood: Journalism and American Film Culture, 1905 to 1915* (Stockholm: National Library of Sweden, 2008).

8. Steven Loza, *Barrio Rhythm: Mexican American Music in Los Angeles* (Urbana: University of Illinois Press, 1993); and Anthony Macías, *Mexican American Mojo: Popular Music, Dance, and Urban Culture in Los Angeles, 1935–1968* (Durham: Duke University Press, 2008).

9. José Vasconcelos, "El México de Afuera," *La Opinión,* June 10, 1928, 9, 10.

10. The Mexican *orquesta típica* (typical orchestra), a primarily string ensemble related to the mariachi, is a popular orchestra of representative Mexican instruments typically used in Mexican ensembles such as *salterio* (a trapezoidal triple-strung metal-string instrument played with finger picks) and *bandolón* (a pear-shaped large guitar with metal strings), in addition to mandolin, violin, cello, guitar, flute, and harp, and sometimes other instruments.

11. Before World War II, much of Southern California's Latino population was of Mexican heritage, but now is much more diverse in national origin. In this study I use the terms "Mexican," "Mexicano/a," and "Mexican American" to refer to individuals of Mexican heritage.

12. The earlier, nineteenth-century history of music and musical theater in Mexican Los Angeles is covered in Kanellos, *A History of Hispanic Theater;* John Koegel, *Canciones del país:* Mexican Musical Life in California after the Gold Rush," *California History* 78, no. 3 (Fall 1999): 160–87, 215–19; and Koegel, "Mexican and Mexican-American Musical Life in Southern California, 1850–1900" and "Calendar of Southern California Amusements (1852–1897) Designed for the Spanish-Speaking Public," *Inter-American Music Review* 13, no. 2 (Spring-Summer 1993): 111–43.

13. "El Nuevo Teatro," *Los Angeles Times,* February 2, 1907, II, 3; "El Nuevo Salon Dramatico," *Los Angeles Times,* February 3, 1907, 14; "Histrionic Art Rudely Shocked in Classic Old Sonoratown," *Los Angeles Herald,* February 12, 1907, 12; and "Theater's Short Season," *Los Angeles Times,* March 9, 1907, 14.

14. "Now Nickel Eats Penny," *Los Angeles Times,* May 31, 1907, II, 8.

15. William Wilson McEuen, "A Survey of the Mexicans in Los Angeles" (MA thesis, University of Southern California, 1914), 74.

16. There is conflicting information about when the Teatro Hidalgo opened, in 1911 or 1912. Kanellos and a newspaper article say September 11, 1911 (Kanellos, *A History of Hispanic Theater,* 21; "El Aniversario del Hidalgo," *La Opinión,* September 9, 1934, II, 3). However, city records indicate that the building was first remodeled as a theater in 1912. See Application to Alter, Repair or Demolish, May 27, 1912, Los Angeles Department of Building and Safety records, www.ladbs.org/services/check-status/online-building-records; and recorded building permits, *Los Angeles Times,* June 2, 1912, VI, 2.

17. "Theater Exchange," *Los Angeles Times,* January 5, 1913, V, 18. It is not clear whether the Portola Theater Company had earlier bought or leased the property that it was advertising.

18. In 1914, McEuen stated that the Teatro Hidalgo printed its posters in Spanish and Italian since a sizeable number of Italians then lived in the Plaza area.

19. Radio broadcast listings, *Los Angeles Times,* August 4, 1934, I, 2, and August 11, 1934, I, 4. Station KELW broadcast several hours of daily Spanish-language programming at this time, including musical performances and discussion by Pedro J. González and his group Los Madrugadores.

20. Tirado's nickname Cachipuchi is a reference to Tío Cachipuchi (Uncle Cachipuchi), a character in Gerónimo Giménez's famous Spanish *zarzuela La boda de Luis Alonso* (The Wedding of Luis Alonso, 1897). Fittingly for Tirado, among other meanings it is also a Chilean term for a comic or circus character.

21. Edna Nahsho, ed., *New York's Yiddish Theater: From the Bowery to Broadway* (New York: Columbia University Press, 2016).

22. Anne-Charlotte Harvey, "Performing Ethnicity: The Role of Swedish Theatre in the Twin Cities," in *Swedes in the Twin Cities: Immigrant Life and Minnesota's Urban Frontier,* ed. Philip J. Anderson and Dag Blanck, 149–72 (St. Paul: Minnesota Historical Society Press and the Swedish-American Historical Society, 2001).

23. Hermann W. Haller, *Tra Napoli e New York: Le macchiette italo-americane di Eduardo Migliaccio* (Rome: Bulzoni, 2006); and Francesco Durante and Robert Viscusi, eds., *Italoamericana: The Literature of the Great Migration, 1880–1943* (New York: Fordham University Press, 2014).

24. Extensive coverage of Adolf Philipp appears in John Koegel, *Music in German Immigrant Theater: New York City, 1840–1940* (Rochester: University of Rochester Press, 2009), 197–380; and Koegel, "Non-English Language Musical Theater in the United States," in *The Cambridge Companion to the Musical,* ed. Paul Laird and William Everett, 29–53 (Cambridge: Cambridge University Press, 2008).

25. I am examining all available issues of the Spanish-language newspapers published in Southern California from the 1850s to about 1950 for a book on Mexican musical theater in Los Angeles. The local Spanish-language press was active sporadically in the second half of the nineteenth century and continuously from the early twentieth century. However, almost all issues of local papers from about 1900 to about 1915 are currently missing or lost. See Nicolás Kanellos, with Helvetia Martell, *Hispanic Periodicals in the United States, Origins to 1960: A Brief History and Comprehensive Bibliography* (Houston: Arte Público, 2000).

26. Janet Sturman, *Zarzuela, Spanish Operetta, American Stage* (Urbana: University of Illinois Press, 2000); and Susan Thomas, *Cuban Zarzuela: Performing Race and Gender on Havana's Lyric Stage* (Urbana: University of Illinois Press, 2008).

27. Manuel Mañón, *Historia del Teatro Principal de México, 1753–1931* (Mexico City: Editorial Cvltura, 1932; reprint ed., Mexico City: Consejo Nacional para la Cultura y las Artes, 2009); Jorge Miranda, ed., *Del rancho al Bataclán: Cancionero de teatro de revista, 1900–1940* (Mexico City: Museo Nacional de Culturas Nacionales, 1984); Gerardo Luzuriaga, "Teatro y Revolución: Apuntes sobre la revista política en México," *Mester* 21, no. 1 (Spring 1992): 11–22; Pablo Dueñas, *Las divas en el teatro de revista mexicano* (Mexico City: Asociación Mexicana de Estudios Fonográficos, 1994); Armando María y Campos, *El teatro de género chico en la revolución Mexicana* (Mexico

City: Consejo Nacional para la Cultura y las Artes, 1996); and *El país de las tandas: Teatro de Revista, 1900–1940* (Mexico City: Museo Nacional de Culturas Populares, 2005).

28. Playscripts and music from Tirado's many *revistas* seem not to have survived. I have searched copyright records at the Library of Congress to determine if Tirado and other local Mexican playwrights registered their works for copyright, but without success; the case is not closed, however.

29. Pola Negri's German film *Carmen* of 1918 was released in the United States in 1921 as *Gypsy Blood*. In Spanish-language theaters in the United States it was called *Sangre Torera* (Bullfighting Blood).

30. Tirado's son Romualdo Arturo Tirado (1912–98) followed his father into motion picture and theatrical presentation, as an owner of Mexican movie theaters and producer of musical variety acts in Southern California and Fresno, from the 1940s through the 1980s. See Manuel G. Gonzalez, "Arthur Tirado and the Teatro Azteca: Mexican Popular Culture in the Central San Joaquin Valley," *California History* 83, no. 4 (2006): 46–63.

31. José F. Elizondo, *El País de la Metralla,* 2nd ed. (Mexico City: Talleres de Imprenta y Fotograbado "Novedades," 1913); and Pablo Dueñas and Jesús Flores y Escalante, *Teatro de revista, 1904–1936,* Teatro mexicano: Historia y dramaturgia 20 (Mexico City: Consejo Nacional para la Cultura y las Artes, 1995).

32. The Teatro Novel was later known as the Teatro Capitol.

33. Eduardo Soto Contreras, "Su Majestad el Hambre, soberana del *País de la Metralla,*" *Tramoya* 70 (January-March 2002): 99–110.

34. The French expression "et tout le bataclan" (meaning "et tout le reste" or "and all the rest") might be translated colloquially as "the whole nine yards."

35. Ageeth Sluis, *Deco Body, Deco City: Female Spectacle and Modernity in Mexico City, 1900–1939* (Lincoln: University of Nebraska Press, 2016).

36. Recordings from *Mexican Rataplán* were reissued on the LP album *El País de las Tandas: Mexican Rataplán* (Mexico City: Museo Nacional de Culturas Populares, MNCP-0011, 1983).

37. Salvador Gonzalo Becerra, "Teatrales," *El Heraldo de México,* February 13, 1925, 5. Numerous reports of the *Bataclanismo* fever in Mexico City were published in Los Angeles's *El Heraldo de México* in the following months.

38. "Nuestros Teatros Locales: Se Bataclanizan en el Hidalgo," *El Heraldo de México,* May 19, 1925, 5.

39. E. de A., "Teatrales," *El Heraldo de México,* June 7, 1924, 5. Guz Águila reportedly wrote more than five hundred theatrical works.

40. Advertisements, *El Heraldo de México,* July 16, 1925, 5.

41. The Teatro Capitol was located at 338 South Spring Street, one block west of Main Street.

42. "A. de la Huerta desea radicarse en Los Ángeles," *El Heraldo de México,* March 12, 1924, 1; "De la Huerta in Los Angeles Saturday," *Los Angeles Times,* November 24, 1924, 2; "Voice Film Gives Exile a Vocation," *Los Angeles Times,* November 16, 1928, II, 5; and Roberto Guzmán Esparza, *Adolfo de la Huerta, el desconocido* (Mexico City: Universidad Autónoma Metropolitana, 2009).

43. Paulina Suárez-Hesketh, "The Frivolous Scene: Cosmopolitan Amusements in Mexico City's 1920s," *Global South* 9, no. 2 (Fall 2015): 103–30.

44. *El Imparcial* (Mexico City), November 11, 1907.

45. Salvador Baguez, "Actress Receives Ovation," *Los Angeles Times,* February 15, 1930, II, 7.

46. For example, "El tango del morrongo" appears in chapbooks illustrated by José Guadalupe Posada, published by Vanegas Arroyo; Tirso Campos included it his *cancionero Lira Mexicana* (Los Angeles: Imprenta de "El Correo Mexicano," n.d. [ca. 1910s]); and it appears, with Conesa's photograph, in *El Ruiseñor Mexicano: Colección de canciones populares,* 3rd ed. (San Antonio: Casa Editorial Lozano, 1924), 63, 111.

47. Francisco E. Balderrama and Raymond Rodríguez, *Decade of Betrayal: Mexican Repatriation in the 1930s* (Albuquerque: University of New Mexico Press, 2006).

48. Robert Berger, Ann Conser, and Stephen M. Silverman, *The Last Remaining Seats: Movie Palaces of Tinseltown* (Santa Monica: Hennessey and Ingalls, 2004).

49. When Laurel and Hardy were honored on Ralph Edward's famous television show *This Is Your Life* in 1954, Frank Fouce appeared as a surprise guest. The episode is included on the DVD set *This Is Your Life—The Ultimate Collection, Vol. 1* (Ralph Edwards Productions DVD set, 2005).

50. Frank Fouce Jr., "A Study of the Los Angeles Spanish-Speaking Television Market" (MBA research paper, Pepperdine University, 1972). For extensive discussion of the involvement of Frank Fouce Jr. and Sr. in the creation of an infrastructure for Spanish-language television in the United States, see Kenton T. Wilkinson, *Spanish-Language Television in the United States: Fifty Years of Development* (New York: Routledge, 2016).

51. Ramón Inclán, "Rescate del Million Dollar," *La Opinión,* August 6, 1999, E1, E7.

52. Luis Gonzaga y Armendáriz, "Balazos después de muchas copas: Como fue el asesinato de Guty Cárdenas, un ídolo," *Revista de la Universidad Autónoma de Yucatán* 239–40 (2006–07): 62–70, www.cirsociales.uady.mx/revUADY/pdf/239-40/ru239-408.pdf.

53. Richard K. Spottswood, *Ethnic Music on Records: A Discography of Ethnic Recordings Produced in the United States, 1893–1942,* vol. 4, *Spanish, Portuguese, Philippine, Basque* (Urbana: University of Illinois Press, 1990), 1739, 1999–2000, 2043, 2157.

54. "Martín," "Comentando Desde el Cuarto Muro," *El Heraldo de México,* December 27, 1928, 6.

55. "Cuatro Años de Vida Cumple el 16 'La Opinión,'" *La Opinión,* September 15, 1930, 1; and Los Angeles radio station KHJ program advertisement, *San Diego Evening Tribune,* November 7, 1930, 8.

56. Álvaro Vega and Enrique Martín, eds., *Guty Cárdenas, Cancionero* (Mérida: Instituto de Cultura de Yucatán, Centro Regional de Investigación, Documentación y Difusion Musicales "Jerónimo Baqueiro Foster," 2006), 38; "El Apoteosis de la Canción Mexicana," *La Opinion,* December 11, 1930, 6; and "Fue un Noche de Arte y Entusiasmo la Despedida de Guty Cárdenas," *La Opinión,* December 13, 1930, 6.

57. *La Opinion* advertisements for those dates; and Alan Gevinson, ed., *Within Our Gates: Ethnicity in American Feature Films, 1911–1960,* American Film Institute Catalog (Berkeley: University of California Press, 1997), 248.

58. Although hardly any issues of *El Heraldo de México* seem to exist past 1928, in which year it was still a daily paper, it was likely published on a weekly schedule sometime thereafter for several decades, at least up to about 1952. Its continued weekly publication is noted in 1947 in Robert F. Brand, "Survey of the Spanish-Language Press in the United States," *Modern Language Journal* 31, no. 7 (November 1947): 434; and in 1951 in Marjorie C. Johnston, "Spanish-Language Newspapers and Periodicals Published in the United States," *Hispania* 34, no. 1 (February 1951): 86.

59. Rodolfo Hoyos and Eduardo Arozamena's recordings of Arozamena's *corridos* "Sidar y Rovirosa" (Sidar and Rovirosa), Brunswick 41034, and "La muerte de Sidar" (The Death of Sidar), Brunswick 41033.

60. Esparza and Camacho's recording of "La Inundación de Santa Paula" (Brunswick 40426); and Cancioneros Acosta recording of "Inundación de California" (OKeh 16285, Columbia 4883X), with lyrics by Esteban V. Escalante, recorded March 28, 1928. See also Agustín Gurza, "Disaster Songs: Telling Tragedy in Any Language," Strachwitz Frontera Collection of Mexican and Mexican American Music, blog post, May 19, 2016, http://frontera.library.ucla.edu/blog/2016/05/disaster-songs-telling-tragedy-any-language.

61. Juan B. Heinink and Robert G. Dickson, *Cita en Hollywood: Antología de las películas norteamericanas habladas en castellano* (Bilbao: Ediciones Mensajero, 1990); John Koegel, "Mexican Musicians in California and the United States, 1910–1950," *California History* 84, no. 1 (Fall 2006): 7–29, 64–69; Charles Ramírez Berg, *Latino Images in Film: Stereotypes, Subversion, and Resistance* (Austin: University of Texas Press, 2002); and Lisa Jarvinen, *The Rise of Spanish-Language Filmmaking: Out from Hollywood's Shadow, 1929–1939* (New Brunswick: Rutgers University Press, 2012).

62. Susan Racho and Nancy de Los Santos, dir., *The Bronze Screen: 100 Hundred Years of the Latino Image in Hollywood* (Chicago: Questar, 2002, DVD).

63. Ernesto González Jiménez was born on July 4, 1888, in Monterrey, Mexico (Declaration of Intention application to become a naturalized US citizen, dated November 30, 1932, Ancestry.com). His date and place of death are currently unknown.

64. *Gracia y Alegría* (Los Angeles: El Heraldo de México, 1921); copy in author's collection.

65. A copy of *Canciones de mi tierra* has not yet been found.

66. Advertisement, *El Heraldo de México*, January 12, 1922, 3.

67. Rodolfo Hoyos, interview, March 26, 1974, Los Angeles, California; quoted in Felix F. Gutiérrez and Jorge Reina Schement, *Spanish-Language Radio in the Southwestern United States* (Austin: University of Texas at Austin, Center for Mexican American Studies, 1979), 6, 16.

68. For Hoyos's recordings, see Spottswood, *Ethnic Music on Records,* 1739, 1840, 1964–65, 1993, 2088–89, 2162, 2330.

69. Although Hoyos made a few recordings of Spanish *zarzuela* arias, it is not known if he made any commercially released operatic recordings.

70. "Rodolfo Hoyos cuenta los dias que faltan . . . ," *La Prensa* (San Antonio, Texas), January 31, 1932, 1.

71. Hoyos's recordings are available on the Library of Congress's National Jukebox (http://www.loc.gov/jukebox/), and UCLA's Strachwitz Frontera Collection of Mexican and Mexican American Recordings (http://frontera.library.ucla.edu).

72. *El Eco de México,* September 1942, magazine article in the possession of John McGowan, Eva Quintanar's son. I thank McGowan for his assistance.

73. Eva Quintanar interview with John Koegel, Fullerton, California, May 4, 2014. See also Agustín Gurza, "Eva Quintanar: A Living Musical Legacy," "Biography, Quintanar, Eva," and "Q & A: John McGowan, Son of Eva Quintanar," blog post, Strachwitz Frontera Collection of Mexican and Mexican American Recordings.

74. The Quintanar family begins to be listed in Los Angeles city directories in 1936, all at the same address on North Grand Avenue; Eva is listed separately, as a musician, for the first time in the 1939 directory.

75. The Los Angeles Conservatory of Music was established in 1883 and merged in 1961 with the Chouinard School of Art to become the California Institute of the Arts, now located in Valencia in northern Los Angeles County.

76. Library of Congress copyright registrations.

77. "Tengo miedo" by Eva Quintanar, recorded by Adelina García in Hollywood, California (Columbia 6099X/OKeh 9420); Spottswood, *Ethnic Music on Records,* 1895.

78. Many of Quintanar's recordings are available on the Strachwitz Frontera Collection of Mexican and Mexican American Recordings website.

79. The UCLA Film Archive, the Library of Congress, and other US archival film collections hold surviving films from Hollywood's Cine Hispano, and many classic Mexican films are available commercially on DVD. The Filmoteca Nacional of the Universidad Nacional Autónoma de México also has a collection of classic Mexican film musicals; see www.filmoteca.unam.mx. See also Jacqueline Avila, "'Los Sonidos del cine': Cinematic Music in Mexican Film, 1930–1950" (PhD diss., University of California, Riverside, 2011).

80. UCLA Sheet Music Consortium, http://digital2.library.ucla.edu/sheetmusic/; and UCLA Archive of American Popular Music, http://digital.library.ucla.edu/apam/.

81. Syracuse University Belfer Cylinders Digital Collection, http://library.syr.edu/splash/cylinders/; and University of California, Santa Barbara Cylinder Audio Archive, http://cylinders.library.ucsb.edu.

ALEXANDRA T. VAZQUEZ

2

RUMBA EMISSARIES

"SHE HURLS CARAMELS TO the patrons, and what's more, they like it." So begins a review of the Cuban stage and film star Ninón Sevilla and her performance at the Million Dollar Theater in Downtown Los Angeles in 1956.[1] Given the wide distribution of her movies during Mexico's cinematic golden age in this same theater, Sevilla was already more than familiar to postwar Los Angeles audiences. This live revue was an opportunity for her to return to her public in a new way. What does she hurl toward audiences and what might be made possible by trying to catch, and catch up with, this gesture? We imagine how folks may have jumped out of their seats to grasp the caramels or others who might have turned to stone to refuse them. Perhaps onlookers wanted to make sure she kept on and so they played along; or maybe the candy was gently placed on the tongue to hold, deep inside, the way Sevilla moved and sang. Some might have read loaded significance into the caramel itself as sugar cooked until it is barely burnt, or inadvertently offered their heads as the perfect ricochets for her act. Sevilla threw her candies during the song and dance number "El Caramelero," an important entry in the Cuban

76

pregón tradition. The pregón is a musical ecology built around a street vendor's cries. Typically suggestive and just barely within the safety of innuendo, the seller in the pregón offers an *experience* alongside the objects they sell. Whether the "cucuruchito" sold by the peanut vendor or the recommendation to "échale salsita" by the sausage seller, whatever is sold by the pregónero offers room for playful intimacy during everyday commerce. In future repetition, the sung pregón carries everything that accompanies it: that vendor, their turf, and all those customers we might never meet in person. There is enough room in the pregón for the performer to impose their own conditions however. Sevilla-as-El Caramelero refuses to be taken as a showgirl and exotic accessory, and so she maintains the masculine pronoun to push "caramelitos para que puede chupar." Buy my candies that you can suck.

Let's take up Sevilla's thrown caramels for all their philosophical volatility, especially for the ways they might catch us by surprise. Many have written about Sevilla and her cohort of performers. This group is categorically named "The Rumberas," an ensemble of rumba dancers that drove plotlines and seized the attention of directors and critics alike. Their singing and dancing bodies were often used to work out the twists and turns of Mexican musical films (often in the Caberetera genre) between the mid-1930s to the later 1950s. Soon after the decline in these films' popularity, the former stars often took to the road. Usually but not always set within and against the environs of a cabaret, rumberas such as Sevilla made profound cinematic and sonic imprints up and down the hemisphere. From the real-time of her film appearances to contemporary feminist and women of color scholars, critics often depend upon Sevilla to signal the critical regimes of race, nation, and gender to the New World culture industry.[2] In the writings about her, we learn how Sevilla and her cohort functioned as exotic presence and "whitened" adaptation of black movement—and how the rumberas often turned their function into conscious play with what was too often imposed on them. And yet, Sevilla's hurled caramels demand us to come to other senses of her and ask: Beyond her service to and for the plots of these movies and their critics, what else did her actual performances *do?* And what does study of her invite in? She interrupts typical ideas for what's worthy in media study by insisting on what, in excess to equipment, makes technology evolve. As a media-savvy performer well versed in the radio-vaudeville-cinema-telenovela continuum, Sevilla was likely aware that the Million Dollar Theater was one of the first cinemas in the United States to offer sound and image together. Her song offered an echo of the venue's history and her candies were DIY additions to the growing 3D viewing trends of the time. Taking the caramels seriously even aids in the disruption of the male lineage behind many art-historical narratives. She can and should be considered a maximalist precursor to the minimalist work of the late-twentieth-century conceptual artist Felix Gonzalez-Torres, who we can be certain (alas, without knowing) would appreciate the relation.

To study Sevilla is to search out, even and especially in highly commercialized performance, all the possible aesthetic legacies offered by those who are dismissed as decorative function. We can keep listening and looking with the certainty that Sevilla and her cabarete cohort were an active part of musical traditions, especially those that have long had to cultivate visual displays to circulate. This certainty resists the trappings of the "exotic," which takes its etymology from the outside and foreign, and is deployed to set many apart from what makes something so. Any history of Los Angeles must begin with the certainties that the outside and foreign have long made it so. Sevilla, as just one of the misfit crew of Mexican screen rumberas, contributed to the development and circulation of Cuban music idioms such as the rumba and the mambo in the Los Angeles scene. Far from empty gestures, Sevilla's rumbic candy selling offered Angelenos in her audience something to work with, something to take with them and make their own. She was a seeming anomaly: she was born Emelia Pérez Castellanos in Centro Habana, became Ninón Sevilla on Mexican stages, and later brought her import-export stage business into the Million Dollar Theater. Such an itinerary might give one pause. And yet, if we proceed with the certainty that she was not an exception, if we slow down how audiences might have encountered her, and if we crack open demographic assumptions of who makes up Latinate Los Angeles, Sevilla is everything but an incongruity.

Sevilla reaches out to us now to revive the fertile deltas collecting dust in the greater American cultural memory, namely, all those venues shared between Cuban and Mexican performers, between Mexico City and Havana before, during, and after the world wars. The movement between these cities was not linear, nor did it follow a predictable path. It was more a dynamic intersection that held Los Angeles as part of its junction, and the experimental laboratory of the Million Dollar Theater was just one of many vitalizing rest stops.[3] This was a widely shared and well-trod circuit. There are material footprints we can hold in our hands, for the rumberas' impact is as visual as it is musical. Simply visit eBay, enter the term "rumbera," and scan its shelves for the dozens of lobby cards and collector's posters that remain lively on the market. The dancers who were drawn, painted, and photographed as marquee figures for the Mexican and Los Angeles culture industry were circulated far and wide. An especially robust location for their making, indicated by online auction sites, was in the former Yugoslavia. No matter how or where their image was set down or ended up, much is retained across their larger collection. Their rendering—across the films' multimedia promotional materials—can't help but make convention of defiant women protagonists who launch powerful sidelong glances. Even in their stilled capture we sense their dexterity as performers who rustle eros and irony together. Take in what Sevilla made possible for the artist of the promotional poster for *Perdída* (see figure 2.1). There are myriad puncta here. The overall composition takes us through the dust of the bullring, a glittery undifferentiated urban horizon, and the smoke of an after-hours cabaret. These are the venues visited in everyday hemispheric fantasy in the same space. Her left manicured ring finger lies in wait for the charging bull; her right tacón posed ready to strike the pianist's keys. Her upward glance toward someone or something doing her wrong is a model for the survivalist tactic of bemusement. This kind of face making seen throughout the visual imprint of the rumberas does not remain in place. These are the engrossed, knowing, pleasurable facial languages necessary to much of Latinate partner dancing. In the tight embrace of the mambo, danzón, tango, son, bachata, one does not neglect the face as part of the repertoire. The

Lobby card, *Perdída*, 1950, Collection of Alexandra T. Vazquez.

face does not wag free with some false sense of abandon; it does not perform "freedom." The face instead suggests its own narrative, and offers its own subtle and serious commentary on any given dance floor.

There are other robust traces that are equally challenging to consider in the junction of Los Angeles. How the aesthetics of popular forms, and performances such as Sevilla's, moved between these hemispheric cultural capitals and venues in ways that were once commonplace now feels mysterious and extraordinary. For some, it might be hard to imagine how people and the things they brought with them *moved,* given the easily identifiable culprits of the US trade embargo against Cuba and the militarization of the border. Although the routes between all these locations were in some ways clearer (at least until the mid-1960s), there nevertheless remain other wonders that sociopolitical qualifiers can't explain. For example, how audiences made instantaneous recording of what they learned on the stage and screen—in irrecoverable flashes, in the blinks of a few frames—and then, by their altered reenactment, transformed everything into new material for the music and movement of Los Angeles. This is the extraordinary capacity of people to innovate all together, even when they're not sharing the same stage or even the same city.

We are fortunate to have at our fingertips Sevilla's filmed version of "El Caramelero" as performed for the camera for the film *Llévame en tus brazos* (Take Me in Your Arms), directed by the prolific Mexican director Julio Bracho and released in 1954.[4] Let's consider that this film occupied the stages *before* Sevilla's live performance in 1956 of one of its hit numbers. In her filmed performance, the camera tightly frames her legs as they dance. Her movements are fluid but deliberate, almost like instructional record sleeves come alive. This narrative film, like most melodramas of the Mexican golden age, experimented with the documentary form by revealing the mechanics behind the movement, the song, the romance.[5] They (by which I mean both the movies and performers) were conduits for new sounds and choreographies. We must remind ourselves, as trite as it feels to do so, that, for the audiences of the time, revisiting Sevilla's performance was not a simple matter of pressing rewind or command-refresh. Audiences had a fleeting relation to clips such as this. And so part of what we honor when talking about Latin America in Los Angeles are those who cultivated photographic/phonographic memories of what they saw and heard, and then made their own, in other venues that aren't recorded or held in proper archives or made value of in auctions. These movements and sounds made anew at the ballroom or at the family party or in the living room all contributed materially to the history of the rumba and of the mambo. All those fleeting relations to the clips—and the creatively faulty memories that helped to invent new forms of movement—make part of the solid, steady infrastructure of Cuban musical worlds in Los Angeles. If Los Angeles was and is a junction of Mexico City and Havana, many performances occasion marvel about what the city itself—its ballrooms and family parties and living rooms—inscribed in these musical worlds during and after moving through it.

Although these everyday innovations by audiences might not be transparent in the written histories about these genres, they are certainly recorded in song. There are songs that exemplify how influence is never unidirectional—how what Mexican and greater Angeleno audiences did *to and with* mambo was not merely derivative of the Cuban—but moves circuitously. Mambo, like all music, depends upon a whole set of noncredited coauthors, and a large population of musical figures who remain nameless in song is dancers. Their imprints are strong but their physical cues are not as easily picked up as when singling out what a particular instrument, say, an upright bass, does to a song. Some musicians make it a priority to vocally notate what dancers do to music. Take a few famous examples by the Cuban musician Beny Moré. Moré was a musician who constantly put volumes of the great uncredited to dance and sound. His greatest hits are often made to function as nostalgic attachments to a past-tense Cuba and part of this circulation prevents our listening to what Moré actually did inside of them. His mambo "Rumberos de Ayer" (Rumberos of Yesterday), recorded in Mexico in 1952, was a swinging elegy to what American popular culture was always invested in forgetting: the contributions of all those "exotic" black composers and dancers that made its music so. The song was set down four years after the murder of the great Cuban musician and composer Chano Pozo in New York. Pozo, whose work offered one of the greatest tributaries to new modes of jazz, is made into a refrain for dancers to work out Moré's and their grief over this collective loss. Moré sings in his haunt-echo, over and over, "Sin Chano yo no quiero bailar," to which the chorus in the song, and the dancers who hear it, answer and amplify: "Sin Chano." Without Chano I don't want to dance. Not without Chano. Vocalizing grief, which resists being productive, Moré sings of not wanting to dance the rumba anymore. But he nevertheless extends his characteristically generous credit and platform. Even as he sings this refusal, Moré makes it so that dancers can still dance to him, and do so for Pozo.

Beny Moré as perhaps one of the most beloved icons of Cuban popular music came of musical age in the Mexican cabaret circuit with El Conjunto Matamoros. He recorded some of the most important mambos with the mambo genre's "King," Dámaso Pérez Prado, for RCA Victor, and spent almost a decade in Mexico before his return to Havana. Although his reputation on the island was always formidable, it was only after Moré spent all that formative time away in Mexico as its rising star that he became a celebrity in and for Cuba. To reiterate: musicians take their cues from dancers, everywhere, and the proof is in their songs. Let's listen in to a theme song for our catalogue-junction, "Bonito y Sabroso," an oft-cited song that famously insists upon Mexican authorship in and as the mambo genre. Moré was one of the many Cuban musicians who performed the musical structures for Sevilla, the rumberas, and all those Mexican films, in addition to playing in Los Angeles with the Luis Arcaráz y Su Orquesta, among others.[6] Here, at least as we're informed by the lyrical part of the song, we have Teflon-like proof of Mexican notation:

Pero qué bonito y sabroso,
bailan el mambo los mexicanos
Mueven la cintura y los hombros,
igualito que los cubanos.
Con sentido de ritmo,
para bailar y gozar,
que hasta parece
que estoy en La Habana.
Cuando bailando veo una mexicana,
no hay que olvidar
que México y La Habana
son dos ciudades
que son como hermanas,
para reír y cantar.
¡Pero qué bonito y sabroso,
bailan el mambo las mexicanas!

Chico Sesma, one of Los Angeles's great musical planners, did much to musically program the junction in Los Angeles. One of his great marquee efforts, a show that featured Moré at the Hollywood Palladium in 1958, left behind a snapshot to help imagine the transaction between musician and audience there (see figure 2.2, Moré at the Hollywood Palladium, 1958). We're asked to do some homework by taking in this image together with "Bonito y Sabroso." Scholar and musician Raúl Fernández featured this image in his groundbreaking exhibition and catalogue *Latin Jazz: The Perfect Combination* and has done much to encourage us to unfreeze this frame, to unfreeze all those documentary frames taken in Los Angeles to ask: What are the conversations that have always happened here?[7] The diagonal composition—the radiant and radiating line!—of this photograph helps us to

Legendary Cuban singer and bandleader Beny Moré appeared at the Hollywood Palladium in 1958, where he was accompanied by the Tito Puente Orchestra..

imagine the creative sinews that attach from Moré's conducting fingertips to the audience and back again. They are the perfect ricochet for this act, as Moré would often sing and lead his orchestra in tandem. Spend time with the faces that line the stage in this image and it is hard to not feel their electrifying effect on Moré and his music. This frozen frame isn't exactly the finite proof we look for (even if it is) on the assignment to write on submerged musical histories of Latin LA. It is a visual guide, a spirit guide that we can consult when taking in a whole other repertoire of the city's songs and dances.

Part of what Sevilla and Moré invite us to ask on the occasion of this exhibition is: How does influence work exactly and how is (or isn't) it recorded? Sevilla makes us come to our senses to respond to that question in a twofold way: influence can announce itself as hard as a caramel can hit your head, and influence resists clear trajectories. Moré shows us that sometimes we can only mark things in song, and that songs themselves carry things and move people in unique and magical ways. What the performances of Sevilla and Moré do to our sense of Latin LA is make us look in excess of those easy indicators of cross-cultural encounters. They make us thrive in what performers bring with them while on tour that we can name and in all of the unidentifiable stuff at play in the colloquial to "bring it." Whether the performers stayed in Los Angeles, made a live cameo appearance on its horizon, or were promotionally plastered on some forgotten wall, something has been altered for good.

NOTES

1. *Los Angeles Times,* June 22, 1956, 22; Proquest Historical Newspapers.

2. See Melissa Blanco Borelli, *She is Cuba: A Genealogy of the Mulata Body* (Oxford: Oxford University Press, 2016); José Piedra, "Hip Poetics," in *Everynightlife: Culture and Dance in Latin/o America,* ed. Celeste Fraser Delgado and José Esteban Muñoz (Durham: Duke University, 1997); Ana M. López, "Caberetera Films," in *Encyclopedia of Latin American and Caribbean Cultures,* ed. Daniel Balderston, Mike Gonzalez, and Ana M. López (London and New York: Routledge, 2001); and Carlos Monsiváis's critical oeuvre on the cinema. Sevilla famously caught the critical eye of Francois Truffaut, who wrote a review of her under the pen name Robert Lacheney in an issue of *Cahiers du cinema* from 1954. See also Raquel Mendieta Costa, "Exotic Exports: The Myth of the Mulata," trans. Eduardo Aparicio, in *Corpus Delecti: Performance Art of the Americas,* ed. Coco Fusco (London and New York: Routledge, 2000), 43–54.

3. The Million Dollar Theater offered new models for programming. According to Roseman and Vigil, the Theater began showing live revues by Mexican and other Latin American entertainers and featured weekly Spanish-language movies in the late 1940s. Given the growth of the Mexican population, neighboring theaters began to copy the format. See Curtis C. Roseman and J. Diego Vigil, "From Broadway to 'Latinoway': The Reoccupation of a Gringo Landscape," *Places* 8, no. 3 (1993): 20–29.

4. www.youtube.com/watch?v = 5vfEd4uepYU; the whole movie can be accessed here: www .youtube.com/watch?v = y-KAzI-FoY8.

5. Of the melodramatic function of melodrama in postwar Mexican films, see the foundational essay by Ana M. López, "Tears and Desire: Women and Melodrama in the 'Old' Mexican Cinema," in *Feminism and Film,* ed. E. Ann Kaplan (New York: Oxford University Press, 2001), 505–20.

6. Radamés Giro, "Beny Moré" in *Diccionario Enciclopédico de la Musica en Cuba,* vol. 3 (La Habana: Editorial Letras Cubanas, 2007), 132.

7. Raúl Fernández, *Latin Jazz: The Perfect Combination/La combinación Perfecta* (San Francisco: Chronicle, 2002).

3

DOING THE SAMBA ON SUNSET BOULEVARD

Carmen Miranda and the Hollywoodization of
Latin American Music

Q: Has this trip changed your views any about Latin America and your policies? Do you see any perspectives differently after this trip?

THE PRESIDENT: Well, I learned a lot, because that's what I went to do, is—I didn't go down there with any plan for the Americas or anything. I went down to find out from them and their views. And you'd be surprised, yes, because, you know, they're all individual countries. I think one of the greatest mistakes in the world that we've made has been in thinking, lumping—thinking "Latin America." You don't talk that way about Europe. You recognize the difference between various countries. And the same thing is true here.[1]

To those who know anything at all about Latin American history, demography, geography, and culture, this epiphany exhibits a curious quality. Still, it is easy to understand how President Ronald Reagan, who had spent so many years in Hollywood, might have come to perceive Latin America as a culturally homogeneous region and be surprised to learn, off the set, that the reality was so different. His career as a movie actor coincided with the emergence of one of the most phenomenal screen figures from Latin America and one who, more than any other person, helped create an all-purpose, homogeneous image of Latin Americans, their culture, and especially their music.

Hollywood used the sensational singer and actress Carmen Miranda as a do-all prop in dramatic settings as diverse as New York, Rio de Janeiro, Buenos Aires, Havana, and Mexico. The resulting conflation of costumes, instruments, musical genres, and languages is highly entertaining on one level but pernicious and (at the time) politically counterproductive on another. As Allen Woll observes, the merely partial coverage by US news media of events in South America leaves a gap that is "often filled by fictional representations in motion pictures and television shows. Film, in particular, has played a major role in shaping modern America's consciousness of Latin America."[2]

LA PEQUENA NOTÁVEL

Carmen Miranda, so closely associated with Brazil, was actually born in Portugal, in the village of Marco de Canavezes (Porto), on February 9, 1909. She was baptized Maria do Carmo, though the family came to call her Carmen because she looked a bit Spanish to them (Bizet's opera from 1875 had made that name very popular). She later adopted her mother's maiden name of Miranda and, thus, her eventual stage name. Desperate economic conditions in Portugal compelled the family to emigrate to Rio the year after her birth, where Carmen's father found work as a barber. In 1925, her parents opened a boardinghouse, which attracted a number of customers in the entertainment business, including composers, who introduced her to the world of radio and recordings.

While her career was in the embryonic stage, she worked in a milliner's shop designing and making hats (a portent of things to come), while softly singing her favorite songs. Many of the earliest tunes she learned and performed were, ironically, not sambas but rather tangos, in the style of her idol, Carlos Gardel. It was not long before Brazilian composers noted her talent and began to collaborate with her. These included such figures as Synval Silva, Ary Barroso, and Dorival Caymmi. Her meteoric rise to fame in the 1930s brought her to the summit of popularity in Brazil, as a recording artist, performer, and even movie actress.

During this early phase of her career, she invented a persona for herself—the brash, liberated, extremely extroverted and showy Carmen Miranda—one quite at odds with her more conservative, retiring, and proper alter ego, Maria do Carmo. This penchant for reinventing herself would be greatly amplified by the mass mediation of her adopted persona. It was also necessitated by the cultural politics of her milieu, as "it was essential that her Portuguesse origin be kept secret because the public might reject a non-Brazilian performer of sambas."[3] Although her physical appearance betrayed European ancestry, she cultivated the *gíria*, or "street slang," of her Rio environs, thus masking her true identity. However, her later addition of North American elements to this character would prove controversial in

Brazil, where she would be accused of having become "Americanized" and making Brazilians look laughable and ridiculous.

Carmen's devotion to samba came at a time when, under the regime of Getúlio Vargas (president 1930–45, 1951–54), a new ideology of national identity was forming, one that embraced blacks and mulattos as distinctive facets of Brazilian society and culture. The samba was the musical icon of this unique Brazilian identity, and the middle and upper classes were now ready for a white woman like Carmen to promote this national art form. In 1930 she signed a contract with RCA Victor and began her ascent to stardom. In that first year she recorded no fewer than forty songs, and by the end of the decade she had recorded 281, with a variety of companies.[4] Half of these were sambas, and the other half mostly carnival marches, rumbas, and tangos. In 1934 she began working with a Rio group called the Bando da Lua (Moon Gang), an association that would last through her Hollywood years. It was during this formative stage that César Ladeira, a Rio radio announcer, dubbed her *La pequena notável,* or "The Remarkable Little Girl." This childlike aspect of hers would take on great significance in the films she made in Hollywood.

One of the major developments of this decade was her emergence as a film star. The most significant of her Brazilian films was the last, *Banana da terra* (1938). Set in Bahia, this film was a collaboration between her and the Bahian composer Dorival Caymmi (b. 1914). Her star turn comes with Caymmi's unforgettable "O que é que a Bahiana tem?" ("Oh, What Does a Bahian Girl Have?"). Caymmi's lyrics clarify what the Bahian girl has that makes her so appealing: turban, earrings, skirt, sandals, and bracelets and other types of jewelry, all adorning a body in seductive movement. Here really was the birth of her Hollywood screen image. But it is important again to understand that this was Carmen's creation, under the inspiration of Caymmi. The Bahian women themselves considered turbans and gaudy jewelry old-fashioned slave attire and rarely wore such things. Thus, Carmen did "not copy the costume worn by the Bahian women [but] took elements from it and then added personal touches" like the strings of beads, bare tummy, exotic hats piled with fruit, and always bright colors.[5] Carmen had now assembled all the ingredients that would make her a Hollywood star. All that remained was to go north.

In 1939 the Broadway impresario Lee Shubert visited Rio de Janeiro and witnessed the Brazilian sensation in action. He immediately perceived Carmen's potential and offered her a contract. She jumped at the opportunity, with the proviso that the Bando da Lua accompany her. Carmen was on her way—to Broadway. Vargas himself took an interest in this development. He hoped she would foster closer ties between northern and southern hemispheres and serve as an ambassadress of Brazil in the United States. This could benefit Brazil economically by increasing its share of the American coffee market. She shared his vision and declared,

> I shall concentrate all my efforts on one objective: to take advantage of this chance to promote Brazilian popular music in the same way I popularized samba in the countries on both sides of the River Plate. What I want is to show what Brazil really is and change the wrong ideas existing in the United States about our country.[6]

Bud Abbott (left), Lou Costello (right), and Carmen Miranda, 1941, Herald-Examiner Collection/Los Angeles Public Library.

It is instructive to bear these words in mind when surveying the actual trajectory and impact of her career. In fact, Carmen and the Bando made their Broadway debut in 1939 in the musical *Streets of Paris* singing a number titled "In South American Way," a rumba instead of a samba (music and lyrics by American pop songwriters Jimmy McHugh and Al Dubin)!

Carmen had the preternatural gift of being in the right place at the right time. Washington was in the midst of rehabilitating its Good Neighbor Policy toward Latin America, in an effort to compensate for overseas markets now closed by the Axis and the war. This effort was put forth on several fronts, including cultural. Hollywood's assistance was vital in this regard, because it was one of the chief means by which the United States could reach out to Latin American countries and win the hearts and minds of the populace and governments there, enlisting their aid economically and, all too soon, militarily. Hollywood was only too happy to comply, insofar as many of its overseas markets were no longer available, and it wanted to build on the substantial market Latin America represented, with more than four thousand movie theaters. In 1940 the State Department set up the Office of the Coodinator (*sic*) for Inter-American Affairs, with Nelson Rockefeller as its head. John Hay Whitney was put in charge of the very important Motion Picture Section of this office. Whitney and Rockefeller worked closely with Hollywood studios, especially 20th Century Fox, to ensure that there would be a steady stream of movies with Latin American themes that could be exported south in the hopes of warming up hemispheric relations. By war's end, Hollywood had produced no fewer than eighty-four such films.[7] The greatest luminary in the cavalcade of Latin American screen talent to demand such an effort was Carmen Miranda. It did not take Hollywood long to notice Miranda's star quality, and her first appearance on the US screen came in 1940 in the musical *Down Argentine Way,* which opens with her singing the now trademark rumba she premiered at the Shubert. Several movies followed over the next decade, including such classics as *That Night in Rio* (1941), *Weekend in Havana* (1941), and *Springtime in the Rockies* (1942). Others, like *Something for the Boys* (1944), *Doll Face* (1945), *Copacabana* (1947), *A Date with Judy* (1948), and *Nancy Goes to Rio* (1950), are not of the same caliber but nonetheless feature some memorable numbers. (And some were just plain bad, such as *Scared Stiff* of 1953, with Dean Martin and Jerry Lewis, in which Carmen appears as the Enchilada Lady, selling Mexican food and doing a crude parody of herself.) Carmen also recorded many of the selections from her films, and they appeared in sheet music. Harry Warren (the son of an Italian American bootmaker, whose musical education had come from being a Catholic choir boy, a carnival drummer, and a saloon pianist) and Mack Gordon were the principal composer/lyricist team who wrote for her, although she also did arrangements of tunes supplied by Brazilian composers. It is from the numbers composed by Warren, however, that we see best how the process of Hollywoodization worked, and in one movie above all others.

THE GANG'S ALL HERE[8]

Critics may differ about the relative merits of Miranda's films; for instance, *That Night in Rio* (*Uma noite no Rio*) is still regarded in Brazil as the best of her Hollywood movies,[9] while few North American critics would assess it that highly. But *The Gang's All Here* (1943), with music by Warren and lyrics by Leo Robin, directed and choreographed by Busby Berkeley, stands out in my mind as by far her best film, and perhaps one of the best Hollywood musicals ever. Originally to have been titled "The Girls He Left Behind" (in Brazil it is called *Entre a loura e a morena,* meaning "Between a Blonde and a Brunette"), the plot is simple. On his last night on leave, an army sergeant, Andy Mason, falls in love with a glamorous showgirl named Eadie Allen (played by the blonde Alice Faye) at the Club New Yorker. However, Andy is already engaged to Vivian Potter (played by the brunette Sheila Ryan), the daughter of the very wealthy and prudish Peyton Potter, who also happens to be business partners with Andy's father. Andy woos Eadie under an assumed name ("Sargeant Casey"), causing all sorts of problems later on. She falls in love with him and sees him off at the train station the next day. Andy returns from the Pacific several months later, in time for a splashy war benefit staged by the club's cast at the Potter estate. Dorita (Carmen Miranda) discovers his ploy, nearly ruining Andy's plan to marry Eadie, who flies into a rage upon learning the truth. In the end Vivian decides to pursue a dancing career, and Eadie, convinced of Andy's sincere love, forgives him. This is basically a morality play about fidelity in wartime.

Miranda adds a splash of local color to the film that audiences found riveting, even hypnotic. Her malapropisms, her gesticulations, her facial expressions, and of course her outrageous costumes jump off the celluloid and command our rapt attention. As *Variety* discovered, "Carmen Miranda dominates whenever the cameras rest upon her."[10] The chief characteristic of this picture, however, is its greater emphasis on song and dance than in most of her other films. The music is integrated into the drama through repeated use of some melodic material, and the actual numbers are far more frequent, elaborate, and extended. Indeed, the slender drama serves as an armature to support the music and dance.

The opening is memorable. From total blackness appears a singing head, that of Aloysio de Olveira, the guitarist in the Bando da Lua. Although he is not playing his guitar onscreen, it is heard in the background accompaniment. He sings the then enormously popular "Brasil" by Ary Barroso, an evocatively wistful serenade meant to instill in the audience a longing for (an imaginary) Brazil, a zone of tropical splendor and insouciant languor, for escape from the terrors and trials of the present moment. "Brazil—the Brazil that I knew / Where I wander'd with you . . . Lives in my imagination." The exotic effect is heightened by his singing in Portuguese.

The text's romantic nostalgia for someplace far away and long ago is reinforced in the music. The initial melodic gesture in the song is an ascending major sixth, an interval that has an enduring history signifying longing and desire, for instance, in such disparate examples as the prelude to *Tristan und Isolde* and the folk song "My Bonnie Lies over the Ocean." Moreover, the elastic rhythm and lack of a strong beat intensify its rhapsodic quality. A thickening of the orchestration and jazzing up of the harmony coincide with a gradual quickening of the tempo as the camera pans left to survey the ocean liner *SS Brazil,* disgorging passengers and cargo at dockside in New York. The song suddenly metamorphoses into a very upbeat samba played by the Bando da Lua, which appears intermingled with the passengers.

Of greatest visual significance now are the sacks labeled "sugar" and "coffee." Here was the Good Neighbor Policy in operation. Brazil was a zone not only of escapist fantasies but of natural abundance. It is precisely at this moment that the camera surveys a large net full of fruit, tilting slowly downward toward the predictable elision of the net's cornucopia with the tutti-frutti hat of Carmen Miranda.[11] She takes up the song in its new incarnation, gyrating in trademark fashion while perched on her platform shoes. In the background one now hears a female chorus singing wordlessly in the manner of sirens from the zone of seduction. The association of the wordless female voice with mystery and exoticism is a powerful one, for example, in *Tannhäuser* and Holst's *The Planets,* or more recently in the theme song of the original Star Trek series from the 1960s.[12] All this precedes a new encounter.

Phil Baker, the bandleader now acting the part of representative of New York's mayor, appears in a car accompanied by a marching band playing "A Hot Time in the Old Town Tonight." Here is the musical emblem of North America, and its brazen bombast effectively interrupts the Brazilian music. Baker immediately asks if Carmen has "any coffee." The quizzical look on Carmen's face and exchange of apparently disapproving glances among her and the Bando are accompanied by an interrogative flourish in the woodwinds that underlines her gestures musically. Here was a moment of self-reflective irony in the context of Good Neighborliness. The greedy, acquisitive *norteamericano* is oblivious to Latin modes of social conduct, courtesy, and transaction. Significantly, Carmen does not answer his coffee question and proceeds into the next tune, a paean to the glories of New York. It represents the full Hollywoodization of Brazilian music, as they are completely inundated by the jazzy strains that flow in a resistless stream from the unseen ensemble.

At this point it is also clear that this is a play within a play, and that the real setting is not at dockside but rather in a nightclub, the Club New Yorker. Only at the end of this number, which introduces Alice Faye as one of the showgirls in the act, does Carmen relinquish the coffee she has withheld to this point. That is, the question highlighted in the woodwinds before is now answered, but only after an appropriate interval of musical introduction. Of course, the action in this scene reproduces the actual journey that Miranda herself had made only a few years earlier. Yet, all of this takes place in a kind of mythic dimension, as there are absolutely no blacks in this number, the one group without whom there would be no samba or jazz! This mythological dimension of Miranda's persona finds its most potent expression in the next scene.

"Did you tell her about me dancing with that South American savage, that gypsy?" The drama's resident puritan, Peyton Potter, has been dragged to the Club New Yorker by his business partner, Andrew Mason, *pére,* and now worries that his wife will learn that he got caught up in an audience-participation dance with "Dorita." His humorous neurosis represents a view of South America as a realm in which savages and gypsies are indistinguishable, a view perhaps shared by many in the movie theaters of the time. The characterization of Brazil as a zone of natural luxuriance inhabited by natives living in peaceful, if primitive, accord with their environment is reinforced by the ensuing song and dance.

The floorshow at the Club New Yorker continues with Miranda's most celebrated number, "The Lady in the Tutti-Frutti Hat." It opens with organ grinders in white suits and real monkeys capering about them and in the trees, in search of bananas. The music evokes the characteristic sounds of the *organillo,* mimicked in the orchestra using a "wrong-note" technique that simulates the misfiring valves of an organ grinder's instrument. This serves to establish the comical, madcap ambience of the number. The music here is simulated in the orchestra rather than reproduced live, and does not accompany a song. The trumpet plays the melody, and the accompaniment in the strings simulates the strumming of a guitar.

The camera pans across a generically tropical "landscape" of a little "island" dotted with "palm trees," and among these there is a generous assortment of leggy, nubile young maidens in bare feet wearing shorts and halter tops. Each wears a scarf tied around her head, the basic design of so many of Miranda's headdresses and one that we recall she herself adapted from the costume of the *Baiana*. Their skimpy *ensembles* are in banana shades of yellow and green. The numerous pairs of long, clean-shaven legs—which the camera thirstily drinks in—were no doubt a welcome sight for woman-hungry GIs on leave, and that is the major part of their appeal.

As the scene opens, the women are all lying recumbent on their little island, apparently in a state of customary tropical torpor. They are roused from slumber, however, by the approach of the Lady. From the back of the set she emerges on a bullock cart drawn by bare-chested young men (whose subservient eunuch-like status does not change during the number and who do not interact with the women at all). Miranda sings, in English, a stylized samba full of references to supposed amorous encounters. But there is something very odd going on here. The fecundity of the region is suggested not only by the scantily clad females cavorting about the set but by the Freudian image of the banana itself (as well as of strawberries), huge models of which are carried about by the maidens. (At one point in the choreography, they form a vulvaesque circle and heft their bananas up and down in repeated simulation of coital penetration; at least that is what we are thinking, even if the censors would have excised anything quite so explicit. In fact, this thinly veiled sexuality caused the number to be censored in Brazil.) Yet Miranda's hair remains concealed under her enormous hat of fruit, except for a little bit of bang. Her hat possesses as a result a curious symbolism in this context. The fruit tells us of her estrous fertility, but the nun-like concealment of her hair declares her unattainability. (It comes as a great surprise in her later movies actually to see her hair.)

With her arrival on a rustic bullock cart drawn by males, surrounded by what appear to be vestal virgins, and by virtue of her unattached/uninvolved status throughout the picture (except for a tenuous and apparently platonic relationship with Phil Baker, the bandleader), Miranda's character takes on a symbolic dimension, a sort of blend of the Virgin Mary (Our Lady) with some tropical fertility goddess (these are common in the Afro-Brazilian cults that gave birth to the samba, especially *Candomblé*). Moreover, she appears as a child-woman speaking fractured English, one who has gotten into mommy's closet and jewelry box and made herself up in a ridiculously incongruous assemblage of baubles, bangles, and beads. The prattle of her lyrics suggests something of childlike naiveté and simplicity, combined with an elusive sexual appeal:

> Some people say I dress too gay
> But, every day, I feel so gay
> And when I'm gay, I dress that way
> Is something wrong with that?

All of this is consistent with her natural persona as the Remarkable Little Girl. These lyrics contain several direct or indirect references to the virginal, unavailable status conferred by her hat:

Americanos tell me that my hat is high
Because I will not take it off to kiss a guy.

And further on:

Brazilian señoritas they are sweet and shy
They dance and play together when the sun is high
But when the tropic moon is in the sky, ay, ay,
They have a different kind of time
And even I forget that I'm
The Lady in the Tutti-Frutti Hat.[13]

The Bando provides visual backup, but they are almost inaudible due to the prominence of the orchestra. The strings especially play an important role in this number, with the occasional highlighting from flutes or trumpet. In fact, to audiences at the time, the trumpet more readily connoted Mexico or Cuba, in the context of Mexican mariachi or Cuban conjunto. In any case, its augmentation of the melody exhibits a rhythmic simplification that reinforces the primitiveness of the setting. Miranda's melody is a very stylized and simplified samba, if compared to recordings she made in the 1930s in Brazil. It is in straight quarter notes, all on the downbeat, with only a bit of syncopation at the end of the phrases. The flat (Johnny-one note) melodic contour suggests an atavistic simplemindedness. This monotone character is repeated at the larger level of the phrases themselves, which are highly repetitive. Also, the melody is very diatonic, contained within a one-octave C-major scale, with only a hint of chromaticism in the third phase. In fact, it all sounds a bit childish, which is exactly the effect intended.

The virginal, childlike quality of this number taps into a deeper preconception of Latin America in the European and US psyche, i.e., that of a virgin region awaiting consummation by the superior, masculine European culture, and of a child who needs the guidance and tutelage of the Protestant, industrial, democratic northern hemisphere.

Miranda's choreography, always the same in every movie she made, includes a spin at a make-believe marimba, made of bananas, of course. The version of the melody she plays is full of "wrong notes," and is thus highly comical, the musical counterpart of her malapropisms. The xylophone, of African origin, has nothing to do with modern Brazil, and is associated with southern Mexico and Central America. Indeed, this entire number is essentially a musical fantasia, a series of extrapolations on the theme that parallels the visual fantasy onscreen. The lush string sound that accompanies the banana choreography leaves the samba completely behind, while the worldless female chorus expresses a siren-like rapture that words could not hope to convey. The string and vocal arranging suggests tropical luxuriance, tending toward a swoon. The "wrong-note" technique is amplified at the end of Carmen's song by a "wrong-chord" arpeggio in the highest register of the harp that emphasizes her bats-in-the-belfry comical nature (she glances upward when this chord is played, as if it had emanated from her head). After she leaves the stage, the maidens return to their slumber, legs conspicuous, and we again see the organ grinders with their monkeys.

From this example, we can extrapolate some general categories of (mis)representation, which in turn merit further exploration by citing examples from others of her films. These categories include (1) suppression of negritude, (2) incongruity of context and confusion of type, (3) racial and gender stereotyping, and (4) stylization and simplification of music and text.

SUPPRESSION OF NEGRITUDE

The suppression of negritude, or "blackness," served a very real commercial purpose. A striking testimony to racial animus, and Hollywood's self-conscious need to pander to it, surfaces in the following letter from Zella Richardson, of the City of Atlanta Board of Review, to E. J. Mannix at MGM, dated January 8, 1944.[14]

> My dear Friend: . . . I had the real pleasure of sitting thro the very pleasing picture THE GANGS ALL HERE and of enjoying the MANY comments such as—"At last the Producers have realized that white people CAN be entertaining without having to inject Negroes" and "Thank the Lord one picture without niggers"—Yes I'm quoting. . . .
>
> We cannot understand the desire to exploit these people [negroes] . . . who to us represent paganism at its height, when they are doing their natural things, and the acts of monkeys when they are aping the white folks. That's the way we feel . . . so I will just continue to cut out the most objectionable parts, and WALK OUT with hundreds of others on the rest. . . .
>
> I have to be fair and say that . . . this IS causing trouble among the races—that this trouble will some day reach a climax not to be desired . . . we will just swallow those things which offend us so, and wait till our boys come home to right them.

Despite her sensational claims concerning incipient race war over Hollywood's "exploitation" (an interesting word choice) of negroes, her sentiments no doubt enjoyed broad currency during that period, and similar suppression of negritude can be found throughout Miranda's movies. For example, *That Night in Rio* begins with a memorable song-and-dance number featuring Carmen and Don Ameche along with several chorus girls in Miranda-style garb. The setting is in the hills of Rio during Carnival, and the samba number is clearly meant to establish the atmosphere. But the cast is totally devoid of a single dark-skinned person, despite the large black population of Rio and its central presence in Carnival celebrations. Once again the music is similarly whitened, absorbed into a lavish Hollywood arrangement with the heavy percussive quality and dense rhythmic layering of Afro-Brazilian Carnival samba largely expunged.[15] But even scenes like this did not go far enough to please some. A critic for *Cue* complained: "I'll never know why Miss Miranda insists on making herself up so she looks like an African witchdoctor's nightmare."[16] Consciously or not, audiences and reviewers did not want negritude.

One hastens to point out, however, that Carmen's own opinions on race did not conform to the racial prejudice that was so obvious in her movies. She addressed this topic frankly and directly when she said, "I never had racial or religious prejudices. I dealt well with blacks, Japanese, and Jews."[17] She could credibly claim an absence of anti-Semitism insofar as she had married a Jew, David Sebastian. Her collaboration and friendship in Brazil with black sambistas like Synval Silva also suggested a lack of racial prejudice.

This was, however, a strategy for placating the racist sensibilities of white moviegoers not merely in the United States, but in Latin America as well. In Miranda's first Hollywood movie, *Down Argentine Way,* the Nicholas brothers make a brilliant appearance in a dance-club scene doing one of their trademark gravity-defying tap numbers. The assistant commercial attaché to the American Embassy in Buenos Aires reported to Fox the reasons that Argentines objected strenuously to this (along with so many other things in the movie). Basically, he explained, it added "to the Argentine impression that all Yankees think they are Indians or Africans . . . a colored person is seen in Buenos Aires as often as a Hindu in Los Angeles."[18] In fact, Afro-Argentines, who often worked as gauchos, made important contributions to Argentine song and dance. But this did not accord with the national self-image the ruling elites in government and culture were striving to cultivate.

Despite the demographic differences between Argentina and Brazil, similar attitudes existed in the former Portuguese colony as well, and this merits closer examination. William Rowe and Vivian Schelling explored racial attitudes in the context of Latin American popular culture and traced the attitudes through several stages. This evolution perhaps allows us to understand the wider cultural significance of Miranda's persona, especially in light of repeated references in the press to her as "savage" and "primitive." In late nineteenth- and early-twentieth-century Brazil,

> the attempt to extirpate the unsightly "barbarian" elements—forms of social life and culture connected to blacks, mulattos, Indians, peasants, illiterates—from the fabric of Brazilian society is manifested in a set of ideas, policies and state actions.[19]

Among these "state actions" was a deliberate policy of encouraging European immigration (like Carmen's father), in order to improve the overall racial stock of the country.

But a shift in attitudes came about in the 1920s and 1930s, especially as a result of the modernist movement, which "called upon the intelligentsia to 'discover Brazilian reality,'" that is, to embrace the various native and African elements in the country's demography and culture.[20] The centerpiece of this ideology was *mestiçagem,* a belief that the racial "melting-pot" was beneficial and not negative. This became "a key feature of a populist programme of national integration" during the regime of Getúlio Vargas, one of Carmen's biggest supporters; nonetheless, there persisted "the widespread notion that Brazil's racial problems were being resolved through ethnic integration, whose goal remained white civilization."[21] Here is a possible parallel between Carmen's Bahia-inspired costumes and the blackface of an Al Jolson, a white person posing as a black. Perhaps the Euro-Brazilian

Miranda represented the *mestiçagem* identity in her appropriation and "sublimation" of black dress and music, thus fulfilling the national goal of "ethnic integration" with the retention of privilege by those of European ancestry (an inherently contradictory and consequently unrealized ambition). It was through this process that "popular cultural forms became important sites where . . . traditional, ethnic and local identities were articulated by the state within the project of national integration and development."[22]

Miranda's Hollywood numbers certainly constituted one such "site." Still, there were those in Brazil who rejected this program and Carmen's projection of Brazilian identity. When she returned to Brazil in 1941, some critics expressed the belief that "Brazil was not well served by a Portuguese who promoted 'vulgar negroid sambas.'"[23] But Hollywood was at pains to try to avoid this reaction. In terms of the Good Neighbor Policy, the American producers felt it necessary not to feature any aspects of Latin America—in either race relations, religion, poverty, or politics—that might be offensive to the middle classes and ruling elite. That Carmen was of European origin, and the Moon Gang was solidly middle class, was advantageous to this policy. This makes it easy to understand why, "in their second trip to the United States, [the Moon Gang] left behind the only member married to a black."[24]

INCONGRUITY OF CONTEXT AND CONFLATION OF TYPE

It is not at all unlikely that a Brazilian entertainer would have been appearing in nightclubs in Buenos Aires or Havana, doing sambas. Miranda herself had become popular in Argentina as a star of stage and screen, performing her Brazilian routine, although she actually got her start singing tangos in Brazil. Still, there is a colossal disconnect between reality and Hollywood in terms of the contexts in which her numbers appear. Take, for instance, the number "Ñango" from *Weekend in Havana*. In an internal document titled "Vital Statistics," by publicist Harry Brand, the claim is advanced that the "Ñango" was based on a "voodoo rhythm of Afro-Cuban origin."[25] Even if such a dance actually existed, that voodoo is associated with Haiti and not Cuba was a detail that either eluded Brand or was considered of negligible importance. He elsewhere claimed that "before writing the number, the song writers (Warren and Mack) secured from Cuba acetate recordings of the jungle rhythms which they have incorporated into the song."[26]

But Carmen's big numbers are done in the Club Madrileño scene, where she sings "Rebola, Bola" (a Brazilian *embolada,* or tongue twister), composed by Aloysio de Oliveira, in Portuguese, despite the fact that her character's name is Rosita Rivas. Moreover, in her choreography there is absolutely nothing to suggest Cuban dances such as the rumba, conga, *danzón,* or anything else appropriate to the locale. She uses her trademark strutting, undulating, and wriggling, which served her equally well in any setting Hollywood desired.

Still, one has to give *Weekend in Havana* some credit. The music is suffused with boleros, rumbas, and typical Cuban rhythms, especially 3 + 2 clave. Alice Faye's enchanting number "Tropical Magic" utilizes the beguine rhythm, and as Roberts points out, the beguine is essentially a rumba (and a Cole Porter trademark).[27] Some trouble was also taken by 20th Century Fox to get the scenery right, and there is actual footage of Havana, including Sloppy

Joe's, made famous by Hemingway. In fact, according to more "Vital Statistics" internal documents, again by publicist Harry Brand, Dr. Oscar Presmanes, Los Angeles Cuban Consul, paid a visit to the set of the movie and, after approving the script, had these words of approbation for the film: "This is the first picture that has been made about my country that does justice to its beauty and charm."[28] But this was mere diplomacy, and the Cuban critics panned the film as a gross misrepresentation of their island home.

The biggest offender, however, was the first movie Miranda made, *Down Argentine Way.* Astoundingly, there was not a single tango in the entire film (if you want to hear a tango, you have to watch her second movie, *That Night in Rio*). Instead, the signature number is a rumba, sung by Betty Grable (who also does a conga), while Carmen sings sambas: "The film received bad reviews in Brazil and was forbidden in Argentina because 'of wrongly portraying life in Buenos Aires' . . . the setting [was] a confused mixture of Brazil, Mexico, Cuba and Argentina."[29] According to the *Examiner:*

> When "Down Argentine Way" was shown in Rio de Janeiro it was hissed off the screen. What made the customers especially bitter was not so much Don Ameche's corny characterizations of a South American, but because Carmen Miranda, cast as an Argentinean, is a Brazilian and does not speak Spanish, but Portuguese.[30]

Don Ameche, however, does his bit for anti-Americanism, as he performs "a rhumba [*sic*] in Spanish with castanets and talks about orchids, as rare in Argentina as in New York." Moreover, there is "a fiesta with mantillas and Spanish combs. One of the songs ends with the Spanish expression 'Olé,' which is never used in Argentina."[31] At one point in the film, Don Ameche spreads out his arm in a sweeping gesture, amid scenery that with its old-style mission architecture evokes Mexico and not Argentina, stating, "Here you have the authentic Argentina." The assembled peasants and town folk proceed to dance to a Mexican *zapateado!*

And yet, the North Americans just did not get it. US reviews of the movie were ecstatic. Without a hint of irony or self-consciousness, *Variety* breathlessly enthused, "The Miranda personality and her swift-tongued song recitals in Portuguese *give an authentic Argentinian note to substantiate the title of the picture*."[32] Hollywood's utter incomprehension of the probably political consequences of pictures like this is beautifully encapsulated in the following assessment by the *Hollywood Reporter:* "In it is a timely and intriguing spirit of good will between North and South America."[33] Even Carmen herself participated in the propaganda parade, proclaiming that, "for the first time, the true imprint of the Brazilian popular soul was portrayed in a Hollywood film as it really is."[34] *Down Argentine Way* complicated the Good Neighbor Policy in Argentina, where there was already considerable sympathy for the Axis, and alienated both the public and officialdom from the United States and its war aims.

In fact, Hollywood never really caught on. In one of Miranda's later films, *Nancy Goes to Rio,* her signature number, "Tico, Tico" (a *choro* by Zequinha de Abreu), was fitted out with "special lyrics" by Earl Brent and Georgie Stoll. The conflation of Brazil and Spanish-speaking realms, especially Cuba, is again on display:

> I know I'll meet myself a couple caballeros
> And maybe learn a couple of sambas and boleros.
> I'll be so happy down in Rio de Janeiro
> With my maracas and a rose in my sombrero.[35]

Adding insult to injury, in this same movie Nancy is feted by her cast mates, who sing of her impending trip to Rio—by singing her an *habanera!* In *A Date with Judy,* Carmen appears as the rumba instructor Rosita Concellas, whose task is to teach Melvin Foster (Wallace Beery) to rumba. In one scene, the old man practices his dance steps at home, clearly grunting out the conga rhythm—while holding a book on how to rumba!

RACIAL AND GENDER STEREOTYPING

Savage, torrid, witchdoctor's nightmare, jungle music: these are some of the ways the press and industry publicists often referred to Miranda and her numbers, revealing attitudes about Latin America in general. Consistent with this role, she always has something "torrid" to sing, never anything lyrical, slow, or sad. "Jungle music" elements were clearly associated with blacks but not presented directly as such. Her public clearly craved upbeat songs and dances, and her handlers were determined to provide them, even against her will. The Brazilian magazine *Manchete* quoted her in 1954 as saying that she had once tried to introduce a slower Brazilian song into a movie, but the director refused, stating, "Carmen, here you have to play the kind of much which Brazilians, Americans and Europeans like. If you could please only Brazilians you wouldn't be here."[36] In fact, in early 1946, she stated in an interview that

> Even before the Brazilians disapproved of my films, I was upset. Many times, as soon as I had seen a new picture at a private showing, I would go to the executives to complain about the kind of repetitive roles of limited range and say that very soon the Brazilian public would dislike me.[37]

And things did not really improve over time. "Despite all our efforts, Americans cannot tell samba from other rhythms from Latin America," Carmen complained.[38] Xavier Cugat had stated along the same lines: "Americans know nothing about Latin music. They neither understand nor feel it. So they have to be given music more for the eyes than the ears. Eighty percent visual, the rest aural."[39] But Miranda never seemed to understand the central role she had played in perpetuating that confusion, precisely because she had supplied the crucial visual dimension that rendered unimportant any attempt at musical authenticity.

If money alone had been her object, Carmen would have had little to complain about, as she was the highest-paid entertainer in the United States by 1945, with an annual income of

$200,000, more than Bob Hope, Errol Flynn, Bing Crosby, or Humphrey Bogart. But she was an artist whose creative impulses needed a better outlet. Sadly, they never got one. She was making lots of money off of these films, but the studios were making even more money off of her, and they were not about to fix a money machine that was not broken.

Time and again, Carmen Miranda and other Latin actresses were described as "torrid." Consider the case of Lupe Vélez, a Mexican actress of the 1930s and 1940s, who starred as Carmelita in a seemingly endless succession of (now forgotten) "Mexican Spitfire" movies for RKO.[40] The series came to an abrupt and tragic halt in 1944 when the actress took her own life. The archetypal Latin female was

> Non-Anglo-Saxon, sexually aggressive, unable to speak proper English, possessive, illogical, jealous, highly emotional, regarded as a sex object, temperamental, and hot-blooded [and] usually native to a tropical, exotic climate. "Hot Tamale," "Firecracker," and "Wildcat" are some of the other names applied to her.[41]

In many ways, Lupe Vélez was to Carmen Miranda what John the Baptist was to Jesus. She paved the way and actively participated in creating a stereotype of the Latin female that Carmen then took to outrageous, even campy, heights (or depths). Words like "savage," "torrid," "primitive," "barbaric," "fiery," "tempestuous," and "volatile" came to be used in an almost unconscious, offhand, and yet very revealing way in US press notices about Carmen's films. They reflect a certain ambivalence, that is, that she is a threatening presence sexually, but her mangling of English and her comic outfits somehow diminish the danger.

The Los Angeles *Herald Examiner* described Miranda as "outfitted in smart, barbaric colors, waving articulate hips and rollicking through the most fun of her Hollywood career.[42] Washington, DC's *Evening Star* titled its review of *That Night in Rio* "Torrid Carmen Miranda Brightens New Musical" and observed:

> The way of progress is indicated clearly. All the boys need to do is improve their contributions ... is to teach this *torrid tamale* from South America more and more broken English until she has a vocabulary larger than those of the other members of Mr. Zanuck's musical stock company.[43]

Variety found that "Carmen Miranda ... chants and dances and wears her bizarre attire with a savage grace which spreads excitement around her in widening ripples to color every scene she plays.[44] The *Hollywood Reporter* said of this same film, "[Miranda's] performance in English is ... vivid, fiery and tempestuous."[45] In regards to *Springtime in the Rockies, Variety* later declared that Miranda was

> colorful, arresting, exerting her forthright, primitive charm through her staccato chanting, her energetic dancing, the way she displays her bizarre costumes, and, above all, her volatile sense of comedy from which all her other manifestations spring.[46]

All of this formed a much less flattering image of Latin America than what audiences and critics in the southern hemisphere were comfortable with. Indeed, the Uniao Cultural Brasil-Estados Unidos wrote to Will H. Hays, president of the Motion Pictures and Distributors of America (and notorious film censor), on January 2, 1942, to remind him of "the great need for teaching the average American citizen the following facts about Brazil," which included its size (largest in South America), language (Portuguese and not Spanish), urbanization (São Paolo is comparable to Chicago), and culture and science (as important as that of the United States), and so forth.[47] To be fair, the studio did run the script and music for *That Night in Rio* by the Brazilian Embassy in Washington, DC.[48] But the stereotyping continued unabated throughout Miranda's career, and beyond.

STYLIZATION AND SIMPLIFICATION OF MUSIC AND TEXT

Miranda's torrid stereotype required a commensurate distortion of the musical and textual materials used to create her character. Again, to be fair, Miranda's movies represented a quantum leap over what American audiences had previously experienced in the way of Brazilian music from Hollywood, especially in *Flying Down to Rio* (although that movie was remarkably sensitive in other ways, including its use of blacks in the song-and-dance numbers and generally favorable depiction of Rio as a modern metropolis). Miranda was the leading performer of samba, backed up by her handpicked Brazilian musicians, occasionally, at least, singing songs written by Brazilian sambistas (e.g., the samba "O tic-tac do meu coraçao" by Alcyr Pires Vermelho and Walfrido Silva in *Springtime in the Rockies*), many for her personally. But the truth is that most of the numbers in her movies were written by Americans possessing only a superficial acquaintance with the genre, and the songs were composed to appeal to a US audience that, at least as far as samba was concerned, was completely unsophisticated. *LA Weekly* certainly saw this many years later when it remarked on "the pseudo-sambas of Tin Pan Alley tunesmith Harry Warren and Mack Gordon, and [the replacement of] her soulful Portuguese lyrics with pidgin doggerel like 'Chica Chica Boom Chick.'"[49]

Mirabile dictu! In fact, internal documents give us some genuine insight into the genesis of this number, which was one of the big hits from *That Night in Rio*. According to Harry Brand, Mack Gordon had this to say about its text:

> Harry [Warren] had the basis of a great tune—we played it over on the piano and I hummed it with him. But I wanted to get the rhythm down so I could take it home with me to work on the lyric. To fix the rhythm in my mind, I hit upon a group of syllables which exactly fitted the music. I sang them out loud. The syllables were "Chica, Chica, Boom, Chic-." "Sing that over again, Mack," suggested Harry. So I did. "That's great, Mack, you've got the title—let's call the song 'Chica, Chica, Boom Chic.'" So that's what we call the song—it's a perfect jungle chant![50]

Despite its dubious association with the jungle, we must remember that the Brazilian Embassy was shown the script and song texts in advance. Thus, it seems incredible they acquiesced to the rest of the lyric:

Come on and sing the chica chica boom chic,
That crazy thing, the chica chica boom chic,
Brazilians found the chica chica boom chic,
They like the sound of chica, chica, boom, chic,
It came down the Amazon,
From the jungles,
Where the natives greet everyone they meet
Beatin' on a tom tom.[51]

That "chica chica boom chic" was more closely situated to the Mulholland aquaduct (*sic*) than the Amazon River and that Brazilian Indians do not play "tom-toms" were fine points of ethnography that the composer and lyricist knew full well would not disturb the sleep of American moviegoers. Moreover, this was conceived as a rumba, not a samba, and therefore has little relation musically to Brazil. In fact, Aloysio de Oliveira had to modify both this rumba and the conga "I, Yi, Yi, Yi, Yi, I Like You Very Much" with elements of samba and *marchinha,* respectively, in order to enhance their Brazilianness.[52]

What so distressed Carmen's countrymen, however, was that through her active participation in this kind of thing, her art had become Americanized. As we have noted, Carmen complained bitterly that she was never given an opportunity onscreen to sing slower, more lyrical songs. The studio executives believed that only her hyperactive numbers had any box-office appeal and that the subtleties of Brazilian popular music would be lost on American audiences. For instance, nearly all her movie numbers are in major keys, while in fact many of the sambas she made famous in Brazil in the 1930s—for example, "Diz que tem" by Vincente Paiva and Hannibal Cruz or the bewitchingly melancholy "Coraçao" by Synval Silva[53]—are in minor keys and exhibit some poignant lyricism. Like so much Brazilian popular music, they convey *saudade,* a sort of wistful nostalgia. But the happy escapism of Miranda's Hollywood movies, and the kind of role in which she found herself frozen in every film, demanded that anything elevated, serious, sophisticated, or reflective be completely expunged.

AMBASSADRESS OF THE SAMBA?

Carmen's expressed feelings about her role as a representative of Latin American culture in general and Brazilian music in particular are somewhat contradictory. On the one hand, she was pleased with her role as a symbol of Latin America and the "proof" that symbol provided of amity between the northern and southern hemispheres:

It is comforting to know that a simple popular artist like me could have been used as a political weapon. But if I didn't have talent and this charisma they attribute to me, I would not have survived, right?[54]

However, she was vehement in rejecting the notion that she was "Latino-americana":

I detest this expression, as it is so generalized. I like to be called a Brazilian, not from South America or Latin America, for I have nothing to do with the descendants of Spain. After all, we Brazilians are the only citizens of Latin America that speak Portuguese, and we really are different.[55]

This statement is highly ironic, because as we now know, her admixture of diverse elements from Mexican, Cuban, Brazilian, and Argentinian traditions created a hybrid that often obscured the Brazilian character of her art. She actively participated in the creation of a mythological, pan-Latin stereotype that incenses South Americans to the same extent it entertained—and misinformed—moviegoers in the United States. But, as Ana M. López has pointed out, this "hybridization [is] potentially inherent to all national cinemas."[56]

We close with another quotation from Roberts's seminal book, one with which this author cannot agree. He states that Miranda's movies "made no statements about Latin music, and to object to their stereotyping is about as valid as objecting that *Oklahoma!* gave a false impression of American farmers."[57] One may or may not choose to object, but the stereotypes possess an importance that transcends mere nitpicking about authenticity. In fact, her movies constitute a very important statement about Latin American music, demographics, politics, women, and culture in general. It is simply that, as many have observed, the statements are misleading. As Shari Roberts proclaims, "Miranda's parodic text works undeniably to reinforce regressive stereotypes of Latin Americans and of women, and to support racist and sexist conceptions."[58] The music plays a key role in such stereotyping.

Yet we need not view the situation as uniformly sinister. In their promiscuous miscegenation of musical types, choreography, and costumes, Carmen's movies could be viewed as a phenomenon nearly half a century ahead of its time. The "ethnofusion" that now drives the popular-music industry exhibits at times bewildering combinations and permutations of styles not only from Latin America but from the world at large. Carmen was, in fact, a prophetess of the musical global village that had not yet fully arrived in the 1940s. Her Hollywoodized eclecticism has a postmodern quality, and we can find meaning, significance, and (yes!) entertainment in it outside the highly political context in which it emerged, whether of Brazilian nationalism under Vargas and his regime of racial reconciliation, or of the Good Neighbor Policy in the midst of a world war.

Miranda revivals have taken place at periodic intervals since her death in 1955. In the 1960s, *tropicália* filmmakers in Brazil were fascinated and deeply influenced by her Hollywood movies.[59] The 1990s witnessed another resurgence of Miranda-mania, especially as result of the brilliant documentary *Banana Is My Business,* released in 1994.[60] Succeeding generations will almost certainly continue to find much in her art that is compelling, relevant, and joyful. To assert anything less would be to diminish her stature as the creative genius she truly was.

NOTES

1. This exchange occurred during a press conference on December 4, 1982, in the early going of Reagan's presidency. I am extremely grateful to archivist Diane Barrie of the Ronald Reagan

Library for tracking down the precise quotation and source for a statement I only dimly recalled from so many years ago.

2. Allen L. Woll, *The Latin Image in American Film,* rev. ed. (Los Angeles: UCLA Latin American Center Publications, 1980), v.

3. Martha Gil-Montero, *Brazilian Bombshell: The Biography of Carmen Miranda* (New York: Donald I. Fine, 1989), 28.

4. For a thorough discography, see Cássio Emmanuel Barsante, *Carmen Miranda* (Rio de Janeiro: Europa Empresa, Gráfica e Editora, 1985), 230–35; see also, for lyrics and further recording information, Abel Cardoso Júnior, *Carmen Miranda, a cantor do Brasil* (São Paulo: Cardoso Junior, 1978).

5. Gil-Montero, *Brazilian Bombshell,* 57.

6. Cited in ibid., 67.

7. Ana M. López, "Are All Latins from Manhattan? Hollywood, Ethnography and Cultural Colonialism," in *Mediating Two Worlds: Cinematic Encounters in the Americas,* ed. John King, Ana M. Lopez, and Manuel Alvarado, 67–80 (London: British Film Institute, 1993), 69.

8. The soundtrack of this movie is available on CD: *The Gang's All Here* (Sandy Hook Records, S.H. 2009, 1978). Other CD compilations of her US recordings include *Carmen Miranda: South American Way* (Jasmine Records, JASCD 317, 1993), and the *Carmen Miranda Anthology* (One Way Records, MCAD 22124, 1994).

9. Gil-Montero, *Brazilian Bombshell,* 121–22.

10. In a review of *Springtime in the Rockies* from September 21, 1942. Unless otherwise stated, this and all other reviews cited below are found in the press files for each film in the Margaret Herrick Library, General Collection (MHL/GC), Academy of Motion Picture Arts and Sciences, Hollywood.

11. The banana possesses considerable symbolism on many levels. It not only is psychological, even Freudian, but also has resonance in the sphere of business and politics. The United Fruit Company had extensive interests in Central America and made its contribution to Good Neighborliness by establishing a Middle American Information Bureau in 1943 to encourage inter-American understanding. The following year, it introduced a Miranda-inspired logo, Chiquita Banana. The feminist dimension of the banana's political economy, using Carmen Miranda as a point of departure, is the topic of Cynthia H. Enloe, "Carmen Miranda on My Mind," in *Bananas, Beaches & Bases: Making Feminist Sense of International Politics* (Berkeley: University of California Press, 1990), 124–50.

12. See Linda Phyllis Austern, "'Forreine Conceites and Wandring Devises': The Exotic, the Erotic, and the Feminine," In *The Exotic in Western Music,* ed. Jonathan Bellman (Boston: Northeastern University Press, 1998), 26: "From the travels of Odysseus to the voyages of the starship *Enterprise,* the Western mind has been called to vicarious adventures in distant lands of pleasure and danger through the voice of an exotic woman."

13. These lyrics were obtained from a typewritten document in the MPAA Production Code Administration file on this film, in the Margaret Herrick Library, Special Collections (MHL/SC).

14. Ibid.

15. Shari Roberts points out that this process of "whitening" the *samba de morro* had begun in Brazil, and the mellower variety was popularized by Miranda and others in the 1930s. Shari Roberts, "Lady in the Tutti-Frutti Hat: Carmen Miranda, a Spectacle of Ethnicity," *Cinema Journal* 32, no. 3 (1993): 3–23. One should keep in mind, however, that many of the composers of this newer type of samba were, in fact, black.

16. In a review of *Nancy Goes to Rio,* dated April 8, 1950.

17. Dulce Damasceno de Brito Consiglio, *O ABC de Carmen Miranda* (São Paulo: Companhia Editora Nacional, 1986), 58. Translated by Sarah Hamilton.

18. Gil-Montero, *Brazilian Bombshell,* 97.

19. William Rowe and Vivian Schelling, *Memory and Modernity: Popular Culture in Latin America* (London: Verso, 1991), 38.

20. Ibid., 41–42.

21. Ibid., 42.

22. Ibid., 44.

23. Gil-Montero, *Brazilian Bombshell,* 101.

24. Ibid., 115.

25. MHL/GC, press file on *That Night in Rio.*

26. In an e-mail message to this author on May 20, 2000, ethnomusicologist Peter Manuel, an authority on Caribbean music, could not identify the *ñango,* except to speculate that perhaps "the word in question is ñañigo . . . a member of the abakua secret societies, derived from the Carabali people. They have distinctive music and dance. But it's not a religion per se, and there is no spirit possession (as there is in voodoo)." Perhaps this was the inspiration for Brand's explanation.

27. John Storm Roberts, *The Latin Tinge: The Impact of Latin American Music on the United States,* 2nd ed. (New York: Oxford University Press, 1999), 83.

28. MHL/GC, press file on *Weekend in Havana.*

29. Barsante, *Carmen Miranda,* 18.

30. Review dated July 17, 1941.

31. Gil-Montero, *Brazilian Bombshell,* 97–98.

32. Review dated October 2, 1940, emphasis added.

33. Review dated October 2, 1940.

34. Cited in Gil-Montero, *Brazilian Bombshell,* 103.

35. Lyrics from MHL/SC, MPAA Production Code Administration file on *Nancy Goes to Rio.*

36. Gil-Montero, *Brazilian Bombshell,* 173.

37. Cited in Barsante, *Carmen Miranda,* 119.

38. Gil-Montero, *Brazilian Bombshell,* 173.

39. Roberts, *The Latin Tinge,* 87.

40. Walters provides a sampling of titles: *Mexican Spitfire* (1939), *Mexican Spitfire Out West* (1940), *Mexican Spitfire at Sea* (1941), *Mexican Spitfire's Baby* (1941), *Mexican Spitfire's Elephant* (1942), *Mexican Spitfire Sees a Ghost* (1942), *Mexican Spitfire's Blessed Event* (1943). Debra Nan Walters, "Hollywood, World War II, and Latin America: The Hollywood Good Neighbor Policy as Personified by Carmen Miranda" (MA thesis, University of Southern California, 1978), 106.

41. Ibid., 61.

42. Review dated October 24, 1941.

43. Review dated November 7, 1941, emphasis added.

44. Review dated March 7, 1941.

45. Review dated March 7, 1941.

46. Review dated September 21, 1942.

47. Letter in MHL/SC, MPAA Production Code Administration file on *That Night in Rio*.

48. According to internal documents, MHL/GC, press file on *That Night in Rio*.

49. Review dated October 2, 1998, MHL/GC, file on Carmen Miranda.

50. MHL/GC, press file on *That Night in Rio*.

51. Lyrics from MHL/SC, MPAA Production Code Administration file on *That Night in Rio*.

52. Gil-Montero, *Brazilian Bombshell,* 120.

53. Both numbers are available on *Carmen Miranda: The Brazilian* Recordings (Harlequin HQCD 33, 1993).

54. Consiglio, *O ABC de Carmen Miranda,* 19.

55. Ibid., 61.

56. López, "Are All Latins from Manhattan?," 6.

57. Roberts, *The Latin Tinge,* 106.

58. Roberts, "Lady in the Tutti-Frutti Hat," 19.

59. For an insightful look at the relationship between *tropicália* musicians and Miranda, see Caetano Veloso, "Carmen Mirandada," in *Brazilian Popular Music and Globalization,* ed. Charles Perrone and Christopher Dunn (Gainesville: University Press of Florida, 2001), 39–45. He speculates that "her great vocation for the finished product, her ability to design extremely stylized samba dancing as though creating a cartoon character, might . . . have been the decisive factor in her popularity [in the United States]."

60. Directed and narrated by Helena Solberg; produced by David Meyer and Helena Solberg. International Cinema production in association with the Corporation for Public Broadcasting, Channel 4 Television, and the National Latino Communications Center. Fox Lorber HomeVideo FLV1211.

4

WALT DISNEY'S *SALUDOS AMIGOS*

Hollywood and the Propaganda of Authenticity

O N THE EVENING OF OCTOBER 30, 1943, when the United States had been embroiled in World War II for nearly two years, a "Latin American Fiesta" took place within the concentric arches of the Hollywood Bowl. This gala event, planned by the consuls of Latin American countries with offices in Los Angeles, fêted with music and dance the newly revitalized friendship between the United States and Latin America. One sponsoring organization was the Office of Inter-American Affairs (OIAA), the sprawling, Washington-based agency charged with advancing the Good Neighbor Policy.[1] Crafted by President Franklin D. Roosevelt and his administration, that policy proclaimed the virtues of hemispheric solidarity in the face of European fascism, often relying on what was openly recognized as propaganda. Among the OIAA's fifty-nine committees was the Motion Picture Section, which collaborated with the Motion Picture Society

I wish to thank Leo Bernucci, Silvia Glocer, Katelyn Welch (Hollywood Bowl Museum), and Kristine Krueger (Margaret Herrick Library, Academy of Motion Picture Arts and Sciences) for their insights and assistance with this project.

for the Americas (MPSA), recently established in Hollywood to oversee film portrayals of Latin America.[2] Other Fiesta sponsors included the University of Southern California, the Los Angeles and Santa Barbara branches of the Pan American League, and other entities.[3]

Serving as emcees were two icons of Good Neighborly music and film. Desi Arnaz, who had wildly slapped his conga drum in *Too Many Girls* (1939), paired up as master of ceremonies with Xavier Cugat, the Latin ballroom star who reputedly appeared on more film footage than any other bandleader in Hollywood.[4] That evening, Cugat also performed with his orchestra, backing up the Mexican American actor and singer Lina Romay, his frequent collaborator on NBC Radio and the daughter of Porfirio Romay of the Mexican consulate in Los Angeles. Other featured artists included the up-and-coming Colombian baritone Carlos Ramírez, a contract actor for MGM, and Aurora Miranda, sister of the flamboyant Carmen. For those with more highbrow tastes, Dolores Niles and Serge Leslie offered the ballet "from the Spanish opera *Le Cid* by Massenet." (Marshaling a "Spanish opera"—by a Frenchman—for the cause of Pan American solidarity surpassed even the usual such gaffes. Not only is Spain well outside the Americas but in 1943 it was a pariah state, having collaborating with Hitler and Mussolini during the Spanish Civil War.)

The Fiesta also offered folk music, hardly a typical offering for Hollywood display. Yet female representatives of the twenty-one American republics processed in a Parade of the Americas, each to the accompaniment of a requisite folk genre—a Chilean *cueca,* a Cuban *son,* a Panamanian *tamborito,* a Peruvian *wayno,* a Venezuelan *joropo,* a Southern Cone *pericón* for Uruguay, and a "Cherokee Indian Dance" for the United States. (A *baile boliviano* and *danza nicaragüense* are also listed in the program although it is not clear which Bolivian and Nicaraguan dances were played.) A subtler reference to folk music figured as well. Walt Disney's animated feature *Saludos Amigos* (1942), which chronicles a tour of Latin America undertaken by a team of Disney artists, was enhanced with "authentic folk music of a far distant day," as one critic enthused.[5] Accordingly, two of the film's cartoon protagonists—or at least their human agents (i.e., the voices of these characters)—made cameo appearances that night at the Bowl. Donald Duck (Clarence Nash) and Joe (José or Ze) Carioca (José Oliveira) both came onstage "courtesy of Walt Disney" and graced the program cover of the "Latin American Fiesta."

Well might this pair figure so prominently. When *Saludos Amigos* premiered just over a year earlier, critics had hailed it as a major step forward in Good Neighbor films, calling it an "amusing and friendship-cementing piece of entertainment," a "beguiling way of helping along the desired hemispheric solidarity for war and peace," and a "strong potential goodwill builder."[6] Clearly it fulfilled the obligations of propaganda. But *Saludos Amigos* was also upheld as "a document of authenticity" in that critics believed Disney and his team had produced an accurate account of Latin American life, one, moreover, that in true Pan Americanist spirit, would intertwine with US values.[7] One critic exulted in Disney's refusal to be guided by "extravagant and mistaken notions about our Southern neighbors," and another insisted, "here at last is cinematic justice and atonement for Hollywood's insults to Latin America!"[8] As we'll see, folk music was an important part of this rhetoric.

We shouldn't be surprised that US critics took this self-congratulatory tone, which they often did when it came to Good Neighbor films. But it is worth noting that *Saludos Amigos* also impressed Latin Americans. This reaction is partly tied to the film's exceptional performance history, for instead of premiering in the United States, it was first shown in Rio de Janeiro (as *Alô, Amigos*) on August 23, 1942. This was no ordinary night at the movies: the previous day, after years of vacillating between the Allies and the Axis, the Brazilian president-dictator Getúlio Vargas declared war on Italy and Germany.[9] By October, *Saludos Amigos* was playing to great acclaim in major cities in Argentina and Chile, as noted in reviews of the Hollywood premiere that December.

Such enthusiasm may surprise us today. After all, in 1971, when the Good Neighbor Policy was but a dim memory, the Chilean critic Ariel Dorfman penned his mordant *How to Read Donald Duck: Imperialist Ideology in the Disney Comic,* in which he likened Disney's cuddly protagonists to an omnipresent "registered trademark," one that spread manufactured "sweetness and light" to subaltern populations enslaved to US consumer culture.[10] As current scholarship on the film shows, recent critics are divided, with some echoing Dorfman, some finding the film relatively benign, and others largely bypassing the political implications of *Saludos Amigos* but agreeing with one of the few dissenting early critics, James Agee, who took issue with Disney's "famous cuteness."[11]

These early critics also applauded the music of *Saludos Amigos.* Several praised the music team of Charles Wolcott, Ed Plumb, and Paul Smith for researching Latin American folk songs and dances, along with indigenous music, which in the United States was often loosely referred to as "folk music" or "folklore."[12] But the film also showcases contemporaneous selections by Latin Americans; further, one critic likened the film itself to a musical composition, calling its four scenes "movements."[13] (Considering the low esteem in which cartoon music was often held, this was high praise.)[14] So conscientiously did the music team approach their project that when they jazzed up their Latin American sources with a "Hollywood" sound, these elaborations seemed to offend no one, not even in Latin America, at least as far as we can tell.

Although many have written about *Saludos Amigos,* no one has addressed the music in any detail. In this essay, I first survey the principal trends in music and Pan Americanism during the Good Neighbor period.[15] I then analyze the music, folkloric and otherwise, and relate it to the film's visual and narrative elements, connecting it to broader themes in Pan Americanist discourse. In addition, I reflect on authenticity in terms of Pan Americanism, that is, a yearning for a "genuine culture of the Americas," as one cultural agent of the period put it.[16] In the end, I argue that, whatever authenticity *Saludos Amigos* proffered through its music, the film as a whole served mainly as a tool of strictly one-sided propaganda—in favor of the United States and the war effort. Authenticity, always an elastic term, becomes even more so when paired with the tools of propaganda, especially as fashioned by Hollywood.

MUSIC, THE GOOD NEIGHBOR POLICY, AND THE SEARCH FOR AUTHENTICITY

First, what did Pan Americanism, a congeries of sentiments and policies dating from the 1890s, mean in Los Angeles? In the program booklet for the Latin American Fiesta, the

Venezuelan consul Alberto Posse-Rivas upheld its virtues, according to which citizens of the Americas share a common history and character that supersede individual countries, regions, or language groups.[17] As Posse-Rivas observed, Americans all strove for "the same ideal," one that had "emanated with refulgent splendor from the minds of those illustrious patriots Abraham Lincoln in the north and Francisco de Miranda in the south." What better setting to celebrate these parallels, Posse-Rivas continued, than "the beautiful city of Los Angeles," which "repeatedly [had] given proof of its sympathetic understanding and appreciation of the Latin American peoples?" With these high-flown phrases, the Venezuelan consul deftly dismissed two centuries of border tensions, including the zoot suit riots that had rocked Los Angeles that very summer.

It wasn't the first time Angelenos had been extravagantly compared to their southern neighbors. In November 1922, when an exhibition of Mexican folk art opened at the Los Angeles Museum of History, Science, and Art, the Mexican consul Leandro Garza Leal set forth Pan Americanist principles. "The ideals of the Pilgrims," Garza Leal declared, "were the same in basis as those of the Mexican Revolutionists, against the Spanish in 1810"; like their Northern brethren, Mexicans "were fighting for life, liberty and the pursuit of happiness."[18] To be sure, during the 1910s and 1920s, Pan Americanism suffered one of its sharpest declines due to US military interventions in Nicaragua, the Dominican Republic, Haiti, and Mexico, along with exploitation of Latin America's natural resources and cheap local labor by US business.

Now with the world at war, the stakes were higher. Roosevelt not only dusted off Pan Americanism but gave the concept new life as the Good Neighbor policy, aided by his personal popularity and by genuine fear of an Axis invasion of the hemisphere. Latin America was no longer a congeries of "banana republics" and dictatorships filled with temperamental "half-breeds," as the rhetoric of the 1920s would have it. Rather, the American republics were to be seen as part of a harmonious whole joined by the values over which Posse-Rivas had rhapsodized.[19] As the administration scrambled to smooth over past tensions with the region, the Good Neighbor Policy took shape. It drew unabashedly on propaganda, the strategies of which had become increasingly fine tuned since World War I and which also reflected the goals of cultural diplomacy, then in its nascent stages in the United States.[20] In 1940, Harold Lavine and James Wechsler of the New York–based Institute for Propaganda Analysis noted approvingly the "appropriation of new instruments for exerting the stimuli," concluding that propaganda was a fact of modern life:

> We live in a propaganda age. Public opinion no longer is formulated by the slow processes of what Professor John Dewey calls shared experience. In our time public opinion is primarily a response to propaganda stimuli . . . it would be more fair to state that ours is an age of competing propagandas.[21]

For generating Good Neighborly propaganda through culture, Los Angeles was indeed the ideal setting Posse-Rivas described. Because the city boasted such a high concentration of Spanish-speaking inhabitants, Spanish-language theater and film had thrived there for over a century; John Koegel refers to "the largest Spanish-language stage in the United States."[22] Of course, Hollywood wielded special power.[23] As with the US government, however, previous missteps were painfully obvious. Ever since the silent-era "greaser," Hollywood had spewed out anti-Hispanic stereotypes—the shifty bandido, the temperamental Latin lover, or the somnolent wastrel snoozing under his sombrero. With the Good Neighbor Policy, a fresh start seemed nonetheless possible. Hollywood, the great popularizer, now popularized Latin America, a subject few US Americans had studied in primary or secondary schools.[24] For example, in *Juárez* (1939), a well-researched film that focuses on the Mexican president's admiration for Abraham Lincoln, Latin America appears in a positive light in comparison with European enemies of democracy.[25] Disney, too, produced educational films in addition to cartoon features.[26]

The advent of the movie musical in the early 1930s coincided both with the Good Neighbor period and with the Latin music craze then sweeping the United States, and studios churned out musicals featuring this alluring music. Yet nearly all Good Neighbor musicals fell short. They tended to be frothy confections with travelogue-style titles that emphasized little more than glamour (*That Night in Rio*) or "tropical" settings (*Weekend in Havana*). Advertisements hawked "torrid" scenes in "gay" Latin America, which teemed with beaches, swaying palms, exotic vegetation, and sexy inhabitants. Even movies that explicitly referred to the Good Neighbor Policy demeaned Latin Americans by depicting either corrupt locals, as in *Escape from Paradise* (1939), or slow-witted locals. Hollywood also made many musical errors. First, it relied on its own composers rather than on Latin Americans. Next, it often portrayed inauthentic musical practices.[27] To take just one example, Argentine moviegoers were incensed by *Argentine Nights,* the screen debut of the Andrews Sisters. Its "Rhumbaboogie" features the high-spirited trio frolicking in Caribbean ruffles to an amalgam of pseudo-Cuban music and boogie-woogie. As one Argentine reviewer concluded, "as long as Hollywood insists on seeing Argentina as an incredibly ridiculous tropical country, no Pan American understanding is possible."[28]

Different approaches to musical Good Neighborliness were tested in other circles. In classical music, critics admired works by the Mexican composer Carlos Chávez (1899–1978), seen to reinforce the ideal of ancient America untainted by "civilization," code for a decadent Europe exhausted by war, whose traditions had held sway in the Americas far too long. Not surprisingly, the notion of the Americas as a tabula rasa, on which a new history would be written, was equally compelling in political discourse.[29] Chávez enshrined the tabula rasa in his music—the "authentic expressive values" of Pan Americanism, as critic Paul Rosenfeld effused—by drawing on well-established signifiers of the "primitive" in his works: "open" intervals (fourths and fifths), ostinati, conjunct melodies, short motivic fragments of limited range (including native melodies), pentatonicism, and even native instruments. US critics thus affirmed New World identity through these exoticist tropes and acknowledged a yet-to-be-fully-discovered Other.[30] In other words, in the Americas self and Other could coexist. Yet Latin American intellectual elites were likelier to revere European culture, especially in

Chile and Argentina. As a result, the notion of a common American culture proved a hard sell for US cultural diplomats.[31]

Classical composers north and south also availed themselves of folk music, weaving dance rhythms or melodies into their compositions. Sometimes they did so to repudiate the avant-garde, following the lead of the musicologist and composer Charles Seeger, who urged composers to avoid elitism.[32] By 1941, as chief of the Music Section of the Pan American Union, Seeger was in a position to advance these principles on behalf of the Good Neighbor Policy, working closely (if sometimes less than smoothly) with the OIAA. William Berrien, another Washington-based cultural agent during the Good Neighbor period, argued that familiarity with Latin American folk songs of "birth and death, heroic deeds, work, [songs] of beggars, muleteers, *vaqueros*" could ensure affective north-south bonds; Berrien also held that folk music study would counteract the perception, relentlessly driven by Hollywood and the music industry, of Latin American music as "very gay and sometimes spicy."[33]

Folk music, which was becoming established in academic departments in the United States and Latin America, thus promised authenticity. To be sure, north and south it was much influenced by Europe, whether in Appalachian ballads in the United States or the common-practice harmonies and instruments of Spain and Portugal in Latin America. Whatever folk music's roots, scholars and performers concerned with preservation held, sometimes nostalgically, that the rural values it represented could protect national identities against encroaching urbanization. Folk music also offered convincing proof of the Americas' common characteristics. In compiling collections of Spanish-language folksongs, US cultural agents sought to win hearts and minds throughout the Americas through shared song. The preface of one such collection rather extravagantly declared, for example, that anyone singing the children's song "El patio de mi casa" would instantly sense that it mirrors the intervallic structure of a certain well-known tune commemorating "our friend MacDonald who had a farm."[34] Like classical musicians, folklorists considered self and Other. As Regina Bendix argues, authenticity "is generated not from the bounded classification of an Other, but from the probing comparison between self and Other."[35] Such probing was the source of both tension and fulfillment during the Good Neighbor period.

Of these three musics, popular, classical, and folk, it was popular Latin ballroom dances—"very gay and sometimes spicy"—that commanded the biggest public. As lyricist and producer Arthur Freed declared in 1940, "hemispheric solidarity, good neighborliness, and the like is [*sic*] only a background reason for the flood of South American features. . . . The actual reason is South American music."[36] Just as in Good Neighbor musicals, US Americans danced the tango and the rhumba (the music industry's spelling of *rumba,* a multifaceted Cuban musical practice).[37] These genres were often reworked with Big Band orchestration; likewise, English lyrics might be sung to melodies by Latin Americans that had nothing to do with the original, a genre Gustavo Pérez Firmat dubs the "latune."[38] Especially compelling was so-called Latin rhythm, consistently understood as "complex" but sometimes simplified by the sheet music industry—and advertised as such—to increase sales.[39] The result was a generic product that could be marketed as "Latin."

It would be easy to claim that Latin Americans uniformly resented US popular music and the inroads it was making worldwide. But if we undertake a "probing comparison," we find that their reactions were by no means monolithic. Arnaz and Cugat (the latter born in Spain) were both delighted with their Hollywood careers. Brazilian artists reversed the latunes phenomenon, singing hit songs from the United States with Portuguese lyrics and creating a genre known as the *versão*.[40] Folk genres such as the Colombian *cumbia* or the Andean *wayno* began to be enhanced with saxophone. Other Latin Americans railed against the Colossus of the North, however. When Carmen Miranda returned to Brazil after cavorting through several Hollywood films in her banana-laden headdress, she was greeted coolly by her compatriots for having sold out. The Mexican composer Manuel Ponce once lamented that the foxtrot had caused Mexican youth to "deliver themselves unconsciously into the arms of the conqueror . . . overlooking the fact that behind the invading dance from the United States, Uncle Sam's coattails were etched."[41]

Racism also affected north-south musical exchange. In the early Good Neighbor musical *Flying Down to Rio* (1933), the central production number features the wholesome, athletic movements of Fred Astaire and Ginger Rogers (onscreen together for the first time), setting them apart from the pelvic thrusting and butt-wiggling of Afro-Brazilians earlier in the same sequence.[42] In 1935, the recently fortified Production Code Administration attacked the film for "sex suggestiveness"; indeed, it deemed the "entire colored troup [*sic*]" objectionable.[43] Various spokespersons for Latin American culture acted no differently. In 1941, when the Brazilian historian Pedro Calmon saw the African American dancer Katherine Dunham and her company in the Technicolor short *Carnival in Rhythm,* he protested that the film conveyed the impression that "all or most Brazilians are negroes, and that all or most of their dances and music are predominantly African."[44] Probably the best-known Good Neighbor project to crash on the shoals of racism was Orson Welles's unfinished documentary on samba in Rio de Janeiro, which the OIAA nixed because, among other reasons, it emphasized samba's Afro-Brazilian roots. Clearly black and mixed-race people weren't good for propaganda north or south, however authentic their contributions to Latin American music.

SALUDOS AMIGOS: PROPAGANDA AND THE LIMITS OF AUTHENTICITY

Disney initially planned twelve cartoons, of which *Saludos Amigos* was the first.[45] The films were conceived to purvey both "direct and indirect propaganda" about and to Latin America.[46] As noted, *Saludos Amigos* more than fulfilled that objective. One critic quipped, "who would have thought in the dim primordial past of five years ago that Donald Duck would be giving the retort perfect to [Hitler's minister of propaganda] Herr Doktor Goebbels?"[47] Likewise, the educator Dr. Lenore Vaughn-Eames asserted, "if this is the type of propaganda film that Disney is going to put out let's have more and many of them."[48] Yet *Saludos Amigos* is also very much about artistic representation. No mere account of life in Latin America, the film gives pride of place to the creative process of the Disney team: how *they* experience Latin America and transform *their* experiences into image, movement, and sound.

Visually, the film operates in three different environments. One, of course, is animation. Two Disney characters already familiar worldwide figure prominently: Donald Duck, as a curious tourist, and Goofy, as a Texas cowboy who unexpectedly finds himself in the pampas. *Variety* described both as "solid Yank symbols."[49] Complementing them were two Latin American characters, a mail plane named Pedro, who crosses the Andes from his native Chile, and Joe Carioca, a natty Brazilian parrot with a flair for the samba. The second visual environment is that of the documentary. Enlarged 16 mm Technicolor footage records the artists' activities—sketching, typing, listening to music—such that photographic reality contrasts with cartoon antics. A third environment is the avalanche of sketches and paintings by the artists themselves that punctuates the film. Boundaries between the three are fluid: often a drawing morphs into a cartoon character, giving birth to a dialogue or a story, followed in short order by the 16 mm footage. In other words, the visual format discourages a "bounded classification" between self and Other.

Nonetheless, the 16 mm footage reinforces the US gaze, as does the avuncular voice of the narrator Fred Shields. As Shields tells it, both the human and the animated travelers are intrigued by the Latin American Other. For example, the Disney team consistently seeks rural settings rather than "modern city life." (One exception is Rio de Janeiro, where the team initially lands and to which it returns; Buenos Aires, on the other hand, was "impressive" but no match for "the lure of the pampas.") Just as sixteenth-century European travelers marveled at outsized plants and exotic blooms, the cartoonists find themselves in a "scenic wonderland," as the *Hollywood Reporter* put it.[50] Superlatives abound, whether in referencing Lake Titicaca (the highest navigable body of water in the world), the Andean peak Aconcagua (the highest mountain outside of Asia), or the "millions of acres of rich grazing land" that constitute the Argentine pampas. Unlike Good Neighbor musicals, usually set in a handful of countries deemed attractive or cosmopolitan, *Saludos Amigos* ventures to Bolivia and the Chilean Andes, not normally part of the Hollywood circuit.

In praising Disney for avoiding "extravagant and mistaken notions about our Southern neighbors," critics wanted to understand the secret of his success. Evidently it boiled down to high regard for his subjects. An anonymous reviewer for *Variety* stated that "Disney took great care to treat the . . . culture of the South Americans with great respect and admiration."[51] A reporter from the same publication, writing from Buenos Aires, noted "the Norteamericanos . . . become the fall guys," adding, "Disney has been careful that in getting his laughs, the gags are not on our Good Neighbors, but rather on the Yanquis."[52] Critics also applauded the team for having "gathered the folk tales and [legends] for the cartoon imagery," ensuring that "the background [was] faithfully followed . . . based on actual customs and facts."[53]

Interweaving with the three visual environments and the narrative stance is the music. As is well known, film music, often perceived only subliminally, is not mere "background" but a set of special codes distinct from other cinematographic elements.[54] Music may even speak to viewers more viscerally than the visual elements. As Pascal Quignard comments, "what is seen can be abolished by the eyelids . . . what is heard knows neither eyelids, nor partitions, neither curtains nor walls."[55] In short, the music of *Saludos Amigos* fulfilled the objective of propaganda defined by Lavine and Wechsler; namely, it was a means of "exerting the stimuli."

Yet the music also explored the relationship between self and Other. As noted, the music team drew on a variety of strategies. To be sure, they showcased folk music. But they also incorporated primitivist gestures, techniques clearly marked as European, contemporary music by Latin Americans, US jazz and blues, and Hollywood tropes. In describing these, the narrator sometimes indulges in clichés not borne out by the score, as we'll see in the scene-by-scene survey of highlights that follows.

Launching this "document of authenticity" is the title song, by Wolcott, with lyrics by Ned Washington. Throughout the film it serves as an idée fixe, transformed according to locale and story line. First heard in the opening credits against the backdrop of a cartoon map, it's pure 1940s Hollywood. Bustling strings fortified by a trumpet motive and descending scales in the brass introduce the expansive main melody, sung in unison by a male chorus. The first phrase spans a descending E-flat arpeggio and the second consists of disjunct leaps, which the singers execute with aplomb. Confidently they proclaim the virtues of Pan American friendship, urging "amigos" north and south to keep "a glad song in your heart." The diction is noteworthy: either the singers are nonnative speakers of English or they are trying to sound as if they were. Neither self nor Other, the diction suggests a shared space between the two. How that space is to be negotiated will be addressed in the rest of the film.

When the voices drop out, the saxophones play the melody, fading to a pianissimo as 16 mm footage shows the Disney team boarding the American Flagship jet for Rio de Janeiro. Just as they settle in for the long journey, documentary melts into animation, again with a map, this time animated. In it, Rio de Janeiro's celebrated Christ of the Redeemer statue looks out over a glistening Guanabara Bay, one of several references to Christianity in the film. (Brazil, by the way, is spelled in Portuguese "Brasil.")[56] Accompanying the animated map is the *Saludos* theme. Now, however, the male chorus sings in close, three-part harmony, a euphonious, even contemplative, conclusion to the perky theme, leaving the viewer with an aural affirmation of a basic Pan Americanist premise, namely, a concordant relationship of parts to whole.

We learn that the Disney team will split up, half traveling to Chile and half "north to the Inca country," as Shields explains. As one animated plane flies over Argentina, the *Saludos* theme reenters in the first of its many instrumental guises, with note values of the melody doubled and a generic habanera-like "Latin" rhythm. The theme also signals the arrival at Lake Titicaca, a turning away "from the modern cities to find the descendants of ancient Incan civilization," all in 16 mm footage. As the artists soak up ancient America, the theme responds accordingly in that the melody is taken by a *kena*, a vertical Andean flute, and harmonized by another *kena*. An agogically accented perfect fourth figures, and the disjunct leaps in phrase two are rewritten as smaller intervals; an ostinato accompaniment replaces the high-energy brass and strings of the opening credits. Clearly the cheery *Saludos* theme can sustain these familiar signifiers of the primitive.

Another such signifier appears via pentatonicism. Still in the world of 16 mm footage, the viewer observes an older man playing a *pitu,* an Incan transverse flute, which confirms that the people of the region play "melodies handed down from their Inca ancestors"; further, Shields intones, "the music is strange and exotic." We hear that most exotic of sonorities, a B-minor triad (albeit in a pentatonic context), and then another pentatonic tune, also played by an Andean flute but enhanced with glissandi of a different timbre. The two pentatonic melodies dominate the rest of the sequence, highlighting, for example, the entry of that "celebrated American tourist" Donald Duck, whom we first see admiring Lake Titicaca through binoculars. When he sets out on the lake in the balsa raft, pentatonic tune two accompanies him, now with *bombo* (an Andean drum) and guitar playing the ostinato introduced earlier. Back on land, Donald visits a market, where three local musicians are playing the *kena, bombo,* and panpipe. We see that it is a panpipe that produces the glissando. But why does its timbre not correspond to the actual sound of the instrument? Nor do we hear the common hocketing technique, which requires more than one panpipe player. As it turns out, once back in Disney's Burbank studio the music team discovered that panpipes not only were hard to find in Los Angeles but did not record as desired. By substituting an ocarina, they effectively doctored the "strange and exotic" sounds, bringing them closer to home but departing from authenticity.[57]

Donald Duck also interacts with a few Andean children. A typically acquisitive US tourist, he spontaneously takes a picture of an Andean baby being carried on his mother's back, to which the kid promptly retaliates by snapping a photo of Donald. This fleeting moment of triumph for indigenous Latin America figured in the Sunday edition of the *New York Times* (February 7, 1943, X3). Donald also encounters a boy playing pentatonic melody one. After using "crude sign language" to communicate with the "wide-awake youngster," Donald tries out the *kena,* spitting out the same tune. But "solid Yank" that he is, Donald naturally slips into hot jazz, to which the llama responds rather confusedly. Jazz closes the scene: as Donald and the llama risk life and limb on a fragile suspension bridge, pentatonic theme two gains energy through ever-fuller orchestration and intensified jazz rhythms. After snapping at the llama, who makes its way to safety, Donald plunges downward, landing safely in the lake and beating a hasty retreat to strains of jazz. In short, the music team upheld the character of "ancient America" according to the codes of the era, leaving hot jazz for Donald's less-than-brilliant moves.

The next "movement" of *Saludos Amigos* departs from the "strange and exotic" with the 16 mm footage taking the viewer back inside the plane, which now flies over the Andes. The *Saludos* theme, enhanced with a woodwind descant, accompanies the drawing, note-taking, and composing of the Disney artists, who capture the Uspallata Pass, with its Christ of the Andes statue marking the link between Chile and Argentina. In reflecting on the pioneer mail planes that once flew the route from Santiago to Mendoza, they conceive of a plucky little plane called Pedro. As his story begins, a dancelike theme in D major played by strings heralds the shift to animation and the melody, with its common-practice harmonies, becomes Pedro's theme, itself redolent of Europe. A prominent *sesquiáltera* (hemiola) suggests any number of Iberian and Latin American genres, including the *cueca,* traditionally a couple dance from rural Chile and invariably in a major key, like Pedro's theme. The customary *cueca* instrumentation, which generally combines guitar, accordion, harp, and *bombo,* is absent, however.

Redolent of a different Europe—and of the "pretend" Wagner common in cartoon music—is leitmotiv, here a six-note fragment of Pedro's theme. When played by solo trombone, it introduces the Papa mail plane; hurried woodwinds playing the same six notes announce the Mama plane. In representing Pedro, the six-note motive hesitates but is then extended to accompany him to flight school. One day, when Papa and Mama are too ill to deliver the mail, Pedro rises to the challenge, and as he takes off, the entire theme resounds in a brisk march tempo with brass flourishes. Shortly thereafter, he catches a glimpse of Aconcagua (depicted as a craggy, ominous face) and the theme flirts briefly with the parallel minor. Pedro nonetheless retrieves the mail in Mendoza and confidently indulges in some trick flying, the theme now in waltz time. But when Pedro reencounters Aconcagua, the weather changes and a rising motive in the trombone and string tremolos signals danger. Pedro struggles to gain altitude and ultimately rises above the danger zone—only to run out of gas. His theme fizzles and then is heard in minor on the English horn as Pedro's parents, back at the hangar, dejectedly wonder what has become of their son. Still, as Disney's determined and diminutive characters are wont to do, Pedro survives, miraculously clanking back home and accompanied by the theme in pseudo-Wagnerian grandeur. The resolution of a prominent 4–3 suspension affirms that little Pedro has imparted an important lesson on responsibility and persistence to the youth of the Americas.[58] Thus Wolcott and his collaborators remained true to authentic folk music while giving the nod to Latin American Europhiles.

The *Saludos* theme leads us across another animated map, this time over the Argentine pampas. Note values in the melody are again doubled, and the accompaniment is rhythmically elaborate. By now, the team has arrived in Buenos Aires, captured with shots in 16 mm footage of the Plaza de Mayo (which the narrator pronounces in Argentine Spanish, that is, *mah-jho*), the Teatro Colón, the Plaza de la Constitución, and the Art Deco Edificio Kavanagh, then the tallest building in Latin America.[59] When the Disney team visits the studio of the Argentine artist Florencio Molina Campos, known for depicting life on the pampas, a new theme, folkloric and in compound meter, is heard, signaling rejection of the Argentine capital's famous cosmopolitanism. Unlike the "strange and exotic" music of the Incas, however, it ultimately evokes the songs and dances of the United States.

Sure enough, no sooner do the Disney artists arrive at Molina Campos's studio then they head for the pampas, where a rodeo is in full swing. The music shifts to a quick triple meter with a long dominant pedal accompanying some of the more energetic maneuvers of the "Wild West show," as Shields calls it, adding that such exertions are "all part of a day's work for the gaucho," the independent horseman of the pampas, immortalized in poetry, prose, and music. What Shields does not mention is that the gaucho population declined so precipitously during the nineteenth century that by the 1940s they were essentially farmhands.[60] In 16 mm footage, the team enjoys an *asado* (barbecue) as couples in folkloric dress perform what seems to be a *gato,* an Argentine folk dance, on a wooden platform. As

Shields remarks, they dance "not the modern tango but the same tunes to which their grandparents have danced." Not only that, but the steps resemble "the old-time square dances of North America." Two men dressed in traditional gaucho costume perform a few steps of the *malambo,* a competitive dance that celebrates manhood and endurance, and the music continues unchanged. Throughout, these "country dances" are dominated by violins, accordion (i.e., not the *bandoneón,* associated with tango), and the *bombo.*

A more extensive sampling of folk genres comes with the next shift to animation, as we zoom in on a map of Texas. In one of the film's not infrequent touches of parody, Shields solemnly describes the territory: "untouched and unsullied by mercenary hand of civilization"—despite the thicket of signs advertising gas, lodgings, and food, along with several oil wells. (In other words, gringos are good sports and recognize their obsession with commerce.) As for the cowboy, a specimen of "strong, silent, and weather-beaten" manhood, Goofy is seen slumping on an old nag. When magically transported to Argentina, he proceeds to test his mettle against gaucho standards. Most of the time, however, Goofy is outsmarted by his horse.

Musically El Gaucho Goofy doesn't fare much better. Under a star-studded sky, he sings a *triste,* a folk genre the narrator describes as a "sad, romantic ballad." The *triste* in question is "Yo soy la blanca paloma" (I Am the White Dove), anthologized by Andrés Avelino Chazarreta (1867–1960), Argentina's first folklore scholar and on whom Wolcott relied by using four of his transcriptions in this sequence. This *triste* appears in a theater work by Martiniano Leguizamón (1858–1935), *Calandria: Comedia de costumbres campestres* (Calandaria: A Play about Rustic Customs). In *Saludos Amigos,* the viewer is initially led to believe that it is Gaucho Goofy who is singing so sensitively. Yet a phonograph is actually doing the work, as becomes obvious when the needle gets stuck. Promptly Goofy bursts into a *chacarera* with his horse, who has changed into a pink dress. A *chacarera,* which is generally in a minor key, is often sung to the accompaniment of guitar, violin, and bombo. Here, the sheer number of violins results in a symphonic sound against the strummed accompaniment, whereas the drum is barely audible.

Again, Shields juxtaposes self and Other by detecting parallels with US music. Just as the folk dances at the *asado* resembled square dancing, the *chacarera* combines "the Bunny Hug" and "a dash of Jumpin' Jive," all adding up to a "pampas version of 'cutting a rug.'"[61] After eight seconds, the horse pounds out a bluesy rendering of the *malambo* on a piano that materializes out of nowhere. Not for nothing does Shields call the traditional gaucho dance "perpetual motion below the equator": Goofy dances so energetically that his *bombachas* (pants) separate themselves from him and dance on their own. Goofy and his horse then dance the *pala-pala,* a dance from northwest Argentina (i.e., bordering Bolivia), generally sung in Quechua. *Pala-pala* dancers often wore animal masks, a tradition subverted in this performance by the two costumed dancing animals. After dancing too close to the campfire and setting his clothes on fire, however, Goofy is whisked back to Texas, filled with pleasant memories of his sojourn in "the gay, romantic land of the gauchos," where folk music holds sway, uniting self and Other in a close embrace. One Latin American Other was not impressed, however. Molina Campos, whose drawings sparked the Disney team's interest in gauchos in the first place, was displeased with the sequence and wanted his name taken off the credits, a wish that was not satisfied.[62]

An animated map leads eastward to Rio de Janeiro as the *Saludos* theme accompanies the travelers' arrival. Again, they are surrounded by natural beauty: the 16 mm footage shows Sugar Loaf, Copacabana Beach, and Guanabara Bay, along with the statue of "the Savior," as Shields notes. The hand of man is also to be admired in the "scenes of active city life," smart cafés, and the mosaic sidewalks common in Brazil. Intrigued, the team decides to linger. A series of their paintings interrupts the 16 mm footage: a street scene that includes three Afro-Brazilians walking along a mosaic sidewalk, several flamingos, Guanabara Bay, lush vegetation, and a parrot (*papagaio*). Then, with a shift back to 16 mm footage, the viewer beholds a real parrot surveying the team at work in the ad hoc studio they set up in Rio. Brazilian music takes over the *Saludos* theme as a conservatively dressed, middle-aged Brazilian woman demonstrates the basic samba step. Three musicians play the piano, the *reco-reco* (scraper), and a shaker, as Shields marvels at "that intricate samba rhythm."

In fact, the music is neither a samba nor especially intricate. It's the children's song "Escravos de Jó" (Slaves of Job), which ordinarily accompanies a circle game. We hear a harmonized version of the tune on the piano with simple ostinati in the percussion, "the same rhythm that captivates the whole city when carnival time comes around," as Shields proposes. To prove the point, Technicolor footage of carnival in Rio is inserted (carnival was some months off when Disney visited in early September). Sadlier speculates that the footage was extracted from Orson Welles's unfinished documentary, minus "shots of black celebrants."[63]

Real samba *can* be rhythmically complex, however. Further, the genre emblematizes Brazil's mixed-race population like little else, and initially many middle- and upper-class Brazilians found the genre distasteful, some objecting to "vulgar Negroid sambas."[64] This situation changed under Vargas, who sought to consolidate his power by instilling *brasilidade* (Brazilianness) through film, radio, architecture, and music.[65] With samba and its mixture of African-influenced rhythms and common-practice harmonies and melodies, Vargas could promote the rosy myth that Brazil's racial diversity was one of its strengths. Fitting perfectly into this scheme was the lyricist and composer Ary Barroso (1903–64), who in 1939 composed "Aquarela do Brasil" (Watercolor of Brazil), a paean to Brazil's beauties. "Aquarela do Brasil" seemed the ideal finale for *Saludos Amigos,* almost like the lavish production-number endings of many a musical.

It is also a fitting conclusion for a film about artistic representation. Not only is the animation at its most spectacular in the Brazil sequence, but the creative process itself takes center stage. It starts simply enough, with a sheet of blank paper affixed to an easel. Then the shadow of an artist flits over the drawing surface and a mysterious hand—a brown one—takes charge, wielding a paintbrush over the tabula rasa. After a slow, string-heavy introduction with tremolos and a recitative-like vocal line, the samba proper begins, the brisk tempo of which unleashes a profusion of colorful transformations. A jot of blue becomes a waterfall (the "murmuring fountains" in Barroso's lyrics) and drips of pink find new life as tropical flowers. Vegetation bursts into animal life and vice versa, as with the tree that turns into a bird and the bunch of bananas that morphs into a group of toucans. A pair of flamingos sways to the music and golden blooms sing backup, all executed by the painting hand.

Confirming north-south amity, Barroso's orchestration for "Aquarela do Brasil" contains elements of big-band style and some jazz-inflected gestures, such as the clarinet "lick" that accompanies a bumblebee's encounter with Donald Duck, who has suddenly shown up in Rio. After mistakenly swallowing the bee, Donald observes his stomach beginning to pulsate, as a rhythmic vamp leads to his encounter with Joe Carioca, whom the painting hand creates before Donald's very eyes. As the two stroll about town, Donald asks, "what's samba?"— a logical enough question given that samba was not as popular in the United States as the tango or the rhumba.

In reply, an extended percussion riff commences, with Joe using his head as a percussion instrument and introducing "Tico-Tico no fubá" by the Brazilian composer Zequinha de Abreu (1880–1935). To be sure, "Tico-Tico no fubá" (Sadlier translates the title as "Little Sparrow in the Cornmeal") is really a *choro,* an older Brazilian urban genre with prominent flute and *cavaquinho,* an instrument similar to the ukulele but with a different tuning.[66] The merry pair sits down in a café and order *cachaça,* a powerful spirit made from sugarcane that causes Donald to hiccup—in rhythm, of course—followed by a reprise of "Aquarela do Brasil." All is led by the painting hand, which dips into the liquor bottle and fashions silhouettes of other hands, also brown, and plays a variety of Brazilian percussion instruments. With kaleidoscopic abandon, the silhouettes turn to blue and then pink, and we see Donald dancing with a woman in a headdress, surely an allusion to Carmen Miranda. They are even at the Urca, the Rio de Janeiro nightclub where Miranda got her start but where she was shunned in July 1940 after making it big in the United States.[67] "Boy oh boy oh boy oh boy— samba!" Donald exclaims, as the scene reaches apotheosis.

But will Disney's "document of authenticity" conclude with all this dizzying movement? As the final cadence approaches, the image of Rio de Janeiro by night—Sugar Loaf and Guanabara Bay enhanced by brilliantly colored flowers against the black sky—begins to recede. The viewer realizes that the animation has ceased, that its ferment and fantasy are no more. Rather, our final glimpse of Latin America is static, a painting fixed to what can literally be described as a drawing board. The creative process thus reified, the camera continues to pan outward and the distance between viewer and artwork widens. The final cadence grandly resolves, affirming that, in Disney's tribute to north-south friendship, the artistic imagination—as manifested by the US self—gets the last word.

Clearly the music of *Saludos Amigos* did not entirely achieve "cinematic justice and atonement for Hollywood's insults to Latin America," even if its research was impressive for the era. The team drew on established musical tropes, which they enhanced with certain clichés, to giddy effect. The protean *Saludos* theme sustains not only the instrumentation of Hollywood but the intervallic structures, ostinato, pentatonicism, and instruments of "ancient America"; the Chilean sequence affirms European strategies whereas Argentine folklore goes hand in hand with US rustic tradition, just as the gaucho resembles the cowboy of the Wild West. In the splashy Brazilian "movement," the brown painting hand pays homage to Brazil's mixed-race heritage, even if critics overlooked it.[68] The finale prompted advertisers to extol "the torrid tempo of the Samba!" in much the same language as was used to entice viewers to Good Neighbor musicals. *Saludos Amigos* even proved that the quest for authenticity could be profitable, for the film grossed 1.3 million dollars.

When Donald Duck and Joe Carioca took their bows at the Hollywood Bowl that October night in 1943, the Los Angeles public that applauded them undoubtedly did not have the music of *Saludos Amigos* in mind. But it did care deeply about the propaganda the movie so exuberantly spread, north and south, and the new direction it promised for the war effort. The formal part of the evening concluded with the singing of "The Star-Spangled Banner," after which attendees repaired to the patio, to dance to an orchestra led by Bobby Ramos. A decade or so later, Ramos would record selections such as "Bongo bongocero" and "Noche de Amor" on the LP *The Arthur Murray Way: Exciting Latin Rhythms.* By then, Good Neighborly enthusiasm had faded, as the United States, a formidable superpower after World War II, was on to other things. In the new global (rather than hemispheric) scheme, Latin American countries were no longer equal partners with the United States in hemispheric governance. Rather, along with Asia and Africa, Latin America was relegated to the category of "underdeveloped" and thus vulnerable to Soviet influence. Worse, the United States resumed intervening in Latin American governments, toppling those seen as receptive to communism, or giving diplomatic recognition to the same. It was as if Disney's frolicsome cartoon characters and "friendship-cementing" music had never graced the screen.

NOTES

1. The organization underwent several name changes. See Gisela Cramer and Ursula Prutsch, "Nelson A. Rockefeller's Office of Inter-American Affairs (1940–1946) and Record Group 229," *Hispanic American Historical Review* 86, no. 4 (2006): 785.

2. On the MPSA, see Darlene J. Sadlier, *Americans All: Good Neighbor Cultural Diplomacy in World War II* (Austin: University of Texas Press, 2012), 40–45.

3. These were the Academy of Motion Picture Arts and Sciences, the Southern California Council of Inter-American Affairs, the Allied Nations Committee, the Nomads, Consular Corps of Los Angeles, Las Américas Unidas, Las Fiestas de las Américas, and the Pan American Club. Program booklet, *Latin America Fiesta,* October 30, 1943, n.p.

4. John Storm Roberts, *The Latin Tinge: The Impact of Latin American Music on the United States,* 2nd ed. (New York and Oxford: Oxford University Press, 1999), 85.

5. Vernon Steele, "Motion Picture Music and Musicians," *Pacific Coast Musician,* February 20, 1932, 9, courtesy Margaret Herrick clippings file (hereafter MHCF).

6. "*Salduos Amigos:* Reviews," *Variety* (MHCF); "*Saludos* (Songs)," n.d., *Variety* (from Buenos Aires) (MHCF).

7. Roscoe Williams, "*Saludos Amigos,*" *Motion Picture Daily* (MHCF), December 14, 1942; see also "Disney Picture No Sedentary Job These Days," *Herald Tribune,* February 14, 1943 (MHCF).

8. Vernon Steele, "Motion Picture Music and Musicians," 9 (MHCF); "The First of Walt Disney's Technicolor Musical Cartoon-and-Travelogue Impressions of South America: 'Saludos Amigos,'" *Film and Radio Discussion Guide* 9, no. 4 (January 1943) (MHCF).

9. On Vargas and *Saludos Amigos,* see Antonio Pedro Tota, *The Seduction of Brazil: The Americanization of Brazil During World War II,* trans. Lorena B. Ellis (Austin: University of Texas Press, 2009), 85.

10. Ariel Dorfman and Armand Mattelart, *How to Read Donald Duck: Imperialist Ideology in the Disney Comic,* trans. and intro. David Kunzle (New York: International General, 1975), 28.

11. James Agee, *Agee on Film,* vol. 1 (New York: McDowell, Obolensky, 1958), 29. See Julianne Burton-Carvajal, "'Surprise Package': Looking Southward with Disney," in *Disney Discourse: Producing the Magic Kingdom,* ed. Eric Smoodin (New York and London: Routledge, 1994), 131–47; see also her "Don (Juanito) Duck and the Imperial-Patriarchal Unconscious: Disney Studios, the Good Neighbor Policy, and the Packaging of Latin America," in *Nationalism and Sexualities,* ed. Andrew Parker, Mary Russo, Doris Sommer, and Patricia Yaeger (New York: Routledge, 1992), 21–41; Eric Smoodin, *Animating Culture: Hollywood Cartoons from the Sound Era* (New Brunswick, NJ: Rutgers University Press, 1993), 138–56; Richard Shale, *Donald Duck Joins Up: The Walt Disney Studio during World War II* (Ann Arbor: UMI Research Press, 1987), 41–49; Sadlier, *Americans All,* 45–50; Tota, *The Seduction of Brazil,* 84–87; Dale Adams, "*Saludos Amigos:* Hollywood and FDR's Good Neighbor Policy," *Quarterly Review of Film and Video* 24 (2007): 289–95.

12. See, for example, Aaron Copland, "Carlos Chávez—Mexican Composer," *New Republic* 54 (May 2, 1928): 322–23. An uncredited member of the music team was German-born Friedrich Stärk (Fred Stark), a music arranger and librarian associated with the Disney Studios since 1938.

13. Bosley Growther, "The Screen," *New York Times,* February 13, 1943, 8.

14. Daniel Goldmark, *Tunes for 'Toons: Music and the Hollywood Cartoon* (Berkeley, Los Angeles, and London: University of California Press, 2005), 4.

15. Discussed in Carol A. Hess, *Representing the Good Neighbor: Music, Difference, and the Pan-American Dream* (New York: Oxford University Press, 2013).

16. Corinne A. Pernet, "'For the Genuine Culture of the Americas,'" in *Decentering America,* ed. Jessica C.E. Gienow-Hecht (New York and Oxford: Berghahn, 2007).

17. Program booklet, *Latin American Fiesta.* Of the vast literature on Pan Americanism, see John Edwin Fagg, *Pan Americanism* (Malabar, FL: Robert E. Krieger, 1982); Ricardo D. Salvatore, *Imágenes de un imperio: Estados Unidos y las formas de representación de América Latina* (Buenos Aires: Editorial Sudamericana, 2006).

18. Quoted in Helen Delpar, *The Enormous Vogue of Things Mexican: Cultural Relations between the United States and Mexico, 1920–1935* (Tuscaloosa and London: University of Alabama Press, 1992), 136.

19. Canada rarely figured in Pan Americanist rhetoric of the period. See Clarence H. Haring, *South America Looks at the United States* (New York: Macmillan, 1928; rpt. Arno Press and the *New York Times,* 1970), 54n30.

20. Richard T. Arndt, *The First Resort of Kings: American Cultural Diplomacy in the Twentieth Century* (Washington, DC: Potomac, 2005), 24–48.

21. Harold Lavine and James Wechsler, *War Propaganda and the United States* (New Haven: Yale University Press, 1940), vii.

22. John Koegel, "Mexican Immigrant Theater in Los Angeles, circa 1910–1940," paper delivered at the Annual Meeting of the American Musicological Society, Louisville, November 14, 2015, 2. I thank Professor Koegel for sharing his work with me. On musical life in Los Angeles, see also Steve Loza, *Barrio Rhythm: Mexican American Music in Los Angeles* (Urbana-Champaign: University of Illinois Press), 1993; Anthony F. Macías, *Mexican American Mojo: Popular Music, Dance, and Urban Culture in Los Angeles,* 1935–1968 (Durham: Duke University Press, 2008).

23. Allen L. Woll, *The Latin Image in American Film,* rev. ed. (Los Angeles: UCLA Latin American Center Publications: University of California, Los Angeles, 1997); Alberto Domínguez and Nancy de los Santos, dirs., *The Bronze Screen: 100 Hundred Years of the Latino Image in Hollywood,* DVD (Chicago: Questar, 2002).

24. An account of this problem is "Report on the Teaching of Latin American History," *Bulletin of the Pan American Union* 61 (June 1927): 547–77.

25. Brian O'Neil, "The Demands of Authenticity: Addison Durland and Hollywood's Latin Images during World War II," in *Classic Hollywood, Classic Whiteness,* ed. Daniel Bernardi (Minneapolis: University of Minnesota Press, 2001), 363–64.

26. Lisa Cartwright and Brian Goldfarb, "Cultural Contagion: On Disney's Health Education Films for Latin America," in Smoodin, *Disney Discourse,* 169.

27. An infamous example is *Down Argentine Way* (1940), Carmen Miranda's first Hollywood movie. The movie contains not a single tango; further, when Don Ameche announces, "Here you have the authentic Argentina," a group of light-hearted *campesinos* dance a Mexican *zapateado.* Walter Aaron Clark, "Doing the Samba on Sunset Boulevard: Carmen Miranda and the Hollywood-ization of Latin American Music," in *From Tejano to Tango,* ed. Walter Aaron Clark (New York and London: Routledge, 2002), 267.

28. Quoted in O'Neil, "The Demands of Authenticity," 360. See also O'Neil's valuable discussion of Addison Durland, the Latin American specialist hired in 1941 by the Production Code Administration to detect script errors and correct false impressions. His impact on music was limited, however.

29. Hess, *Representing the Good Neighbor,* 26.

30. Ibid., 28–31; Leonora Saavedra, "Carlos Chávez's Polysemic Style: Constructing the National, Seeking the Cosmopolitan," *Journal of the American Musicological Society* 68, no. 1 (2015): 99–150.

31. Carol A. Hess, "Copland in Argentina: Pan Americanist Politics, Folklore, and the Crisis of Modern Music," *Journal of the American Musicological Society* 66, no. 1 (2013).

32. Carol A. Hess, "Competing Utopias? Musical Ideologies in the 1930s and Two Spanish Civil War Films," *Journal of the Society for American Music* 2, no. 3 (2008): 330–32.

33. William Berrien, "Report of the Committee of the Conference on Inter-American Relations in the Field of Music. Digest of Proceedings. Principal Addresses," cited in Pernet, "'For the Genuine Culture of the Americas,'" 145.

34. Carol A. Hess, "Anti-Fascism by Another Name: Gustavo Durán, the Good Neighbor Policy, and *franquismo* in the United States," in *Música, ideología y política en la cultura artística durante*

el franquísmo (*1938–1975*), ed. Gemma Pérez-Zalduondo (Madrid: Ministerio de España y Fundación Brepols, 2013), 367–81.

35. Regina Bendix, *In Search of Authenticity: The Formation of Folklore Studies* (Madison: University of Wisconsin Press, 1997), 17.

36. Cited in Woll, *The Latin Image in American Film,* 58. See also Hess, "Copland in Argentina," 199.

37. Yvonne Daniel, *Rumba: Dance and Social Change in Contemporary Cuba* (Bloomington and Indianapolis: Indiana University Press, 1995). The aggressive stride of the tango was often sanitized. See Susan Cook, "Passionless Dancing and Passionate Reform: Respectability, Modernism, and the Social Dancing of Irene and Vernon Castle," in *The Passion of Music and Dance: Body, Gender, and Sexuality,* ed. William Washabaught (Oxford: Berg, 1998), 133–50.

38. Gustavo Pérez Firmat, "Latunes: An Introduction," *Latin American Research Review* 43, no. 2 (2008): 180–203.

39. For example, the publisher E.B. Marks issued the celebrated song "The Peanut Vendor" ("El Manicero") in a "simplified version in 4/4 time." As John Storm Roberts points out, virtually all Cuban popular music is in 4/4 time. Storm Roberts, *The Latin Tinge,* 77.

40. Tota, *The Seduction of Brazil,* xv.

41. Manuel Ponce, "S.M. [Su Majestad] el Fox," *México Moderno* 1, no. 9 (April 1921): 180–81.

42. See Rosalie Schwartz, *Flying down to Rio: Hollywood, Tourists, and Yankee Clippers* (College Station: Texas A & M University Press, 2004); Todd Decker, *Music Makes Me: Fred Astaire and Jazz* (Berkeley, Los Angeles, and London: University of California Press, 2011), 171–77.

43. Letter, Vincent G. Hart, to Sidney Kramer (RKO Distributing Corporation), July 19, 1935, Margaret Herrick, Special Collections Correspondence File.

44. Quoted in O'Neil, "The Demands of Authenticity," 369–70.

45. Shale, *Donald Duck Joins Up,* 44.

46. Robert Spencer Carr, "Ideas for More Walt Disney Films for South American Release," document cited in Burton-Carvajal, "'Surprise Package': Looking Southward with Disney," 133.

47. Theodore Strauss, "Donald Duck's Disney," *New York Times,* February 7, 1943, X3.

48. "The First of Walt Disney's Technicolor Musical."

49. "Saludos Amigos," *Variety,* December 15, 1942 (MHCF).

50. "Disney's Charm in 'Amigos': Mono. 'Rhythm' Girly Flash," *Hollywood Reporter,* December 15, 1942 (MHCF). See also Sadlier, *Americans All,* 48–49.

51. "Reviews: 'Saludos Amigos,'" *Variety* (MHCF).

52. "Saludos (Songs)," *Variety* n.d. (MHCF).

53. "Reviews" (MHCF); "Saludos (Songs)" (MHCF).

54. A classic source is Claudia Gorbman, *Unheard Melodies: Narrative Film Music* (Bloomington and Indianapolis: Indiana University Press, 1987).

55. Quoted in Alex Ross, "The Sound of Hate: When Does Music Become Torture?," *New Yorker,* July 4, 2016, 66.

56. As Sadlier notes, the animated maps so integral to *Salduos Amigos* are a nod to contemporaneous cinematic technique: Nazi films showed troop movement and indicated conquered

territories with moving arrows on maps, a strategy Hollywood promptly imitated in films such as *Casablanca*. Sadlier, *Americans All,* 46–48.

57. Steele, "Motion Picture Music and Musicians" (MHCF).

58. The one postcard in Pedro's mailbag reads (in Spanish), "Having a wonderful time, wish you were here," and is addressed to Jorge Délano Coke of *Topaze,* a Chilean magazine, who hosted Disney and his team in Santiago: http://disneyenchile.blogspot.com.ar/2007/03/parte-8-pelicula-saludos-Amigos.html.

59. Although not shown on screen, the team promptly set up a makeshift studio in the roof garden of the Alvear Palace Hotel and got to work. See www.elliberal.com.ar/noticia/234810/dia-walt-disney-conocio-folclore-mano-don-andres-chazarreta.

60. Richard Slatta, *Gauchos and the Vanishing Frontier* (Lincoln: University of Nebraska Press, 1992).

61. The song "Jumpin' Jive," recorded in 1939 by Cab Calloway, was popularized by the African American dance duo the Nicholas Brothers. The Bunny Hug, an earlier dance genre, is associated with ragtime. Shields also refers to the minuet, a comparison that will likely remain a mystery.

62. Shale, *Donald Duck Joins Up,* 46.

63. Sadlier, *Americans All,* 48.

64. Quoted in Clark, "Doing the Samba on Sunset Boulevard," 265. See also Lisa Shaw, *The Social History of Brazilian Samba* (Aldershot, UK: Ashgate, 1999), 7–14.

65. Daryle Williams, *Culture Wars in Brazil: The First Vargas Regime, 1930–1945* (Durham and London: Duke University Press, 2001).

66. Sadlier, *Americans All,* 49; Tamara Elena Livingston-Isenhour and Thomas George Caracas García, *Choro: A Social History of a Brazilian Popular Music* (Bloomington: Indiana University Press, 2005), 52.

67. Tota, *The Seduction of Brazil,* 5.

68. The music team also omitted those lyrics of "Aquarela do Brasil" that hinted explicitly at this heritage, retaining the first line, "Brasil, meu mulato inzoneiro" (Brazil, my sly mulatto), but not the references to a (black) "wet-nurse from the fields," the "Congo king," or the "headstrong mulatto girl with the indiscreet look." Translation in Shaw, *The Social History of the Brazilian Samba,* 169–71.

5

A CENTURY OF LATIN MUSIC AT THE HOLLYWOOD BOWL

MOST MAJOR CULTURAL INSTITUTIONS in Los Angeles took time to warm to the idea of diversity. Until the 1950s, when whites still made up almost 90 percent of the county's population and minorities were still geographically segregated in inner-city neighborhoods, the city's arts establishment was content to cater to that seemingly homogeneous majority culture. It would take the social upheavals of the 1960s for society at large to accept the multicultural concept that multiple cultures can be appreciated on an equal par.

The Hollywood Bowl, however, stands out among these institutions as a pioneer in cultural diversity before that term even entered the popular lexicon. Since its very inception, the lineup of artists featured on the stage of the fabled outdoor amphitheater has included artists from Mexico, Latin America, and Spain. The Bowl didn't need political pressure, a cultural revolution, or a population explosion to voluntarily open its doors to Latino performers. On the contrary, multiculturalism seems to have been an artistic cornerstone of the venue almost since it was carved into the hillsides of Bolton Canyon.

Nowadays, however, Latinos and other ethnic groups have become the majority in Los Angeles and diversity as a policy has become commonplace. Perhaps because memories are short, the Hollywood Bowl, summer home of the Los Angeles Philharmonic, doesn't always get full credit for its long-running practice of sharing its prestigious stage with Latino artists working in a wide variety of musical genres, from classical to mariachi, romantic boleros to hard-driving salsa and Latin jazz. In 2009, there was much ado, and rightfully so, about the arrival of Gustavo Dudamel as the Philharmonic's latest musical director. The appointment of the charismatic young Venezuelan was hailed by some as the ultimate fulfillment of the progressive vision of the Hollywood Bowl's founders: the notion that the elite world of classical music was indeed accessible to all, regardless of race, social status, or national origin.

Many of those cheering the move as a breakthrough, however, may not have been aware that more than half a century earlier, two Mexican classical composers and conductors— Eduardo Vigil and Carlos Chávez—had taken up the baton as guests of the Philharmonic, performing on separate occasions at the Hollywood Bowl during its first two decades.

Latin music programming at the Bowl was inconsistent and uneven, with ups and downs throughout its history. But considering the state of race relations in Los Angeles during the Bowl's first, formative decades, what's remarkable is that it featured any Latin programs at all in the early years. In the seven decades before the Bowl was founded—from the time of the US victory in the war with Mexico and the resulting white expansion westward—the Latino population in Los Angeles had been falling steadily and precipitously. By 1920, the year the first outdoor show was held on the current Bowl site, Mexican Americans had gone from being a majority in the city to being a small minority.

For at least the next three decades, powerful forces in Los Angeles aggressively attempted to suppress multicultural mixing. Racist real estate practices, legally written into deeds, worked to contain minorities to their ghettoes and barrios. Meanwhile, during the swing era, police crackdowns violently suppressed the street exuberance of Chicano zoot suiters while municipal policies worked quietly to discourage young whites from "slumming" in South LA at the hopping jazz clubs along Central Avenue.

The Bowl was born and raised, so to speak, in that segregated environment. And though it was no interracial utopia, its founders shared the era's progressive faith that music, when democratically shared, could bring people together. Thus in 1924, during only its third official season, the nascent venue offered its very first "Spanish Program," featuring Vigil, the bearded and bespectacled Mexican opera conductor, and the soprano Alma Real, also from Mexico City, who sang folk songs in costume. Remember, this was a time when Mexican American children still attended segregated public schools and Mexican men were still being publicly lynched in California. Despite the overt racism and the dwindling demographics, the Bowl quickly established itself as a safe harbor welcoming Mexican artists.

Over the years, the Bowl managed to keep its pulse on cultural trends in Latino arts, and even occasionally featured the avant-garde in some fields. The appearance in 1937 by

Chávez, perhaps the most renowned of Mexican classical composers, was a case in point. That year, the Bowl's sixteenth season, Chávez led the Los Angeles Philharmonic (without a baton, as was his preference) in an eclectic program that included Rossini's "William Tell" overture and Tchaikovsky's "Pathétique." The composer's own *Sinfonía India,* written the year before, captured the spirit of the explosive nationalist movement in Mexican arts that celebrated the country's normally disdained indigenous cultures. As Chávez once explained, he sought to project "what is deepest in the Mexican soul." That same ethos fired the imagination of Mexico's great muralists, such as David Alfaro Siqueiros, who had earlier shocked LA's arts establishment with his controversial anti-imperialist mural *América Tropical,* painted at Olvera Street in 1932.

But while the city's scandalized cultural elite immediately ordered the Mexican mural whitewashed, along with its central figure of a crucified Indian, the Hollywood Bowl would continue to feature concerts with Chávez as guest conductor, right through the 1960s. By then, concerts featuring Latin music of all kinds, both classical and popular, had become a regular part of the Bowl's annual programs.

THE BOWL CELEBRATES A GOLDEN ERA IN LATIN POP MUSIC

During the 1940s and 1950s, the Bowl's Latin programming became safe and predictable, often reflecting the mambo dance craze that swept America with watered-down versions of Afro-Cuban music. In 1943, the bandleader Xavier Cugat starred in a program titled "Latin American Fiesta," emceed by Desi Arnaz, the young Cuban who would become a trailblazer of television sitcoms with his wife Lucille Ball, his conga strapped over his shoulder, his shock of hair dancing on his forehead, and his screams of "Babalu!." The Bowl show also exuded Hollywood influence with the onstage appearance of Donald Duck and Joe Carioca, characters from Walt Disney's animated feature film *Saludos Amigos* who also appeared on the program cover along with a third stereotypical figure, a gun-toting Mexican rooster in a big sombrero. Pure Americana!

Sixteen years later, the Bowl would once again turn south of the border, but this time for genuine Latin music, unprocessed through a Hollywood filter. In 1959, the venue featured a show starring two superstar vocalists, Mexico's Lola Beltrán and Chile's Lucho Gatica. Though generically (and strangely) titled "Pops," the concert faithfully embodied the best of Latin music from the postwar decade, specifically the *boleros* and *rancheras* that were so popular throughout Latin America at the time.

The songs performed that night represented perhaps the last truly great era in Latin pop music, before rock 'n roll had a chance to invade and overpower global pop culture. It was a repertoire composed of such beloved standards that a reprise of the very same concert might be a draw today. The dignified Beltrán offered classics—"Paloma Negra," "Cucurrucucú Paloma," "Qué Bonito Amor"—that helped define the golden age of mariachi music, which dominated pop culture in Mexico for three decades, from the 1940s through the 1960s. For his part, Gatica reached for the same gold standard in his set of boleros—"El

Reloj," "La Barca," "Total," "Nunca"—reflecting the genre's international origins in Spain, Cuba, Mexico, and elsewhere.

As if to underscore the authentic quality of the evening, the emcee, Ricardo Montalbán, addressed the Bowl audience in Spanish, with apologies to non-Latinos in the crowd. But in keeping with the Bowl's cross-cultural spirit, the show was cohosted by the American crooner Nat "King" Cole, who had ingratiated himself to Latinos the year before with his phonetically learned interpretation of Latin standards on his hit album *Cole Español*. The suave Mexican actor Montalbán introduced the orchestra under the direction of his compatriot, the composer, pianist, and arranger Chucho Zarzosa. Anybody even casually familiar with Mexican pop music at the time would have recognized the name of the bandleader, who worked with the biggest pop stars of his day—Pedro Vargas, Agustín Lara, Toña La Negra—and whose credits are listed on scores of popular Mexican recordings.

That show sent a signal that Latin pop music was to be appreciated for its own intrinsic value and on its own terms. The following decade, the Bowl built on that premise with big shows featuring artists from across the Latin music spectrum. In 1966, for example, one such concert, under the music direction of the local Latin jazz luminary René Touzet, featured the mariachi singing stars Miguel Aceves Mejía, Tito Guízar, and Lucha Villa, as well as the Afro-Cuban stalwarts Xavier Cugat and Miguelito Valdés. LA's own Nati Cano, head of Mariachi Los Camperos, served as the evening's "director of Mexican folklore."

Though classier than the typical vaudeville-style revue, the show resembled in its size and variety the large Latin tours called *caravanas,* or "caravans," that typically toured the Southwest in the 1960s, playing popular Mexican venues like downtown's Million Dollar Theatre. For its show, the Bowl picked a title that was a historic misnomer—"The Bowl Goes Latin," as if this were a first. To set the record straight, the program carried a clarifying headline: "The Bowl goes Latin *all the way.*"

BEATLEMANIA AT THE BOWL, CHICANO-STYLE

The Bowl's showcasing of international Latin stars didn't always satisfy local audiences. While big on mambo, flamenco, samba, and mariachi, the venue was late to embrace the talented Mexican American musicians making exciting pop music in its own backyard.

In Southern California, Chicano rock traces its roots to such Top 40 hits from the 1950s as Ritchie Valens's "La Bamba" and The Champs's "Tequila." But it really flourished during the 1960s in East LA where a dynamic garage band scene fused Latin stylings with doo-wop and R&B to create the fabled Eastside Sound, bringing national attention to a handful of top exponents such as Thee Midniters. In the barrio, the movement was such a powerful cultural force that the musicians were seen as "symbolic shamans who led their audiences in their inborn passion for musical expression and life," writes the UCLA musicologist Steven Loza in his comprehensive study, *Barrio Rhythms*.[1]

Clearly, it would be important for Mexican American fans to see one of their bands take the stage at a hallowed cross-town venue like the Hollywood Bowl. Some observers suggest this happened for the first time when Thee Midniters, fronted by the singer Little Willie G., performed at the Bowl as part of the 1967 edition of "The Bowl Goes Latin." However, that milestone actually came two years earlier when another pioneering Chicano rock band, Cannibal and the Headhunters, opened for the Beatles at the Bowl on two consecutive nights in late August 1965.

The vocal quartet had been founded barely the year before and was composed of four young friends from Eastside housing projects, Richard ("Scar") Lopez, Frankie ("Cannibal") Garcia, and the Jaramillo brothers, Robert ("Rabbit") and Joe ("Yo Yo"). They quickly scored their one and only Top 40 hit with "Land of a Thousand Dances," featuring Cannibal's famous novelty hook ("na-na-na-na-na"), created by chance one night when he forgot the lyrics during a live performance at an Orange County club.

At the urging of Paul McCartney, the Beatles had invited the East LA lads to join them on their tour in 1965, the year before Chicano guitarist Carlos Santana formed his own band, which would come to define Latin rock. As the story goes, the charismatic Cannibal and his Headhunters played up such a storm that they were asked to tone it down, so as not to upstage the more sedate Fab Four from Liverpool. For those now legendary Bowl shows, East LA fans came out in force to give their hometown boys a welcome that rivaled Beatlemania.

"They rocked the house that night!" said the UC Riverside Ethnic Studies associate professor Anthony Macías.[2] "Mexican Americans still remember that performance because it showed how we can break through to the mainstream culture on our own terms, without going Hollywood, without being too schmaltzy. It proved that pop culture is important, even if it's not political. Black and brown representation in such a venerated highbrow venue sends a powerful social message. Here are these kids from East LA singing soul music on that famous bandstand, under that shell, opening for the Beatles. Back then it proved we could make it in a white man's world."

RETRENCHMENT AND RECOMMITMENT

The Hollywood Bowl hit a lull during the 1970s and 1980s, a period that paradoxically saw the start of a massive explosion in the Latino population, which spread throughout Southern California. Simultaneously, Latino pop stars like Julio Iglesias started breaking down the entertainment boundaries that formerly had restricted them to certain favored venues, such as downtown's Shrine Auditorium. In 1984, for example, Iglesias did a record-breaking stand of ten nights at the Universal Amphitheatre (now the Gibson) before a newly found crossover audience of adoring Anglos. No neighborhood and no concert hall seemed off-limits to Latino artists any longer.

Meanwhile, the Bowl retreated from its Latin pop experiments, falling back on more conservative, classical programming that was respectable but not daring. The venue seemed to be taken over by Spaniards—José Carreras, Plácido Domingo, Paco de Lucía, and The Romeros. Or by Brazilians—Sérgio Mendes, Flora Purim, Eliane Elias. As far as the music of Mexico and the rest of Latin America was concerned, the middle-aged Hollywood Bowl seemed to be telling its new competitors: Been there. Done that.

Toward the end of the 1980s, there were signs that augured a new direction. In 1987 and again 1989, the Playboy Jazz Festival featured one of the most provocative and ground-breaking artists in all of Latin pop music, the Panamanian singer/songwriter Rubén Blades, who had launched a brilliant solo career on Elektra Records in 1984. Blades would return repeatedly during the next decade, including once in 1997 for a thrilling reunion concert with the Puerto Rican bandleader Willie Colón.

Once again, the Bowl stage resonated with the most powerful expressions of Latin pop music. The venue came roaring back in the 1990s with a series of shows that spotlighted two enduring strains of popular music: the Mariachi USA Festival, now in its twenty-eighth year, and the Hollywood Salsa and Latin Jazz Festival, which ran for seven consecutive years during the salsa revival sparked by the rise of the young Nuyorican singers Marc Anthony and La India. At the same time, the Playboy Jazz Festival, which had featured West Coast Latin jazz greats like Willie Bobo and Mongo Santamaría since its very first year at the Bowl (1979), intensified its programming with a roster that reads like a who's who of the genre—Tito Puente, Poncho Sanchez, Arturo Sandoval, and Chucho Valdés. In 1997, the festival featured Los Van Van, the cutting-edge Havana dance band that overcame the US embargo to launch its very first US tour.

That show put the Bowl at the center of an exciting and historical cultural opening between Cuba and the United States. The subsequent Bowl appearances by members of the more traditional Buena Vista Social Club seemed anticlimactic to Cubanophiles.

MORE TO COME

The most recent decade has been the biggest for the Bowl, in terms of the number and variety of Latin artists who performed there, including for the first time some big names in Latin alternative music, such as Café Tacvba and Aterciopelados. But oddly enough, not all the barriers have been overcome. Now, they're internal. Some big Latin pop stars still don't recognize the importance of playing the venerable venue, says the concert promoter Martin Fleischmann, who coproduced the Bowl's salsa festivals and many other Latin music shows at other locations.

"Once you get to the level of being able to sell 10, 12 thousand tickets or more, it's the only place to play," says Fleischmann, son of the late Ernest Fleischmann, the music impresario and veteran LA Phil executive. "For Latin artists of any stature, it should be a goal to play there. If they haven't already figured it out, when they get there they do figure it out.

"The Bowl is a pinnacle."

NOTES

1. Steven Loza, *Barrio Rhythms: Mexican-American Music in Los Angeles* (Champaign-Urbana: University of Illinois Press, 1993).

2. Anthony Macías, *Mexican American Mojo: Popular Music, Dance, and Urban Culture in Los Angeles, 1935–1968* (Durham: Duke University Press, 2008).

6

VOICE OF THE XTABAY AND BULLOCKS WILSHIRE

Hearing Yma Sumac from Southern California

A S A KID, I REMEMBER picking through my Peruvian father's record collection, between the LPs of Peruvian creole waltzes and Mexican ballads, to regularly admire a strange album that featured an alluring woman dripping in jewelry, posing ceremoniously before an erupting volcano, crimson lipstick applied to perfection.

The album was *Voice of the Xtabay* and the woman was Yma Sumac. Sumac was the Peruvian songstress known for her four-octave voice and for pretty much launching the musical category known as exotica, a cinematic fusion of international styles that allowed mid-twentieth-century American audiences a taste of the mysterious and the remote. (The South Pacific, Africa, and the Amazon were favorite themes.)

To me, a Peruvian kid who grew up in Southern California, Sumac was infinitely more than that: a rare representation of the Andean in US popular culture (albeit one distorted by the funhouse mirror that is the entertainment industry). And it was a representation soaked in glamor. Sumac was the imperious, raven-haired Inca princess (at least

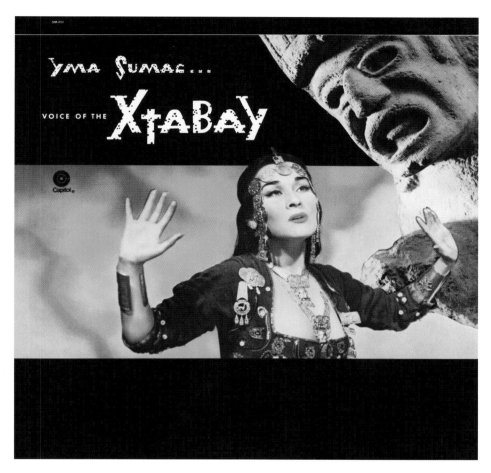

Yma Sumac, *Voice of the Xtabay,* Capitol Records, 1950 (original release), Idelsohn Society for Musical Preservation Archive.

according to the lore) who maintained an extensive wardrobe stocked with sumptuous gowns. It was a Peruvian girl's ultimate fantasy.

Xtabay, the hit album from 1950 that introduced her to international audiences, seemed like otherworldly evidence of her power.

It opens with the smash of a gong with "Taita Inty," a song described as a "traditional Incan hymn that dates back to 1000 B.C." (Never mind that the Inca civilization didn't get rolling until more than two thousand years later.) And from there it segues to tunes like "Tumpa," full of guttural scatting that evokes the sound of a wah-wah trumpet. All of it is held together by Sumac's operatic trills, which could leap from low growls to high-C color-atura that sounded as if it could shatter glass.

"She took Peruvian traditional music, set it in the popular music vein and sang it with the voice of a coloratura soprano, but infused it with jazz and blues," says her biographer, Nicholas E. Limansky, author of *Yma Sumac: The Art Behind the Legend.* "It's a fascinating concoction."

Xtabay bore no resemblance to any Peruvian music I grew up with or have heard on any trip to Peru. (Gongs, for one, are from Asia, not the Andes.) With its symphonic interludes, the album sounds more like a soundtrack for a 1950s-era jungle epic, featuring the sorts of melodies that beg for a rum drink in a ceramic Polynesian tumbler.

It was irresistible. It was also a piece of fiction. Yma Sumac may have been from Peru. But her exotic Peruvian persona was invented in Los Angeles.

Xtabay was successful for myriad reasons. First, there were the contributions of composer Les Baxter, who set Sumac's Andean stylings against groovy beats. And, perhaps more significantly, there were the machinations of the overheated publicity department at Capitol Records in Hollywood, which fabricated all manner of legends about Sumac as a way of drawing the public's attention.

Among them: That the singer was a "descendant of the last of the Incan kings" and that the title song, "Xtabay," was about the legend of a "young Incan virgin" who had a "forbidden love" with a "high prince of an Aztec kingdom." (No such legend exists.)

"Hollywood took this nice girl who wanted to be a folk singer and dressed her up and said she was a princess," says Limanksy. "And she acted like it."

And audiences ate it up. In fact, that epic piece of myth-making—of Sumac, the Inca blue-blood, singing her "mysterious" Andean hymns—helped feed a surprisingly long-running career.

Sumac's boom years were in the 1950s and 1960s, but she performed all the way into the 1990s, when she was well into her seventies.

Her first significant appearance was a show at the Hollywood Bowl in August 1950, which was received with astonishment followed by rapturous applause. From there flowed numerous albums—including my favorite, the relentlessly fabulous *Mambo!* from 1954—as well as performances all over the United States and Europe. In 1960, she undertook a historic forty-city tour of what was then the Soviet Union, which lasted for months.

Over the course of her life, Sumac appeared on television talk shows from Steve Allen to David Letterman. Her music has appeared in commercials and on numerous Hollywood soundtracks, including that of *The Big Lebowski* and of *Mad Men*. It has even been sampled by hip-hop musicians—such as the Black Eyed Peas, who employed the groovy opening from "Bo Mambo" in their single "Hands Up" from 2003.

In 2017, eight years after her death at the age of eighty-six, Sumac remains the subject of fan sites, Pinterest pages, and Facebook groups, and she has inspired a veritable rabbit hole of lip sync videos on YouTube. (One by the Argentine actor Luciano Rosso, looking piratical, is particularly delirious.) In the fall of 2016, she received the ultimate digital nod when she was featured as the Google Doodle on the ninety-fourth anniversary of her birth.

Sumac could have easily gone down in the history books as a musical footnote. And certainly, if she had remained a run-of-the-mill folk singer, she probably would have. But the combination of her beauty, her unusual music, and the colorful stories that surrounded her transformed her into a legend—attracting a devoted cult following in the process. (I was once chastised on social media by a fan for not being sufficiently reverent.)

The high camp didn't hurt either: the feathered headdresses and eyeliner on fleek—not to mention her stage design, which often featured Styrofoam volcanoes and totems. A *Los Angeles Times* review of a Sumac concert at the Shrine Auditorium in 1955 makes note of the singer's "phenomenal voice," as well as the fact that the whole display featured "a touch of the ridiculous"—namely, a stage studded with "pillars of fire."

"She was unique in the combination of things that she embodied," says Peruvian anthropologist Zoila Mendoza, chair of the Native American studies department at UC Davis—whose mother was close friends with Sumac as a teen. "It was a whole fantasy."

That fantasy emerged out of a confluence of social factors in both Peru and the United States.

Yma Sumac was born Zoila Augusta Emperatriz Chavarri del Castillo in the region of Cajamarca in the northern Peruvian Andes on September 13, 1922. (She later took on the name Imma Summack, her mother's name, as her stage name—which morphed into Yma Sumac after she moved to the United States.)

She was not, as one Parisian publication once wrote, raised in a "miserable hut of dried earth." In fact, Sumac was raised in a well-to-do family whose ranks included a physician and a judge. Her father was involved in local civic affairs; her mother was a schoolteacher.

"Definitely she was elite in the area," says Mendoza, who has studied indigenous performance in the Andes and written on the subject of Sumac in the past. "They did have economic resources."

As a teen, Sumac relocated to the capital city of Lima to go to school, and it was there that she met Moisés Vivanco, a noted folk musician who would shape her early career—and whom she would ultimately marry and divorce (twice). One popular Sumac legend, crafted by the fabulists at Capitol Records, has Vivanco traveling for days to a "remote mountain region" to seek out the singer known for "talking" with the "birds, the beasts, the winds."

Not quite. Vivanco met Sumac at a rehearsal in Lima, where, after hearing her sing, he invited her to participate in a folkloric event.

Naturally, all of this raises the issue of Sumac's supposed Inca lineage. Her mother carried the surname Atahualpa, that of the last Inca emperor. But whether that made Sumac a real-deal royal (or someone who could even reasonably claim indigenous identity) can't be determined.

She likely spoke some Quechua, one of the principal indigenous languages of the Andes, as did most people who lived in the highlands at the time. But, physically, she was a fair-skinned mestiza, a mix of Spanish and Indian. "She was white compared to most Andean people," notes Mendoza. "She had green eyes. She and my mother were very close friends. My mom also has green eyes. So they were these two pretty Andean women with green eyes."

But Sumac emerged at a time when Peru was beginning to pay more attention to its indigenous roots. Indigenist movements across the continent were bringing attention to native culture and history. The wide dissemination of the archeological wonders at Machu Picchu after 1911 brought attention to the country's resplendent Inca past.

"In that context, the whole institution of folklore emerged," says Mendoza, referring to the burgeoning musical industry built around Andean indigenous music. Recordings were made, radio programs were launched, and contests and festivals were held.

Sumac's early repertoire reflected this musical current, including, for example, traditional Andean *huaynos,* brisk highland ballads featuring strings and flute. (Some of these have been collected in the compilation album by Blue Orchid Records *Early Yma Sumac: The Imma Summack Sessions,* released in 2003.)

"By the time Yma Sumac came about, there was a whole infrastructure that allowed her to become a national figure," Mendoza explains. "Before that, it wouldn't have happened. The infrastructure didn't exist."

As a result, Sumac and Vivanco became quite well known in Peru and had successful engagements in the important Latin American media centers of Argentina and Mexico, including a successful recital at the prestigious Palacio de Bellas Artes in Mexico City—at the invitation of the Mexican president. In 1946, the pair moved to New York City, figuring that their success in Latin America boded well for the US market.

But American audiences weren't exactly rushing out to see Andean folk music—and Sumac's early years in New York, as part of a group called the Inca Taqui Trio, were Spartan. They played supper clubs, Borscht Belt resorts, business conventions, and, for a time, a delicatessen in New York's Greenwich Village, where a magazine writer for *Collier's* would later write that Sumac could be found performing "in a back room richly blanketed with the aroma of pickled herring, salami and liverwurst."

The trio nonetheless developed a following, which resulted in some local television appearances—one of which sparked the interest of a talent agent, who helped Sumac land a deal at Capitol. The Inca Taqui Trio was too folkloric for the label, so they settled, instead, on building an album around Sumac's voice.

Enter the exotica master Baxter, and a post–World War II US public that was ready to be seduced by fantasy.

Also, enter Los Angeles.

The deal with Capitol necessitated a move to Southern California, and by the late 1940s the couple was comfortably ensconced in tony Cheviot Hills, on the city's Westside. (One can only imagine what Sumac's Cheviot Hills neighbors thought of the pack of Peruvians practicing their drumming in the garage.)

The move would be a key factor in Sumac's metamorphosis from talented Peruvian folk singer to Inca exotica pioneer.

"I don't know if this could have happened in another city," says Limanksy. "New York has Carnegie Hall and the Metropolitan Opera, these famous classical institutions, and things were geared around that. But in Los Angeles, you had the film industry and everything that entailed. Her whole transformation, it does smack of Hollywood . . . It was very cinematic."

But the tarted-up Inca princess identity was not something that Sumac was initially wild about. "She wanted to be a folk performer," says Limansky. "She really didn't like it at all."

But like many performers forced to embrace a new sound in the name of success, Sumac reinvented herself. And she did it with haughty grandeur. The singer was known for striding on stage as if she had arrived to reclaim her empire, demanding the undivided attention of her public—to the point that, in later years, she became known for storming off if spectators so much as opened their mouths.

"She looked like a princess and she acted like one," says Limansky, who attended some of her shows in New York in the 1980s. "She was entertaining, but not in a 'let me get in your face and laugh with you' kind of way . . . She was very formal with the audience."

This regal quality translated to her roles in Hollywood films. In 1954, she appeared in the Charlton Heston adventure flick *Secret of the Incas* as the Quechua maiden Kori-Tika. In it, Sumac gives a pair of surreal mountaintop performances at Machu Picchu. She also throws serious side eye at Heston's European love interest, played by Nicole Maurey. When Maurey tells her, "You speak English very well." Kori-Tika replies cattily: "So do you."

It's a very different depiction from that other mid-century South American icon: the Brazilian Bombshell Carmen Miranda, who was often shown as the flirty Latin party girl in the towering fruit hat. Sumac was way too royal for that.

On another level, Sumac's embrace of the role of Inca noble (a role some say she came to believe) was various levels of meta.

Her whole notion of Inca identity was built around ideas of Inca culture that had blossomed during Peru's indigenist period—ideas that weren't always rooted in historical fact.

"When she became a folkloric artist in the 1930s, there had been a couple of decades in Peru of composers and musicians who had been creating symphonies and these really sophisticated pieces of music based on an invented idea of what the Inca sound was like," says Mendoza. "It had very little to do with what contemporary indigenous people were actually playing."

Sumac, therefore, was channeling a concocted notion of Inca identity as an invented Inca princess. A fiction born in Peru adds another layer of fiction once it lands in Hollywood, and from that fiction rises Yma Sumac. What could be more Los Angeles?

Which brings me to an aspect of the singer's life that intrigues me the most: Sumac's profound connection to LA, where she lived longer than she ever did in Peru. (After landing in the late 1940s, she never left—and, in the process, became a US citizen.)

In my work as a culture reporter, I feel as if I continually find residue of her presence.

There is her star on the Hollywood Walk of Fame—the only Peruvian with that honor—which I frequently pass on my way to shows at Los Angeles Contemporary Exhibitions (LACE) across the street. Last year, in an improbable coincidence, I discovered that Sumac had once performed at a fundraiser for LACE in the late 1980s.

"She was exactly what you would imagine," says Joy Silverman, who oversaw the organization at that time. "You were in the presence of this dramatic Peruvian songbird. She was never out of character."

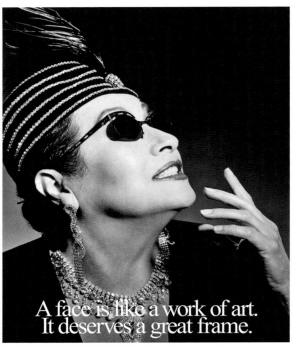

A face is like a work of art.
It deserves a great frame.

Designers of limited edition frames for sunglasses and prescription eyewear

l.a.Eyeworks

Face: Yma Sumac. Frame: Carmen. Hair & Make-Up: Eric Barnard for Cloutier, LA.
Photographer: Greg Gorman. ©1989, l.a.Eyeworks. www.laeyeworks.com

Courtesy l.a.Eyeworks
(photo: Greg Gorman).

At around the same time, Sumac also appeared—in sleek shades and plumed hat—in one of the iconic magazine ads for l.a.Eyeworks, part of a campaign that featured entertainers such as Grace Jones and Iggy Pop.

"It was Yma Sumac—we *had* to do it!" says l.a.Eyeworks cofounder Gai Gherardi, who recalls a petite woman of monarchical bearing with a taste for bananas. "Her image, she knew what it looked like, and she lived up to it."

In her late years, Sumac played regular cabaret engagements at the now-defunct Cinegrill and the Vine St. Bar & Grill jazz club in Hollywood—events that brought out a crowd that was only in LA.

Author Tom Lang, who worked at Vine St. in the 1980s and is now based in Bali, described a scene that was "Sunset Boulevard on ayahuasca."

"The pre-show atmosphere was anticipatory, a legend returns," he stated via e-mail. "Opening night, sold out. A group of tiny Peruvians, impeccably dressed, at one table. [Pianist and author] Leonard Feather in his regular booth (throne). Bill Murray and his entourage, up front."

Late in life, Sumac was an uneven performer—with good nights, as well as terrible ones, her voice cracking, her temper foul. The show at Vine St. was one of the latter. "I wanted to take her off the stage and hug her and tell everyone else to leave her alone," recalls Lang.

There are other LA stories, too. About her taste for El Pollo Loco and her shopping trips to Bullocks Wilshire. "She must have had 300 pairs of vintage shoes from throughout the '50s," recalls her friend and former assistant Damon Devine, who runs the tribute website yma-sumac.com.

The singer, who was sold to American audiences as a wonder from a strange land, was, in the end, just another grand dame living on the Westside (she later moved to West Hollywood) who might enjoy an afternoon of listening to Eurodance with her assistant.

"L.A. is full of people like her," says Silverman. "People like Angelyne—these self-invented people."

And it was in LA, the city that made her who she was, that she would ultimately come to rest.

On a warm afternoon in early January, I paid a visit to Sumac's grave at Hollywood Forever Cemetery. It's in the same mausoleum building as Iron Eyes Cody, a performer who was also known for a manufactured indigenous identity. (A second-generation Italian American, he frequently played a Native American in the movies, and told the press he was Cree and Cherokee.) In another part of the building lies Constance Talmadge, the renowned silent screen star.

In the photo displayed on her tomb, Sumac is perfectly made up, wearing an indigenous textile and earrings as big as chandeliers. My father used to roll his eyes at Sumac's claims of Inca nobility. But Los Angeles, a mestizo city and land of the faux historic, requires a ruler. All hail the queen.

7

MUSICAL ANTHROPOLOGY

A Conversation with Elisabeth Waldo

WHEN I THINK OF THE history of Latin American music in Los Angeles, one of the first musical figures who come to mind is the great composer, violinist, and musical anthropologist Elisabeth Waldo.

My first encounter with the music of Ms. Waldo was upon finding her *Rites of the Pagan* LP from 1960 at a thrift store during my high school years. The cover art popped out at me and immediately grabbed my attention. I knew I had to investigate. It was clear to me that this record encompassed a touch of exotica as well as a reverence and respect for the Aztec musical traditions from which the theme and song titles were derived. Upon listening to the record, my expectations were greatly surpassed. This music not only offered an authentic glimpse of ancient Mexican tradition but also incorporated a tasteful and sophisticated sense of orchestration.

Ms. Waldo's work, in my opinion, differed from other works that were classified under the label "exotica" in that she went deeper into the archaeological and anthropological aspects of the music rather than simply making the music sound exotic in a general

ELISABETH WALDO and her concert orchestra

STEREO

RITES
OF THE
PAGAN

MYSTIC REALM OF THE
ANCIENT AMERICAS

WITH AUTHENTIC
PRE-COLUMBIAN
MUSICAL INSTRUMENTS

Elisabeth Waldo and Her Concert Orchestra, *Rites of the Pagan,* GNP, 1960, Idelsohn Society for Musical Preservation Archive.

sense. As I investigated her music further, albums like *Maracatu* from 1959 and *Realm of the Incas* from 1961, I found that she took this approach on many of her other records as well, all while showing off her symphonic abilities as well as her skills on the violin (she was both first violin for the Los Angeles Philharmonic and a member of Yma Sumac's band).

One of my favorite records of hers is the *Viva California* LP from 1969, which takes a look at the musical history of California and how it bridged the Mexican and Native American traditions in a unique and far-reaching manner. I feel that her work in this area is of great historical import when looking at Latin American music as a whole and specifically that of Los Angeles. As far as I know, she was one of the first musicians in LA to explore the musical history of the city and bring it to the public at a time when there were hardly any resources available on the subject at all.

Elisabeth Waldo, *Realm of the Incas,* GNP, 1962, Idelsohn Society for Musical Preservation Archive.

Her works have inspired many of mine, which also draw from Native American and Latin American traditions. In my opinion, Ms. Waldo is a living legend and an unsung hero who has quietly yet significantly influenced much of how Latin American music as a whole is both explored and received in Los Angeles and beyond today.

This conversation for the online radio station Dublab took place October 17, 2015, at her home, the Rancho Cordillera del Norte, in Northridge.

———

GR-W: Thank you for agreeing to this conversation Ms. Waldo

EW: Thank you for being here. I'm so pleased to share my various approaches to classic ethnic music, if you can describe it that way.

GR-W: I think for the majority of our listeners who might be familiar with your music it is probably in the context of some of the records you put out many years ago. One that comes to mind is *Realm of the Incas* and another is *Rite of the Pagan*. We'd love it if you could give us a brief history of your musical background.

EW: Well, yes, I was thrilled to have those two records produced by GNP Crescendo records because it was very unique for them to do something other than a strictly pop generation already and I was a little far out from them but they took the chance. Those two records are still marketable here, Japan, in England that I know of. As a performer and with an ongoing ensemble I've always had my educational shows, which I've loved doing very much because all age groups including universities were not familiar with what I was attempting to do, to show the music of the New World that they hadn't heard about or historically thought about. It was always in the Western European tradition, of the symphony world, and the Curtis Institute, where I was a scholarship student—that was all Western European. And then in the youth orchestras with the great Leopold Stokowski and others I discovered Latin America and that became my destination to create what I am up to today.

GR-W: So it was through your work with the National Youth Orchestra that got you over to Latin America, is that correct? I was reading on your website about some of what you were involved with at that time.

EW: Oh yes, well, when I decided to go on my own and be a featured violinist I started in Panama. My classic production was with William Grant Still, the famous Afro-American. I was not into composition on my own at that time so I said let's do something together for string quartet and string and symphony and it's played all over the world. It's called *Danzas de Panama*. So then after that I kept going back on my own and doing it all through Mexico, Latin America, everywhere. That's just part of it, of course.

GR-W: I also read that some encouragement in the direction of combining the pre-Columbian, pre-Hispanic instruments with the Western music you were already well familiar with and performing, that some of that encouragement might have come from Diego Rivera?

EW: The art and music are such a combination. When I played for him in his beautiful studio in Mexico City I played Bach for him and he said that's OK but I want to take you to the marketplace tomorrow morning. So I was thrilled. He was six feet tall with a big sombrero, "Gasp, there goes Don Diego," but he said what about this music, these are the people, look at these instruments how they are created. He gave me that inspiration to start with it. I have enlarged upon that over the years.

GR-W: There aren't too many other musicians from when you started putting out music who were combining music from the pre-Columbian culture with modern music, with Western music. I can think of a couple but what comes to mind for me would be the composers who were associated with what is known as exotica music, for example, Martin Denny and Les Baxter. I think your music is quite different from their music.

EW: Yes, see, they wanted me to be like them because they were big sellers but I said, "No, to me it's not authentic, its very pop-oriented." I don't like the synthesized flutes because I'm so used to the real concert flute or these Aztec flutes that are over a thousand years old. They have such a beauty and I think that's the best.

GR-W: The difference as well for me is that when I hear guys like Martin Denny it's background music in a way—

EW: But he did start something good and that—like his Hawaiian records—at least made people aware that music is coming out these wonderful areas that are not known or accepted yet and he did that. I admired him a lot for that reason.

Were there other composers prior to the exotica wave you were inspired by?

GR-W: There were composers such as Silvestre Revueltas but he did it in a symphonic sense and that's more what I am in tune with. I worked with Alberto Ginastera in Argentina and he said, "I think you are doing great to try to get this into the symphony world." Because you have to love the culture in order to do it and have to be interested to make research and explore and see what the curiosity brings to you.

GR-W: How long has this center been open?

EW: My late husband [Carl S. Dentzel, former director of the Southwest Museum] named Northridge. I started here as a young bride. I tried to make it into a cultural center because the history is so wonderful here. It combines many cultures: the Hispanic, the antiques, Afro, and I am very strongly into Chinese. That will be my next recording, about the Chinese in the Gold Rush period.

GR-W: I love the integration of the historical aspects into your work.

EW: This rancho area when I moved here it was very in the boonies and the guys were coming to trim the walnut trees and the orange and lemon trees and I tried to keep that with it here too. I spent years on the educational circuit, introducing this place to all age groups and UCLA came three years to this rancho because they said nobody knows the background and how do we get it into the music part of our courses. I like to do lecture demos. I have people from all over the world coming here. We have our own little teatro. It's a salon accommodation, with recording and all of that . . . It's my honor to have people come here to enjoy the natural rancho atmosphere of over seven acres.

GR-W: Are you still actively composing?

EW: Oh yes. All the shows that I do here, usually once a month . . . I did decide to have my own label so that I don't have to talk to a producer who says I don't think this will sell. I have to do what I believe in and what I want to create. I have a piece called "Messages in Clay" featuring all the ancient instruments, I have my opera about Natividad and all the history of that was done at the period of the conquest. I love doing that for voice, quartet, and symphony, including as many ethnic styles and instruments as I can.

GR-W: Ms. Waldo, thank you so much. You are a big inspiration to me. We will keep our listeners posted on what you have coming up and we look forward to talking again in the future.

EW: Oh I can hardly wait. Let's do it, *muy pronto*.

8

ESQUIVEL!

————

HANS ULRICH
OBRIST: My first question is about the exclamation mark
that always follows your name.

ESQUIVEL!: It's true that I don't generally use my full name,
Juan García Esquivel; I just use Esquivel! with
the exclamation point. I took it as a trademark.
The first time it appeared as such was in a place
in the States called Lake Tahoe, and voilà! It's a
place of gambling and casinos, about a four-
hour drive from Las Vegas. Tahoe is a kind of
border between the states of California and
Nevada. This was a long time ago. I performed
in a very nice hotel resort called Harvey's, quite
a beautiful place, both in winter and in summer.
But I've been out of circulation because I broke
my hip in an accident. They had to operate on
my leg and so for almost seven years I've been
bedridden. It's a shame, but I'm doing physical

therapy. They're giving me some exercises, so I hope I'll be up and around again soon.

HUO: You are a pianist, a composer, an arranger, and a conductor. You were called the King of Space-Age Pop and the Busby Berkeley of Cocktail Music.

E: In my day, one thing led to another. I started as a piano player, then, at fourteen, I played on a daily radio program that starred the comedian Panzón Panseco [Arturo Manrique] that became very popular. Then, three years later, I decided to form an orchestra because people wanted to see me. I had to learn how to write music, so I started studying different instruments. At my school I gathered twenty or thirty musicians and asked them what instrument they played. "I play trombone," "I play trumpet," and so on and so forth. "And what can you do with your instrument? What's your range?" I was learning to write music, and then the orchestra boy (I had a boy who used to help put up music stands for the orchestra) would give each of the musicians a sheet of music paper and a pencil, so every one of them had to write down their parts. I was conducting from the piano in the middle. There were twenty-four musicians; it was quite an experience for me. But that's how I arranged and how I learned to conduct, and how to arrange music, all the while playing the piano. One thing led to another: first piano playing, then arranging, then conducting. I had to understand the instruments.

HUO: Understanding them enough to invent new ones, to innovate.

E: I tuned bongos chromatically. I used twenty-four bongos to play melodies. It was very unusual, as the bongos are used mainly as accompanying instruments, just in the background. But I also gave craftsmen ideas about what I wanted them to make. I designed a steel guitar, a lot like the one that the very famous musician in the States uses. I don't know if you've heard of Alvino Rey? He plays the console [steel] guitar.

HUO: Did Alvino Rey really play your guitar?

E: Actually, we performed together. When I arrived in the States, I asked the music contractor if he could find someone that played like Alvino Rey, and he said, "You can have Alvino Rey—he will play for you." In the States, I found it very easy to hire whoever I wanted—it's not like in the Latin countries. Here, when a musician gets famous, he refuses to play as a sideman; but in the States, whatever you want, you just have to ask someone. Any name, you make an appointment with a music contractor and he asks you what you want. And I would say, "I want five voices, two girls and three men," and what kind of ranges I needed. He would willingly find for me whatever I wanted. I used the best trumpet players. In the States, I had a large orchestra of five trumpets and four trombones, five saxophones, four French horns, two alto flutes, and all the rhythms—organ, bass, guitar, drums—until I started thinking about not having such a large orchestra. For the music contractor, it's much easier to pay for six or ten musicians instead of thirty plane tickets and thirty rooms. I started thinking very seriously about writing music for six guys and four girls, which turned out to be a very nice group.

HUO: That was your Las Vegas band—the Sights and Sounds of Esquivel! You once said that, to a certain extent, the conductor has to be a dictator.

E: Yes, as a matter of fact, I once conducted the Boston Symphony Orchestra. Victor Young asked me to make an arrangement for the film *Around the World in 80 Days* (1956) and he said, "This is your turn, maestro," and then I had the pleasure of conducting an orchestra. It was a very important moment in my life. Now I'm trying to make some new music because my manager in New York was asking me for new material. I'm writing a piece titled "Guacamole." It's a nonsense thing, done on a synthesizer, and it's nothing but rhythm and the orchestra, but once in a while in the arrangement, the words "guacamole, molé, molé, molé, molé."

HUO: "Guacamole, molé, molé, molé, molé" reminds me of your famous "Zu-zu-zu" and "Pow! Pow! Pow!" Can you tell us a little more about the time you spent in Las Vegas?

E: I was in Vegas for about twelve years, from the early sixties to the mid-seventies. I was quite busy. My contract with the Stardust Hotel was for twenty-six weeks a year. One of my roles was as a communicator. I presented my show, my arrangements, and sometimes I would try to make jokes, subtle jokes. I learned how to live by night and sleep in the daytime. I had to go to bed at four in the afternoon and get up at twelve at night, take a shower and go to work. I would perform two shows a night; one of them was at one thirty, the other was at four. And sometimes after the show I would call for a rehearsal and work with the orchestra. We would go to the cafeteria and have something to eat, then we would rehearse from eight to eleven in the morning. At eleven, I would go home. I had a nice large swimming pool; I would sunbathe a little. At noon, I would go inside the house

to write music and to make phone calls because of the time difference between Las Vegas and New York. So life was very busy.
Working at night and rehearsing in the morning, and off to bed at
four in the afternoon. Tremendous fun.

HUO: Was Vegas a generous place?

E: Oh, I learned a lot of things there. Do you remember Frank Sinatra?
Frank used to come and see me when he was in town. He used
to come to my show, and I would always know he was there
because he would send notes in the napkins saying, "Play
'Bye Bye Blues'!" That's how I would know he was there. And he
used to go with many artists. He took Shirley MacLaine and Ann-
Margret Olsson.

HUO: And the Las Vegas years were also the time that you started to make
music for television?

E: I wrote a lot for television. I wrote music for *Kojak* and for *The Six
Million Dollar Man*. And for *Columbo*, who was a detective. I wrote
close to two hundred songs for Universal Studios. I have an infection
in this eye from watching so much TV, I guess. I wanted to put music
to what is happening. I have a knack for descriptive music, you know,
like when a girl is walking at night, alone, and suddenly a hand grabs
her. I have a disposition for putting music to all kinds of scenes: music
for love, music for storms, electric music, horse music—I even wrote
music for Indians and for cowboys.

HUO: You invented groundbreaking multimedia shows in the sixties with
incredible light effects. These shows influenced the pop music
industry. You invented a new medium.

E: You had a lot of big bands then, and I was one of the last ones to
perform with a big band. Rock 'n roll came, and I knew it was the
trend to follow, but I wasn't ready to change my style so I chose to
make it a smaller show. I had to leave Hollywood. I had to leave town
and go live in Las Vegas. I would perform every night and when I
made my recordings I often had to fly from Las Vegas to Hollywood.
Every night, every week, I had to fly, and I recorded in Hollywood.
Then I would fly back to Las Vegas. Wow. It seems like such a long
time ago—forty years! That's a long, long time. And almost all the
recordings I made in the early sixties were only released in 1998. And
suddenly all the recording I had made almost forty years ago came
alive again.

HUO: *See It in Sound* was your last album to be released in 1999, although
it was recorded thirty-nine years ago. RCA thought it would be too
jarring for the audience's ears.

E: When I made that recording, they didn't like it. It's not that I don't like RCA—they never said no to any of my ideas. As a matter of fact, for an album I used two, no actually three studios at the same time. One studio had a piano and the rhythm section, and then in another studio I had the trumpets and the trombones, and in another studio I had the saxophones. The musicians could see me through a closed-circuit TV. I was lucky because RCA gave me all the facilities. They never said no to me.

PEDRO REYES: I have a friend who has all your LPs. When he finds your records in flea markets for ten or twenty pesos, he goes to the United States and sells them for a hundred dollars apiece. They're collectors' items.

E: [*laughs*] I know. Once, a friend of mine told me that he had gotten $150 for one. It's amazing.

HUO: What's the title of the album that you recorded in different studios?

E: That was *Latin-Esque* (1962). At that time, when they sold stereo equipment, they would give away an album with the machine. They gave away about sixty thousand copies of *Latin-Esque*.

HUO: In *Other Worlds Other Sounds* (1958) and *Exploring New Sounds in Hi-Fi* (1959) you sought to push stereo music to its limits, weaving unusual sounds into your music, ping-ponging them from one side of the headphones to the other.

PR: It's interesting that you have a degree in engineering. Maybe this explains why you've always been able to take advantage of the latest achievements in stereophonic sound. You studied in the fifties, at a time when Mexico was a very experimental place. Color television was developed in Mexico; it was a good period for technological and scientific research.

E: It was my ambition to become an engineer. I learned about microphones when I was a student. That was very helpful during recordings because I had all these ideas that I was able to develop. Also, because of my desire to invent new things, I don't think I could have done it without knowledge of how things are made in my head. And as I said, I'm very grateful to RCA. By the way, do you know that they're going to make a film about my life?[1]

HUO: No, that's fantastic.

E: It will be a movie with a young American actor, John Leguizamo. I had a visit here from the director, Alexander Payne, and from the scriptwriter. He came all the way from Spain to visit me here, to get information. They sent me a video of John Leguizamo in New York performing to a full audience, by himself, just one man filling the

LATIN - ESQUE

ESQUIVEL
AND HIS ORCHESTRA

La Raspa · Adios, Mariquita Linda · Jesusita en Chihuahua · Cachito (Pedacito) · Latin-esque · La Paloma · Estrellita (Oyeme) Cachita · Jungle Drums (Canto Karabali) · Mucha Muchacha · You Belong to My Heart (Solamente una Vez) · Carioca

Esquivel and His Orchestra, *Latin-Esque,* RCA Victor, 1962, Idelsohn Society for Musical Preservation Archive.

stage. He talks and dances; he's very talented. Of course, people will want to know what I looked like sixty years ago. But I guess he will wear glasses like I used to.

HUO: You've led a very interesting life.

E: Actually, I was very surprised because I didn't think my life was worth making a film about. But on the other hand, I'm very flattered, of course, and very anxious to see what they're going to do. My life has been very interesting. It is nice to know that, in spite of all the time that has gone by, people are still interested in my work. My life has been full of experiences—photography, engineering. I was in the home of a son of mine who lives near here in Taxco. I decided to go over and spend some time there and I lived

Esquivel and His Orchestra, *Other Worlds Other Sounds,* RCA Victor, 1958, Idelsohn Society for Musical Preservation Archive.

with him for almost a year after I finished my contract in Las Vegas. In this bedroom there was a very slippery floor and I fell down four times and hurt my leg. I never imagined that I was going to live here again. I fell down and broke my hip and that's why I've been in bed all this time. But I kind of like it. My brother's home is a few blocks away. I found this place by chance because it's secluded. And now I live here with no problems. I'm happy. Two girls take care of me. I have my studio across the room with a synthesizer and my piano.

HUO: Do you have unrealized projects that you never got to do, or projects still left to do?

E: One thing was working with Yma Súmac. Do you know her? She's a singer. She has one of the widest ranges, from the very low notes to the highest note. She was very popular. I don't know if she's still living, or what she's doing, but all my life I tried to find a way to work with her. She's fabulous. I will quote General MacArthur: he used to say to his troops during the war, "I shall return," but then one last time, he said, "The forecasts for the war I have ahead of me are not as clear as they used to be, so this time I can't say I shall return." Right now, I can't say I have any ambitions or any desires. I don't know. I'm eighty-two years old, so who knows what destiny has to serve to me. But if time allows, I'll be ready for any new venture. If not, all I can say is that I have had a beautiful life. I have had six different lives, as you mentioned before: as an engineer, a composer, a pianist, an arranger, a conductor, and a communicator.

HUO: What's really fascinating is how you've been at the forefront of pop avant-gardism, working very experimentally, and yet you've never had a problem with the mainstream.

E: I have never said no to any job. Someone would ask me, "Will you write music for this?" And I would say yes, even if I didn't know how to do it. I had to invent new forms. But I don't remember having turned down an invitation to write music for anything. That has led me to very particular circumstances, because even if I didn't know anything, I would learn about it. If you asked me to write Chinese music, I'd say yes even though I don't know anything about it. I would find a way to learn about it. It was a funny thing. I said I wrote music for Indians and cowboys; I had never written anything for Indians before. I remember a very famous actor, Randolph Scott—who said he was as famous as John Wayne—heard my music for Indians, and he said, "This guy must have some Indian blood, because this is the best music for Indians I have ever heard." That was a compliment, especially because it was the first time I had ever written for Indians and for cowboys. But like you said, I was always using different aspects of music. I would use different instruments. It was a very nice experience; I love working that way. And since I'm experimenting all the time, I can never guarantee that, yes, this is going to be all right. They let me do it, so I tried. It's a little immodest on my part to say, but I think that most of the time I succeeded. To me, making music is like giving me a doll, and I take the clothes off and I can put anything I want on her. I can put Greek or Swiss dresses on her, or her hair, or I can draw a moustache, or I can put a cigar in her mouth. Experimenting—and that's very gratifying—thanks to the good will of the people who let me do my experiments. Because if I were in other people's shoes, I don't know if I would hire myself. [*laughs*]

NOTE

1. The film was under production by Fox Studios until 2004, when the project was postponed indefinitely.

DAVID F. GARCIA

9

LISTENING ACROSS BOUNDARIES

Soundings from the Paramount Ballroom
and Boyle Heights

O N SATURDAY NIGHT, AUGUST 28, the group led by Cuban
composer and *tres* player Arsenio Rodríguez headlined
the Paramount Ballroom in Boyle Heights. That same night,
local television station channel 9 aired *The Beatles are Back* at 9:00 PM
in anticipation of the Beatles' concerts at the Hollywood Bowl set to
take place the following two nights. About two weeks prior, residents
of Watts rebelled against police brutality and poor living conditions.
These two events captured and shaped the attention of people locally,
nationally, and internationally. For residents of Los Angeles, August
1965 was indeed a tumultuous, violent month: arrests were made at
the Beatles' concerts and (many more) in Watts.[1] For those dancers
and listeners who attended the Paramount's entertainment that night
in August, it's hard to imagine that all the unrest in the air and on radio
and television—the heavy presence of riot police and the California
National Guard in the city—wasn't on their minds and wasn't somehow filtering through the music coming from the Paramount stage. It
is also reasonable to believe that, once Rodríguez's group finished
their last set for the night, everyone returned home from 2706

Brooklyn Avenue a little different, perhaps tired from a night of making music, dancing, and listening, but different nonetheless.

Rodriguez's performance in an East Los Angeles ballroom wasn't a fluke. The history of Cuban music in East Los Angeles may be little known, but musicians like Rodriguez and Cuban flutist Rolando Lozano are an important part of the story of how Latin American music took shape across the greater LA landscape. "Rolando [Lozano] and I played together I forgot how many times because we were in the same band," recalls Nicaraguan pianist Rocky Moran, a member of Rodriguez's *conjunto*. "[But] he limited himself to working in some areas because he didn't drive. I remember driving him—I still remember he lived on Wabash Street—and he was afraid to drive. So, most of his gigs were in East LA, and in fact we worked together for many years at the Paramount Ballroom on Brooklyn Avenue.[2]

In preparing to write my contribution to this collection of essays, I reengaged the historical documents on the Paramount Ballroom that I had collected from 1996 to 2003, when I was a doctoral student researching the life and career of Cuban musician Arsenio Rodríguez. I have continued to struggle with negotiating the temporal and spatial distances separating me from Rodríguez and the ten months in 1965 when his *conjunto* played many weekends at the Paramount Ballroom. Whereas as a doctoral student I traveled around Los Angeles to interview musicians like Moran, other Cuban groups like Lozano's, or their own groups at the Paramount Ballroom, now I find myself in Durham, North Carolina, attempting again at even greater distances to understand what this place meant to Rodríguez's career, the local music and dancing communities, and the histories of Boyle Heights and Los Angeles. Yet, as I reexamined these materials and collected new documents, it became apparent to me that such distances from the Paramount Ballroom, 2706 Brooklyn Avenue (its address until 1994), and Boyle Heights applied no less to many people living in Los Angeles in 1965 and before. This may seem for some readers an obvious point, but one which is necessary to make in order to begin to account for the complex nature of such distances. If we, thus, rethink the nature of our temporal and spatial distances from 1965, from the Paramount Ballrooms of the past, and seek to understand this place's meanings via people's movements of all sorts across time and geographic space, then we might retrieve the Paramount Ballroom's historical significances from vantage points of a different epistemology altogether. My goal is to listen between and across boundaries of all sorts, including "between the lines" of archival newspaper reports.[3]

One of Los Angeles's most persistent spatial binaries—real and imaginary—is the political, economic, cultural, geographical, and infrastructural fault line that separates East Los Angeles from downtown and everything west, north, and south from there. In *Arsenio Rodríguez and the Transnational Flows of Latin Popular Music,* I depended on (and perpetuated) this logic to explain what his performances at the Paramount Ballroom tell us about his career in Los Angeles. I claimed, for instance, that "audiences from other parts of the city avoided the Paramount because of the area's notoriety." In characterizing his performances in Boyle Heights as "relegated" to a lower status and the Paramount itself as a "peripheral location compared to places in downtown and Hollywood," I discursively silenced alternative voices that did not fit the binary. For example, I wrote, "The audience that Arsenio evidently had at the Paramount Ballroom represented a distinct and marginal section of the broader Latin dance music audience."[4] Did his audiences, for example, really feel marginalized while dancing across the ballroom floor? In his book *City of Quartz,* Mike Davis similarly silences the people and histories of East Los Angeles as he critically analyzes the very political forces (Downtown and Westside elites) whose development and redevelopment projects, dating at least to the turn of the twentieth century, determined to a great extent the abstract and real spatialities that distinguished everyday living in South and East Los Angeles from the rest of the city.[5]

This time, instead of taking the silences of Boyle Heights as empirical evidence of its residents' marginal status, I trace people's movements and soundings in, out of, and around the Paramount Ballroom in an attempt to reveal and let resound their impassioned declarations of economic and educational equality, political enfranchisement, and racial, ethnic, and national identities. By "declarations," I mean the actions—planning, marching, protesting, distributing, singing, dancing, teaching, musicking,[6] broadcasting, and so on—taken by people at particular moments from 1929 to 1965 for important reasons. This approach to studying the Paramount Ballroom not as one building but as many lived spaces over time, where the movements and soundings of people engendered its historical and cultural significances, is in the end how I propose we critically listen between and across the spatialized boundaries of geographical place and historical time in order to access its stories.

To get started, I should explain how I understand and am using the notion of spatiality. Not only is spatial thinking concerned with unpacking how boundaries of all sorts (historical, geographic, and ideological included) structure the ways we move and think our way in the world. It also and ultimately should bring to bear on our analyses of what Michel de Certeau describes as the "dispersed, tactical, and makeshift creativity of groups or individuals already caught in the nets of 'discipline.'"[7] Perhaps the clearest example of how spatiality operated in the daily life of a professional musician in Los Angeles in the 1960s is the system of scheduling venues imposed by the American Federation of Musicians Local 47. The union mapped locations that hosted live music into nine rankings. Those locations with a schedule one or two ranking included the city's major concert halls and hotel ballrooms, whereas the places that fell under a schedule eight or nine ranking included nightclubs and "holes in the wall," as one former Local 47 member put it.[8] Examples of schedule two locations included the Zenda Ballroom (936 W 7th Street and Figueroa) as well as the Latin Quarter and Crescendo (both on the Sunset strip). The Paramount Ballroom and Virginia's (W 7th Street, west of S. Alvarado Street in Westlake), on the other hand, were both schedule nine locations, whose scale in 1965 the union set at $25.80 for the leader and $17.20 for side musicians total for four hours and thirty minutes of work. The scale for higher-scheduled locations was at least twice this amount, if not more.

How a locale received its scheduling depended on a number of factors, including its paid audience capacity, which did not always have to coincide with the location's size. In spite of its characterization as a "hole in the wall," for instance, the Paramount Ballroom was larger than a nightclub. In fact the building itself was divided into two spaces for live music and dancing, the upstairs ballroom and a nightclub on the ground level.[9] The venue's location, also, did not always determine how Local 47 (located on Vine Street, Hollywood) set its pay scales. Virginia's, for example, was located close to downtown, where Davis located the city's downtown elite power structure. While the Paramount Ballroom's schedule nine ranking helps us understand how musicians' earnings there compared with those at other venues, it also serves to show how the activities in one place—musicking and dancing in Boyle Heights—were tangled up in, but not entirely dictated by, the nets of a disciplining entity, in this instance, the musicians union's board of directors and trial board, both of which were invested with the power to stop union musicians from accepting contracts from noncomplying venue managers as well as to suspend and expel a musician's membership.[10] To place the Paramount not only in spatial contexts but also across temporal boundaries provides a different set of perspectives into the ways in which its occupants and their activities intersected and got tangled up with city, statewide, regional, and national forces belonging to other historical narratives.

One of the earliest sources documenting 2706 Brooklyn Ave is a series of advertisements for Brooklyn-Boyle Heights Investment Co., which was published in the *Los Angeles Herald* in October through December 1906. By the 1920s the building at this address became known as the Co-Operative Auditorium, which, as Daniel Hurewitz writes, served as a multipurpose community center for members of Los Angeles's Communist Party.[11] The building's spaces at this time included a meeting hall, bakery, barbershop, and restaurant, while its political activities centered on debating issues, strategizing for action, printing pamphlets and circulars, and organizing youth, workers, and the unemployed in Boyle Heights and adjacent areas. For instance, two such circulars, as reported by the *Los Angeles Times,* carried the headings "Fight against Police Brutality" and "Come in Mass to Protest against the Destruction of the Workers' Children's Summer Camp," the protest meeting of which was scheduled to take place at the Co-Operative Building on August 16, 1929.[12] The *Times,* titling their report "Police Arrest Suspected Red," reported that the LAPD arrested three men for "distributing communistic circulars" in violation of a city ordinance banning the distribution of such literature. One arrest occurred in downtown (21st Street and Griffith Avenue), while the other two were made in Boyle Heights (2000 City View Avenue). The political activism taking place in and moving through 2706 Brooklyn Avenue was clearly at the crosshairs of what Davis referred to as the city's "de facto dictatorship" of *Times*'s owner Harry Chandler, the Merchants and Manufacturers Association, and the LAPD, whose "infamous 'red squad' kept dissent off the streets and radicals in jail."[13] As we know now, stock market prices would begin to fall two weeks later, leading eventually to the market crash of October 29 and, as a result, increased repression of worker organizers and Communist Party members.

It is the *movement* of so-called agitators and their communistic literature from the Co-Operative Auditorium out toward the city's center of political and economic power that compels us to further rethink the nature of 2706 Brooklyn Avenue's presumably marginalized status. Its occupants' disruption of officially sanctioned modes of everyday thinking, talking, walking, and working was indeed the red squad's and the *Times*'s target of intensified repression and biased reporting, respectively, one year into the Great Depression. To "break up," "cordon" off, and "spike" the movements and actions of demonstrators in downtown's Plaza (N Main) on September 2, 1930, as reported by the *Times,* were the tactics implemented by police, whereby "spasmodic outbursts," "distributing," and "singing inflammatory songs" were the countertactics of the activists, including two—Anna Rexnor and Harry Snyder—who gave to the police their home addresses as 2706 and 2708 Brooklyn Avenue.[14] Rexnor and Snyder were among seventeen people arrested that day. Their handbills included "pleas for defense of the Chinese revolution and release of Imperial Valley sabotage-plot prisoners," who were in reality Communist Party leaders arrested earlier in the year for helping Mexican and Filipino farmworkers to organize a strike against their deplorable working conditions.[15] Clearly, the appearances of the Co-Operative Building and 2706 Brooklyn Avenue in the *Los Angeles Times* in the 1920s and 1930s resound with intensity, urgency, and movement, much of which had been planned within that location with the ultimate goal of taking it to the belly of the beast (downtown elite), ending more often than not with beatings and arrests.

One of the earliest printed appearances of the actual name "Paramount Ballroom" occurs in an advertisement published in the *Times* in April 1949, announcing the opening of a branch dance studio at 2706–08 Brooklyn Avenue directed by Eduardo Cansino.[16] The ad identifies Cansino as the "father and teacher of Rita Hayworth" and indicates that his new dance studio will specialize in Spanish, Mexican, flamenco, tap, ballet, and boogie woogie. Earlier in the 1940s Cansino rented studio space throughout downtown and surrounding areas including on S La Brea and S Vermont Avenue. Although Cansino's use of the Paramount Ballroom as a dance studio seemed short-lived, the space's occupancies and uses in the late 1940s and 1950s indicate Boyle Heights's increasing Mexican presence, but more than simply a growing demographic presence. The *Times* reported that the Mexican-American National Association was to hold a public meeting "on behalf of civil rights and the organization's other purposes" at 2706 Brooklyn Avenue on Friday, August 8, 1952.[17] The association, which formed in 1949, attempted to organize Mexican Americans throughout the Southwest to address discrimination at the workplace, in schools, in housing, and in other public places as well as advocate for representation in city and statewide government. Moreover, the group's president, Alfredo Montoya of New Mexico, said to the *Times* that "Mexican-Americans should be proud of their cultural and historical background," adding that "the ancestors of many of them pioneered in the Southwest long before the coming of people of English speech."[18]

As Gaye Theresa Johnson argues, in the face of Los Angeles's long-established power blocs of racial and class oppression, Black and Brown communities "created new articulations, new sensibilities, and new visions about the place of Black, Brown, and working-class people on the local and national landscape."[19] These articulations, sensibilities, and visions, which Johnson terms "spatial entitlements," are certainly audible in Montoya's quotations, specifically in his assertion that the sounds of Mexican Americans' speech not only preceded the migration of "English speech" into the Southwest but should resound proudly once again. We can also apply the strategies for imagining and articulating new or renewed modes of social citizenship that Johnson describes to local radio stations. According to one ad, KWKW was scheduled to broadcast from the Paramount Ballroom on Sunday, December 18, 1955, at 3:00 PM.[20] As Steven Loza and others discuss, Mexican Americans in Los Angeles, particularly in Boyle Heights, increasingly advocated for political, economic, and cultural participation on the local, state, and national levels through the 1950s and 1960s.[21] Radio stations KALI and KWKW contributed uniquely to these striations of Spanish-speakers' lived spaces across the city by including programming in Spanish. In the case of KWKW their programming, according to Loza, went to Spanish exclusively by 1962.[22]

Among the spatial formations that Johnson details are the interracial gatherings that Black, Brown, Jewish, and other White R & B musicians, dancers, and listeners forged together. Fostering such musical sensibilities and social interactions were radio DJs such as Dick "Huggy Boy" Hugg, who in addition to broadcasting on several local radio stations, including KALI, KWKW, and KBLA, hosted dances in South and East Los Angeles as well as in the San Fernando Valley. Huggy Boy hosted one such show, featuring the African American doo-wop group the Six Teens, at the Paramount Ballroom in July 1963.[23] As the ad to Cansino's dance studio shows, the musicking and dancing that reverberated in the Paramount Ballroom from the 1940s through the early 1960s encompassed those encoded as Black as well as Brown. Indeed, as the construction of the Golden State Freeway created a new infrastructural boundary that further marked Boyle Heights as marginalized, the Paramount's reverberations broadcasted on radio across the county challenged, as Communist party members had done, the city's power brokers. In other words, broadcasts of live music from the Paramount encompassed a spatially diverse listening and dancing audience that Local 47, city developers, and housing associations implanting segregationist practices could not quite completely control.

By 1964 the Paramount Ballroom was hosting live music and dancing every weekend, including *tardeadas* (afternoon dances) on Sundays at 4:00 PM. Based on its ads published in *La Opinion,* the Paramount featured mostly Cuban, tropical, or Latin dance music groups, the bandleaders of which were either Cubans, Puerto Ricans, or Mexican Americans. For example, Mexican American band leader Johnny Martínez and Mariachi Los Reyes performed on Saturday evening on June 6, 1964. The next day, Tito Puente's band along with Martínez's group performed a tardeada.[24] Later that month Cuban bandleader Mariano Mercerón and Mariachi Los Reyes were Saturday night's entertainment, and Puerto Rican Orlando Marin from New York and Martínez performed the next day.[25] Other local bandleaders who performed Latin music regularly at the Paramount included Rudy Macías, who was born in El Paso, Texas, and Cuban leader Albertico Pérez. Other clubs in Boyle Heights such as Lalo's Nightclub on 4209 Brooklyn Avenue, owned by Lalo Guerrero, provided a diverse repertory of live music, including *música tropical* and Tex-Mex. Club Culiacán at 4164 E Brooklyn Avenue specialized in mariachi music and catered to the *sinaloense* community.[26] Meanwhile, young Mexican Americans and African Americans continued to forge meaningful interracial spaces of music making and dancing, sometimes within spaces shared with their elders. For example, Mexican singer Sonia López, accompanied by Mercerón's orchestra, headlined a New Year's Eve dance at the Roger Young Ballroom in downtown. The program also included the Harptones, a popular local African American doo-wop group.[27]

The acts hired by the Paramount management, however, suggest that their regular clientele were perhaps first-generation Cuban and Mexican immigrant dancers and listeners. For instance, after beginning a successful performance and recording career in Cuba in 1941, Mariano Mercerón first performed in Mexico in 1947, and by 1948 he decided to move to Mexico City, where his reformed big band, the members of which were Mexican musicians, recorded regularly for RCA Victor.[28] Mercerón's band had many hits in Mexico, including "Margarita" and "Florecita," which were recorded in 1957 and 1959, respectively. His band also performed in Corpus Christi, Texas, as well as throughout Southern California between 1962 and 1964.[29] It is likely, then, that first-generation Mexican as well as Cuban immigrants in Los Angeles were particularly attracted to acts such as Mercerón, whose music they may have remembered while still living in their home nation. Indeed, bandleader Johnny Martínez had a particularly unique perspective on the Paramount's audiences, given that his band performed there as well as throughout the city:

> I kept working at the Paramount with my band. People would ask me, "Hey, you work up at the big high-class joints. What are you doing down here at the Paramount and all these other places where the poor people are?" I'd say, "To me, people are people. I don't care whether they're rich or poor. They still like music and it doesn't matter to me. I'm enjoying my band." You know where the Paramount Ballroom was, don't you? It used to be on Brooklyn Avenue, gung ho Mexican, but they used to love my band.[30]

Bandleader Rudy Macías was less enthusiastic about recalling his experience performing at the Paramount, characterizing it as "not hot" and not comparable to the Hollywood Palladium, Zenda Ballroom, or the Cocoanut Grove:

> I played there for six months, at the Paramount Ballroom. When I came to that place [in 1964], it was dying. Then we started bringing people and then they started hiring bands from Mexico too. . . . It was a different crowd, entirely different crowd. A little lower level.[31]

The bands that Macías referred to included Mercerón's. Latin bandleaders from New York, like Puente and Marin, also performed at the Paramount to supplement their more lucrative performance contracts at schedule one and two locations like the Hollywood Palladium. They also came as leaders and not with their entire bands from New York, which meant they hired Local 47 musicians to perform their music under their direction. Thus, on the one hand, Martínez and Macías mark the difference of the Paramount's clientele in terms of their first-generation immigrant and class-level status. On the other, this clientele's tastes in *música tropical* from Mexico and Latin music from New York suggest a cosmopolitan worldview, one that problematizes characterizations of Paramount dancers and listeners in solely national, class, and immigrant terms. The fact that Black Cuban musician Arsenio Rodríguez also led a group at the Paramount for many weekends in 1965 further conveys a clientele with diverse tastes in dance music, even though Rodríguez's manager at the time, Pedro Ferro, believed that the Paramount's owner, Mitch Rodríguez, did not know his music.[32]

Arsenio Rodríguez started his career as a composer and bandleader in Havana in the 1930s, and by 1940 his *conjunto* had a contract with RCA Victor, for whom he would record until 1952 and again in 1955 and 1956. By 1952 Rodríguez had settled in New York City, where he led his *conjunto* of mostly Puerto Rican musicians. Because his performance career slowed down, however, in the late 1950s and early 1960s, he and his brother Israel Rodríguez ventured out in late 1964 to Los Angeles, where their younger brother Raúl had moved the year before. The brothers lived on Exposition, where they formed a new *conjunto* with local Puerto Rican, Mexican, and other Latino musicians. After initially failing to secure well-attended performances, Rodríguez hired fellow Cuban Pedro Ferro to manage him. Ferro had never managed a musical group. Instead, he was a prominent leader of the Cuban exile and anti–Fidel Castro community in Los Angeles. In 1961, as a member of Bloque Anti-Communista Latino-Americano (Latin American Anti-Communist Block), or BALA, Ferro helped recruit volunteers to aid in the doomed Bay of Pigs invasion.[33] Ferro was eventually named president of BALA the following month, continuing his activism against the Castro government for years after.

In spite of his inexperience as a band manager, Ferro did succeed in jump-starting Rodríguez's performance career in Los Angeles. The first performance contract Ferro secured for Rodríguez was with Mitch Rodríguez. In recalling this contract, Ferro stressed that the Paramount was a *nightclub mexicano* in a *barrio mexicano*. He was also aware that Cuban musicians Mariano Mercerón and Albertico Pérez had performed there regularly, his rationale being that Rodríguez would have to *saber pasar hambre,* or "pay his dues," at the Paramount if he wanted better-paying gigs at the Hollywood Palladium and Million Dollar Theater. In fact, Ferro secured contracts for Rodríguez to perform at the Hollywood Palladium on February 21, a mere two weeks after his first performance at the Paramount, and the Million Dollar Theater on March 26, 1965. During this time Rodríguez's *conjunto* performed at the Paramount on two more Saturday evenings (February 13 and March 20).[34] He returned to the Paramount in May, performing there regularly through August. Thus, the notion of having to pay one's dues by playing at the Paramount did not necessarily mean that the Boyle Heights ballroom could not also be a steady gig for musicians. This was, indeed, the case for Rodríguez, whose LP *Viva Arsenio!* (Bang Records BLPS-216), which he recorded in New York City in 1966, offers perhaps the only insight we have into the impact the Paramount's dancers and listeners as well as Boyle Heights's Mexican and Mexican American communities across generations had on his music.

Three tracks on *Viva Arsenio!,* the popular Mexican songs "La Bamba" and "Cielito Lindo" and the R & B hit "Hang On Sloopy," are indicative of Rodríguez's longtime practice of appealing to the musical and cultural tastes of his audiences, whether Cuban or non-Cuban. For example, he had composed and recorded Puerto Rican *bomba* and *plena* music in New York City in addition to *guaguancós* dedicated to the Black working-class neighborhoods of Havana. His rendition of "La Bamba" on *Viva Arsenio!* is performed in a Cuban *son* style, featuring Cuban percussion, bass, *tres* guitar, lead vocal, and *coros* (chorus). "Hang On Sloopy" is similarly performed in a Cuban *son* style, though Rodríguez sings the lyrics in their original English. That these songs' simple harmonic structures and verse-chorus forms lend themselves to easy adaptation suggests that Rodríguez may have even initially played these songs with his *conjunto* upon request at the Paramount. The simple production value of the recorded performances, especially "La Bamba," seems to bear this out.

Much has been written about the Eastside Sound of the 1960s, in terms of both its eclectic stylistic characteristics (ranging from R & B, soul, and rock to Latin tropical and Mexican popular and traditional music) and its political resonance as a voice of the Chicano youth of East Los Angeles.[35] What the Paramount Ballrooms of the 1920s through the 1960s do to this history is open new modes of listening to Boyle Heights's eclecticisms and resonances, from those encompassing Communist Party activism to classes in Mexican, flamenco, and boogie woogie dance, broadcasts of doo wop, and making and dancing to *música tropical,* Latin music, and Cuban *son.* Likewise, listening spatially to the Paramount Ballroom—its distance from the higher-scheduled, upper-class, and "hotter" venues of musicking and dancing in downtown and Hollywood—and its Cuban musical histories lends further insight into how this building and the movements and soundings within it were always already entangled in a wider web of musical, social, and political forces.

NOTES

1. "100 Arrests Made While Beatles Sing," *Los Angeles Times,* August 20, 1965, 23.

2. Rocky Moran, interview by author, Monrovia, CA, May 25, 1997.

3. See Gilles Deleuze and Félix Guattari, *A Thousand Plateaus: Capitalism and Schizophrenia* (London: University of Minnesota Press, 1987), 492–99.

4. David Garcia, *Arsenio Rodríguez and the Transnational Flows of Latin Popular Music* (Philadelphia: Temple University Press, 2006), 104–6.

5. Mike Davis, *City of Quartz: Excavating the Future in Los Angeles* (New York: Vintage, 1992).

6. Coined by Christopher Small, "musicking" serves as a framework for understanding music in action, as a human activity situated ontologically to embody a unique mode of knowing the world and inspired by the desire to live well in it. Small, *Musicking: The Meanings of Performing and Listening* (Middletown, CT: Wesleyan University Press, 1998), 50.

7. Michel de Certeau, *The Practice of Everyday Life* (Berkeley: University of California Press, 1984), xiv–xv.

8. Alfredo Rubalcava, interview by author, Los Angeles, CA, July 31, 2001.

9. Rudy Macias, interview with author, August 16, 1999.

10. *Constitution and By-Laws of the Musicians Union Local 47, A. F. of M. and of the Musicians Club of Los Angeles* (Los Angeles: American Federation of Musicians, AFL-CIO, 1965).

11. Daniel Hurewitz, *Bohemian Los Angeles and the Making of Modern Politics* (Berkeley: University of California Press, 2007), 155–56.

12. "Police Arrest Suspected Red: Taken in Act of Distributing Communistic Circulars," *Los Angeles Times,* August 17, 1929, 16.

13. Davis, *City of Quartz,* 114.

14. "Red Raid Jails Seventeen," *Los Angeles Times,* September 2, 1930, A1.

15. See Hurewitz, *Bohemian Los Angeles,* 156–59.

16. *Los Angeles Times,* April 7, 1949, 7.

17. "Mexican Group to Meet Friday," *Los Angeles Times,* August 5, 1952, 13.

18. "U.S. Mexicans Will Have Their Own Association," *Los Angeles Times,* October 23, 1949, 36.

19. See Gaye Theresa Johnson, "Spatial Entitlement: Race, Displacement, and Sonic Reclamation in Postwar Los Angeles," in *Black and Brown in Los Angeles: Beyond Conflict and Coalition,* ed. Laura Pulido and Josh Kun (Berkeley: University of California Press, 2013), 165.

20. *Pasadena Independent,* December 18, 1955, 89.

21. See Steven Loza, *Barrio Rhythm: Mexican American Music in Los Angeles* (Urbana and Chicago: University of Illinois Press, 1993), 41–53.

22. See also "Danielson Radio Talk To Be Given in Spanish," *El Sereno Star,* October 29, 1964, 19.

23. "Summer Sounds," *Los Angeles Sentinel,* July 25, 1963, C8.

24. *La Opinión,* June 6, 1964, 7.

25. *La Opinión,* June 27, 1964, 3.

26. See Loza, *Barrio Rhythm,* 74, and *La Opinión,* December 18, 1964, 5.

27. "Candilejas Ideas . . . y Televisión," *La Opinión,* December 31, 1964, 5.

28. See Gonzalo Martré, *Rumberos de ayer: Músicos cubanos en México, 1930–1950* (Veracruz: Instituto Veracruzano de Cultura, 1997), 17.

29. *The Corpus Christi Caller-Times,* September 27, 1961, 28; *Los Angeles Times,* December 21, 1962, 8; and *The San Bernadino County Sun,* December 12, 1964, 38.

30. Johnny Martínez, interview with author, August 11, 1998.

31. Rudy Macías, interview with author, August 16, 1999.

32. Pedro Ferrer, interview with author, October 20, 2000.

33. "Local Cubans Continue to Enlist for Invasion," *Los Angeles Times,* April 21, 1961, 5; "Anti-Castro Group Will Meet Friday," *Los Angeles Times,* May 24, 1961, 6; "Anti-Castro Group Asks Exile Leader to Resign," *Los Angeles Times,* May 27, 1961, A8.

34. See *La Opinión,* February 5, 12, 19, and March 19.

35. See Loza, *Barrio Rhythm,* 95–107.

10

STUDIO STORIES

Interviews with Session Musicians

TRANSCRIPTIONS BY BERENICE ESQUER AND
YATRIKA SHAH-RAIS

THROUGHOUT 2016, WE SAT down with some of the most prolific Latin American session musicians in Los Angeles. Between them, they have played on thousands of recordings for some of the world's most influential and most popular artists. Their contributions—delivered through percussion, bass, saxophone, and clarinet—helped shape songs that became international hits and albums that are still studied as masterpieces of jazz, funk, rock, pop, and R & B.

They are on the speed dial of film score conductors and orchestra leaders. Among musicians, they are legends, indispensable and reliable shape-shifting experts who can be counted on to play anything, produce any sound, slide into any groove, and lock into any genre. They show up. They work hard. They play until they get it right. And then they pack it up and head to another studio for another session. As Abraham Laboriel Sr. remarks in his interview here, they are willing "servants" to someone else's vision. They don't take over a session— they dwell in the background and on the side, and make sure they help the session get to where it is supposed to go. They are professional copilots, team players, and chameleons. Generosity and openness are at the core of their craft: *How can I play in a way that helps you be the you that you want to be? How can my music help you make your music?*

While we may know some of their names and maybe even some of their stories, the depth of their accomplishments and their profound influence on constructing contemporary music have still not been sufficiently documented and celebrated. There are traces in album credit personnel listings, specialty musician magazine interviews, and increasingly in historical essays by hip-hop heads obsessed with tracking down the musicians responsible for their favorite samples (that's Laboriel's bass on Herb Alpert's "Rise," which is sampled on Notorious B.I.G.'s "Hypnotize").

Their status as "session" players, or "side men" and "side musicians," became a guiding metaphor for how we thought about the role of Latin American music in Los Angeles as a whole. Like the percussion of Paulinho Da Costa on a song like Michael Jackson's "Don't Stop 'til You Get Enough," it is at the center, it is foundational, yet it lives on the side. It is a building block not always seen in the finished construction, yet without it, the building loses its character. Without it, things topple. And while literally a "session" refers to a contracted assembly of musicians in a recording studio, it is also something more: a meeting together, a sitting together, a communing. These extraordinary master musicians work in the name of communion. They are invisible craftsmen of togetherness. The sessions they helped make possible have changed the way millions of listeners—strangers living on their own sidelines, working in their own sessions—have felt and danced and moved, and come to know something different about the world.

In our conversations with them, we were interested in learning a few key things: their journeys to Los Angeles from Cuba, Brazil, Mexico, Peru, and Colombia; their experience as working musicians over decades in the city's entertainment industry; their thoughts on the politics of authorship and credit; their sense of how their Latin American backgrounds have influenced, if at all, the session work they've done; and how the politics of race and immigration in Los Angeles have impacted their work. Our interviews typically lasted two or three hours, but in all cases we could have stayed for days.

INTERVIEW WITH ABRAHAM LABORIEL

Abraham Laboriel Sr. was born and raised in Mexico City as the son of Garifuna parents from Honduras. He is one of the most recorded bass players in the world. His work has appeared on nearly five thousand recordings by artists such as Leonard Cohen, Henry Mancini, Quincy Jones, Paul Simon, Michael Jackson, George Duke, Stevie Wonder, Dolly Parton, Gilberto Gil, Joe Sample, and Herb Alpert, and in film scores that include *Saturday Night Fever, Tootsie, Forrest Gump,* and, most recently, *Rogue One: A Star Wars Story.*

We spoke to him at Center Staging studios in Burbank, California, in March 2016.

BA: Tell us about your family history.

AL: My father, Juan José Laboriel, moved to Mexico in the early 1920s [from Honduras]. He first worked in Chetumal, Quintana Roo. In Mérida, [Yucatán,] he became part of the "Trovador" scene. From there, for whatever reason, he went to Tampico and became a cab driver (and then to Mexico City). My father is an integral part of the fabric of the entertainment business in Mexico. Since the 1920s he became a founding member of the actor's association, the musician's association, the composer's association, and of the film worker's association. Since then, my father has participated in over two hundred films, either as an actor or composing music or in the sidelines. As part of the staff of the film company. Then in 1939, he went back to marry my mom. He went to Honduras and they had decided to move to Brazil. But because during the Second World War all the waters of the Atlantic were mined, he brought her back to Mexico. The rest is history.

BA: Mexicans associate the last name Laboriel with a major figure of pop music in Mexico, Johnny Laboriel.

AL: Yes . . . (When) my brother was sixteen years old, he became a member of Los Rebeldes del Rock. They became the most important rock 'n roll band of a pioneering movement in Mexico. And then all the American publishing companies would send him songs for him to consider recording in Spanish. So he will have to make translations of those songs and then record them with a band. And all the songs that he didn't like, he would give to me. So then I started listening to American music very intensely, and play along with the guitar, the 45s he would give to me. And that changed my life forever.

BA: There are three siblings who are in music in the family: you, Johnny, and Ella.

AL: Right. Ella, then my younger sister [who] died, Francis. In my opinion, she was the most talented of all of us. She could sing, arrange, compose, play guitar. Five years before she passed she [played the role of] Mamá Dolores, in the soap opera *El Derecho de Nacer*. [He indicates a picture of her.] In that picture her name was "Fanny." So the name of the group was "Fanny and Her Lollipops." We are an integral part of the entertainment business in Mexico. We represent the soundtrack of generations of Mexicans. Either through movies, TV, or records.

BA: When did you decide you wanted to be a musician?

AL: When I dropped out of engineering school [at the Politécnico in Mexico] I went to the Escuela Nacional de Música [in Mexico City]; to become a composer was an eleven-year program. So I started to visit different embassies to find out if there were other schools that offered a shorter time to get a degree. And I discovered that the United States had a four-year career (program) where you could become a composer, instead of eleven. So I got a scholarship for the Boston Conservatory. That was amazing. So I went to do my audition at the

Boston Conservatory, and the guy that auditioned me says: "you know, Abraham, have you heard of the Berklee School of Music?" I said no. He says, "I have the feeling that you would be happier there." I was really disturbed. I was crying, thinking that I had failed my audition. He says, "here the only modern music that we teach is Stockhausen and Schoenberg and you don't seem to be that kind of musician." So he says, "go and explore there and if you don't like it, you could always come back here." And says, "the only thing is that over there they don't have scholarships because it is not an accredited school. Here you have a scholarship but you would not be happy here." And so I went to visit Berklee and I walked into the room of the guy in charge of admissions; he puts on a record of one of the students to the school and I freaked out. And it was Quincy's music when he was a student there. And I did not know that Quincy Jones had gone there. And I said, "man I'm home!" He says, "if that's what you want this is the only place where you could learn that."

And so that's why I left Mexico—because it was going to be eleven years to get a degree in composition. I came to the United States and it was a fantastic decision. After three years at Berklee, I discovered that I could play the electric bass. And then all the doors opened, wide open. I sat in to make records with Gary Burton, with a rock singer named Andy Pratt, and then I started to travel with Johnny Mathis, Henri Mancini, Michel Legrand. Then eventually we moved to Los Angeles. From 1977 to the present, I've done more than five thousand recording sessions, each session being around three hours.

BA: In the mid-1970s, when you first arrived here, where did you live and what was your sense of the city and the music industry?

AL: We arrived July 4 of 1976. We had to decide to either go to New York or come to Los Angeles. A year before, Henry Mancini found me in Cleveland and he asked me if I would be willing to come to Los Angeles to do a record. He wanted to feature me. So I said yes. And he says to me, "there's nothing I can do for you, the only people that can help you are your fellow musicians. And if they like you, they'll help you and you'll be fine." So in that recording session that he asked me to play and be the featured bass player, he introduced me to Lee Ritenour, Harvey Mason, Joe Sample, Emile Richards, Artie Kane, and Dennis Budimir, all [of] which were the top musicians in their fields, in the studios, and they had been for many years by then. They all said that if I came to Los Angeles that it would be great, that there was room for another bass player. But I was not able to come until a year later when my wife finished her internship. So when we came in '76, they all had beautiful bass players that they were very happy with and there was no work for me. Lee Ritenour had Anthony Jackson, Harvey Mason, Louis Johnson. Joe Sample had Robert "Pops" Popwell, and then everybody else had Chuck Rainey. So there was no work for me, and for two years, I was just (getting) by with my other job and jamming with this wonderful musician, Greg Mathison, and we would perform in different night clubs. And lo and behold, that created a wonderful two years where I was able to cement many things in my heart, including becoming born-again Christian and then all the doors became wide open. I went on the road with Olivia Newton-John. And then with Al Jarreau we did a European tour of six weeks where we made the recording of *Live in Europe with Al Jarreau*. And that was the official beginning of my full-time studio career in Los Angeles, after I moved here.

BA: During that period, were there any other Latin American musicians that you recall?

AL: There was a nightclub called "Virginia's," it was on Alvarado Street. And all the big deal Hollywood people would go dancing every night. Tito Puente performed there and Joni Mitchell would go and dance; she loved Latin music. There was a band called the Latin All Stars. Eventually Alex Acuña was the drummer. The leader of the band was the bass player Oscar López. [It was] like a Tito Puente type of (band), four horns, six in the rhythm section. And they would play in that nightclub, and then there was another nightclub on the corner of La Brea and Sunset that had Latin music every night. And then there was another Latin club on La Brea near Fountain. My life was such that going out dancing was not the thing that I did. When I traveled with Mongo Santamaría, we played lots of dances. On the stage I'm comfortable, but in the audience I was not comfortable. And then Joni Mitchell told me that one time, dancing in that nightclub on Alvarado Street, next to her somebody got knifed. So they were all dancing and somebody came and she saw the guy fall down, the blood and all that stuff. That's not my idea of a good time.

BA: What was it like for you here in LA? You've told us about your long friendship with Justo Almario since the early seventies, but did you have any other interactions with union musicians, other Latin musicians, African American musicians?

AL: Yes, I was a member of the union right away. The Latin musicians that I would hang with came later, Carlos Vega being one of the most beloved and respected drummer[s] of Cuban ancestry. It's hard to be brief because I have so many memories. Alex Acuña also came in 1977. In 1977, while I was working in Los Angeles at a nightclub called the Baked Potato with Greg Mathison. And the percussionist in that band was Manolo Badrena, who at the time had just left Weather Report. One night Alex Acuña came to visit and Greg had this rule that nobody was allowed to sit in that band period. Because the majority of people in the audience were musicians. And he says, "if I let anybody sit in everybody's going to want to, it's going to become a different kind of night." When Manolo saw Alex—they had been touring with Weather Report—Manolo leans over to Greg and says, "Man, Alex Acuña is here. Do you mind if he plays?" And Greg says "absolutely not!" And we were doing a complicated song written in 7/8, that in the middle of the 7/8 there was a bar of 7/4, which means two bars of seven, in a very unusual way. Something that you just don't walk in and sit in. So we started to play the song and Manolo yells, "Alex come!" And Manolo sits on the congas, stops playing timbales, tells Alex Acuña to take over the timbales. And that's the first time that Alex and I met. Literally the roof came off! Greg was very upset, because, he said, "this is a very difficult song and there's this policy; Manolo disobeyed me." And pretty soon the love of the music and the beauty was coming out. It was obvious that he had never heard his song played that well. The music was ridiculous! So then, one of the musicians that was eventually very close to Greg was Carlos Vega.

I want to tell you a story. When Fidel took over Cuba, Carlos's father had been the executive of General Electric in La Habana. So his father left and became a dishwasher in Miami, trying to raise money to be able to bring the rest of the family. So the best they could do was to get the family out of Cuba and they moved to Mexico City. And they stayed in a hotel, near downtown. They had to live there for about two years in that hotel. Carlos was [about] nine years old. And this is really emotional to me. He says you know, "it's amazing that you're from Mexico, because we lived in Mexico City in this hotel. Have you seen that hotel?" Absolutely, I would see it on my way to the Politécnico. He said, "eventually my father was able to bring us to the United States. But during that time I was very upset that we had to leave Cuba and that my father was gone. And there was a song called 'Cachito Cachito,' by Consuelo Velásquez." And he says, "my mom would sing that song every night for me to fall asleep." Thirty years later Carlos Vega came to Mexico City with Herb Alpert, and Consuelito Velásquez was the head of the composers association that my father was a founder of, and she threw a party in honor of Herb Alpert. At some point Carlos says to Consuelo, "you wrote the song that my mom would sing to me every night, to fall asleep." And Consuelito says to Carlos, "Let's get out of the party, I want you to sit next to me on the piano and I'm going to sing that song for you right now." She sang that song for him. Seven years later, Carlos died. So it's a very special connection between Cuba and Mexico. My father being a founding member of the composers association, my going to school, seeing this hotel where Carlos lived. We did endless numbers of recording sessions.

BA: So there were really only a handful of Latin musicians of this group that played back then.

AL: Yes. The people that really crossed over into the mainstream recording studio world were very few. People like Alex Acuña and Justo Almario, for instance, they are much more aware of the hardcore Latin musicians; even to this day that would play every night in all those nightclubs and they knew all the repertoire, all the songs. Ramón Stagnaro, a great guitarist from Peru, he learned how to play Cuban *tres,* so he would do all these gigs, backing up all these different people, all over Los Angeles. One night we went to hear him (and his band) downtown; they were opening for Armando Manzanero. In Cleveland I met a great jazz saxophone player. His name was Ernie Krivda. He traveled with Quincy Jones and they came to Los Angeles to do a rehearsal, and he says to me, "the Latin scene in Los Angeles was very different from the Latin scene in New York." Because the Latin scene in New York was more [focused on] traditional Cuban [music], whereas the Latin scene here was strictly geared for dancers. So the Palladium club and all these places that would house all these dances all the time, when they had to move into the small clubs, that's what they did. Eventually, Jorge Calandrelli came to town, from Argentina. He became very crucial to the recording world. Carlos Ríos, to this day, is still one of the "indispensables." Carlos Vega for a long time was the most sought-after drummer. He traveled for many years with James Taylor. Justo Almario right now is exploding, everybody wants him, they are all using Justo again. Alex Acuña he's a legend. Luis Conte, dear Lord, he's magical! I have a huge space in my heart for Luis.

BA: Did you have interactions with African American musicians?

AL: Yes, I always loved African American music. In fact, when I went to do my audition at Berklee, they asked me, "what is your favorite music?" And I said, "soul music." And the teacher says, "do you mind if we call it rhythm and blues? Because soul is too modern." It's still my favorite music. Joe Sample hired me to do a record of his called *Carmel.* Joe auditioned me and he says, "I'm looking for a Latin bass player but since you're from Mexico, we need to audition you to see if you are right for the material that we want to record." And then that became ten albums! I started to do all kinds of records with Joe and with the Crusaders. When Wilton Felder did his record, he also hired me to do a couple of albums with him. And the connection with The Crusaders became really important. During that time I met Greg Phillinganes. I've done countless recordings with Paul Jackson Jr. There was this producer named Frank Wilson, who was one of the original composers of Motown songs. So he would hire us and he would produce all of our records. We would do Peabo Bryson, Roberta Flack. So I was part of that whole scene . . . I was blessed to do one of the last recording sessions for TV, arranged and produced by J.J. Johnson, and 90 percent of the musicians were all African American.

BA: What does it mean to be a session musician?

AL: The whole thing started at Berklee. When I graduated from Berkeley in 1972, there was this impromptu gathering of all the people that were about to graduate, and the teacher said, "Be careful not to become a specialist, because if your specialty becomes out of fashion you're going be out of work." Very important advice. He says, "try to be as versatile as you can. That way you can either make a living playing live or doing jingles or writing, or session work, or touring." So I remember there was this guy, he was the king of disco music. And people would wait for him to be available to record. I mean if he was not available they would not call anybody else. And then when disco music was no longer "the thing," he was out of work. And nobody would call him to do anything else, which is bizarre. They did not believe that he was capable of doing anything other than disco. So that was a beautiful illustration: my teacher had spoken the truth. What it means to me to be a session player is literally to have a servant's attitude. You walk into the studio, and the question that you have to ask all the time is "what can I do with my instrument to help you achieve your vision?" And so, once the people, the producers and the artist, sense that from me, that I'm there to help them, not to impose my style or my approach. And pretty soon the calls start to multiply.

JK: What do you think Latin American musicians, such as Luis Conte, Alex Acuña, and you, have contributed, specifically with regard to American music?

AL: One night we were performing at the Baked Potato [on the Cahuenga Pass in Studio City] with Lee Ritenour, Harvey Mason, Dave Grusin on piano, and Patrice Rushen. The regular percussionist was not available, so Luis Conte came and played. And then we finished playing at one in the morning and Harvey Mason kept playing with Luis for another forty-five minutes, just the two of them. Harvey says, "man I cannot stop playing, the music feels so good playing with Luis. I cannot stop. So the two of them just kept going, and just playing groove. They were not soloing or anything but the music felt so strong. And I said to Luis, "Man how did you learn to do that?" And he says, "well, I'm Cuban 100 percent, what I play is Cuban. But I'm young enough to know how to adapt my playing to whatever style of music I'm called to do." And that's why he's qualified as a session player. Because if they ask him to play tango, rock, film music, jingles, whatever, he knows how to adapt his "Cubanness" to make the music feel as good as it possibly can. And to see Harvey just literally infected with Luis's groove so strong that he just couldn't stop, to me that's the epitome of being a session musician. Whatever you do to make the music feel good.

BA: You've recorded on thousands of sessions with so many different artists with many different styles. When you started doing this, did you think that you would be doing it today, twenty, thirty, forty years later?

AL: No. But I have to tell you, one of my mentors was this guy named Graham Young, a trumpet player who traveled with us and Henry Mancini, and he was the head of the music department of the schools in Burbank. He says to me, "Abraham, the most important thing that you need to remember is that there are over ten thousand musicians living in Los Angeles and every imaginable style that you want, you will find people that can teach you and show you how to play that style the best that it can be played. So rule number one: you are not indispensable. You need to carry yourself with that attitude that you know that you are not indispensable. The second thing is that the studio musicians of the 1920s in Los Angeles were people like Rostropovitch, Artur Rubinstein, Jascha Heifetz, Aaron Copland. Even the Gershwins came here to do experiments with recordings, Schoenberg, Hindemith." He says, "but they were just the studio guys, not realizing that sixty years later we were going to refer to them as these undisputed masters of music and that's how you need to treat each of the musicians that you meet. Treat them with utmost respect because you don't know, fifty, sixty years from now, they are going to be the Stravinskys. That's what it means to be a studio musician, to validate everything that exists, to know that any style that you're interested in is valid and that you can surround yourself with people that can teach you the secret of how to do certain things just right.

BA: How busy are you now?

AL: Well, we're going to be doing another animated film . . . we're going to be doing a beautiful week of double sessions, which have become rare, where they call us for an entire week, two sessions a day. I was able to do that for the film *Jurassic World,* and recently we just won a Grammy for *Inside Out.*

JK: Were there moments in your career in the United States where you faced feelings of exclusion or being locked out or not invited to sessions to play because of how you look?

AL: Well, yes, but in a sense it goes deeper than that. And I think part of the reason why I'm so positive is because people, when they found out that I was Mexican, they say, "no, no, no, no, we don't want no Mexican bass player." Then, they would try all kinds of things and eventually they would call me and they say, "man, we like the song now, but we thought you were going [to] give us a Mexican bass line." I say, "what I gave you was a Mexican bass line, but now that you met me and you're hearing it, it sounds to you like music, whereas you closed the doors when you found out that I was Mexican." So when people realize what they're really dealing with, they don't maintain that automatic hatred or "you're not welcome." Another time Joe Sample says to me, "Abraham, I come from Texas, man. And in Texas the bass player has to play the down beat, and you don't play the downbeat all the time, so don't give me no Mexican ideas." I went, "give me the downbeat." And then he says, "man, wow! when you play, I'm able to use the whole range of the instrument. Whereas when I play with other people I always have to play on the center of the instrument so that it can speak." And I says, "that's because I'm letting you take care of the downbeat."

JK: It's interesting to know that there might have been more discrimination on Mexicanness than on blackness.

AL: But also there would be discrimination because the Latin bass lines traditionally don't play the downbeat. For many Americans, and especially for R & B musicians, that's very uncomfortable. So that's why my teacher says to me, "Be versatile so that when you identify what's missing, what's making people uncomfortable, you can make the adjustments." Luis Conte told me a beautiful anecdote about the same thing. He was recording with Linda Ronstadt, and one of the great legends of Cuban music was playing, sitting next to Luis, and he kept saying, "something is wrong, something is wrong, something is wrong." I says, "what!?" He says, "I don't know." And it had to do with Luis. He was playing a typical bolero conga pattern, but what the guy wanted to hear was one instead of two beats, and when Luis did that, just casually, this older man says, "yeeah! now I can play."

JK: I remember you once told me about Johnny, that part of what made him so successful in rock in Mexico was that he actually brought in Caribbean and lots of calypso rhythms into Mexican rock for the first time. Could you tell us a little bit about how that happened?

AL: When they would do songs like "Melodía de Amor," which was a calypso, that was not a traditional part of what Mexican youth would like, and to watch thousands of Mexicans just doing this was so unusual because then he captured the hearts of the entire nation. And to have stadiums of people going, "cuando te conoci . . . " It was a different Mexico, like a Mexico that we had never seen before. As opposed to, you know, "Mexico lindo y querido." That's more what we were used to.

Q: And were those rhythms part of your musical upbringing with your father?

AL: Yes, because—because we are Caribbean, the word "Garifuna" means black Caribbean or black Carib. Carib being one of the tribes that when they came from Africa they mixed with the Arawak Indians outside the island of St. Vincent. So my parents belong to that particular ethnic group, and our upbringing was informed with those rhythms and that way of phrasing. Then my mother particularly would encourage my brother Johnny to not feel trapped by the actual rhythm of the melody in time, but to phrase with the lyricism that would really communicate the heart of what the words were saying. And pretty soon, people sing, "Pareces una rosa . . . ," instead of the way the Coasters did in this country. And I was a stickler for that. And I would say to him, "no, you have to do it rhythmically. Rhythm is the whole thing." And my mom would say to him, "no, the words, you have to communicate something that goes beyond the song." And she would insist that he had to feel something. And then my father, who traveled with my brother at the beginning of his career, and my father being a consummate guitarist/composer, he would infuse my brother with a deep respect for the audience. My brother really stole the hearts of Mexicans because my dad would always say to him, "they are the kings. They are the rulers, and you have to submit yourself to the calling of doing whatever it takes to help them forget their daily troubles." And so that became a mantra for my brother, and as a family we have a very special heritage. And rhythmically, in the very first calypso ever written in the Garifuna language was written by my dad. My mom went to school in Kingston, Jamaica. She had a degree as an executive secretary, so all those rhythms from Jamaica we were bombarded from both sides. And then my parents together wrote a song called "Kingston Girl."

JK: How do you talk about the impact of all the stuff you just mentioned? All the rhythms you heard growing up, your parents writing a song influenced by Jamaica, calypso, your brother, but also all these different geographies, Jamaica, Honduras, Mexico. The mixture of geography and style—is that something that you can tap into? Or is it more part of who you are?

AL: It is part of who I am. But when I listen to different recordings that I've done, and the way I approach different passages, for the lack of a better expression I have become a mosaic of all of the different musical influences that I've been exposed to. So when I play rhythm and blues, because my brother would receive all of this music from the American publishing companies, I am deeply affected by Motown, James Brown, Stax, all of these things moved me very very deeply. And when we moved to Cleveland, we met a Mexican family from Toluca, la familia Martínez, and I remember Mr. Martínez saying to me, "Abraham, you are the only Mexican I know that is deeply moved by a Mariachi, and by James Brown at the same time." And I felt that was a very eloquent way of putting it.

There is a feeling amongst Latin musicians—when, when we get together to talk—that I really don't understand. But I know that it has a lot to do with the hurt. They say, "Abraham, this is a Latin gig"—and they immediately start apologizing. "We know that you are more used to things being well organized, well run, this and that, but this is a Latin gig so it might start on time, it might not start on time, we might get paid whatever they say, we might not get paid whatever they say, we may have a dressing room, we might not have a dressing room." I always, I hurt for them, that they present it to me as "this is the way things have always been and this is the way things are—because it has the name 'Latin.'" And, I think, it's been a long time, this has to stop.

JK: I want to go back to something you said when you were talking about your dad, about the advice that your dad gave your brother, about being of service to the fans, and then when you were talking about how you think of yourself as a side player, as a session player . . . as a servant. It struck me as a really powerful thing, part of the kind of philosophy of the family in a way, the importance of service, which goes against stardom, and celebrity, and ego. I don't know if there was more you wanted to say, but it just struck me as a really beautiful thing that is clearly part of the Laboriel tradition.

AL: This is very emotional, because we're talking about how, as a family, the impact that we have with people that have hired us through the years. There is that legacy that says, "you really are not here for yourselves, or to take advantage of the people that hire you." That's when you really figure out how to be. We grew up in an atmosphere of genuine peace, you know. The amount of yelling in the house was not a lifestyle. We always gravitated toward resolving things in a way that made everyone participate and feel included. And not, "my decision has to go, and therefore everybody else has to live with whatever I decide." That said, I have to share with you guys that one time I met a musician from Israel who blew me away by sharing the saying that comes from the Klezmer musicians. That in Israel, they say, "he who plays music, prays twice." And that just . . . stayed with me forever, that when you are having an opportunity to play your instrument, it is a form of connecting with God, and bringing the people that are going listen into that connection. So you're praying not once, but twice.

JK: The one thing we didn't get to ask you and that we would love you to just elaborate a little bit, you went right from Mexico City to Berklee. In Mexico City were you not playing bass? Were you playing anything?

AL: I was playing rhythm guitar. That was part of what I did to prepare to go to the United States. I did these arrangements for my sister Ella. I arranged "Mrs. Robinson" and "Think," by Aretha Franklin.

JK: For your sister's record.

AL: Yes. Two years before I came to Los Angeles, conducting for Cesar Costa.

BA: How old were you?

AL: Around seventeen. I was rhythm guitarist. I was the house rhythm guitarist for Capitol Records in Mexico City.

JK: What other bands you were in?

AL: Los Profetas from Mexico City. Then when we left, they tried to keep the band going and some of them were from Tijuana. We did a theater play called *Dimension Sesenta y Seis,* written by Alejandro Jodorowski.

Q: What is your personal sense of the role of Latin America in the music of Los Angeles?

AL: Many things. I get so emotional, man. Growing up in Mexico, when I was six years old every year I would get asthma and I would have to spend two months with oxygen. And so, during those two months I could not go to school and I would listen to the radio and the only music that I liked was American music. So I was immersed in all kinds of American songs in a way that no Mexican musician or no Mexican youth was, you know. Not realizing all the miracles that were going to happen as a result of that. While I was a student in Berklee, I got an opportunity to do a job as a substitute, and when I went to the job, the trumpet player says to me, "Do you know 'Sweet Lorraine'"? And I said, "Yes, and I love 'Sweet Lorraine.'" He says, "You are the first Berklee musician that knows that song." You know! "How come you know 'Sweet Lorraine'?" I said, "because when I had asthma, when I was six years old, I would listen to this on the radio." And we played it, and the guy started to cry. And he says, "You're hired." So even though I was the sub, from that day on they hired me every weekend to do all these gigs. Then, I come to Los Angeles, recommended by Henry Mancini, Michel Legrand, and Johnny Mathis, and I am part of the mainstream of musicians. And I'm hanging with people like Shelly Manne, and Pete Candoli, and all these heavyweights. Plas Johnson. And finally Dave Grusin comes to me and he says, "You know, Abraham, do you realize that [at the beginning of the eighties] you are the most famous Mexican musician outside of Mexico?" And I said, "wow! What does that mean?"

And then eventually I got called by Manzanero to be part of Luis Miguel's *Romance* records. So they hired Ramon Stagnaro, Carlos Rios, Carlos Vega, and myself. And on piano they had Bebu Silvetti. And then when we saw that millions of Latin people that were living in the United States, that their lives got transformed, that Luis Miguel had to do a whole week at Radio City Hall theatre in New York as a result of what we had done, then I understood that the impact that the Latin community is having in this country cannot happen unless they have great music to listen to, and we are a part of that. We are an eternal part of that and what you guys are doing, you are championing and documenting what it took for all of us to leave our countries, some of us have come to Los Angeles, and to find or break the doors open for the Latin people to inform mainstream American music with what's in our hearts. So, you know, this is great.

INTERVIEW WITH JUSTO ALMARIO

Justo Almario was born in Sincelejo, Colombia. After touring with Mongo Santamaría as musical director, Almario came to Los Angeles to record and tour with Roy Ayers's Ubiquity. Since then, his saxophone, flute, and clarinet performances have appeared on hundreds of recordings by artists that include The Commodores, Freddie Hubbard, Jennifer Lopez, the Winans, Patrice Rushen, Luis Miguel, Charles Mingus, Chaka Kahn, and Cachao and on the scores of films like *Dirty Dancing, Happy Feet, Rio,* and *Sideways.*

We spoke to him at the USC Annenberg Research Park in Los Angeles in March 2016.

BA: Justo, tell us about your family history, the place you were born.

JA: I was born in Sincelejo, Colombia, [a small town] in the Caribbean coast of Colombia, near Cartagena. At the time that I was born, there was no running water, no electricity, so the people got entertained by musicians playing live. There was no radio, no record player, nothing like that. I remember my father was a conga player, and his band used to play a lot and they would take me as a little kid to watch them. Sometimes they would come and practice at my grandmother's, she had a big house and she would make a big pot of *sancocho* for all the musicians, with a bottle of rum. I was there as a little kid you know, watching all these things. That was a big influence on me, music was a very important part of my upbringing, that that was it, there was nothing else as far as entertainment in Sincelejo.

BA: When did you take up an instrument to play?

JA: Well, they said that since I was six months, or a year old, I already wanted to be a musician. I was always doing things. I actually started playing my father's drums, a little bit, the conga drums, and things like that. Many musicians that would come to the house played many different instruments. I always liked the saxophone, the clarinet, the little flute. When I was about four years old, they got me two instruments: a little flute called piccolo and they got me a short clarinet, in the key of E flat, so my fingers would reach. Since then, I loved it. I always dreamed with being a musician since I was four years old. And the other kids they used to call me "Justico" like little Justo: "Justico come over here, let's play *fútbol!*" I didn't want to go, I wanted to stay listening to the musicians, or the instruments, which is something weird when you think about it. I'm not normal, it's completely abnormal.

BA: You grew up during the glory days of Colombian music, with the big bands led by Lucho Bermúdez, by Pacho Galán. Did that have any influence on you?

JA: Of course it is because of Lucho Bermúdez. I'm related to him. When my mother, in this little town, when they heard that, when they saw that I really like music, they sent me to study with one of the family friends (that) already lived in Barranquilla. I was about six years old. And that friend, he was the uncle of Lucho Bermúdez. I was raised practically by this guy, Jorge Rafael Acosta. I remember Lucho Bermúdez coming to the house to visit when I was there, and they would say "come and listen to this little kid play his clarinet." I was always playing. So I knew Lucho Bermúdez really well and also Pacho Galán. Pacho Galán was from Barranquilla and I was in Barranquilla at that time with this family, studying. One of the sons, who is a great saxophone and clarinet player, was [a] member of the Pacho Galán Orchestra. They used to take me when they did the shows on the radio stations, to watch them play. Then, when I was ten or eleven years old, they were asking me to sit in with them to play. Because it was sort of a novelty. this little kid playing. "Justico is going to play for you." So I would play. They would play a *cumbia a porro,* or a fandango, and I just improvised solos with my clarinet on the radio broadcast.

BA: Let's fast-forward a few years. When did you start working in a band in Barran- quilla?

JA: Unfortunately, the people that I was living with in 1961, when I was twelve years old, they died. So I moved to Medellín, because my mother had moved there. And she had remarried and I became part of that household. Medellin had a lot of record companies, and great musicians. I started to study also with the musicians. There was a great teacher there named Gabriel Uribe, who was a great saxophone player, and I started playing, working, and studying with him. And then, there was a band that was made of Italian immigrants, that had come (to Colombia) in the '40s and they had a band called "Italian Jazz" in Medellín. They played American music and *cumbias*. It was a society band and I started playing and working with them too. I was fourteen, fifteen years old. And then, when I was fifteen, I moved to Bogotá, to be with the son of the guy who raised me, Alex Acosta, that used to play saxophone with Pacho Galán. He had his own big band in Bogotá. So I started to work and live with him, to be part of the scene that was happening in Bogotá, and recording. I remember that one of the recordings I did was with an accordion player named Lucho Campillo. They asked me to come and play in this one song. The song was "Rosa María se fue a la playa. . . ." We did the original. Later I found out that the song was being played everywhere in Mexico. That was when I was sixteen years old.

BA: What brought you to Los Angeles?

JA: Well, what took me to the United States is the fact that I fell in love with Jazz. Because of Alex Acosta, the saxophone player. He loved Cannonball [Adderley] and Charlie Parker. Sometimes, someone would bring him records, from America. And when I was about fourteen, fifteen, he shared those records with me and I had those recordings and it totally changed my life. When I heard Cannonball Adderley play the saxophone, it sounded like a little bird that was released from the cage and said, "wow!" Because I had never heard something [like that]. The music of Colombia is very rhythmic and I loved it a lot, but never at that level of freedom for the saxophone to play. So since then I said I want to go to the US to study. And then I had an opportunity when I was about seventeen years old. There was a band formed in Bogotá called Cumbia Colombia that came to the US to do some shows as a cultural exchange and we went to Miami and played. At that time they gave us resident visas to come over here. It was like, wow! I'm talking about 1966 . . .

BA: So it was sort of the way Cubans were once treated in the US. You arrive and automatically you get residency.

JA: Yeah. So, eventually I wound up in Boston, Massachusetts, at the Berklee College of music. And then, when I was finishing my college education, I received a call from Mongo Santamaría to come and join his band. He was living in New York at that time. In Boston, they had a very important jazz club called the Jazz Workshop. And they would bring bands, all the famous bands, Miles Davis, Thelonious Monk, the Jazz Messengers, Mongo Santamaría and his band, to play at the Jazz Workshop, and they would stay there for a whole week, Tuesday to Sundays. On Sundays they would do a matinee. So Mongo called me one time, and he said: "Justo, I'm here in town playing at the Jazz Workshop tonight, the saxophone player couldn't come, but they recommended you. Can you come and play with me tonight? The other guy will come tomorrow." I already knew who Mongo was! I said, "yeah!" I couldn't believe it! I said, "yeah, I'll be there." He called me around five; I was there at seven. We played that night, a lot of people were there. Everything went OK. And Mongo at the end of the night asked me: "Can you play the whole week?" And I said, "sure!" After the whole week he said, "man I'm playing in Atlanta in three weeks, can you come with me?" I said, "well I have to arrange my schedule with the school and everything." So I did. Eventually one thing led to the next and he said: "Justo why don't you move to New York, to be part of my band?" And I did, eventually when I finished school. That was in 1971.

Eventually, I became his musical director and I would do arrangements and compositions and I recorded with Mongo on, maybe, eight to ten LPs. Some of them included my arrangements and my compositions. He was very busy at that time. [Back then] musicians would travel to places like Chicago, Atlanta, and play in a club for six, seven days, and stay at that city for that week. And we'll play three shifts per night . . . But on Sundays we will play a matinee and then the three sets, so there was a lot of playing!

I stayed in New York with Mongo until 1978. In that era, Fania Records was booming. Everything was over there: Willie Colón, Hector Lavoe, the salsa scene was happening. And I was part of that because we used to record for Fania, too, with Mongo. In the studio I did things with Barreto and Pacheco, Ismael Rivera, Tito Puente, and Machito's Orchestra. They used to play in New York at the Palladium Dancing Club every night. Sometimes they had to do two gigs: one in Brooklyn, one in Queens, and then the other one in Manhattan, at the Palladium club. So the saxophone player . . . would play with them, but sometimes they couldn't do [all the gigs] so they would call me: "Justo, can you play a show with me, or with Machito, if you're in town?" Yeah! I would go and do those things. That was [such a] great, great experience for me. And I also started to work with jazz musicians . . .

BA: You mean, straight-ahead jazz.

JA: Straight-ahead jazz yeah. I started to work with Freddy Hubbard, the trumpet player. One time Charles Mingus wanted to do a project based on *cumbias* and someone told him, "call Justo, because he's from Colombia." So he called me and I was able to help him and gave him some LPs that I had such as Los Gaiteros de San Jacinto, Lucho Bermúdez—all those for him to listen—and he returned the albums. I don't know if you ever heard [his album] it's called . . . *Cumbia Fusion*. I helped him with that. So, it was very good.

Then, I started working with Roy Ayers, the bass player, and we were recording for Polydor Records. And he became really popular. The name of his band was Ubiquity and he signed this group to Elektra Asylum. And Elektra Asylum was based here in Los Angeles. We did *Vibrations, Everybody Loves the*

Sunshine, all of those albums. So we came over here to do them. I wound up staying here and I loved it. I've been here since 1978 now.

BA: That's the reason you ended up moving here?

JA: Well yes, but also because of my wife, she's from here, and she has family here. So we moved and we had my oldest daughter, one daughter already. So it was better for her to be near her family. I was traveling, and I was doing all kinds of work. So, we moved here and stayed. I was really happy that I did. In the beginning I wasn't too happy because I was used to the New York energy, walking in Manhattan with my saxophone at three in the morning, man! And all of a sudden I see Joe, the saxophone player, walking too, and we would take a taxi and go together [to] uptown Manhattan. Something like that . . . But then I really love Los Angeles and I love California. It's a very important musical city and there's nothing like the weather over here. Because I have traveled all over the world. That's the blessing of my life, being a musician. And people often ask, "of all the cities that you've traveled, what's your favorite?" And I say here, really. Because, right now it's March, and, look, the sun is out. If we were to be in the French Riviera right now, it would be cold and grey. The French Riviera is a beautiful place. I've been to Nice, Cannes, all those places, and it's beautiful, in the summer, but not now! Over here it's like this all year!

Q: What was the music scene like in Los Angeles at the time, as a musician, but also as a Colombian, as a Latin American in LA. What was the scene like?

JA: Well, it was quite different than New York. At that time it didn't have, as I said before, that energy. I think you didn't feel that energy because of the . . . geographical aspect of the city. In New York everything is right there. Here, you have to drive to get to another place and everything over here at that time was closing at 1 AM at night. In New York it's all night. Remember I was coming from the Fania boom. Everything was happening! . . . When as a Latino musician you came over here, and nothing like that was happening over here. But the reason I was over here is because I came as a member of this band. So that kept me busy. I was touring with Roy. It wasn't really until maybe the latter part of 1979 that I got a call from Freddy Hubbard, the trumpet player, to come and be part of his group. He was living here. So then, all of a sudden, I started to make living just staying here, playing here. And then sessions started to happen. I reconnected with Abraham Laboriel; we had met in Boston. The two of us were the two Latinos that were in Boston, at that time, at Berklee in 1969. There was no one else. That was it. And when we saw each other: "Man, you talk like me and I talk like you!" So we've been friends ever since. When we reencountered here, we started to share things. One other thing that happened is that he had started a band called Koinonia. He asked me to be part of the band. That was very important, because, through that, I started to meet other people and make other connections [that helped me] to be involved on sessions.

BA: Tell us about that world. When was your first studio session?

JA: Well, I remember that one of the first sessions that I was called to do was done at the A&M studios, on La Brea, and it was for that group called the Commodores [in 1981].

BA: That group!

JA: I did a session and, from then on, I started to do not only that but some TV shows.

BA: Such as . . .

JA: Let me see, I have to think: *Dear John,* I think one called *Amen, Amen, Equal Justice.* And then TV commercials. Then I started to do some soundtracks. I play in the soundtrack of that movie called *Dirty Dancing.* That was one of the first ones that I did.

BA: Do you remember a story from the sessions? Anything that you remember about working with musicians and what they were asking you to do.

JA: [In New York] we used to do the recordings live. Everybody was playing together at the same you know. When what happened over here, recordings that I did, they already had the rhythm section recorded. And then they have the horns overdubbed. So you needed to play with the rhythm section and also you need to have what they called the click. Which is like the metronome, what they give you to keep the time. And for me you know I always was playing with the drummers. So it was a new thing for me to get used to. Because when they would ask me to play a little solo over here, I would play and the click would happen. And they said, "but how come you stopped?" And I said "because I'm trying to leave the room for the click to groove. And they said, "No, no, but the click is not going to be in the album!

   Such a different world, the world of doing recordings where you're asked, "What would you play here?" For instance, the composer will say, "let me hear what you would play with this type of thing. I like that, yeah! Let's keep it, let's keep it, OK"? They never say, "this idea was given by such and such guy. No, no, no forget about it."

BA: No credit?

JA: No, no credit. I have to tell you something about the scene over here in general, and in Hollywood as a player, as a Latino: it is hard. Because doors are not as open for you to work. I have opportunity to work. You can see my résumé, and I've done things. But it's been because the people that hired me are the composers that know me, like Dave Grusin. These people know me so they say, "No, I want Justo to come and play." But in this system they have what is called contractors. And contractors, they have their people already, that they want them to play. So for a person of color to get in, this is not easy. This is a system of Apartheid, I can say that, in Hollywood, when you're coming to do a recording. There are a lot of recordings being done, but not all the time do they include people of color . . . Whenever they would have a Latin act, they would call me to play, with Julio Iglesias, El Puma. But when they had Frank Sinatra or . . . No! . . . And I think I was as capable of playing (with him too). So they had me stereotyped.

BA: From the time that you got here?

JA: Yeah, yeah.

BA: . . . to the present?

JA: Yeah, to the present. Even more so in the present now.

Q: What's your experience working with African American musicians?

JA: If it weren't for them, I would've probably really been pinpointed to just work on Latin music. But these people included me. Right now I work with Kenny Burrell's Jazz Quintet. I play with his big band too. So, that was very positive. I also met a saxophone player named Frank Foster in New York, who included me in his band, and became also a mentor for me . . . I felt welcomed by African Americans. One time we went to Africa with the Roy Ayers Band, which was composed by African Americans. And we played with Fela Kuti. He was the opening act, and we were the headliners. But check this out: Our first concert in Lagos, Nigeria, was supposed to start at 8 PM at a stadium. And Fela Kuti and his band, which had ten dancers, ten female singers, six brass musicians, six percussionists. . . . It was like thirty people on stage. And all of those ladies were his wives. We were the headliners and we were waiting in the dressing room, to play a set. And it's eight o'clock and nothing. The audience is there, nine o'clock, nothing, ten o'clock nothing. And at eleven o'clock Fela Kuti starts playing but each of his songs is like a story, each song lasts an hour. We didn't know that. We weren't aware of it. We never heard of such a thing . . . So he started at eleven. It was three in the morning and he was still playing! So by the time we played it was like four in the morning.

So the next day—because we did like four weeks of touring—we said to him, "Fela, starting tomorrow we're going to open the show." And that's the way we did it. And it was, it was amazing! We did a recording with Fela too. That's one of my highlights, actually. It's called *Two Thousand Blacks Got to Be Free*. Fela played piano and saxophone a little bit. So there's a part where the two of us are trading saxophone lines. Yeah, myself and Fela. We recorded in Lagos.

BA: I remember something you said to me in an interview, many years ago: Americans think that Latin music is only Cuban music.

JA: When we say the term "Latin jazz," for instance. When you hear Latin jazz, the rhythms that are used is Afro Cuban music. And I love Cuban music. But if you're going to call it "Latin," we need to include the music from Colombia, Argentina, Brazil, Peru, Mexico. It's so rich. I've been doing arrangements to feature all of that and I have an ensemble here in Los Angeles, that we perform. When we do a Latin jazz concert, we don't play Cuban rhythms. We play

Colombian rhythms, some Peruvian rhythms. We even do a little bit of "Son Huasteco." Because it's so rich. And that's what I can contribute to bring this thing to people to [show] that it's not just one thing. Of course it started like that. It's started with Chano Pozo, Dizzy Gillespie, Mongo Santamaría. They brought the rhythms. And at that time they were calling it Cubop, which means Cuban and Bebop. But then they started calling it Latin jazz, and they started excluding all those other rhythms. And we have such a mine of rhythms that come from all the countries in Latin America. Mexico has so many grooves man! *Sones, huapangos,* music of Veracruz, so rich, so important!

I always loved Mexican music. And I'll tell you why. At one point in Latin America, the movies that we would see, the record companies that were popular, were all from Mexico. The Spanish-language movies all were made in the studios Churubusco, Estudios Azteca. With all those great actors: Cantinflas, Los Hermanos Soler, Pedro Infante, Jorge Negrete, all of them. And the music was amazing! I remember hearing all that. Today in Colombia we have mariachis! There are mariachis all over the world, I think because of that influence.

BA: In any of the recordings that you've done over the years, were you able to incorporate Latin American rhythms into the music? For example, with Roy Ayers.

JA: I did, actually. And I did with Mongo. There's an album that we did for Fania Records, where we recorded a *cumbia,* "Cumbia Típica." I have Mongo playing *cumbia*-style. He'd never done it before, and he loved it.

BA: It's interesting that there is this idea that you guys are putting in these secret codes.

JA: Exactly! Because of all these things, all these roots. And that's the thing that's amazing because those are the things that we want to share with everyone. We want to share with the studios over here. Imagine when the music of movies. It's getting a little better now [with music] from South America! In the sound-tracks sometimes they use music that sounds Mexican.

BA: As a Latin American immigrant in the United States, is that a different perspective than a US-born Latino playing in the music world?

JA: Definitely. Because as a Latin American playing in Los Angeles, I have more direct [connection to] that culture. You know what I mean? That I can share directly. Because I'm fresh off the boat. I'm supposed to compete with someone who is a Latino born here, that's maybe second-generation, third-generation?

BA: Yes, there's a significant difference. At the moment you arrived in this country you brought your "spirit" from Colombia.

JA: Yeah. I brought that cadence, that is very important, musical cadence; that's part of the vocabulary and that it's been appreciated and accepted.

INTERVIEW WITH PAULINHO DA COSTA

Paulinho Da Costa was born in Rio de Janeiro. One of the world's most sought after percussionists, he has played on over two thousand recordings and with over nine hundred artists. In addition to his solo albums for jazz legend Norman Granz, he can be heard on recordings by Dizzy Gillespie, Sérgio Mendes, Earth, Wind & Fire, Quincy Jones, Rod Stewart, George Benson, Barbra Streisand, Aretha Franklin, and Madonna, as well as on Michael Jackson's *Thriller* and *Off the Wall*. He has appeared on over 150 TV and film scores, from *Ally McBeal, Sex and the City,* and *Knots Landing* to *Purple Rain, Flashdance, Footloose,* and *Selena.*

We spoke to him at the USC Annenberg Research Park in Los Angeles in August 2016.

BA: Tell us about growing up in Brazil. Was music part of your family?

PDC: In Brazil, wherever you go, in every neighborhood, there is rhythm and singing. My mother used to love to sing. My father sometimes played accordion for fun. I used to always listen to the radio and loved tapping on tables.

BA: Which instrument did you first pick up and why?

PDC: My first instrument was the *pandeiro,* which I practiced seriously for hours. I would listen to the rhythms from diverse musical cultures, like African, Puerto Rican, Cuban, as well as funk and other rhythms played on the marimba. Then, I would play them on the *pandeiro.*

BA: When did you join the Escola de Samba?

PDC: I was about five years old. I was already playing enough to be part of this small group called "Mirim," which is the group consisting of kids that are part of the Escola de Samba. Our samba school was Portela. There were many talented kids there and about three to four small groups. We used to travel all around Brazil to play and it was very helpful for the kids' musical formation.

BA: How did you eventually go to the music industry?

PDC: I used to dance. I combined the rhythms of the *pandeiro* with dancing styles of *frevo* and samba. Some of the big promoters who came to see us were impressed by what I was doing and invited me to play at events. Things started to progress from there. I was considered a *ritmista,* a percussionist. The Escola de Samba would also go to professional events. From there I was invited to participate in recordings, festivals, and to perform in different countries. So, I became a professional musician.

BA: How did you end up leaving Brazil and coming to LA?

PDC: We were invited to participate in a festival in Russia. I was on stage playing and dancing and there were members of the Soviet Ballet in the audience in Moscow. After the show, they came to talk to me and offered me a dance scholarship to study in Russia, because the way I was doing the *frevo* was unique. I was honored but I couldn't accept the invitation. I was sixteen at the time and wanted to see the world and to learn more rhythms. In Brazil, people always encouraged me to go to the US. Then, Sérgio Mendes made me a good offer to join his group. At that time, my wife had just had our first baby, so I thought it was a good opportunity to come to the US. I had always admired the jazz and the Latin music scene in the US, so I was excited for this experience. I arrived in Los Angeles on January 4, 1973.

BA: What was the music scene like in LA?

PDC: I met many great players. All the Latin and jazz players embraced me fully. It felt like I had known them for a long time.

JK: Were you surprised how popular Brazilian music was in LA?

PDC: I never expected it to be so popular. I was taken by how our music was so well received. The music industry was powerful in promoting it. They promoted all the greats, including Tom Jobim, João Gilberto, and Baden Powell.

BA: Who connected you with this long list of musicians?

PDC: The first album I recorded in LA was with a group called the Miracles; I played on their song "Love Machine," which was number one on the charts for a long time. Then, Freddie Perren, their producer from Motown, asked me to record with Minnie Riperton. When you do a number one song, it opens doors and the opportunity came for me to work with Dizzy Gillespie. This was in 1975 at RCA studios. Dizzy became the main connection between me and Norman Granz, who produced his album *Bahiana*. Norman and I really got along well. Then, Quincy Jones found my number somehow and called me to work on *The Wiz*. From then on, I played with him on everything, including Michael Jackson's *Thriller*. I don't know why, out of all the artists, this was happening to me. I was working like crazy. I got so many work offers that I had to turn down many of them and referred other musicians I wanted to help. There were many percussionists around but I was very lucky.

JK: In LA, were you on a work visa?

PDC: I was on an H1 work visa then. I had an exclusivity agreement with Sérgio Mendes. In 1976, when I decided to pursue other music opportunities, I gave Sérgio notice and then I was ready to sign a contract with Norman. We hired a lawyer to finalize my immigration status and I got my green card through his label, Pablo Records. Eventually I got my citizenship and my dual passport. The recording industry was very nice to me, and I can't love LA more than I do.

BA: How many recordings did you do on Pablo?

PDC: Three solo albums. Norman usually liked structure but he gave me freedom on those recordings. The logo of Pablo Records is a Pablo Picasso design. Many people don't know that. That's why the label is called Pablo. Norman and I became really close friends. He used to come over to my place and I would

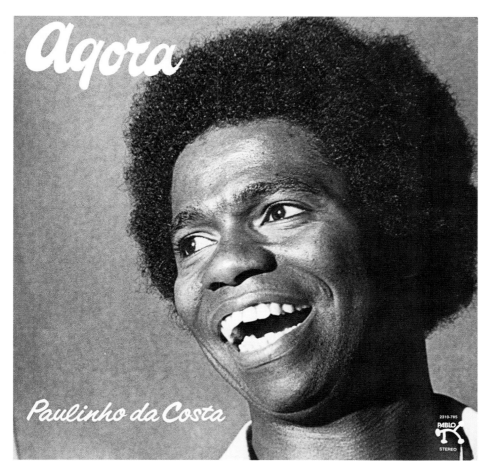

Paulinho Da Costa, *Agora*, Pablo Records, 1977, Idelsohn Society for Musical Preservation Archive.

cook *feijoada* and teach him how to dance. Once when we were in London with him, he invited us to his apartment and all the walls were covered with Picasso paintings and drawings. I asked him if he was worried about theft. He said: "Don't worry! All the good ones are at the museum!" Norman knew all the Latin musicians, but he'd say to me, "Paulinho, you've got something special on your plate." He really cared about me and I truly cared about and respected him. Lalo Schifrin was also a dear friend whom I admired and who taught me a lot. With the label, I also recorded and coproduced *Ella Abraça Jobim* with Ella Fitzgerald, and I worked with Joe Pass and Milt Jackson.

BA: I am curious about the seventies when you recorded all these disco songs.

PDC: During that time I didn't even have time to sleep! I recorded with tons of amazing artists, like Donna Summer, Tavares (for *Saturday Night Fever*), Michael Jackson, Madonna, Rod Stewart ("Da Ya Think I'm Sexy?"), Quincy Jones and many others. They were putting all the Latin stuff into the music, so it gave me a great opportunity to be a part of these records.

BA: Tell us specifically about instances where you feel that the sound of the percussion and rhythm that you provided influenced the way the song came out.

PDC: Many of these projects, from jazz, to disco, to rock 'n roll used Latin rhythms. American artists accepted me because I always put my flavor in there by assimilating many rhythms. I'd spice it up with Mexican, Cuban, and African textures, and would break the disco rhythm with some Latin ones. With Earth, Wind & Fire, I had a metal spoon, which I played in a unique way on "Brazilian Rhyme." On "Serpentine Fire," I used African cowbells against the groove. Even today, members of Earth, Wind & Fire tell me that I made that song come together, so that means a lot. I also played on "I Will Survive" with Gloria Gaynor, with the Jacksons on so many of their great songs, on Lionel Richie's "All Night Long (All Night)," with the Commodores, Kenny Rogers, Kenny Loggins, and the list goes on.

JK: You can take the music of the seventies and one thing they have in common is YOU. Unlike other instruments, because rhythm is a language that holds everything together, you became the thread that pulled everything together. You can tell musical history through the artist. But you can also tell it from the back end, from the perspective of the session player. How does that change musical history? Suddenly Brazilian music is no longer this marginal exotic sound but at the center of virtually everything that people are listening to. How did you see yourself? Were you a session player? A contracted worker? A collaborator?

PDC: I always felt like I was invited to be part of a project. I never felt like a musician sitting in a corner because they treated me with so much respect. I think they inspired me to raise myself to a higher level. I felt I was collaborating. While I was there, I was doing the job, but in retrospect, I realize how important my job was. I'm deeply grateful for everything, and, even now, I still think sometimes about whether I am good enough and can do better. But what is the most rewarding is that percussionists tell me that the reason they play is because they listened to me. That is the best compliment that no money can buy.

JK: In the late seventies you collaborated with Earth, Wind & Fire, Milton (Nascimento) was working with Wayne Shorter, George Duke was getting into Brazilian music. So what was happening then in LA?

PDC: LA is a mecca for the recording industry. We were lucky and our time was right. I did so many projects with Earth, Wind & Fire and George Duke. LA was the perfect place for it. Everything was happening here, the queen of soul, Aretha Franklin, Gladys Knight, Natalie Cole, Deniece Williams, Bill Withers, the Crusaders, Joe Sample, the Emotions, George Benson, Bonnie Raitt, Barry

Manilow, B.B. King, Barbra Streisand, David Sanborn, and so on. I played with all of them. Pop, rock, jazz, R&B, country and Latin, it all happened at the same time. Brazil's flavor and color was in there because they all listened to the music.

BA: Música popular brasileira (MPB) was huge and American musicians were tuned in.

PDC: Stevie Wonder listened to Brazilian music and he actually wanted me to be in his band.

JK: How were you paid for your sessions? Did you receive royalties?

PDC: You have a fee established by the union. When you become recognized you can charge double, triple, or special scale. Many times, there would be a song, and I would suggest other ways to play the rhythm or do the rhythmic arrangements. And, many times I was not credited for that. If your name is not on a contract or on the liner notes specifically for that song, you won't get any performance rights or royalties. I consider myself very organized and my wife, Arice, who manages me, has a lot to do with that (we have been together for forty-six years and are a team). But it is still difficult to get credit for every piece of music that you're on.

JK: Could you talk about the meeting between Afro-Brazilian and African American music. Was that a natural fit?

PDC: It was a natural fit. As an example, Maurice White of Earth, Wind & Fire used Brazilian and Latin grooves. In my case, there were so many that I worked with: Lamont Dozier, Barry White, Miles Davis, Ray Parker Jr., and Jimmy Jam and Terry Lewis. Plus, many other African American artists, composers, producers, and drummers, like James Gadson, Ndugu Chancler, and will.i.am, appreciate Brazilian sounds. The rhythms, the songs, the dances came from the same roots. African American music, the Brazilian groove, and most importantly "the feeling" are very much connected.

BA: Tell us of one memorable session that is close to your heart.

PDC: Looking back, what I did on "(I've Had) The Time of My Life," which was part of the soundtrack to *Dirty Dancing*, was very special and they told me that I saved the song. And I did get credit! The track became huge, and won a Grammy, Oscar, and Golden Globe.

JK: Did you ever face discrimination based on where you're from or what you look like?

PDC: Believe me, I have been very aware of what people of color have gone through and still go through. Things need to change. But I never felt any major discrimination, maybe one or two bad looks here and there, and occasional disrespect, but no major incidents. I always fight for the respect of musicians. Norman Granz taught me that. He always took us through the front doors!

BA: How much do Brazilians know about your contribution to American music?

PDC: The music industry knows. The public does not know as much. For example, Madonna wanted the title of the song "The Beautiful Island" to be in Spanish, and she asked me how they said that in Spanish. So I asked our good friend, Manuel, who is from Mexico. This was pre-Internet, so he also gave us the correct pronunciation: "La Isla Bonita." Madonna later signed a picture for him.

JK: Do you think the song "Don't Stop 'til You Get Enough" is a Brazilian song?

PDC: I don't think it is a Brazilian song, but there is a lot of Latin influence in it. You hear the samba feel in it, also some Latin and pop. It is a mix of musical cultures and one of my favorites.

JK: Would you say that the role of Latin music in the music that comes out of postwar US has been properly credited?

PDC: Well, we're trying and we're going to get there.

JK: The Escola de Samba is a living tradition, but much of your career has been playing nontraditional music. Tell us about tradition vs. modernity.

PDC: Tradition is everything. That is the foundation. The Escola de Samba is even more organized than when I was with them. They gave me foundation and they taught me history—the themes become a history school. Each guy in the Escola played one instrument and if you were not good, you would be out. The music has to be part of your culture. Never forget where you come from. New styles of music are great and important, but traditional rhythms will last forever.

INTERVIEW WITH ALEX ACUÑA—DRUMMER, PERCUSSIONIST

Alex Acuña was born in Pativilca, Peru. After working as a percussionist with Pérez Prado, Diana Ross, and Weather Report, Acuña became a Los Angeles session fixture, playing on albums by Joni Mitchell, Paul McCartney, Ella Fitzgerald, Chick Corea, Whitney Houston, Milton Nascimento, Carlos Santana, Yellowjackets, and Herbie Hancock, among many others. He has recorded on over three hundred film scores for composers such as James Newton Howard, Bill Conti, and John Williams.

We spoke to him at his home studio in Van Nuys, California, in May 2016.

BA: Where did music start for you?

AA: I come from a family of musicians. My father was born in the north coast of Peru, in Chiclayo, in the state of Lambayeque. He was the first musician of his family. His teacher taught him music for a couple years. Then he had to work two years and give some kind of payback to the teacher. That's how he became a musician. Then he really went on his own, playing more instruments. Then he became a teacher himself, teaching (music) in high schools. I come from a (family of) eleven children: six boys, five girls. I'm the number ten, the last of the boys. The five musician (brothers), older than me, studied different instruments with him: piano, sax, trumpet, trombone, flute, guitar, drums. My father was able to teach everything. [He was] very intelligent, one of the most accomplished musicians I've ever known.

His name is Fernando Neciosup. That's what my [real] last name is. Acuña is my mother's name, Victoria Acuña. So it's Alejandro Neciosup Acuña. When I came here it was changed. Because here everybody is Bob Hope, Tom Jones, things like that. So, [that's why] Alex Acuña.

I was the only one that he never taught music to, because my mother told him, "you already have five musicians." I was the youngest one. But every time they rehearsed I was under the table listening. Then, when they left for a break, I played. They wanted me to be a pianist. Later on, I played piano, trumpet, but percussion called me: the touch of the instrument, the skin; [not like it is today, made with plastic], wow! the bongos, congas, *cajón!*

BA: How old were you when you felt that calling?

AA: Three years old. To make a long story short: one of my brothers . . . left with his girlfriend. He was the drummer and they had Friday, Saturday, and Sunday gigs. By then I was already ten [years old]. They said: "who is going to play the drums?" I was always around them; they never talk to me because they thought I was "little Alex." I said come on. They said, "We never saw you play before. Daddy never showed you anything." I said, "You're right, because my Mom didn't want me to be a musician, she wanted me to be a carpenter or a mechanic, or not a musician." They said: "you sure you can play?" I said, "yeah." That was the first, the last, and only audition that I've done in my entire life. It was with my family.

By age five, six, seven years old, I listened to the radio: Oscar Avilés, Chabuca Granda, just master musicians. Pérez Prado, Sonora Matancera . . . Duke Ellington, Miles Davis, John Coltrane. So when they auditioned me, I knew all the songs by Pérez Prado. And they said, "wow! How do you know these songs? I've been here listening to your rehearsals, and when you leave these instruments I play everything here. And when my mom is not home, I even play more. But I'm a natural, I told them. It's natural for me. So they hired me.

My brothers moved to Lima . . . and when I was about fifteen, sixteen, they started calling me. Because they used to come home [to visit] and play with me, and they saw that I was growing up. They would say, "you should come to Lima!" I said, "yes, but I'm taking care of my mom. I'm paying for the rent, I'm paying for the telephone." By age twelve, I had become a financial supporter of my mother, my two sisters, and a nephew. That's when I was playing with the local bands.

BA: What kind of music where you playing?

AA: In those days, with my band, La Orquesta de los Hermanos Neciosup, the Tropical Boys, that was the name of the band, the orchestra. We played everything. We played Cuban music. We played jazz, big band, Glenn Miller, Ray Conniff. So people danced because Peruvians, they dance to everything. They dance to Peruvian music but they also dance salsa, mambo, and they dance swing, rock 'n roll. I used to listen to Bill Haley, all that. We played all kinds of music. It was for me a great training, to really appreciate everything, every style, every genre. And it's been like that all my life and still is, and it will be.

BA: Once you moved to Lima, how did you connect with Pérez Prado?

AA: When I was eighteen, Pérez Prado came to Lima. He didn't audition me. They recommended me for his band. He says, "I'm going to take the whole band to do a South American tour, but I want to take a good drummer." Even in those days, even before Colombia, Peru played better Latin music. In South America, Peru was the one that played Latin music. Cubans were living there. That's why he came to Peru. He said he wanted to start his tour in South America, [and go to] Colombia, Venezuela, Argentina, Chile, Brazil, Peru. So he went to the manager of the band, you know, the contractor, and said, "I want to take him." I said, "take me where?" Take you on a tour South America and then he wants to take you to the United States. I laughed. He says, "Why are you laughing?" I said, "he's going to take me to the USA? I wish I could." He said, "Would you like to come?" I said, "let me tell you something. The best drummers in the whole world are from United States." I start mentioning Buddy Rich and so on. Because I listened to everybody and I read who's playing drums. Dizzy Gillespie's drummers, Miles Davis's drummers, J. J. Johnson's drummers. I said: "You want to take me to United States?" That sounds funny. I told him. He said, "you're right, how do you know all of that?" I said, "I import records from the USA. There's a place here where they import the records that I want. I listen to the radio and I know what record and what music I like. So I order them." "Wow, you are very well informed." I said, "yes, I am very well informed." "You're right," he said, "but all those drummers that you mention, they don't have the feeling that you have for my music. That's why I want to bring you to play with me to United States." So that's how I came [to the USA in] 1964 and I came with a green card, a permanent resident. I never had a working or a touring visa. I came when we went to sign the contract. My parents signed because I was a minor. My tour with him in the United States was before we did the South American tour: ten months here in the United States, all over. We started in Las Vegas and from there Arizona, Colorado, New York, Chicago, Washington, DC, Philadelphia, and we came back. Ten months touring the United States.

BA: After leading a band in Puerto Rico, what made you come to the US?

AA: I went to New York, to check things out, the scene and everything. The first thing I felt was that New York was too big for me. I already had been in New York, when I was in Puerto Rico; I went to record a lot with RCA Records. But I say when I say too big, [I meant] it was too big musically. I noticed that they would box me in to a Latin musician and I don't play one genre. Next, I went to Atlanta, and five, six months later, we land at the Playboy club here in Los Angeles, on Avenue of the Stars. So we got a gig here for one, two months. I'm going to check out Los Angeles. I was here ten years ago; now I'm going to check it out again. Again, too big musically; I wasn't ready for Los Angeles; I said they're going to box me again. I'm going to play just Latin music. So I had some friends in Las Vegas; I called them. They said, "Alex, come over, man!"

So I found somebody to cover for me in the band, at the Playboy club, and I left for Las Vegas on April 1974. A month later I'm playing in Las Vegas at the International Hilton. That's where Ann Margret, Elvis Presley, and everybody [were performing], and I played with all of them: Diana Ross, the Temptations. In Las Vegas I was only playing in that orchestra, at the International Hilton, for one year. One day, the main guy from Weather Report called me, because they heard about the New York sessions I did. He said, "are you the percussionist, Peruvian, drummer that lives in Las Vegas?" And they invited me to play, no audition either. I went and started playing. That was my new career . . . I stayed with Weather Report for three years, 1976 to 1978.

Later I came here [Los Angeles], I bought a house, brought my family, and I soon as I got here, I started working on recordings, drums and percussion, and playing in movies with Lalo Schifrin. Lalo Schifrin called me and said, "Alex Acuña is here!" I started working on movie soundtracks and doing albums . . . The recordings here, I start recording at ten in the morning and I end recording every day at midnight, every single day, even on Sundays. I'm talking from 1978 to 1983.

I played with everybody. I had no time to practice, but playing with Herbie Hancock and Chick Corea, Wayne Shorter, and make records with Whitney Houston, Blondie, Barbara Streisand, you name it: movies, composers, jingles, . . . television, I mean, so much music. The reason they hired me was to play every kind of fusion, some pop, a little bit of disco, but mainly percussion, because a lot of the Latin percussionists, they don't read music that well. I was privileged to be able to read music because I studied in a conservatory in Puerto Rico. So I know classical, and when you play in the movie soundtracks, it's eighty musicians with a conductor and you have to know when to land. You got to understand conducting. That's what has sustained my life in California. The reason why it was difficult to get together with you guys is because I've been so busy. From November till now I've done eighteen movies. And a lot of those movies went to the Oscars. Before, it used to take me six years to make eighteen movies. Now, it took me six months!

JK: Let's talk about a couple of specific recording sessions. Talk about one of the most memorable sessions, in the context of Hollywood, scoring a Hollywood film with Lalo Schifrin.

AA: My admiration for Lalo was even before he became a composer. Lalo had similar story. Dizzy Gillespie brought Lalo to the US. Lalo was a jazz pianist. And so I followed his career. Lalo said, "Alex, I need you to play congas. These two are just going to record trumpet, rhythm section, no drums, congas, and then the whole orchestra is waiting, I want you to play drums, and then you're gonna overdub congas later." And everything sounded beautiful. I was listening to, the other day, some of those tracks; they are on YouTube. I don't know if that was the first one, but the one that I was listening to [was] "Boulevard Nights" Classic! That was the first session that I did. Then the next session was with Bill Conti. This is Sean Penn's first movie, with Esai Morales, *Bad Boys*. Remember, when you knew a new musician in a town like Los Angeles, there is a line from here to San Diego to get into the movies, you know. The reason they call me is because Weather Report. So I start working with Dave Grusin, jazz composers too, jazz players. They knew me and they called to me to do those movie sessions. I was doing a lot, and going from studio to studio, day and night, recording, everybody, crowded house.

JK: Can you tell us a little bit about Joni Mitchell? We heard a story that she was in Las Vegas at one of those sessions, in the garage, and she was there hanging and singing, and doing her thing. Was that the first time you met her?

AA: No. The first time I met Joni Mitchell was with Jaco, when we were doing *Heavy Weather* in 1976. She started dating a friend of mine, a great percussionist that used to play with Miles Davis, Don Alias . . . He's the one that recommended Jaco and me to do a record with Joni Mitchell . . . And that's when I met Joni Mitchell in 1977.

BA: And that was recorded here in Los Angeles?

AA: That was recorded here, I think [it] was at A&M

BA: Tell us about that, that session with Joni and Jaco.

AA: In those days, they had a budget to record for four or five days. It's not like today—they want to do the whole record [in] one day—so it was kind of nice. And I recommended Airto; he did one song or two with us; and Manolo Badrena. One of the songs, I don't remember the name, we did some kind of a groove that I heard. I said, "I have an idea with the stomping, with ankle bells." So, dancing like a Peruvian. It sounded amazing, with the ankle bells. She said, "yeah!" So they found a piece of wood. And I have my shoes for the ankle bells, and I danced in that song ["Dreamland"].

JK: But then there is the other song, "Tenth World," right?

AA: Oh yeah!

JK: She just lets you guys go.

AA: Bananas.

JK: Was that part of the pitch for the record? Did she want it to have a kind of South American feel to it? Or was it just mixed into her style?

AA: She wanted it to be creative. She always called the musicians that could do that. "I want to hear what you want to do. This is the song. What can you do in this one? Express yourself." That's what it was. Because she's like that. It was amazing.

JK: When you were telling us that story about that one session, and the moment that you put on the ankle bells, Joni Mitchell was in that scene. She was hugely influential in shaping what many people called "the California sound," a very southern California sound. And yet, here you are, being able to put Peruvian ankle bells, into the heart of what people think is Californian. Was that something you were conscious of? This is a great opportunity to put Peru or to put South America into LA?

AA: I never thought of it in that way. Music is music. Especially rhythms from all of the world are welcomed in my soul. I grab them and when I think that I can fit in that piece of music and that song—yeah, I will let it happen. It's not that they have to be perfect, or they have to be Peruvian—oh no no no. I like to blend. Make it happen. Maybe the sound of the instrument, or the concept of the rhythm, is quasi-Peruvian. My approach is what the music needs more than how I am going to shine. I like to respect that very well. I never think about "this is my chance to put my *cajón,* my Peruvian beats, or anything like that. I think the music feels better if I do this . . . And since she [Joni Mitchell] was so open. OK, let's try it! And she said, "yeah, I love it!" And everybody said, "yeah man! That was beautiful! OK, great! Got the take!"

BA: Is that what being a session musician means for you then?

AA: There are many kinds of session musicians. There are the thirty-six string players. They're all playing long notes. Those are different. They're just called to read, and to play those notes. Now, a percussion musician is different. When we did *Jurassic World,* there's a lot of percussion. I just did *Jungle Book,* a lot of percussion—we're using *taiko* drums, it's four times bigger than a regular drum (from a drum kit). That red drum, *taiko,* Japanese drums have bass drums for the low ends. I have four trucks that bring my stuff to the studio, because the percussion section is from like the entrance of my house all the way to this studio in the backyard. The eighty musicians, we use the sound stages: Fox, Sony, Warner, etc. Sometimes, you learn while you are doing a session . . . I'm doing a session one day, with Robbie Robertson. The singer. The producers say, "Alex, the conga patterns you're playing sound too Latin!" Other people get offended. And I said, "oooh! OK. How do you want it?" "Can you make it more African?" "Sure!" You know what I did? I just switched the congas around. I played the same pattern. But they were in different places. I played and they said, "Yeah! That's what I want!" That's how you have to respond. . . . A couple days ago, I just finished recording the third *Star Trek.* I've been so blessed that I'm playing in the big movies, more than before. Because when I decided not to travel anymore, I called the contractors and the composers, and the main musicians of this town; I said, "you know what I can do. I'm available. I don't want to take anybody's position, but if there is a space for me, remember, I'm in town. Call me, and I work with you." Because sometimes when you become a famous musician, [people will say,] "no, he's too expensive." They don't call you because you charge $100 more than the other one. No no. I work with your budget. I work with you. Call me. I want to play; I want to stay in town. So that's why they're calling me, more and more, because I'm available. You have to bring charisma. You have to bring your professional musicianship.

BA: Are there a lot of Latino musicians in studio orchestras now?

AA: You can count them with your own hands: bass player Abraham Laboriel, of course, on the movie sessions; sometimes another flute player that came from Venezuela, Pedro Eustache; and me. I introduced a new guy from Puerto Rico, plays very well, young guy, Walter Rodríguez. His very young and he plays tablas and reads well and everything, very well prepared, but he's also a great drummer and he's also become friends with everybody . . . Paulinho Da Costa, all those guys are really great people, besides being great musicians. But there aren't that many really, especially in the movie business.

JK: I have to ask you about one more: "The Tide is High," the Blondie song.

AA: Oooooh!

JK: Can you tell us about that session? Who was in the room? Who played on it? Because there's very little information.

AA: I played percussion.

JK: I'm particularly interested in the horn section, which I had heard was Doc Severinsen, *The Tonight Show* band director, and the horn players from that *Tonight Show* band?

AA: Yeah! Snooky Young! Another two trumpet players from here. Wow! As you know, I'm very bad with names. I know Snooky Young was there. Snooky Young played in New York and he moved out here with Doc Severinsen, from New York. But I don't remember the other ones.

JK: Did they give you instructions about what they wanted? Because it's a reggae song . . .

AA: Right!

JK: That becomes mariachi. [We play the song.]

AA: The trumpet player is Chuck Findley! He came to town playing with Buddy Rich, in the '70s . . . Oh, I hear this sound, we put a little bongo, and put little woodblocks and things like that.

BA: What about the mariachi-sounding horns?

AA: That's Chuck Findley! Because Chuck Findley also played with the Tijuana Brass![1]

JK: Was there a violinist on it?

AA: Oh my God! I think so. But I don't remember who it was. That's amazing! That's a great example, I love that! It still sounds like it was recorded yesterday! That groove is happening . . . Rhythms, Latin music. Put some of the flavors inside the pot. You have Colombian, Venezuelan, Brazilian, Uruguayan, Peruvian, and definitely Mexican and flamenco, Argentine. Right now, most of the recordings, they have two, three percussionists. They always have a demand for percussionists, for Latin musicians to record, to put that "flavor." That's why a lot of good percussionists from Puerto Rico and Cuba are moving to town. Younger, amazing, great! And they all call me. I know because they all call me: "Alex! I'm in town! Throw me a bone!" I say, "of course I will!" And I do. I help everybody here. Because I was one of the first ones to arrive in this town in 1978! And that's before Luis Conte, Justo Almario. Paulinho Da Costa was already here. Michito Sánchez, Tiki Pasillas, Walter Rodríguez, Efraín Toro, Richie Gajate García, Walfredo de los Reyes Jr. I call everybody to record with us in the movie soundtracks too. I said, "I need four percussionists, can you have four?" "Yeah yeah!" So I bring them. I open the doors for all my friends. "Come with me to the session." Wear headphones, listen to the click, look at the conductor, look at the music, and listen to the band. That's the thing, right there . . . Watch the conductor, read your music, and play your instrument!

INTERVIEW WITH AIRTO MOREIRA

Airto Moreira was born in Itaiopolis, Brazil. He came to the United States in 1967 and was soon playing percussion with jazz greats like Lee Morgan, Joe Zawinul, and Cannonball Adderley, including a storied string of legendary tours and recordings with Miles Davis. He settled in Los Angeles in 1973. In addition to a lengthy solo career (his first LA album was *Promises of the Sun* in 1976), Moreira has played with Weather Report, Santana, Mickey Hart, Antonio Carlos Jobim, Gil Evans, Keith Jarrett, George Benson, and Chick Corea, among many others, as well as on numerous collaborations with his wife, vocalist Flora Purim.

   We spoke to him in the living room of his home in Studio City, California, in July 2016.

BA: Tell us about growing up in Brazil.

AM: I grew up in a small town in the south of Brazil. I did not receive any education in anything. My father was a barber and we were poor. I always liked to play on things that were not musical instruments and I would make percussion instruments out of them, like birdcalls and shakers. Most of the time I had no idea what I was doing because at that time there was no TV. I would listen to the radio but they didn't play percussion on the radio.

I was seven or eight years old when I started playing in Ponta Grassa [Paraná], first with an Italian accordionist at weddings and festivities for about a year. Then at the age of fourteen I started playing drums with this band called Jazz Estrela, a family of four musicians and myself. The way it all started is that there was a carnival ball I went to with my family but they would not let us get in. It was raining and my father was trying to get us in. Finally the director said, "The kid can come in but he has to sit on the side of the stage." I was very happy because that's what I wanted anyway. So I was sitting there and they were waiting for the drummer, who was the best drummer in town, and he wouldn't show up. He was already two hours late. So they asked me, "Do you know how to play drums, because we see you playing percussion?" I said, "Well I have never played drums but I watch all the time." They asked me to play two basic rhythms, a samba and a march. I played an old-style Carmen Miranda kind of samba. They liked it and asked me to play with the band. There was no bass player, but there was a tuba. We went over an hour; the drummer did not show up, so we played the whole night. When we finished, the bandleader gave me some money. At first I refused, but he insisted. When I went home and showed the money to my parents, they were overwhelmed because at the time it was a lot of money for them. My father went back with me and tried to return the money but the bandleader would not hear it. They haggled and the leader put the money in my father's pocket and that was the end of it. That money helped my family a lot. A few days later, Pedro the bandleader came to our house with two of his sons and asked my parents if they would let me play with them. They said they'd teach me more rhythms. At first my parents refused, but they finally gave in, making Pedro promise that they would take care of me and not let me drink any alcohol. I played with them for over a year. When I was sixteen, we moved from Ponta Grassa to Curutiba, the capital of the State of Paraná. My mother asked the bandleader of a twelve- to fifteen-piece orchestra to check me out. But they already had a very good drummer from São Paulo, so they asked me to audition on percussion and vocals. They were blown away and they hired me. We worked a lot. Then for a while, I started playing in bordello-type nightclubs and I felt a little lost. Eventually I started playing with really good small combos. I moved to São Paulo but couldn't find any work because they preferred female vocalists.

When I was eighteen, I moved to the US. It was the sixties. I first went to NY and then moved to LA. There were no Brazilian bands in

NY, so I decided to sit in with salsa bands but they did not welcome me. Then one day, I went into a jazz club and Walter Booker was playing bass. I think Cannonball Adderley was also playing. Booker asked me what the hell I was doing there! It was Harlem and I was white, and at that time Black Power was very strong. I told him I was from Brazil and that I needed work. I ended up moving in with him and sleeping on his apartment floor. He was living with his wife and three or four more other musicians. It was dirty and full of leftover food and roaches and we'd be up until four or five in the morning playing with Booker, who was recording. One day I went to the Village and asked to play at a piano bar. It was a very intimate acoustic space where people sat around the piano and drank as you played. I played with two brushes on a pizza tray. The bassist and piano player liked it and asked me to come back, and the owner told me I could eat there when I played. From there I got a gig playing percussion with Cannonball Adderley and then other players started hiring me. I didn't speak English at the time, but I watched Sesame Street whenever I could and I learned a lot.

JK: When did you and Flora Purim begin to work together?

AM: After meeting Flora, once I went to her apartment and she played this incredible music! It was Gil Evans with Miles Davis. It made me want to cry. When she saw my reaction, she said, "This is called inspiration." From that time on, we started playing with one another although we also pursued our own solo careers.

I formed a group in NY called Fingers, which was fairly successful. We were on CIT Records [the best jazz label at the time] and we toured for about two years. After Fingers, one day I was at Booker's apartment and the phone rang. I picked up and a guy told me he was Jack Whitmore, Miles Davis's manager, and that Miles wanted me to record with him. I hung up the phone thinking it was a joke. I was alone at Walter Booker's apartment and Lee Morgan called for him. It was Thanksgiving and I was all by myself. So he offered to pick me up and take me to his home for Thanksgiving. When he came over, the phone rang again and it was Jack Whitmore again. Lee spoke with him and they set up a recording date for me. I took all these instruments that they had never seen before. We recorded *Bitches Brew*. After that I started getting solid recording dates and worked a lot. I recorded with Wayne Shorter, Ron Carter, Herbie Hancock. After that, one day Miles said, "Brazilian (that's what he called me), do you want to sit in at the Village Gate with us?" So I went and there was Chick Corea, Dave Holland on bass, and Jack DeJohnette on drums. I did not take my percussion gear because I was not sure if they would accept me. When I arrived Miles asked, "Where is your stuff?" He was pissed and told me to get out of there. So I jumped on the subway and went all the way uptown, took my gear, and rushed back. Miles was not pleased at all, but he let me play. Everybody liked it. I was not playing congas and timbales but my own percussion instruments. After that Miles offered me a gig in DC with no pay and I accepted. We played there for a week and it was recorded. At the end of the week, he gave me $300. I had never seen so much money! From that time on, I started playing with Miles Davis and made more money and it was very good for me because from then on everyone wanted me to play or record with them. The tours were not necessarily focused on *Bitches Brew* but on whatever Miles wanted to play.

JK: After going from anonymity to a successful career on the East Coast, what drew you to the West Coast?

AM: I didn't go immediately to the West Coast. Wayne and Jack left the band but I stayed in NY. Chick Corea was rehearsing a band with Stanley Clark and Hubert Laws, and Chick asked me to show the drummer some Brazilian rhythms. The drummer took me aside and told me he did not want to be in that band, so when he told Chick, I got the gig instead. The band was Return to Forever and I stayed with Chick for two years. Meanwhile, I also played with Cannonball's band and my own group. I recorded over two hundred albums. Return to Forever split up because Chick wanted to go more electronic. Joe Farrell quit, saying he did not want to play the electronic stuff. At the time, we had to have someone dedicated just to take care of the technical part of the electronics and it was complicated [interviewer's wordings to make it more intelligible]. So I quit with him. And here I am in LA.

BA: What brought you here?

AM: There were Brazilians here. There was Sérgio Mendes. I would talk to Brazilians and they would all encourage me to come to LA, saying it was like Brazil, sunny, clean, organized, and with Brazilian bands. I was going to audition with Sérgio Mendes, but a drummer from Brazil, Dom Um Romão, got the gig. So I put together a group with musicians here and we started traveling and recording for many years. In LA jazz was not really happening and it is still like that. Jazz was in NY. They had smooth jazz, but I was going on the road with people from NY and my own little band.

JK: What was the first album you recorded with your group in LA?

Airto Moreira, *Promises of the Sun,* Arista, 1976, Idelsohn Society for Musical Preservation Archive.

AM: It was called *Promises of the Sun,* followed by *I'm Fine How Are You?*

JK: What about the *Identity* album? Was that part of the earlier recordings?

AM: Yes.

JK: Did LA impact the sound of your music?

AM: I always recorded what I liked. Bob Marley was happening. I used to listen to him and other musicians. But I never wanted to play what everybody else was playing. I always tried to play my own music, my own style.

JK: The *Identity* album, like much of your work in LA relied on a good deal of traditional Brazilian music. What does it mean to be a Brazilian musician outside of Brazil? How much of tradition stays with you?

AM: My plan was to come to the US and stay for a year and go back. But I never did. I didn't go back for eight years. I always felt like a foreigner, because here in America, if you have an accent, you are an outsider. When I was playing I was not a foreigner, but when I was not playing, I was a foreigner. So if it were not for Sesame Street, I would have had to go back!

JK: In the late '60s into the '70s, Brazilian music had a strong influence on the music scene. Can you talk about the spreading of the Brazilian influence on the music of LA?

AM: Brazilian music was well known at the time because of a big music festival at Carnegie Hall. There was another theater in LA that also presented Brazilian music. The jazz scene was always small in LA, but Brazilian music, mainly the bossa nova and more commercial jazz like Stan Getz and Astrud Gilberto, became very well known. There were good musicians in LA—Lee Ritenour, Dave Grusin . . .

BRIAN CROSS: Through Cannonball there is a definite thread of Brazilian music in American music. George Duke, Ndugu, Earth, Wind & Fire, although pop, Sérgio Mendes always covered Caetano Veloso and Gilberto Gil, you and Flora, Deodato. There is a Brazilian sprinkling that happened here.

AM: Bossa nova was very influential in LA and NY, the same way that jazz and funk were influential to Brazilian music. Cannonball recorded an album called *Happy People,* on which I played and I wrote the title track. Stan Getz used to come to LA and play. He brought jazz and bossa nova together . . . The drummer who invented the bossa nova beat was João Palma. He was playing with Sérgio. Sérgio recorded songs with that beat. Cannonball was a beautiful human being. He was aware of politics and Apartheid because he was friends with Jesse Jackson, but he would accept everyone. He really knew about race relations but that didn't influence his music.

JK: How about Jobim? Was he living here in those days?

AM: Jobim came here to record part of his albums. But most of them were recorded in NY. I played on two of them.

BA: The album *Elis and Tom,* which he recorded with Elis Regina, was recorded at Capitol Records.

AM: You are right. It was recorded in LA. Jobim is the most important Brazilian composer whose music went around the world. People loved him because he was a beautiful person, he was a family man, and everything he did at that time was good. They put English lyrics on his compositions. Some of them were nice, but others had

Flora Purim, *Open Your Eyes You Can Fly,* Milestone Records, 1976, Idelsohn Society for Musical Preservation Archive.

nothing to do with the original lyrics. He was and still is the best from Brazil. When you talk of Brazilian music, you talk about Jobim. Of course today we have Caetano Veloso, Gilberto Gil, and other new composers that I am not very familiar with. I have lived outside of Brazil since 1967, so what I hear these days are recommendations from other people. In those days there was a big marriage between Brazilian and American music, but in LA, it was a little more soft and structured than in NY.

JK: I wanted to ask you about the music you made with Flora in LA but specifically about the *Open Your Eyes You Can Fly* album, which struck me as an important one historically and musically. Tell us about the context of that record.

AM: We did two albums with Chick Corea's Return to Forever, and then *Light as a Feather*. We were already performing that kind of music all over, so it was easy to record. When Flora was at Terminal Island, she used to tell the other inmates that she was a jazz singer, but they would not believe her until the day they heard her on the radio. Mo Ostin, who was then president at Warner Bros., heard her too and decided to sign her. But nobody could find her because she was in prison. When he found out, he sent a big shot lawyer, Warren Miller, to LA, and within a few months, she was released on parole. She used to go on furlough to Long Beach University, where someone would sign for her. Then they would drive her to LA to record. Then she'd take the bus back to Long Beach. She did in part *Open Your Eyes You Can Fly* like that.

Everything that I have done, from the little boy in southern Brazil with no education to what I became never ceases to amaze me. I can hardly believe it myself. And when I say I did (in the past tense), I mean it. Since five years ago, I cannot even think about playing. Also something happened with Flora that very few people know. She had a Brazilian passport and we used to travel in and out of the US. Five years ago, we were returning from Europe. I went through immigration but Flora was stopped and told that she could not come in because she had three names (Flora Purim, Flor Moreira, and Flora Bank, which was that of her parents). But her fingerprints were the same for all those names. They said, "You are one person with many names and you were incarcerated." By that time, the computer systems were all linked. They wanted to deport her, but she bought a ticket to Portugal. I went to see her but it was very hard over there coping with everything. She got very affected. Can you imagine? We were together for fifty-five years and we're not together anymore. She is now in Brazil. I went to see her, but we could not make it work, so I came back. I have been talking to her every day for four years. Some days she is OK, some days not. Some days I am OK, some days not.

Gilberto Gil was once on *The Tonight Show* and Johnny Carson asked him if he was afraid of death. Gil said, "No, I'm not afraid of death. I am afraid of dying!" What an answer, man! We're going to die and we'll find ourselves living in a different place as spirit. Then you detach from your physical body, you try to talk but there is no sound. But you're there. And we have to reincarnate many lifetimes in order to learn. Some of us don't learn what we should learn and it takes a lot of pain to come back here.

INTERVIEW WITH LUIS CONTE

Luis Conte was born in Santiago de Cuba. He came to Los Angeles in 1967 and became an active member of the local Latin music scene. After touring as a percussionist with the Hues Corporation, he went on to record and tour with artists such as Madonna, Maná, Phil Collins, Shakira, Dave Matthews, Randy Newman, Ray Charles, Celine Dion, Eric Clapton, and, most frequently, James Taylor.

We spoke to him at his home studio in Thousand Oaks, California, in May 2016.

BA: How did you come to music?

LC: I really owe it to my grandmother and my parents. They loved music. As far as I can remember in Santiago de Cuba, where I was born, music was all the time present in our house, either on the radio or my dad playing the new record of Orquesta Aragón. He was a doctor and would play *danzones* on Sundays. He loved music so much and was into all the instruments, pointing out what they were doing on a song. He used to listen to all kinds of music, including jazz and opera. He loved Glenn Miller, Tommy Dorsey, and all the big bands. He was very open-minded and so I was exposed to all that. And my grandmother, who used to live in Havana, also had a strong influence. When I was a little boy, she would see me banging on things when the radio was playing. So every time she would come to visit, she would bring me an instrument, a *guïro,* maracas . . . As far as I can remember, I had musical instruments.

BA: So when did you actually start playing in a group or a project?

LC: That was not until much later. I didn't really play until I got out of high school in the United States. I played for fun in Santiago. My dad had troubadour friends like Compay Segundo and Ibrahim Ferrer, and we'd have parties and I played clave with them. All those people were from Santiago. We actually lived a few blocks away from La Casa de la Trova . . . I left Cuba when I was fourteen and eleven months, and I got to the US when I was fifteen and two months old. A hell of a trip! I got enrolled in Hollywood High School. I played in the small school bands then but was not thinking about making music my profession. Let me just say that I was just living. Due to the embargo and the political situation back then, I had lost connection with my parents, who had stayed in Cuba, and I was living in Hollywood with a second or third cousin of my dad. After I graduated from high school, I got a job bagging groceries at a supermarket while taking night classes at Los Angeles City College. It may have been 1972. One night I heard congas coming out of the Black Student Union. I skipped class and went over. I asked the guys playing where they had gotten their drums. They said, "Oh man! There's this place in Micheltorena and Sunset Boulevard that sells congas." So I went there. They were super expensive but I was able to get hold of a drum.

BA: Why Los Angeles? Obviously the family relationship was a connection but you could've gone to Miami or New York.

LC: My cousin—whose name is also Luis Conte and who is still alive (he is eighty-eight)—had decided to come to the US during the Batista regime. He was a young man then and he went to NY and married a Jewish American lady. This is before the Cuban exodus. Because of his job he had transferred to Hollywood. And he was my only relative outside of Cuba, man! I had to go somewhere and he was kind enough to take me in.

BA: So, can you talk to us a little bit about of what it was like arriving from Santiago in the middle of Hollywood in 1967?

LC: I remember one of the funniest things like it was yesterday. When we were living in Cuba, we had ration cards and it was rough. You could only get this much milk, one pair of shoes for sports, and one pair for school, once a year. So if your shoes got worn out, you were in trouble. I was coming from that kind of world. I got to my cousin's house and he said, "We've got to sign you up for high school." And he gave me directions on how to get there from the house. So on my way there, as I was walking on Sunset Blvd in my Cuban clothes, a car pulled up and these two girls got out. They were wearing bellbottom pants, tiny T-shirts with no bras . . . and no shoes! And I went: "Wait a minute, you can't get shoes here either?" I was thinking: "The trouble we are going through over there with the ration cards and these guys have no shoes! What am I doing here?"

BA: And did that rock scene start to become part of your life as a teenager in LA?

LC: Most definitely. In Cuba, when I was about eleven or twelve, The Beatles came along. Because of the embargo, you couldn't get anything, but somehow some friends would get hold of records and we'd listen to them and the Rolling Stones. I was intrigued and wanted to know more about them, and then suddenly here I was, right in the middle of Hollywood! And in high school I immediately met some guys with whom I played guitar. We created a little band and we just played. And I discovered Hendrix . . . that was the scene. I was still too young to be admitted into clubs.

After I got my conga drum, I found out that I could go to Griffith Park on Sundays and play with other people. Of course, coming from Cuba, I expected to see "Una conga, una comparsa," drumming, singing, dancing. But it was like a thunderous lot of people playing just drums. I met this person who said he was related to Tito Puente and he told me of a record store downtown called Doran Music. Downtown in those days was rough. He had a cassette of Willie Colón, which he had got there. So I went there and they had Willie Colón, Eddie Palmieri, and more . . . This was in 1973. It was the heyday of Fania All Stars, so I got reconnected with Cuban music. I knew these guys were in New York, but wondering where was the Latin scene in LA? Then an older Cuban musician told me to go Chez Pico! So I went and Chocolate y Sylvia were playing there. Chocolate was a much older percussionist, solid real Black Afro-Cuban man and his wife was Sylvia. In Cuba, if you're Black and real dark, they call you Chocolate. It's not a racial thing but really out of love. The pianist in that quintet was João Donato. I asked Chocolate if I could sit in with the band, and he said yes, so I got my congas and that started the ball rolling.

BA: What was the audience like at that club?

LC: It was a Cuban nightclub with no food! There was a restaurant next door called El Colmao. The audience was a mixture of Latinos, like you find in LA.

BA: And what were you guys playing?

LC: We played Cuban songs—standards, Arsenio Rodríguez, Chapotín, cha cha chas, dance music. It was all Afro-Cuban music but the crowd was mixed.

Chez Pico burned down. There was another club, Virginia, and another one next to the Madrid Theatre on Sunset. I played with Chocolate but also with a Nicaraguan band. And there was this other guy called Peckito y su Boogaloo and he played piano. He was from Panama, I think. And I started playing with him in a club all the way close to Inglewood. We played three or four sets on Friday and Saturday nights and I made $25 a night. That was it! No more bagging groceries! By that time I was eighteen, I was done with high school.

BA: Was there any moment that you realized that you were living in a heavily Mexican Latino city? Or was it like you were in this separate, kind of Caribbean bubble?

LC: No, it wasn't a bubble, because right from the beginning, it was so mixed. There were many Mexican American bandleaders I played with, like Rudy Macías. There were also South Americans. The musicians were mixed but the music we played was mainly Afro-Cuban-based, salsa, and also boogaloo.

BA: Were you connected at all with the Central Avenue, African American jazz world at all?

LC: Not yet. What happened next is that I met Munyongo Jackson, a well-known African American percussionist in LA, who played with Stevie Wonder. I met him at a club called the Mardi Gras in MacArthur Park, where Joe Cuba played. I snuck in because I was still underage. I was watching Joe Cuba's killer band and saw this guy behind me and we struck a conversation. He told me of the club, Virginia's, that was a good place to start connecting with musicians. I started going to the club. Johnny Martínez played there five nights a week. I met Perico José Hernandez, who is like my brother, one of my mentors. He pointed out a man to me by the name of Camilo Azuquita, a Panamanian of Cuban descent, who was putting a band together. I went over and introduced myself and gave him my number. He never called but I found out about a rehearsal at Munyungo's house, down on 43rd and Western, and I just crashed at the party. They were waiting for the conga player to arrive, so they could rehearse but he never showed up (by the way, that was my dear friend Hector Andrade). I told them I played congas and I got the gig. That was my first break in LA. The name of the band was Azuquita y su Melao!

We worked on the nights when Johnny Martínez was off. And when Willie Colón or Eddie Palmieri and other musicians came to play in town, they would come afterward to the club and that's how I met them. My first recording session was with Azuquita y su Melao in 1974. Roberto Durán was coming to town to fight a championship, and being from Panama, Azuquita wanted to record a 45. I wrote a couple of songs for him. The first song I recorded was called "Durán Mano de Piedra," which is what they called him, "stone-hands." It was there that I first realized I could play congas, and then play maracas on top, and then bongos! The trumpets would double themselves too. I had no idea you could do that. I had never been to a recording studio and that mesmerized me. And the fact that I would be able to hear it later without playing live, like on the radio, blew my mind! The trumpeter was a jazz player called Oscar Brashear. Oscar told me he that he played at the Baked Potato. When I went there, it was a whole other crowd! They were playing jazz. I started going there and meeting musicians and playing with them.

One day I decided to go to the musicians union, thinking of signing up and meeting other musicians because I also liked pop, funk and rock 'n roll. While I was there I saw Johnny Cheda. He gave me the number of a couple of Americans looking for a conga player to do a recording. I called them from a payphone and asked a friend to give me a ride to the studio. The song I auditioned for was "Rock the Boat," which is the first, original disco song. I got the gig and I was off to the East Coast to record for RCA Records, and before you know it, I was on the road for a promotional tour for the Hues Corporation. It was in 1975 and I was twenty. The first gig was in Newark, NJ. The other band sound checking was the O'Jays! It was incredible! We played on all the popular night shows on TV. It was a blessing! I had to take a break from Azuquita, but when the tour ended, I came back to LA to my roots again and picked up with Azuquita.

JK: Over the course of your career, you've played more with non-Latin acts? Is that right?

LC: Yes. More non-Latin.

JK: So was going back to your roots, Cuban music, still the foundation? No matter who you're playing with, when you're done with a James Taylor tour, a Phil Collins tour . . . When you go back to you . . . Is it the original songbook that you started with?

LC: Yes. When a tour is over, I go to Mambo's Café in Glendale and play with my six-piece Afro-Cuban band. It's always been like that . . . I always go back to my roots. It's all related. It all came from Africa. This is one way of playing the funk, and we got a different way of playing the funk. But the result of both is funky. With the Hues Corporation, or after playing with Diana Ross, I would come back and play with Tony Martínez or whoever, until the next thing.

JK: Did that ever feel like a dual identity, a split identity? Like there were two Luises?

LC: No . . . Not at all

BA: What's the next big . . . break?

LC: Well I went back to my roots playing with Azuquita, at Virginia's! . . . One Saturday night this guy walks in and introduces himself as Alex Acuña. He said he played with Weather Report. Now I had no idea who they were. He explained that they were a jazz band. He sat in with Azuquita on the timbales. We exchanged numbers. At the time he was living in Las Vegas. But he was in LA recording *Heavy Weather*. . . . And another stroke of luck—my friend told me of an audition to play with the Supremes (by that time Diana Ross had left). I got the gig and we got to play two weeks at the Caesar Palace in Las Vegas! That's my next break. And when I got there, the first day was our day off. I called Alex. He invited me over to his place and when I got out of the car, I heard drumming. I banged on the door and Walfredo Reyes Sr. opened the door. Walfredo just pointed at a congas set and I started playing. They were rehearsing a Louie Bellson recording for Pablo Records. It was kind of American jazz meets Afro-Cuban drums and the idea was to mix it all together. We played all afternoon and then at the end Louie asked me if I wanted to play on it. He was the sweetest guy. I couldn't believe it! I get goose bumps thinking about it!

JK: And did Caldera[?] grow out of those meetings . . . with Acuña and others?

LC: No . . . Well maybe Acuña might have had something to do with it. I heard about a club called the Sound Room in the San Fernando Valley. I met there the late Carlos Vega playing in a band. Carlos was Cuban and had come to the US when he was six years old. He was in Caldera. Through him, I met Jorge Strunz and Eduardo del Barrio, who were the leaders of Caldera. Steve Tavaglione was also in Caldera. When they decided to record, they wanted a couple of extra hands, so they hired Hector Andrade and me. I recorded two records with Caldera. *Dreamer* was the first one, and the second one was *Time and Chance*.

BA: So when do you start getting into the rock scene?

LC: I was getting calls to do recordings and go on tour. Jackson Browne asked me to record on *I'm Alive*. That's the first record I did with him and we toured it. I started working with James Taylor in 1998 but before that I worked with Phil Collins. I worked with Pat Metheny, Helen Reddy, Doc Severinsen from *The Tonight Show*. That came through Walfredo Reyes. Walfredo had been playing with Doc, but because of a parallel gig, he could no longer do both and he recommended me. While I was going back and forth, I didn't play much Cuban music. Then later in the nineties, the Phil Collins gig came in through Helen Reddy's piano player, who was playing for him . . . I only recorded on *Testify* and on his *Tarzan* soundtrack. The track "You'll Be in My Heart" was a powerful ballad that became a big hit. I also played with Claire Fischer, who introduced me to the great Poncho Sanchez, and I played with Salsa Picante.

In the eighties Herb Alpert was reappearing after laying low in the seventies and doing label work. I met the Toussaint Brothers, Eugenio, Fernando, and Enrique, through Claire Fischer. They were like brothers to me. Herb wanted to take us on the road in 1982 and put the band together with sax player John Cross, John Pisano, Julius Wechter from the Tijuana Brass, Bob Edmondson, and a rhythm section. We rehearsed at A&M for three months. During breaks I would peek in on Paulinho Da Costa recording with George Duke. And as we hit the road, Herb came down with hepatitis. So after all the work, we ended up only doing two gigs.

I started getting back to the roots and teaching hand percussion and Afro-Cuban drums and playing with local salsa bands. Next thing I know, I am called in for an audition with Madonna. I got there early and Jonathan Moffet, "Sugarfoot," her drummer, had also turned up early. He had this big beautiful setup with all these shiny symbols and my set was ragged, and after all these years, I didn't even have an endorsement. Nobody else was there so we started playing together, and when we stopped, I heard someone clapping and it was Madonna up on the balcony! That was the audition right there! She said, "I love your hands . . . You're on the gig and going on tour with us." That was 1987. Being in LA, there was a lot of Mexican music and artists recording too, like Luis Miguel and all the big names. So I start recording with all these major Spanish artists . . . I recorded on Miguel's *Romances* series albums. The first one, *Romance,* was a big big record! Carlos Vega was on drums, Abraham Laboriel on bass, and the genius Bebu Silvetti was the producer, arranger, and pianist.

BA: Tell us one or two stories of the recording session, just like the one you told us about Madonna where you went in to audition. A recording session that meant—that means to you something special that you'd felt that you did something that was different and that the person in charge of that project said, "hey I want that!"

LC: Working and recording with Cachao at Capitol Studios here was memorable. He was the Charles Mingus of Cuban bass. He would just go [to] the studio with nothing prepared and put it all together right there, just like that. Playing on the Eric Clapton song "Change the World" was special. Babyface, who was producing it, played me the song and I asked him where he wanted me to play and he told me to play wherever I wanted. There was a lot of programming on it and he said if I wanted to take the programming out and play the rhythm myself, I could. I played percussion instruments that are not usually played on a pop record and it became a huge song.

JK: Do you have a sense that Latin American music and musical styles or traditions, whether Cuban music or Brazilian, have influenced American music in some way? And if so, how?

LC: Chano Pozo influenced American music in the forties . . . And it has been continuing since then. René Touzet was a Cuban bandleader who influenced rock 'n roll. The song "Louie Louie" has claves. I'm working right now on a tour with James Taylor, and we're doing a song called "Snowtime," which is on his latest record. We were in Montreal, and I went for a walk. I heard live music. It was a Caribbean festival. There were people from Barbados and a float from Trinidad and one from Puerto Rico, and there were bands playing on top of them. I called James and asked him to hurry down and check them out. He actually tells the story in his shows now. So he came down and we got behind the Barbadian float while I was trying to find a piece of metal or something to bang on. He just walked for about four blocks and stayed there, but I kept going with them until the very end. But the inspiration for "Snowtime" came out of there, seeing people from other cultures in Canada, in the cold, going there for a reason, maybe for a better life, or better work . . . And the song is a cha cha cha. And this is a James Taylor song. That's an example of an influence. There's a song called "Niño" on Jackson Browne's *Looking East* and it is a kind of merengue! Latin music has influenced every form of music. New Orleans jazz is connected with the islands and to Cuba, like the first habanera. All that is influenced by *la raza*.

BA: What does it mean to you to be a session musician, a studio musician?

LC: To me it means I'm a good musician that gets hired to play on other people's music. A session musician has to have a lot of versatility and has to be able to change colors like a chameleon in a way, change dresses because today it is a Caribbean song, tomorrow it's a rock song, and the next day is with a jazz artist, and the following day it might be a movie. And it could be *Mission: Impossible* with a lot of bongos or it could be *Jurassic Park*. Another day it could be a Barbara Streisand record. For example, I'm coming from a James Taylor tour, and then I do two days of recordings with Barbara Streisand, and one night I had a recording for a jazz artist. A day I will always remember is when I started the morning with Andy Narrell, who had come down here for a recording, and in the afternoon I worked on a session with Guns N' Roses. It was the remake of "Sympathy for the Devil" by the Rolling Stones. It was for the soundtrack of *Interview with the Vampire*. Then later that night, I went to Conway Studios, and recorded a song with Diane Reeves. So this is a studio musician, being a . . . chameleon! You know you're changing coats! And none of it was my music! But I do my best, I give it 100 percent and with no ego. That's what it means to be session player.

BA: Where is the you in all of it? You kept saying, "it is not my music." So what's the core?

LC: Well the core is still me. I say, "it's not my music," out of respect but I am still in it, because they wanted me for who I am. For example, when I made suggestions to George Duke, he would always say, "Hey man, you're the cat!" So I'm there because they know what I do.

INTERVIEW WITH RAY YSLAS

Ray Yslas was born in Los Angeles, the son of Mexican immigrants. He performed on the title song to *Sex and the City* and has toured and recorded with artists such as the Backstreet Boys, Juan Gabriel, Christina Aguilera, Alejandro Fernández, Joan Sebastian, Stevie Nicks, Babyface, Willie Nelson, and Maxwell. He has performed on TV with *The Voice, Lopez Tonight,* and the *Grammy Awards,* and his film work includes *Zorro* and *The Longest Yard.*

We spoke to him at his home studio in San Gabriel, California, in March 2016.

BA: Tell us about your family history, where you grew up, how you started playing music.

RY: My parents are from Sonora, Mexico. I was born in El Sereno, in the 'hood back then when I was growing up, it was *cholos* everywhere, man! One day I was walking home from school, I took the alley and there were some 'hood guys, young cats, all tattooed-up, bandana. And one of them said, "hey man, come join our gang, you're going to be part of it!" I was scared. "No, I don't want to be" . . . "Come on man, you gonna be in the gang." And then, one of the other guys said, "Wait a minute, that's the dude that plays drums! I saw him play at a party the other night. No, he's cool man, leave him alone, he's cool, he's a really good drummer." And they said, "alright man, go ahead." And from there on, I told myself I'm going to keep playing drums, 'cause that got me the pass. That got me the "cool guy," that opened the door to keeping away from being in the gangs and that whole scene. So I must've been like maybe eight, nine years old when that happened.

I started studying privately. I went to Pasadena City College, to Grove School of Music in Van Nuys. Then I started doing a lot of local playing, a lot of touring. I didn't take music seriously in my high school years. But I still played in rock bands and then I started getting more local gigs, and then some out of town. One of my first [gigs with an] artist that actually had been signed to a label was a band called Shadowfax. And they asked me to play on a track and I went to the studio and played on the album. And then the leader, Chuck, asked me to be a band member . . . So then we started touring, all over the East Coast. The album got nominated for a Grammy . . . I was in the band for about four years. We did three albums and it was an experience; it was my introduction to touring and performing and learning odd-time-signature music and playing electronic instruments. It wasn't just jazz. This is way before the term "contem-porary jazz" I think was even in the in the picture . . . And then I started working with different artists. A lot of Latin artists: Álvaro Torres, Joan Sebastian, and other Latin artists. The Rippingtons, I played in that band for a while.

BA: Why percussion, why drums?

RY: I think it just called me, it just had the energy. For me it's like the—the driver of every song, whether [it] is live or recording, is the drums. It's the heartbeat, and that got me and that told me: you got to learn how to do this. I first started playing drum set, but I didn't study it. I just learned by ear. I would sit with records and headphones and watch whatever I could and mimic it and then realize, "ah, that's how you get those sounds" . . . But then I started doing more research on drums and percussion and I realized I want to get more into percussion. The cultural element of it drew me closer to percussion, so then I started studying, a lot of private study. One of my first teachers was Luis Conte. I would drive to his house and borrow money from my parents to take lessons from him.

JK: You said that drums and percussion are culture and there's a "cultural thing" behind it. Can you expand on how you got introduced to that notion?

RY: The music that my parents would play in the house, whether on the radio or albums like José Feliciano, I would hear drums. I would hear bongos, the bongo pattern, the martillo pattern playing in a bolero or the congas. And then I would think, "wow that sounds so beautiful! There's no drum set, yet the energy and the drive is there." And then I realized, "I'm hearing this in Latin music, I'm not hearing it in Western pop music" . . . you would hear that later in the dance music where they would add percussion, like Miami Sound Machine. But [here's] the difference for me that drew that: I was noticing [that] every song that I heard percussion as a kid was in Spanish, everything, and I liked it. And being a kid trying to be cool with your friends: no, I don't like that music, but yet I was drawn to listening when it was playing in the house. That's really nice, it's really cool. What pattern, what does that mean? And then you would hear the elements: that's a Cuban drum, it's a Cuban rhythm being played on top of a trio, which is more Mexican music. More of the Mexican culture. But the blend of the percussion in that element really got my attention. I mean, they don't play the same rhythms as the drums, as we know.

The drums are keeping a separate beat, a two and a four perhaps. Whereas the percussion is making that groove sweeter, it's delivering more of a—just a solid groove. It enhances the drum part. That's what got my attention as a kid and made me want to study it, made me just want to learn that.

BA: You were initially a drummer but then you transitioned to playing everything. How does that open up your world and your opportunities as a musician?

RY: It definitely opened up a lot of doors. I was able to play a lot of different styles of music. I remember one time driving in the car with my wife, I turn the radio on—this is when we were dating. She put on KLVE, the Spanish-language radio station, and then I hear "Secreto de Amor," the Joan Sebastian song that I play percussion on. And I thought, "oh that's cool, Latin radio." Then changed it to [smooth jazz station] the Wave and I'm hearing a jazz song on the radio that I played on. And then I hear "Ain't No Other Man" by Christina Aguilera that I played on, on pop radio! Wow, man, I'm able to play jazz, Latin, and pop and it's on the radio, all within two or three hours of each other!

BA: You've played with a lot of major pop music figures: Stevie Wonder, Carlos Santana, Christina Aguilera, Willie Nelson, Juan Gabriel, Paulina Rubio, the Backstreet Boys. How much of an influence do you think Latin music has had in pop music?

RY: I think the key is to give little hints here and there. You learn after years of playing. One thing I've always forced upon myself is working with a drummer . . . I approach music by the structure of the song. I want to make the song sound better. Not every song needs congas, not every song needs a bell; it may be just something really light. I want the artist to just do their thing, play their song, and I want to enhance it. I don't want to get in the way of the song. Ever.

JK: So the clave becomes a way of decoding all of these different styles. As a drummer you're playing patterns. We can go through the history of Western pop and actually pull out these little "secret codes."

RY: Yeah, you know it's in there, it's a rhythm, it really is. It's in there and without you even knowing. There is Latin music hidden in there! But yet you hear the backbeat, which kind of takes it away from being a Latin song. I love how Sting's music, certain songs are in odd time signatures, and yet you don't even know it. All these little beautiful elements that are hidden within the songs. Like clave, even a conga pattern, if it's played right, it won't be Latin. If it's played right, within the song.

JK: Do you see yourself, when you show up to a session, as representing a tradition? Do you feel that weight at all, that there's a tradition behind you?

RY: For some gigs, yes. When I worked with Strunz & Farah, that's tradition. You got to play "martillo" pattern on the bongos. You're representing the percussion section or the percussion part of these songs as a traditional element. Even when I was playing with Joan Sebastian, there was a very traditional aspect to it. He was very proud to have Latinos in his band, but he wanted LA-based musicians. He wanted to go to Mexico with LA cats. Pepe Aguilar too.

BA: And why did Joan Sebastian want LA players?

RY: He felt they were delivering his music properly, especially on the pop side. On that stage, he had *banda*, mariachi, and the pop setup, three different bands. I remember we played at the Universal Amphitheater, and I looked at the stage and there must've been thirty musicians up there, but three different bands! When he wanted to do *banda*, that *banda* was from Mexico. And then the top mariachi band. And then us, with Enrique Martínez conducting the whole show. I mean, it was solid. It was probably one of the most beautiful concerts. Pepe Aguilar, the same way. We do the same thing.

BA: Have you seen an increase in interest of Latin percussion, for pop music?

RY: It comes and goes. My first introduction to being involved in the pop stuff was with 98 Degrees and then immediately I went from 98 Degrees to the Backstreet Boys tour. And then it was insane. This is when Backstreet was at their peak. We were playing stadiums and arenas multiple nights in the late nineties, early 2000s. And then from there I went directly to Patty Labelle. And then from Patty Labelle to Christina Aguilera. I did two tours with Christina. But percussion was very important for those artists. And there was a lot of electronics involved as well, whether it's claps or sound effects or grooves. But then I would go to congas a lot, but I wouldn't stay on the congas. That to me would be too much Latin. People see congas they think "Latin music." It doesn't have to be, because if you listen to funk to all that '70s music, the congas are slamming and that's funk.

BA: Tell us about a session that you remember as a special experience.

RY: I was actually very proud to be on [a recording by] an artist named Luz Casal. Oh my God! We did her album. Another one who came to LA to record the project here, from Spain. When I got called to the session I didn't know who she was. Her voice just got me by surprise, that day in the studio. So we show up in the studio. It was Luis [Conte] and myself on percussion, and Alex Acuña on drums, René Camacho on bass, Ramon Stagnaro on guitar.

BA: All Latin session musicians.

RY: It was amazing! It was one of those days . . . So we are in the studio and all I'm playing on the session—because you got Luis on percussion and Alex is on drum set—is maracas, bell, and bongos. Bongos in two songs. All I did on three songs was maracas. Alex was not playing hi-hat. Alex was playing brushes on the snare and very light, beautiful textures. And at one point I went slightly off the pattern with the maracas, just give it a little color, and the producer goes, "Ray, oye Yslas, save that for your album! I just need the [basic pattern]." And I thought that was the funniest shit, man! So then it became, "I'm the hi-hat now, I'm the time keeper on this track." And it became one of those things where I just planted my feet. Like a batter getting ready to bring in, with bases loaded. But the simplest little tiny thing that you take for granted, that I would take for granted—maracas, shaker—I had to nail it. And you don't want to be the cat who has to fix your parts while everybody goes into the room. Stay in the click.

There was another session I did for *American Idol*. That was with Ricky Minor. Ricky was amazing throughout my career; he has given me work here and there, on TV, he got me on the Christina Aguilera gig, Backstreet Boys, Patty Labelle. This is at Capitol Records, Sunday morning you show up and you look at the charts. I'm scanning to see how many songs we're doing; we had to do thirteen complete songs. In that session was Abe Laboriel Sr. and Abe Laboriel Jr., Paul Jackson Jr., a full string section in the other room that we're hearing thru the headphones. Everybody is tracking live. Talk about charts. You're following the charts, playing little things here and there. Then, let's move on to the next song. Sometimes we'd get it in one take. And the funny thing is that Abe Laboriel Sr. and Jr. never made a mistake. The producer would say, "alright you guys, any fixes?" I have to do a tambourine part now; a guitar player says, "I have to fix a bar." Abe Sr. and Jr. would look at each other and say, "I'm good. Are you good, dad?" "Yes, I'm good. Vámonos!" They'd go back into the room, groove locked. One of the most beautiful things I've ever seen, working with both of them. We did thirteen songs in eight hours, one right after the other, half-hour lunch break, then back in the room.

JK: What's been the role, on the arc of your career, of your parents' background from Sonora. What's been the role of Mexico, culturally, musically, on you as a Mexican American in LA?

RY: Growing up, you don't think about that. My kids aren't thinking about that now. The older I got, I realized I started to get more calls to play Latin music. And back then my Spanish wasn't up to par. Because I grew up speaking more English than Spanish. My Spanish consisted of talking to my parents. But that was it. Outside of the house, it was just not there. But when I started doing more Latin gigs, I realized, I got to communicate more in Spanish. Where you start to respect, and look back at your upbringing, right? You look at your parents and you start asking more questions, about their history and everything. It's interesting, neither one of them played instruments. We had relatives who played instruments, but they weren't popular instruments. My aunt was a poet, not a songwriter. She wrote books and books of poetry. She was my mom's sister. She wrote a few poems that Juan Gabriel put into songs. No credit. But he gave her cash. He gave her gifts. But did it come from there? I don't know . . . As I got more exposed to the Latin artist side of playing percussion, [it became] more important to me. Me being me. I took it more to heart. I realized that this is just not my last name. This is something that is in my blood, this is my family. Especially when I work with artists like Pepe Aguilar, people from Mexico. I just recently worked with Natalia Lafourcade. I played the Latin Grammys with her . . . And, you know what was cool, all I played was *cajón* on that gig. It was fun. And another thing which just made me proud: another Latina, from Mexico. She took the Latin Grammys that night. She took home like five Latin Grammys. It made me really proud to be Mexican American, to be working with her.

BA: Twenty years from now, what do you think would be the sound of LA?

RY: I think it's going to be heavy on the Latin side. I'll tell you that. I think the creativity side. I get really impressed when I hear young Latin music, creative minds that are learning the technology, that are blending the DJ element, of electronic music with a little bit of culture, which I really dig. I really dig that part. What La Santa Cecilia is doing. I remember when I first saw them, years ago we were doing a show with Cesar Castro . . . I remember seeing them and thinking, "wow!" It wasn't completely different, or brand new, but the elements were just a little bit spicier. It was like the food was a little bit spicier; it had more of a taste to it. And that's the thing . . . When I saw La Santa Cecilia, I said, "OK this is going to be big. This is going to be a new representation of East LA."

The percussionist, Miguel Ramirez, he took my percussion class at Pasadena City College when I was teaching. He was in my class back in the day. But he already knew how to play. I said, "why are you here? This is beginning percussion." And the original drummer, he also was in my class . . . I told him, "You better be careful what you wish for man, because when that boat sails, you're going to be out there for a long time."

NOTE

1. Acuña's memory of this session contradicts the Musicians Union personnel credits, as discussed in the introduction. We left his memory of the session here because even if inaccurate it speaks to the fluidity of culture among session players at the time, from *The Tonight Show* to the Tijuana Brass.

11

FROM BAHIANAS TO THE KING OF POP . . .

A Speculative History of Brazilian Music into Los Angeles

O QUE É QUE A BAHIANA TEM?
WHAT DOES A BAHIANA HAVE?

Ladies and gentlemen, Carmen Miranda—no other. You know ladies and gentlemen now there's a lot more to samba, as I just found out, than meets the virgin ear. Now I've got a full complement of really top samba players here at the microphone and they are going to help us now to investigate the anatomy of samba. Now I'm no authority but plenty of authorities are standing by. . . .

Brazilian babies can beat out samba rhythms before they can talk and dance the samba before they can walk, at least that's what I was told and I believe them.

—ORSON WELLES FROM THE END CREDITS OF
IT'S ALL TRUE WITH CARMEN MIRANDA.

The journey of the collation of rhythms known as samba into the rest of the Americas during the Getulio Vargas regime was a huge success. Samba was a real cultural pawn in the Good Neighbor Policy—a scheme to ensure that the Germans or indeed Japanese wouldn't open up another front against the United States. Samba itself, it has been argued, is what makes Brazil Brazil.

Photo archive from Dori Caymmi's House in Woodland Hills, 2008. Included with Dori are Chico Buarque, Quincy Jones, Pelé, Milton Nascimento, Gilberto Gil, Branford Marsalis, Antônio Carlos Jobim, and, of course, his father Dorival Caymmi.

In the 1910s Rio de Janeiro was in flux. Many people from the former capital of the country, Bahia, came south in search of better lives away from the treacherous ways of the *coronel* system (similar to share cropping in the United States). In the city itself there was development and displacement. Praça Onze was being torn down and old geographical alliances were being moved to the Morro (hill) and the first favelas were being constructed. Out of this chaos several young musicians began to play a new style, a blend of *batuques*, or rhythms. A hybrid, urban, modern style birthed from the *terreiros* (sacred spaces for the practice of candomble Afro-Brazilian religion). The Mae de Santos, the elder women priests, many of whom sold fruit on the street during the day, known on the street as Bahianas (women from Bahia), acted as midwives for these young musicians as they manifested this new style. This music was samba. Samba and its cousin *capoeira* become the first social institutions created by blacks newly freed from slavery in Brazil.

Samba was indigenous to Brazil, new, modern ("Pelo Telephone," the first samba recorded in 1917, is an homage to the new technology of the telephone), and yet deeply routed in the narratives of Afro-Brazil. It attracted and inspired many of Brazil's intellectual elite. Hermano Vianna conclusively argues that samba itself helps to create the modern nation of Brazil.

Carmen Miranda, Portuguese by birth, Carioca by culture, became an early star of the music. Her quick wit and strong voice captured the imagination of many and popularized the style through the new mediums of radio and cinema in Brazil. Since the mid-1920s the Bahiana had been a popular trope for the Carnivalesque in the Rio Balls, and many white women adopted the garb of the women who cultivated samba. In 1939 Miranda adopted the headdress of the Bahainas of Praca Onze and sang the Dorival Caymmi tune "O que é que a Bahiana tem?," a song of empowerment honoring these women from Bahia. Shortly thereafter she was spotted by a promoter from the United States; he offered her a contract for a musical on Broadway. She insisted on bringing her band—that was her commitment to samba. The promoter refused to pay for the group's travel and the Vargas government stepped in to save the day, making Miranda a proxy ambassador for Brazilian culture to the United States. She made her stage debut in 1939 and quite quickly was cast as Argentinean, Cuban, or often just "the Latin chick" She became a big star on Broadway and moved to Hollywood. Filmmakers there had little desire for cultural specificity, yet Miranda fought through and became the highest-paid female star by 1945. Her work with Busby Berkeley on the film *The Gang's All Here* singing "The Lady with the Tutti Frutti Hat" has inspired thousands of impersonators, mostly oblivious to its Afro-Brazilian root.

The constraints of the Good Neighbor Policy, the extreme insecurity of the marketplace, and ultimately the difficulty of being the best-paid woman in Hollywood put Miranda's cultural position in a precarious place. It was always going to be a fight with stereotypes, a collision with a country that looked to Europe rather than the south for culture. However, Miranda's minstrelsy earned her many fans in the United States and introduced samba to an eager American public. She built a cultural bridge that somehow made invisible black cultural and diasporic production but opened up a discussion that had began earlier and would flourish in the ensuing years. Her impact is immeasurable; she is still a popular icon; her fruit-adorned turban and exaggerated makeup are instantly recognizable. The United Fruit Company came up with the Chiquita to sell bananas as an imitation of her iconic character.

In many ways her work is emblematic: she reveals little about history or origin but had a huge impact in both worlds, linking the postslavery survival strategies of Brazil's newly urbanized populations to the excessive high stakes world of 1940s Hollywood. As Caetano Veloso has said, to think of Carmen is "to think of the complexity of the relationship between the US and Brazil."

She died tragically at the age of forty-six after feeling ill while performing on the Jimmy Durante show in Los Angeles. Her funeral in Rio was a huge public display of grief.

A few months after Carmen left on August 7, 1940, the *USS Uruguay* sailed into Rio de Janeiro harbor with a young orchestra (the All American Youth Orchestra) eager to play North American music for a Carioca audience, no doubt bemused by all this new attention. The orchestra was led by Leopold Stokowski—he had been the music director of the Philadelphia Orchestra and was a well-known figure, not least for his role in *Fantasia,* the animated film from the Disney Studios. Perhaps this is what had prompted the US government to send Stokowski to South America on this huge vessel as a further extension of the Good Neighbor Policy.

Stokowski was friends with Heitor Villa Lobos, the acclaimed father of modern Brazilian music. Villa Lobos, for his part, was a huge fan of samba and indeed connected not only to its biggest stars but to the men and women who originated the music, many who had never been recorded, let alone seen the kind of stardom that Carmen Miranda was enjoying. On the night of August 7 (meticulously documented by Daniella Thompson on her blog),[1] Villa Lobos and Stokowski conspired to create one of the most beautiful documents of Brazilian music of the prewar era. They had invited some of the most important musicians of the Rio scene—Pixinguinha, Cartola, João Do Bahiana, Donga (cowriter of "Pelo Telephone"), and Ze Espinguela. Also part of this session was a young classical guitarist who was also a fan of the new music, Laurindo Almeida.

From midnight on August 7 until 10 AM the following day forty songs were committed to wax. According to liner notes on the double set of 78s, the music was "All personally chosen and supervised by Leopold Stokowski"—however, according to the Rio press from the following day, Stokowski went to bed around 3 AM, leaving the majority of the recordings to those there. The result is an invaluable record, one that basically vanished into the Columbia vaults. Most of the musicians were never paid (Cartola only heard his recording years and years later through a record collector), but they remain a fantastic document of an early exchange between North American record men and Afro-Brazilian music. Stokowski came back to the United States and within a year or two had formed the Hollywood Bowl Orchestra.

Clearly North America was ready for the pizzazz and comedy of Carmen, but more serious investigation of Brazilian music was going to have to wait.

JAZZ SAMBA AND SAMBA JAZZ TO BOSSA NOVA: ALMEIDA, SHANK, DONATO, SERGIO MENDES, AND CANNONBALL

Bossa Nova had its fling with American Jazz, especially the West Coast jazz, but it never lost its Brazilian character. What was called "samba-jazz" from the West Coast had nothing whatsoever to do with Bossa Nova. It was only a laminated hybrid.

—VINICIUS DE MORAES, LINER NOTES FOR PAUL WINTER'S
RIO ALBUM, 1965.

"To Sid, Viva in the South American Way . . . Carmen Miranda March 24th 1941." Carmen Miranda's footprints in front of Sid Grauman's Chinese Theatre, Hollywood Boulevard, January 2017.

> Bossa Nova has often been derided as a whitening of samba for cocktail drinking sophisticates. But the Brazilian jazz musicians of the late 1950s knew that by incorporating greater blues influence into their playing they were tapping into the headwaters of African American music. Bossa Nova proved compelling in part because it offered both exciting new terrain for musical experimentation and a path back to a parallel musical tradition.
>
> —BRYAN MCCANN, "BLUES AND SAMBA: ANOTHER SIDE OF BOSSA NOVA HISTORY," *LUSO BRAZILIAN REVIEW*, 2007.

There are many accounts of how "The Girl from Ipanema" and its new rhythm conquered the popular music world. And to run in the face of the great Vinicius, few, however, give ample credit to the collision that was already happening between samba, blues, and jazz. In the United States there was jazz samba and in the Rio there was samba jazz.

One of the many legends that had played on the *USS Uruguay* made his way to Los Angeles in the 1940s. Laurindo Almeida had moved from Rio through Europe to the United States in 1947—he was an adept and sensitive (self-taught) classical guitarist. While in Paris he had seen Django Reinhardt and it forever changed his life. He went on to play with the great Stan Kenton Orchestra. Kenton ran a progressive orchestra more concerned with complex ideas and finding new idioms than with being merely a dance band.

Almeida and Bud Shank, both alums of the Stan Kenton Orchestra, went into the World Pacific studios in Los Angeles with Richard Bock in 1953 and rewrote the playbook for Brazilian music and jazz. Shank was part of a crew of reed men that later would be known as the West Coast Cool school; it included Art Pepper, Gerry Mulligan, Shorty Rogers, and Stan Getz, all Kenton alums. *Laurindo Almeida featuring Bud Shank,* later known as *Brazilliance,* was their combined effort and it was a massive success. Backed by merely Harry Babasin on bass and Roy Harte on drums, Almeida and Shank worked their way through an esoteric collection of great Brazilian music.

The album opens with "Atabaque" by Radamés Gnattali and its economy and overwhelmingly Carioca melody instantly conjure what could be possible in the collision of the two musical styles. The record is primarily written by Brazilians: Gnattali is represented with several pieces; samba and *choro* founder Pixinguinho is represented with "Carinhoso"; Carmen Miranda collaborator and giant of Brazilian song Ary Barrosso has two compositions; most surprising, however, is Almeida and Shanks's version of the classic *"Baiao."*

Baiao is a rhythm from the northeast of Brazil created by *sanfonista* (accordionist) and cultural superhero Luiz Gonzaga with lyrics by Humberto Teixeira; the song "Baiao" entices the listener to dance to this new rhythm; it was a hugely popular hit in Brazil in 1946, but ostensibly would have been considered regional music. Almeida and Shanks's "Blue Baiao" begins in a wonderfully restrained way, Shank following the classic northeastern melody—however, about half way through, he takes off on a series of runs that would make Gonzaga or even Dominguinhos proud. In a spectacular turn, the popular dance floor smash from the Pernambucano hit factory gets a West Coast jazz workout.

On World Pacific Jazz, recorded in Los Angeles a good five years before Gilberto's *Chega De Saudade, Brazilliance* was hugely popular and wonderfully preemptory.

Bryan McCann tells of how at the same moment Rio was alive with new experiments and extraordinary virtuosity in the mid- to late 1950s. The influence of big band swing from the United States, combined with the growth of the radio orchestras under the Vargas regime, had led to a new professionalization of the music in Rio. This new concentration of music professionals led to new possibilities for musicians in the late 1940s into the mid-1950s.

Moacir Santos, Edson Machado, Paulo Moura, and Booker Pittman all were extending the vocabulary of jazz and blues into a new idiom samba jazz. Samba jazz bristled with influence from its neighbors to the north; however, it would be foolish to think that this was merely imitation. Santos was an extraordinary arranger-composer in his own right, and while his first solo record—the exemplary and beautiful *Coisas*—didn't emerge until 1965, his influence was felt either through his arrangements for others, through his teaching, or indeed in his playing. He was the first Afro-Brazilian to write for the Radio Nacional Orchestra.

Booker Pittman, on the other hand, was an American who had come to Brazil through some European dates with a big band. He had taken a gig and disappeared in the state of Para in the mid-1940s. He reemerged in Rio in the 1950s with arrangements from the great Lindolfo Gaya and, with his stepdaughter Eliana, and took the city by storm. His swing and style were influential in that burgeoning scene. McCann conclusively argues that blues, at the root of jazz, was a driving force in the Brazilian pre-bossa moment. Pittman's jazz credentials were secure and his reemergence in the mid-1950s was instructive.

Listening to any of the Edson Machado albums from this period yields a perspective on this Brazilian scene virtuosic, bristling and full of originality. His *É Samba Nova* album from 1964 is a head-spinning journey through eleven chunks of extraordinary trill-brass-filled energy. Four of the pieces are by Moacir Santos, four are by the young J.T. Meirelles, and the band is a who's who of Brazilian jazz at that moment. Moacir Santos, Paulo Moura on sax, Ed Maciel on trombone, J.T. Meirelles on sax, Pedro Paulo on trombone, Sebastião Neto on bass, the incredible and tragic Tenorio Junior on piano, and of course Edson Machado on drums. All these figures would go on to record vast amounts of music in the ensuing decade, not just contributing to the instrumental tradition but writing and playing with all the greats of popular Brazilian music. Moacir Santos moved to LA in the late 1960s and made several albums for Blue Note, but more on that later.

Needless to say, bossa nova superseded samba as the main cultural export from 1959 onward. The ground paved by Laurindo Almeida, Bud Shank, and indeed Chet Baker and the many more commercial or popular jazz experiments primarily happening out west made an intervention by João Gilberto and Antonio Carlos Jobim possible. It was merely a matter of time before a huge hit would happen and in 1964 it did. Kenton orchestra alum Stan Getz and João Gilberto recorded an album under the guidance of the great Creed Taylor—which yielded the monster hit "The Girl from Ipanema," penned by Antonio Carlos Jobim and Orson Welles's drinking buddy, poet and diplomat Vinicius DeMoraes. The version that was released on 45 was an edit that cut out Gilberto's singing and left his wife Astrud's vocal. A brilliant cut by Taylor, a man who played a huge role in Brazilian music's proliferation.

Bossa nova became a huge cultural force. As North American popular music heated up with the new rhythm and blues–inspired rock 'n roll, another path emerged with bossa. It would be silly not to also mention here the Marcel Camus–directed *Orfeu Negro* (which had won Cannes that year) and has been considered a classic since. Adapted from a play by Vinicius De Moraes—*Orfeu Negro* was a great international vessel for the new music. The producer commissioned new music for the film (in an attempt to keep the publishing) and Antonio Carlos Jobim, Vinicius de Moraes, and Luiz Bonfa wrote the music and its popularity hasn't diminished to this day. The theme "Manha De Carnival" remains one of the most recorded songs of that period.

Sadly it clearly exoticized Brazil, glossed over the social conditions of the Rio favela dwellers, and maligned the play Vinicius had written. Vinicius walked out of the premiere appalled. But the world loves the film regardless. Curiously enough, one of the great contributors to the local Los Angeles Brazilian scene is Carlinhos Pandeiro de Ouro; he is one of the children in that famous scene when they ask, "please play your *violao* to make the sun rise."

Brazil was entering a period of profound cultural activity: in theater Augusto Boal was reinventing the relationship of theater to the public sphere; in visual arts Lygia Clarke and Helcio Oiticica and many others were finding new ways to make art post the object; Glauber

Carlinhos Pandeiro de Ouro (child actor from *Orfeu Negro* and esteemed percussionist, in Los Angeles, 2006).

Rocha and Nelson Pereira Dos Santos were breaking the shackles of Italian Neo-Realism and inventing Cinema Novo; and in music Jobim, Vinicius, Gilberto, and a young accordionist from Acre in the far west of Brazil called João Donato were inventing the new thing bossa nova with their young, upper-middle-class friends on the Zona Sul of Rio.

All of these cultural gestures would have a huge impact inside Brazil and later on outside, but bossa struck first. After the song "Chega do Saudade" was released by João Gilberto, things began to shift quickly in Brazil. In the United States, almost immediately Charlie Byrd and Stan Getz began to cut versions of the new music and it wasn't long before Quincy Jones cut "Soul Bossa Nova" and then Floridean Miles Davis alum Cannonball Adderley cut "Jive Samba."

In jazz there was certainly always room for new ideas and it seemed that the pop inklings of bossa nova were a good fit. According to legendary drummer Leon Ndugu Chancler, the bossa nova is just an extension of the New Orleans Second Line and Afro-Cuban clave; the root is there and the rhythm misses a beat—which gives it that inclusive samba swing. Melodically João Gilberto innovated with the *violao;* the *violao* is a six-string acoustic guitar, similar to the classical guitar, with nylon strings. Bossa nova was popular so quickly in Brazil that the *violao* replaced the accordion as the most popular instrument for young Brazilians in a matter of a year. The accordion had been the most popular instrument since the 1940s, clearly in no small measure due to the efforts of Luiz Gonzaga and his *baiao.*

The *violao* is so soft that its dynamic affects all the other instruments: everything needs to be either quiet or sparse. The new music clearly benefited from new recording technologies being developed after World War II that allowed close micing and wide dynamic range. Gilberto, up to today, is a master of the quiet. He famously is a nightmare for live sound technicians because his voice is never more than a whisper and he is forever unsatisfied with his microphones.

Jobim, continuing in the tradition of the great Villa Lobos, brought extraordinary, modern, lush arrangements and a unique new voice in his compositions. His undeniable pop skills, underwritten by the sophistication of his orchestrations, put Jobim's catalogue up against any of the twentieth century. There are just so many great songs. By any measure he is clearly one of the greatest postwar composers.

Jobim's first arranging gig in 1956 is the debut album of a young pianist and the mysterious musketeer of bossa nova João Donato.

Originally from Acre, deep in the Amazon, on the border with Peru, he began as an accordion player. João Gilberto claims that he envisioned bossa nova while watching Donato play piano, much in the same way that Charlie Parker claimed to imagine what he wanted to do musically while listening to Art Tatum. Donato, just as bossa nova began to become popular, got an offer to come to the United States. Panamanian bandleader Wally Fernez offered him six weeks of work at Harrah's in Lake Tahoe. And unbeknown to most of the music community a real treasure snuck in and began working in the Bay area from October 1959.

Donato was a child prodigy. His first professional gig was at fifteen. He was the main pianist at the Sinatra fan club, which was the social hub that produced most of the stars of bossa nova. His memories of this time in the United States are remarkable: "Stan Getz wasn't really popular at that time—it was the bossa nova that saved his career . . . I wasn't fortunate enough to meet Carmen Miranda—she was already dead—but I did meet Cannonball Adderley. I played with Bud Shank at a place in Sausalito called the Trident—its still there. I played there with Chet Baker and Bud Shank; we lived in House Boat there side by side . . . And Cannonball showed up there; he was playing at the Jazz Workshop in San Francisco and we found ourselves walking on that little deck there . . . 'Hi, Cannonball!' . . . 'Hi. João, are you living in that little boat?' In that one over there, it was a joke, as if we were in Thailand."

In truth Donato, in his own humble way, came in the backdoor and then was the best-kept secret in the West Coast jazz scene. He played with Shank (most notably on *Bud Shank and His Brazilian Friends* with Rosinha Da Valenca), Cal Tjader on several albums (including *Solar Heat*), Mongo Santamaría on two albums (*Arriba* and *Live at the Blackhawk*) and even Tito Puente on *Vaya Puente.* All the while, bossa nova became a bigger and bigger influence on pop music worldwide. "The guys came around asking about me about João [Gilberto], they wanted to know 'Who is this cat?' They then began to listen to the album there in the United States. And they became interested . . . Stan Getz ended up appearing; he was gone, Stan Getz; nobody knew who he was—nobody was talking about him when he recorded

João Donato with Gaelle Cross (daughter of the author), Urca, Rio de Janeiro, 2014.

'The Girl from Ipanema.' He got pop—became a star on the charts. Then jazz became popular again, because jazz was never that popular it was always . . . jazz."

João went back to Brazil for two years in the middle and cut two albums, both classics: *A Bossa Muito Moderno* and *Muito a Vontade,* highly sought after records that display an equally original vision for the new music as anything Gilberto or Jobim were doing. Then he returned to the United States and began recording in earnest. Between 1965 and 1972 (when he returned to Brazil for good), he recorded three solo albums with varying degrees of success. *The New Sound of Brazil* for RCA, *A Bad Donato* for Blue Thumb Records, and *Donato/Deodato* a colloboration with Eumir Deodato.

But the real breakthrough came on his second return to Brazil. Donato was almost a mystical figure; his records were hugely regarded but few had met him because he was living in the United States. Through a meeting with Agostinho dos Santos he decided to collaborate with lyricists. Within a year he was working with all the best Brazil had to offer: Gilberto Gil, Caetano Veloso, Marcos Valle, Nana Caymmi, Emiliano Santiago, and even Milton Nascimento—his solo record from this period, *Quem É Quem,* is regarded as one of the five greatest Brazilian records of all time.

The impact of bossa nova in the United States between 1960 and 1968 is vast and unprecedented. "The Girl from Ipanema" is the second-most recorded song in pop history after "Yesterday" by the Beatles. We are used to clichés about the Brit Invasion; we never hear of the Brazilian one. Antonio Carlos Jobim's record with Frank Sinatra, recorded at Hollywood Sound Recorders, was nominated for a Grammy for best album in 1968, only to be beaten out by *Sgt. Peppers Lonely Hearts Club Band.* Absolutely everyone tried their hand at the new thing, from jazz legends to pop ingénues. Getz's and Gilberto's success had prompted a veritable stampede to the rhythm of this international samba. However, the subtle poetry of Vinicius De Moraes that accompanied the Brazilian music was often lost to mediocre translations or approximations.

At the height of the first wave of bossa nova in December 1962, the Brazilian consul in New York decided to organize a show at Carnegie Hall. It was a huge investment in the new music and introduced several of its new stars to a North American public. It was given mixed reviews back in Brazil, although generally it was considered a big success. The show led to some serious copyright issues, though, as several publishing companies claimed to have rights to administering the music after the concert. The complexity of the exchange between north and south seemed to be intact; nonetheless, the Carnegie Hall concert made a big impact and also helped pave the way for the success that would follow.

A chance meeting in New York after the infamous concert would lead to the apex of Brazilian music into Los Angeles. Cannonball Adderley, the great alto player, who, along with John Coltrane, Bill Evans, Jimmy Cobb, and Paul Chambers, had made up the band that played *Kind of Blue* with Miles Davis, was playing at Birdland. Cannon had been introduced to bossa nova music by Miles Davis a few years earlier. Lena Horn had given Miles *Chega De Saudade* by João Gilberto, and of course he played it for his friend.

One of the Brazilian visitors for the Carnegie Hall show, a young pianist, a student of Moacir Santos, and a leader of the Bossa Rio Sextet, decided to go down to Birdland and see the great Cannonball Adderley. After the show they hung out and decided to make a recording. By 1962, Cannonball was no stranger to the new music and was astute enough to recognize the difference between playing with a Brazilian band, especially one of this stature, and playing with a US one. In picking the repertoire, he also knew that it would be "artificial to twist either pop standards or jazz originals into a Bossa Nova format."[2] The album *Cannonball's Bossa Nova* makes it seem, for all intents and purposes, that he went to Rio, hooked up with the hottest young band (several members were part of the samba jazz scene; both Paulo Mauro and Pedro Paulo are on the Edson Machado record mentioned above), and really made something that bridged the two worlds. Cannonball was a unique musical figure. His taste was wildly popular, but he was deeply rooted within the jazz idiom. He was constantly on the lookout for young musicians and new places to take the music. The meeting with Sérgio Mendes started a series of events that would result in the most fertile period of Brazilian influence in popular music that the United States has ever seen.

Everybody talks about Brazil, but they don't talk about Brazil making the African connection. That's why Bahia is so important, because when you deal with the Miltons and all of those guys, that African connection, that African root is what drives that rhythm. That African root is what drives all those dudes and their samba, not the bossa nova, but the African root is all embedded in that samba. So we, as African Americans, we already have a natural tendency to feel the pulse of that samba before.

—LEON "NDUGU" CHANCLER

Cannonball's Bossa Nova is a great example of what might be possible. Sérgio Mendes's band is taut, full of ideas, and Cannonball is clearly excited by the new possibilities. There's two Jobim compositions and even one by the new California resident João Donato. Subsequently Mendes made two records with the Ertugun brothers for Atlantic, which weren't particularly successful, and then came directly to Los Angeles to record with Herb Alpert and Jerry Moss. Alpert's idea was a more mainstream one—get singers, take the bossa nova to the pop market—clearly feeling the glow of Getz and Gilberto's success with "The Girl from Ipanema."

The Bossa Rio Sextet had given way to Brasil '65, which birthed Brasil '66, and on their first album with Alpert and Moss's A&M label, they completely broke the bank. Mendes inverted Cannonball's intuitive authenticity and cracked the musical clam of pop success.

Young Carioca Jorge Ben had written a completely perfect pop song in 1963 with "Mas Que Nada," and he recorded it with J.T. Mierelles and his band. Only recently was the song discovered to be an adaptation. In Europe and the United States there's a long tradition of adapting folk themes or airs into contemporary music. Beethoven had song collectors who fed his creative needs; Gershwin, Villa Lobos, and Caymmi transcribed the

Sérgio Mendes, during the recording of *Timeless* with will.i.am (not pictured), São Paulo, 2006.

songs they heard fishermen or cattle hands sing; and "Mas Que Nada" started off as a song on a record called *Tam Tam Tam* by Jose Prates. Prates, a pianist, is an interpreter of the music of the *terreiro*. The *terreiros* are the sacred church spaces of *candomble*, the Afro-Brazilian religion. Prates was part of a touring stage show put together by Mieco Askanasy, a Polish promoter and bookstore owner from Rio, in 1949 that had traveled the world as a

Cannonball Adderley from the house of David Axelrod, North Hollywood, 1998.

kind of folkloric theater show. Their first record, *Drums of Brazil,* came out in 1950 and, as you might expect, is a document of a theatrical show. However, in 1958 they cut record in the studio for Polydor. It is stunning, and track three of side one is "Nana Imboro," clearly a reference to Jorge Ben's early masterwork and one of the greatest pop songs of the post-war era.

Heliópolis, São Paulo, 2002.

It is hard to understand now just how remarkable it was, but Mendes and Brasil '66 with the *sambalanço,* or samba swing, were classic. It is really stunning. The song had been recorded by the great Tamba Trio earlier, but Mendes and Alpert gave it that big sound and the vocal by Lani Hall was perfect. This cemented Mendes's place in Los Angeles music. He had a hit, he had a new sound, and he had the attention of a great recording team in Alpert and his partner Jerry Moss.

A&M became the home for the new post-bossa Brazilian sound in the United States. Pretty soon they would record with Edu Lobo, Tamba Trio, and the man who would drive the influence of Brazil even further into the roots of African American music, Milton Nascimento.

POST-BOSSA AND MINAS GERAIS: MILTON NASCIMENTO, LUIZ EÇA, DEODATO, WAYNE SHORTER, AND EARTH, WIND & FIRE

The thread of this music runs through a lot of musicians. People go to the well of this kind of music as they would jazz, as they would classical music. This is Brazil's classical music.

—VERDINE WHITE, EARTH, WIND & FIRE, INTERVIEW WITH AUTHOR, DECEMBER 2016

By the late 1960s there were Brazilians all over the country making waves with their swing. In New York, Sivuca, the savant musician, was bandleader for South African refugee Miriam Makeba; Bossa Tres stayed on after the Carnegie concert and made several albums, most beautifully *Jazz Tempo, Latin Accents* with Clifford Brown, Prince Lasha, and Sonny Simmons. Bossa vocal group Quarteto Em Cy became the Girls from Bahia and "changed their address from Bahia to Burbank, even managed to bring the great Dorival Caymmi to Los Angeles to record."[3] Bola Sete was traveling the country with his tremendous trio, including hugely influential Paulinho Magalaes on drums. Donato was living between Los Angeles and the Bay Area, playing with Bud Shank, Sebastião Neto, and Rosinha Da Valenca. Marcos Valle was beginning to have traction with pop crooners like Andy Williams and Tony Bennett, eventually collaborating with the great Leon Ware. Edu Lobo, one of the greatest songwriters of the era, was penning tunes for Augusto Boal (*Upa Neguinho*) as well as making records for A & M. His catalog from this era is monumental. Flora Purim and Airto Moreira had just arrived from Brazil in New York. Even Mexico was feeling the benefit of many Brazilian extended-stay musicians. Amazing string arranger and pianist Luiz Eça and his Sagrada Familia were there, as was Tamba Trio, now Tamba 4.

The truth is that between 1964 and 1974 was a terrible time to be in Brazil. In 1964 João Goulart, a left-leaning, democratically elected president, had been overthrown by a carefully planned, US-backed coup. The nightmare of the 1960s in Brazil had begun. The 1950s had been an optimistic time for Brazilians; there was a palpable feeling that the moment was coming when they could finally take their place among the developed world. Brazilia, the new capital city, was constructed and Amazonia had begun to be opened up with the Trans-Amazonica highway. But darker forces loomed. In much the same way that the United States was terrified of another front for the Germans and Japanese during World War II, the possibility of a left-leaning South America with Russian sympathies became a strategic priority. A social-democratic government in Guatemala had been averted in 1954 with the use of a CIA-backed force. However, Fidel and Ché led a popular revolution and beat US-backed dictator Bautista off the Island of Cuba in 1959, and this was a huge cause for alarm among the anticommunist powers deep within the US government. This potential threat had to be assuaged immediately. Thus, in 1964 Brazil became the guinea pig for what was to come in Chile, Mexico, Argentina, and many more. Torture and the suppression of unions, students, and organizers of all stripes became the new normal, and by the time of the fifth decree in 1968 the democratic state had been abandoned entirely in favor of martial law.

Resistance among artists and musicians was both confrontational and often allegorical. From 1964 until late 1968 the social space for resistance seemed possible; however, after the death of high school student activist Edson Luis and the protests that followed, the government introduced the infamous fifth decree. Brazil had entered a new phase of its repression. This political reality drove and forced many Brazilians into exile. The censorship of lyrics, the internment of artists, the collapse of the public sphere, and the normalization of torture and disappearance all contributed to one of Brazil's darkest periods, but, as Christopher Dunn has noted, "one of its periods of greatest creative joy."

Sérgio Mendes's success at A & M and the presence of those great musicians in Los Angeles were a lure for many Brazilians. Airto Moreira, the legendary percussionist from Santa Catarina in the south and part of Quarteto Novo with Hermeto Pascoal, had been in New York with his partner Flora Purim, but he got word that Sérgio might be in need of a percussionist: "There were Brazilians here. There was Sérgio Mendes. I would talk to Brazilians and they would all encourage me to come to LA, saying it was like Brazil, sunny, clean, organized, and with Brazilian bands. I was going to audition with Sérgio Mendes—but a drummer from Brazil Dom Um Romão got the gig."

Dom Um Romão is an extraordinary and singular percussionist. His work with Weather Report later is shocking in its beauty. Famously, from time to time he played a solo with his shoes—no drums, just shoes. Airto may have been mistaken though, as Dom Um had played with Sérgio since the beginning and it seems implausible that Sérgio would have been hiring him when Airto came to LA in the late 1960s. Nonetheless, many Brazilians had found their way out west.

Ralph Gleason writes at the beginning of the liner notes for Milton Nascimento's *Courage* album on A & M from 1969, "Brazil is one of the oldest cultures of the Americas and certainly one which has gone far along the road to solving some of the social problems which haunt the United States." Clearly Gleason was writing about North America's racism in relation to Brazil's racial democracy narrative with little or no connection to what was happening on the ground—the dictatorship, the continuing exclusion of Afro-Brazilians and indigenous folks, and the suppression of many activists and artists, including Nascimento himself. The album's title, *Courage,* clearly didn't extend to Gleason's liner-note writing.

Milton Nascimento, the adopted child of a student of Villa Lobos and a mathematician and radio station owner from Tres Pontas in the state of Minas Gerais, had shot to fame from his early days as a rock 'n roller to a real post-bossa phenomena. He entered a song competition in Rio in 1967 and was heard by arranger and composer Eumir Deodato and the great American engineer and producer Creed Taylor. He had already recorded an album with Luis Eça when he went to New Jersey to make *Courage*. Creed Taylor and Deodato were taking no chances: the band was stellar—Herbie Hancock on piano, Airto Moreira on percussion, and a host of great string and horn players. In truth the arrangements aren't as stark or unique as what Luiz Eca had managed in Rio, but the record sounds bigger, and while it may not have broken Milton into a mainstream American audience, clearly folks were listening.

Jazz saxophonist Kamau Kenyatta from Detroit told me he remembers clearly listening to Milton on the radio at the University of Michigan in the late 1960s. Ndugu Chancler explains, "I was wondering how a lot of people got into him, like Maurice White from Earth, Wind & Fire in Chicago. Well here's the thing; they did play Milton in 1969 because he had an album on A & M called *Courage,* and it featured Herbie Hancock. That opened the door for me—that and an album by Paul Desmond that features some Milton music called *From the Hot Afternoons*. Both of those were on A & M, and that was in '68 or '69. It was starting to creep out by then."

Wayne Shorter had been paying attention too. He had recorded *Super Nova* with Airto in 1969 and even covered the Jobim song "Dindi." *Super Nova* is blisteringly beautiful; where Airto plays is full of rattle, counterrhythm, and feel. Miles Davis hired Airto not long after, and he became part of the rotating crew that made *Bitches Brew.* Walter Booker, bassist for Cannonball Adderley, is on *Super Nova,* and we may suspect that he was the one who brought in Airto.

It seems these were the last moments when African American jazz musicians were testing the water; after 1970 and especially after 1972, as we will see, there is a flood of Brazilian influence and musicians into jazz.

It is worth noting here that Bola Sete was also impacting the way the young jazz musicians were hearing the music. Ndugu Chancler explains again: "We never talk about Bola Sete at the Monterey Jazz Festival, and I want to say that was '68. It's a trio. You've got to hear it because the drummer, Paulinho [Magalhaes], did the samba; he did the *cuica;* he did all of that; and it was just a trio. They did "Samba de Orpheus"—the music of *Black Orpheus*—and it was one of the best treatments of that. Again, that was another introduction to the whole Brazilian thing that the world slept on—because it was coming from that jazz arena, it didn't get the commercialization."

It really feels as though these years were the tipping point. Jazz was changing to a more improvised, inclusive approach; Brazilians were now not just sending records or songs, but were already in the United States—a number of them with high profiles—and the language of the Brazilian approach, be it in jazz, samba, or bossa—was being understood.

In another chapter of Cannonball Adderley's involvement, he gathered his band and went to Brazil in 1972. According to his producer, David Axelrod, he came back a changed man: "He fell in love with Brazil, he came back and he would say, 'David, David, wherever you go, to whatever funky little bar there's music, I need to make enough money to where we can charter a jet to bring the entire family down, not just Adderleys and Axelrods but the entire family.'"

Cannonball went straight to the Capitol studios and made *The Happy People*. "Inspired by a trip to Brazil, the new music of Cannonball Adderley—like flesh and blood and Rio . . . hot and humid and happy and unimaginably real," reads the back of the record. Recorded in the unique Axelrod/Adderley style of live performance in front of an audience at the Capitol studios in Hollywood, *The Happy People* is impulsive, new, inspired, and ambitious. Axelrod arranged the title track: "He [Cannon] didn't know what the fuck was happening, the arrangement caught him by so much surprise . . . He had no idea I was coming back on the second day with singers. Well, I've always liked Brazilian music—who doesn't like Brazilian music—but I made it a samba; it is not a bossa nova . . . I made sure of that; it says over everybody's part, 'SAMBA' [followed by an] exclamation point."

The song, an Airto Moreira composition, is a roaring vamp. The lyrics say,

I want to tell you about this samba, samba, samba,
Samba do and Samba la,
In Brazilian carnival the people dance all day long

The only solo is Cannon, filled with happiness, clarity, and fire. His playing is full of emotion, and just when you think he has ventured too far, he falls back in with the rhythm, understated and somehow perfect. Cannonball's gift would be taken from the planet three years later at the age of forty-six. I dare say he never sounds happier than he does on this cut. The voices, the whispering, the crowd brought in for the session by Axelrod. The family was happy and it showed. Many of Axelrod's recordings are known for their tension but here the happy people won. The engine (or kitchen, as the Brazilians would say) is the percussion section of Airto and Mayuto Correa and the wonderful vamping of the young George Duke. This happiness was infectious and to me sustained this group of musicians after Cannon's passing. They would form the hub of Brazilian Los Angeles.

Joe Zawinul, the great improviser and writer of the huge hit "Mercy, Mercy, Mercy," left Adderley's group after nine years to play with Miles Davis. There was a revolving door between Miles's and Cannon's groups, which led to some tension at times, according to Axelrod. But, unfazed, Cannon brought in the young George Duke. Duke was something new. Born in San Rafael in Northern California, he was an entirely different generation than Zawinul or Adderley. He had played with Frank Zappa and was already making records for MPS in Germany. Brazil seemed to blow his mind. "George came back talking to us and turned us on," explained Ndugu.

On his record *Faces in Reflection* from 1974, Duke covers Milton Nascimento's "Maria Tres Filhos." He had first written an arrangement of this song for *The Happy People*. It is the only tune George Duke didn't write on *Faces in Reflection*—and the treatment is stunning. *Faces* is a trio record, with John Heard on bass and Leon Ndugu Chancler on drums. The Milton melody gets a full run, rinsed to its full beauty, constantly looping back to its emotional root. Ndugu is pressed to play big but quietly, and he plays perfectly, finding new pockets, playing the outside of the kit, discovering new ghosts and bringing the samba to Ike

Leon "Ndugu" Chancler, the Mayan Theater, Los Angeles, 2012.

and Tina Turner's Bolic Studios in Inglewood. Duke's music from here on out takes a distinctly Brazilian flavor, and, whether working with Airto, Flora, or indeed Ndugu, Duke never stopped paying attention to what was going on five thousand miles to the south. *Faces in Reflection* is but a sketch for what is to come, but clearly the trip south with Cannonball had set Duke on a path. Los Angeles music would now never not have the tint of its southern neighbor.

Cannonball Adderley helped Airto and Flora get their papers to stay in the United States: "He made us legal for this country, me and Flora. He signed everything, nobody wanted him to do that. His manager was pissed. He was a beautiful cat, man, him and Gil Evans. I cannot believe how good he was."[4] They had met in the Village Vanguard. Cannon already knew Flora, who was singing backup for Miriam Makeba and Sivuca. George Duke made the introduction and told Cannon, "You should see this guy on percussion he is serious." Of course Adderley never saw a Brazilian opportunity he didn't like! "Why don't you sit in with us."

Airto Moreira, at his home studio, Studio City, 2006.

Airto became the go-to percussionist, from Cannonball to Miles Davis to the early Weather Report. His unique style, homemade instruments, singing, and vast knowledge of Brazilian folkloric traditions became a wellspring for jazz folks, opening up a new vocabulary, a new palette.

Airto Moreira was born in the small town of Itaoipolis in the southern state of Santa Catarina. He played percussion before he could walk, a perfect example of a Wellesian Brazilian (see quote above). He traveled from a young age with the itinerant dance bands that played throughout rural Brazil. He always made a point to go out during the day and listen to the local sounds and rhythms. His first group, the Sambalanço Trio with Cesar Camargo Mariano, was a smash but the real breakthrough came with Quarteto Novo. Airto, Hermetto Pascual, Theo de Barros, and Heraldo Do Monte made up the group, and even though they have only one album, the eponymous recording from 1967, they continue to have a profound influence on Brazilian music.

Brazil was never just one thing. Bryan McCann, among others, has argued that the samba itself, in its ability to incorporate many rhythms, from *jongo* to *maracatu, lundu, coco,* and *repente,* and the invention of radio as a means to broadcast it are, in fact, the thing that made Brazil possible. Up until the late 1930s Brazil was still an aspirational idea. In the north there had been several breakaway states, including most heroically the one led by Lampiao and his wife Maria Bonita. Their story of tragic repression and beheading by the state in no small way captures the popular imagination in Brazil to this day. Luiz Gonzaga's *baiao* and its popularity bear the trace of this dissident Brazil. Samba may have become the national rhythm under Getulio Vargas with the help of Carmen Miranda, but that is merely one version. There are many more. Airto opens up other Brazils with his rhythmic vocabulary.

Natural Feelings is Airto's first solo record in the United States, recorded for Buddah Records in 1970. The lineup is a new kind of formation. He is joined by wife, Flora, and Sivuca, with Hermeto Pascoal from his Quarteto Novo days and the Miles Davis alum and legendary bass man Ron Carter. Airto, Sivuca, and Hermeto are not just multi-instrumentalists; they are feral imaginations. The record is brimming with echoes of regional Brazil. Gone are the limits of a micro Brazil, replaced with the huge palette, fitting for a country that is spread like a tropical picnic across the southern subcontinent. Airto had brought it all with him somehow—afro, *caipira, arabe, cangaçero, pescador*—and none of it sounded like a folk experiment ; it sounded completely urgent and contemporary.

In this period between 1970 and 1980, Airto filled up the musical lane with a huge volume of recordings. His rhythms launched many groups, from Weather Report to Return to Forever, from Opa to Fingers. He played behind way too many jazz greats to mention, but let's just name drop a few: Dizzy Gillespie, Miles Davis, Donald Byrd, Santana, Randy Weston, Wayne Shorter. He did this all the while maintaining a generous catalogue of solo recordings and producing and playing with his wife, Flora.

Flora herself is a pure lightening rod. Her albums from this period bridge jazz, vocalese, and rhythm and blues. Starting out as a post-bossa singer, Flora had grown into a firebrand vocalist backing up Miriam Makeba. Her unique free jazz vocals—part screech, part harmonies, part guttural reaches—made her an enormous draw in this era. Her bands were always exemplary and her performances often controversial but never dull. The fact that Airto and Flora maintained such a prolific recording schedule at this time—each developing separate audiences and different repertoires—is a testament to just how powerful their influence had become.

This hub between George Duke and Airto and Flora supported a huge group of Brazilians in Los Angeles that would lend their *ginga* to many records. This group included Raul De Sauza the trombonist, Robertinho Silva the great drummer, Oscar Castro-Neves, who had been part of the original bossa nova group and had played at Carnegie Hall, Hermeto Pascoal, guitarist and composer Egberto Gismonti, percussionist Mayuto Correa, percussionist Dom Um Romão, session percussion legend Paulinho Da Costa, and the great Moacir Santos.

Moacir made some beautiful records for Blue Note in this period, but, as Ndugu has pointed out, "Moacir was ahead of his time. Moacir was deep and then the concept of them recording that album *Maestro*—the record company didn't really understand what they had so they didn't market Moacir. They didn't market Moacir because they didn't understand what he stood for."

Moacir Santos from Pernambuco was the best that Afro-Brazil had to offer. He had already scored ten features, had arranged more than fifty albums, and was the first Afro-Brazilian to conduct the National Radio Orchestra, but Blue Note wasn't sure what to do. A young educator and recent alumni of Willie Bobo's band was given the job of producing. Reggie Andrews is an LA legend and this perhaps forgotten part of his story is worth remembering. The teacher of many of the previous three generations of Brazilian music would be produced by the teacher of the next three generations of Los Angeles music. Reggie Andrews went on to teach Patrice Rushen, Ndugu, the Pharcyde, Thundercat, and Kamasi Washington. It is also worth noting here that all of these artists have a deep appreciation for the music of their friends to the south. On that memorable album *Maestro,* two very powerful vocational traditions are linked indelibly. When I hear Patrice Rushen's "Jubilation" from the album *Before the Dawn,* a perfect *baiao* fusion with Ndugu on drums, or "Runnin," produced by J Dilla for the Pharcyde, with its Getz/Gilberto sample, I humbly remember that their teachers had met, had worked together, and, in a perfect way, had joined the traditions.

Brazil saved me. I enjoyed going there more than anything I ever did in my life. I returned to Los Angeles ready to pour that experience into the new record, to bring the sights, sounds, and smells of Brazil to the palette of Earth, Wind & Fire.

—MAURICE WHITE, EARTH, WIND & FIRE

Maurice listened to a lot of Sérgio Mendes back then, but of course Sérgio was very commercial but it was actually Sérgio that brought a lot of the music to America. He commercialized it of course. And "Zanzibar"—those great vocals that was on there—that was Philip and 'Reece doing those top vocals. And then we did "Caribou"—that was actually all of us. That's kind of how it started. 'Reece was actually the person who really brought it to the band.

—VERDINE WHITE, EARTH, WIND & FIRE

As the 1970s wore on and the dance floor became an important part of American popular music again, it seemed only likely that the Brazilian palette would emerge in an even more mainstream way. Sérgio Mendes was still making valid pop statements: his record from 1973, *Raizes,* or *Primal Roots,* as it was badly translated into English, is an outstanding example of this. Fired by traditional rhythms and including some inspired Dorival Caymmi tunes, it is Mendes at his best as the broker of Brazilian culture.

By the early 1970s the producers and arrangers that had absorbed the first wave of bossa nova were still going strong. Quincy Jones was still very much in demand. Henry Mancini was one of the best interpreters of bossa nova in the English language. Jobim was signed to Creed Taylor's label CTI, making his great herbal statement, *Stone Flower.* Clare Fischer, the prolific composer and arranger, was still exploiting the possibilities of Brazilian rhythms and melodies. Even Laurindo Almeida was still making interesting records with Bud Shank and their LA 4.

In 1973 Sérgio Mendes brought another stunning session player from Rio to Los Angeles, Paulinho Da Costa. Paulinho Da Costa said, "In Brazil, people always encouraged me to go to the US. Then Sérgio Mendes made me an offer and as my wife was expecting a baby and the offer was good, I thought it was a good opportunity to come to the US. I had always admired the jazz and the Latin music scene in the US. I arrived in Los Angeles on January 4, 1973. This was in the second wave of Sérgio Mendes."

In this period Sérgio had kept the formula but shifted emphasis from straight bossa nova into something more diverse. He introduced the US pop world to the songs of Edu Lobo, Gilberto Gil, João Donato, and Dorival Caymmi and began a longtime collaboration with Stevie Wonder, another fan of the Brazilian thing. In sending for Paulinho, he must have known he was revitalizing his "kitchen" with a spark of new energy. Paulinho Da Costa has the broad palette of Airto, but is a much more controlled, pocket kind of percussionist. He was already a veteran of the Portela Samba School from Madureira in Rio. Paulinho within a few years became the first-call percussionist on every pop record recorded in the city. He took over from King Errisson (the Bahamian giant) the mantle of pops percussionist. Paulinho's résumé is almost unstoppable in terms of 1980s pop, from Madonna to Kenny Rogers, from the Temptations to Rod Stewart, from Minnie Ripperton to Lionel Richie. (Rod Stewart's "Da Ya Think I'm Sexy?" with percussion by Paulinho is an adaptation of "Taj Mahal" by Jorge Ben.)

But the two main sessions that really changed pop music in my humble opinion are "Don't Stop 'til You Get Enough" by Michael Jackson and "Brazilian Rhyme" by Earth, Wind & Fire. As it turns out, both tracks include Paulinho on percussion.

"Brazilian Rhyme" is attributed to Milton Nascimento; it was recorded after a retreat to Brazil taken by Maurice White in 1977.

In his book *My Life with Earth, Wind & Fire,* Maurice White explains:

There's a sound track to my memories of Brazil; every remembered picture has a melody or groove. I had always loved Latin music, from those days down in Chicago's Old Town neighborhood, but the deeper rhythms and the Afro-Cuban influence opened me up. This wasn't Sérgio Mendes and Brasil '66. This was a tribal, earthy, barefoot-in-the-dirt experience. Brazil's music contained a heavy emphasis on drumming. I discovered there were these little drum schools all over Brazil. I visited three of them and roamed around those rooms like I was a hall monitor in junior high. The talented young musicians had amazing flavor: I soaked it up. I hadn't felt that way since I was a kid back in Memphis with Booker T. and Richard Shann, listening to the new jazz records of Monk and Coltrane . . . I also met the one and only Milton Nascimento. Since Milton and I didn't speak the same language, we would communicate through a funny sign language of sorts. Between those two incredible musicians [Milton and Deodato], the rhythm in the country's very soil, the food, and the beautiful Brazilian people, I left there floating, fully inspired.

Maurice White's moving testimony links his experience with Milton and Deodato in Brazil to hearing Monk and Coltrane in his youth. Perhaps through the language barrier Milton may have told him that his holy trinity from when he was a teenager was Mingus, Miles, and Coltrane.[5] It is beautiful to imagine these meetings, and clearly the energy they manifested is marked in the wonderful music that was produced afterward. "Brazilian Rhyme" is that. A clear riff on the Milton song "Ponte De Areia"—it begins as a mere interlude. But by the time it was finished, it was one of the most recognizable dance floor fillers of the 1980s and 1990s and up into the present. Sampled by the great A Tribe Called Quest on their first album for the track "Mr. Muhammed," it is a proper stripped-down, ultra-catchy finger snap with a vocal—the kind of music that White was critical of as popular African American music moved into the 1980s—but it's a stone-cold classic: Minas Gerais through Los Angeles onto every dance floor in the world.

Earth, Wind & Fire is a great example of how pop incorporates Brazilian music in a way that most of us don't even recognize. American pop expertly does this, feeding itself on the blues, the clave, and eventually Brazilian rhythms in discreet ways that make the inclusive leanings of samba part of our aural experience without openly exclaiming it. Earth, Wind & Fire had been influenced by Brazilian sounds since early on. Maurice White had played bossa novas with Ramsey Lewis when he took over from Isaac Redd Holt in 1966. Earth, Wind & Fire's first producer, Charles Stepney, was steeped deeply in the feel of Brazil, as is evidenced on his compositions and arrangements for Minnie Ripperton's first album, *Come into My Garden.* So Earth, Wind & Fire's version of Edu Lobo's "Zanzibar" from the album *Head to the Sky* from 1973 should have come as no surprise; however, it is new, long dynamic and a full exploration of Lobo's wonderful instrumental. The Zimbo Trio had made a hit of the song, but Earth, Wind & Fire made an epic of it. The forty-five second *cuica* solo at the beginning is instructive, humorous, and sexual. Somehow it had worked for the Earth, Wind & Fire format: they turned "Zanzibar" into a thirteen-minute-long extended soul jazz journey. In their follow-up record, *Open Our Eyes,* Earth, Wind & Fire showed that they could create music like this on their own. "Caribou" is a beautiful Brazilian-inflected vocal jam that could well be Azymuth under the direction of Marcos Valle or Burnier and Cartier, but it is really just a band from Chicago making a song about the little town near Denver that they had decided to record in.

But after the trip to Brazil in 1977, Maurice White wasn't just interested in quotations or covers; he felt Brazil coming through his experience. Curiously enough, in Brazil at this same moment in 1977, two Brazilian arrangers were channeling Earth, Wind & Fire. Robson Jorge and Lincoln Olivetti had already heard the cues and were making samba swing–style productions for many of the soul groups of the day in Rio. One wonders if Maurice White had heard them.

By the time Earth, Wind & Fire as a group made it to Brazil, ten thousand Cariocas met them at the airport. Samba-soul Brazil was ready for its heroes, and from the evidence of the live recordings the exchange was immense.

Michael Jackson began working with Quincy Jones on the making of *The Wiz* in 1978. Later that year Jones began production of Jackson's solo record *Off The Wall*. Michael Jackson had four solo albums to that point, but he felt as though he hadn't let loose yet. He wanted to develop his own repertoire, find his sound, and he trusted Jones to help make this happen. Many songwriters were brought in, from Stevie Wonder to Paul McCartney and Rod Temperton of Heatwave and even George Duke. "Don't Stop 'til You Get Enough," however, was all Michael.

The Jacksons had worked with Paulinho Da Costa previously. The result was the completely infectious "Shake Your Body (Down to the Ground)." But "Don't Stop 'til You Get Enough" is a different beast—even the demo version is completely Brazilian. When you hear the demo, its rhythm is basically shakers and a bottle; this is the *samba de roda* rhythm section. *Samba de roda* is the backyard samba, the circle samba, the small session that happens in bars, at the schools on a Saturday afternoon when they make a *feijoada*. But as soon as Michael starts to sing, it becomes clear what's up—to me this is one of the greatest pop songs of the contemporary era. Somehow, Michael Jackson produced by Quincy Jones (by then a real Brazilophile) is moving from child star to the biggest pop star of all time—it seems weirdly fitting that those hits were being driven by a samba rhythm. The same music that had made Brazil was now making the king of pop. Paulinho Da Costa inscribed the samba school tradition into the popular music of the 1980s and Michael Jackson exemplified this. By the time Michael went to Bahia and Rio with Spike Lee to make the music video for "They Don't Care about Us," featuring Olodum, it was as though they were closing a certain kind of loop. The influence that had begun with the Baianias in the 1910s had found its way back to Pelourinho in Salvador da Bahia and the Dona Marta favela in Rio—through the feet and falsetto of one of pop's biggest and most embattled icons.

POSTSCRIPT

The difficulty of these kinds of arguments in many ways is that they are made from inferred evidence. As music moves, it operates according to its own logic. Influences are fluid: a bossa nova rhythm can morph easily into a second line, a two step can slide into a samba, and writing music is, thankfully, a far more interesting way to write history than history writing. But it is undeniable that, since the late 1930s, the language, swing, and palette of Brazilian music have influenced the world and changed music in the city of Los Angeles profoundly, while very few of us noticed.

Today when we hear Madlib collaborate with Azymuth[6] or Jurassic 5 rework Baden and Vinicius's "Canto de Ossanha," it feels very much part of the extended musical vocabulary we have access to. Yes, this music feels different in its swing and language, but it also feels familiar—we have a place for it. It would be an exhaustive and pointless task to itemize all the places we can feel Brazilian music in our music by now—its openness, the infectious

Azymuth with Madlib, Echo Park, 2008.

ginga of the rhythm, the curious way that out-of-tune sounds right or behind-the-beat seems perfectly on time—but it is there. So when Tyler the Creator samples Wilson Das Neves[7] or Kaytranada builds a song around Gal Costa,[8] we can know that this is a part of a larger conversation, one that has many voices and that isn't always just in its outcomes, but one that contains the possibilities of diasporic understandings far beyond written history.

NOTES

1. http://daniellathompson.com/Texts/Stokowski/Stalking_Stokowski.htm.
2. Liner notes to *Canonball's Bossa Nova* by Orrin Keepnews 1962.
3. Liner notes to the Warner Records release *Revolucion Con Brasilia!* by the Girls from Bahia, 1965.

4. Airto Moreira interviewed by the author published in *Wax Poetics,* 2006.

5. As noted by Edu Lobo in the liner note to Milton's first record.

6. Jackson Conti: *Sujinho* is a collaboration between Madlib and Ivan Conti of Azymuth.

7. "Lone" from the album *Wolf* by Tyler the Creator.

8. "Pontes Da Luz" from the album *99.9%* by Kaytranada.

12

HEROES AND SAINTS

―――――――

The first place that I went to when I was coming out
was the great Latino watering hole
Circus Disco!
Tried to get into Studio One,
but the doorman asked me for two IDs.
I gave him my driver's license and my J.C. Penney card,
but it wasn't good enough.
Hey, what did I know,
I was still wearing corduroys.

Circus Disco was the new world.
Friday night, eleven-thirty.
Yeah, I was Born to Be Alive.
Two thousand people exactly like me.
Well, maybe a little darker,
but that was the only thing
that separated me from
the cha-cha boys in East Hollywood.
And I ask you,

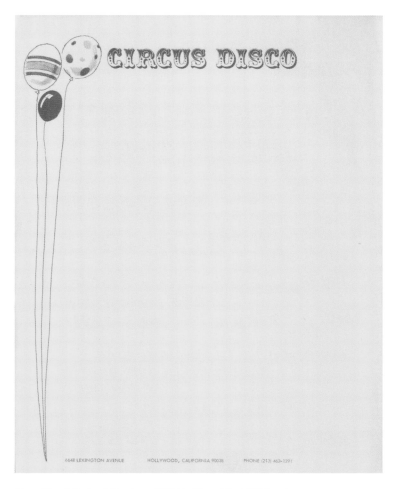

Circus Disco letterhead, Courtesy of ONE Archives at the USC Libraries.

Where are my heroes?
Where are my saints?
Where are my heroes?
Where are my saints?

First night at Circus Disco
and I order a Long Island ice tea,
'cause my brother told me
it was an exotic drink,
and it fucks you up real fast.

The bartender looks at me
with one of those
"Gay people recognize each other" looks.

Gay Latinos Unidos flyer, "A Latino Happening at Circus Disco," 1981, Courtesy of ONE Archives at the USC Libraries.

I try to act knowing and do it back.
Earlier that year,
I went to a straight bar on Melrose.
And when I asked for a screwdriver
the bartender asked me
if I wanted a Phillips or a regular.

I asked for a Phillips.
I was never a good drunk.
And I ask you,

Where are my heroes?
Where are my saints?

Where are my heroes?
Where are my saints?

The first guy I met at Circus Disco
grabbed my ass in the bathroom,
and I thought that was charming.
In the middle of the dance floor,
amidst all the hoo-hoo, hoo-hoo,
to a thriving disco beat,
he's slow dancing
and sticking his tongue down my throat.
He sticks a bottle of poppers up my nose,
and I get home at five-thirty the next morning.
And I ask you,

Where are my heroes?
Where are my saints?
Where are my heroes?
Where are my saints?

Sitting outside of Circus Disco,
with a three-hundred-pound drag queen,
who's got me cornered in the patio
listening to her life story,
I think to myself,
One day
I will become something
and use this
in an act.

At the time I was thinking
less about performance
and more about
Las Vegas.
And I ask you,

Where are my heroes?
Where are my saints?
Where are my heroes?
Where are my saints?

A guy is beating the shit out of his lover
in the parking lot of Circus Disco.
Everybody is standing around
them in a circle,

but no one is stopping them.
One of the guys is kicking and punching
the other guy, who is on the floor
in a fetal position.
And he's saying,
"You want to cheat on me, bitch?
You cheating on me, bitch?
Get up, you faggot piece of shit.
Get up, you goddamn faggot piece of shit."
It was the first time I saw us act
like our parents.

I try to move in,
but the drag queen tells me
to leave them alone.
"That's a domestic thing, baby.
Besides, that girl has AIDS.
Don't get near that queen."
And I ask you,

Where are my heroes?
Where are my saints?
Where are my heroes?
Where are my saints?

I get home early
and I'm shaken to tears.
My mother asks me
where I went.
I tell her I went to see a movie
at the Vista.
An Italian film about a man
who steals a bicycle.
It was all I could think of.
And she says,
"That made you cry?"

I swear,
I'll never go back to Circus Disco.
I'll never go back to Circus Disco.
I'll never go back to Circus Disco . . .
But at Woody's Hyperion!
Hoo-hoo, hoo-hoo.

I met a guy there
And his name is Rick Rascon
And he's not like anyone else.

No tight muscle shirt.
No white Levi's.
No colored stretch belt.
He goes to UCLA
and he listens to Joni Mitchell.
Is that too perfect or what?
He comes home with me
and we make love,
but I'm thinking of him
more like, like, a brother.
And I know, I know.
we're gonna be friends
for the rest of our lives.
And I ask you,

Where are my heroes?
Where are my saints?
Where are my heroes?
Where are my saints?

Started working at an
AIDS center in South Central.
But I gotta,
I gotta,
I gotta
get out of here.
'Cause all of my boys
All of my dark-skinned boys
All of my cha-cha boys
are dying on me.
And sometimes I wish
it was like the Circus Disco
of my coming out.

Two thousand square feet
of my men.
Boys like me.
Who speak the languages,
who speak the languages

of the border
and of the other.
The last time I drove
down Santa Monica Boulevard
and I passed by Circus Disco,
hardly anybody was there.
And I ask you,

Where are my heroes?
Where are my saints?
Where are my heroes?
Where are my saints?
Where are my heroes?
Where are my saints?

13

STAGING THE DANCE OF COALITION WITH VERSA-STYLE AND CONTRA-TIEMPO

A T THE END OF *AGUA FURIOSA,* a dance piece from 2015 inspired by *The Tempest* and performed by Los Angeles company *CONTRA-TIEMPO,* the character Ella shimmers among the dancers, from Caliban to Caliban, saying: "What if in the beginning, middle, and end a beat and a beat join together, creating and bearing all songs for us to dream and seek one another?" Ana Maria Alvarez's choreography provokes the question "What if?" throughout the performance, in which four different Calibans experience the turmoil of latinidad and blackness. Alvarez deeply layers the contemporary tensions and solidarities through references to violence and struggles that have affected relationships between African Americans, Latinxs, and Afro-Latinxs.

Even as I watch *Agua Furiosa* on a password-protected Vimeo video, I am moved as I witness bodies dancing together through slavery, the murders of unarmed black people, the aftermath of Hurricane Katrina, the floods of climate change, and struggles at the US-Mexico border. And I'm moved to see black and brown Latinx bodies on stage, activating these eras, events, and moments that haunt the present—

because the bodies dance the question "What if we could come together to fight these racialized injustices?" They dance their histories as black and brown people in the Americas but the choreography compels me to step back, to see the histories as interconnected rather than distinct. Through such a suturing together of histories and bodies, I argue, borrowing the words of Jack Halberstam, the work makes "common cause with the brokenness of being."[1]

This essay is written in the spirit of Anani Dzidzienyo and Suzanne Oboler's call to attend to the challenges of racial injustice and the practices of building coalition among Afro-Latinxs, Latinxs, and African Americans. I follow their lead in putting race in a transnational context in the Americas, expanding their framework to the context of dance, music, and performance. I address the ways that two Latina-originated dance companies in Los Angeles stage coalition from the placeless realm of the undercommons. Ana Maria Alvarez's CON-TRA-TIEMPO Urban Latin Dance Theater and Miss Funk Jackie Lopez's hip-hop and house-based Versa-Style theorize the complex dance and musical migrations that underscore their experiences and visions of latinidad in coalition.[2] Both companies have a foundational connection to dances of the African diaspora. Using choreographic analysis of dance and performance studies as well as interviews with the choreographers, I will examine the coalitional dimensions of their works. At the heart of this work is the question "In this contemporary moment of Black Lives Matter, how do these Los Angeles–based companies cultivate alternatives to racialized violences?"

In September 2016, Versa-Style premiered *Box of Hope* at the Ford Amphitheater, choreographed at a time of increased state-sanctioned police brutality against black people, anti-immigrant violences, and the social alienation of communities of color. Influenced by Black Lives Matter, *Box of Hope* in part explores the way that the different bodies in Lopez's community come to dance together. She directs the company with cofounder Leigh Foaad (also known as Breeze-lee). "I have amazing young dynamic dancers in this piece: African American, Latino from East Los Angeles, Filipino, Egyptian, Hmong, and White. I think about how their experiences overlap and how they do not," Lopez tells me.

At the center of the stage, Breeze-lee trembles with fear, with excitement as he reaches for the lid to the closed red box at his feet. He opens it, reaches in, and removes the energy of hope. His jittery gestures begin to flow as hope enters his body and he holds it, shapes it. At first glance, Breeze-lee's body seems to be alone in the spotlight as small circles of light glide across the darkened backdrop. But the small circles of light illuminate the still bodies of others who silently observe Breeze-lee tenderly deposit hope back in the box and fit it with the lid once again. He picks up the box and holds it to his heart as the bodies of the witnesses step toward him. The scene propels me to feel this moment deeply as I think about the box and what lies inside. For Harney and Moten, a box is a shipping container holding bodies of the dispossessed. It is also a boxcar, prison, and hostel.[3] And in that box, bodies are together. "Though forced to touch and be touched, to sense and be sensed in that space of no space, though refused sentiment, history and home, we feel (for) each other."[4] What becomes important, then, is not a simple feeling of utopian hope, but the shared sense of love created by the hold. In the logic of the undercommons, the box created the conditions for this love, an inheritance, a history to be cherished.

DANCERS IN COALITION

As I consider the ways in which Versa-Style and CONTRA-TIEMPO form their companies, I am struck by the political engagement of the productions and the dancers that come to coalition through Latinx social dances flowing out of the African diaspora, including hip hop.[5]

For Lopez, the dancers who make up Versa-Style must come from the dislocated location of the undercommons, must be able to directly identify with the kind of dispossession she herself experienced. With parents who migrated from El Salvador to escape the Civil War, Lopez was born in Los Angeles in 1979. "I grew up in Echo Park around gangs and drugs in a very tough time," she says. "With a dad not so involved because of his own addictions. My mom was so fearful of this culture and she missed her family in El Salvador. As a kid I was angry because I didn't understand: Why am I starving? Why am I not eating? I was fifteen, working full time at Kentucky Fried Chicken. I barely graduated high school." Versa-Style grew out of Lopez's senior project at the University of California in Los Angeles in 2004 when she invited members of her dance community to join her on stage. "They were street dancers that wouldn't necessarily think there was any space for them in an institution like UCLA," Lopez tells me. The people in the piece were Latinx and black, from Echo Park, Silver Lake, the San Fernando Valley, and North Hollywood. "We're all spread out," she says, "and hip hop brings us together."

Most of the Versa-Style dancers come from Next Generation, an arts program for high school students that Lopez now runs. "The students I find are the ones that come from very hard backgrounds like my own," she says. "I'm very specific to serving this demographic. There's a huge Latino population, mostly Mexican and Central American from El Salvador, Guatemala, and Honduras." She is dedicated to teaching hip-hop movement based on "the ground being the essence of how you groove. Because when you go in the industry for commercial hip-hop dance, it's very choreographic-based. It almost looks jilting; the essence is lost."

I ask Lopez about the way she has integrated Latinx popular dances such as salsa with hip hop in some of her work. "I grew up doing *cumbias* and salsas," she says. "But all the hip-hop street party dances also attracted me. I was able to see the overlap between both cultures in many ways. The social aspect, for example, . . . I recall being able to go to *quinceañeras* with my family and dance salsas and *cumbias* and merengues. And when there was a dope hip-hop song down the street and people would just improvise and freestyle. But the way that we were grounded, the way my upper body would move, I was able to connect both Latino dance and hip hop because neither were foreign." So it was not difficult for her to intertwine salsa, *cumbia,* and house moves in her choreographies: "There is an overlap in the footwork, the grooves, the intricacy, the rhythms, and the way we approach social dance. It's so improvisation-based. It's connected because of house dance, which was created by the Latino and black communities. The movement in house is a lot of improvisation—you can pop, lock, break, hip hop, salsa, all of it. What does the music call you to do? In hip-hop and Latino dance music it's a call and response constantly."

When Lopez and Foaad choreograph work, they are bringing into coalition dancers from multiple backgrounds who form a connection primarily through hip hop but also, for some dancers, through Latinx popular dances such as salsa and *cumbia*. Though one might argue that Lopez articulates a desire for an elusive "authentic" hip hop in binary opposition to the "jilting" commercial hip hop of the industry, her discriminating lens through which she invites dancers with varying economic histories of dispossession to join the company simultaneously builds coalition across race, culture, and nation. As I continue to ask Lopez questions about Versa-Style and hip hop in Los Angeles, she shakes her head like I will never understand. "You have to live it to know it," she tells me.

Like Lopez and Foaad, CONTRA-TIEMPO's artistic director Ana Maria Alvarez also runs a youth training program through which several young dancers have been able to join the professional company. Futuro is a summer intensive that began in 2011 for high school– and college-aged participants. Instructors teach urban Latin dance theater grounded in dance practices of the African diaspora in the Americas and social theater techniques based in Augusto Boal's Theatre of the Oppressed.[6] They teach practices at the intersection of social dance, concert dance, and the Afro-Latinx diaspora, making salsa and hip hop crucial to the choreographic theorization of social justice.

When CONTRA-TIEMPO was founded in 2004, salsa was the base practice. Part of CONTRA-TIEMPO's salsa training used to happen at the King King, a nightclub in Hollywood. "The King King was our hangout while I was teaching there every Tuesday night, until 2008," Alvarez says. "Tuesday night was Afro-Cuban salsa, Afro-Cuban jazz, *descarga*. Sono Lux was the band there, led by Willie McNeil." Rumbankete, a *timba* band formed by Sono Lux trombonist Denis Jirón, also played there, and its singers had previous experience with well-known bands from Cuba—Gonzálo "Chalo" Chomat (formerly of Conexión Salsera) and Iris Sandra Cepeda (formerly from Arte Mixto in Cienfuegos). Rumbankete has played at other Latin American dance venues in the city like El Floridita, the Mayan, and the Conga Room. "Mario, the owner, allowed me to bring in my company every Tuesday night," Alvarez recalls. "Part of our rehearsal process was freestyling. I recruited half the cast for my company at the King King. As the instructor, I got to initiate the night, undermining heternormative gender rules. Men could lead or follow. Men could dance with men, women could dance with women. There would sometimes be crazy resistance. We always packed the place so Mario let us do our thing."

It is possible that the social space she created sparked her creativity for a section in *Full Still Hungry*: As the salsa rhythm plays, two men enter the stage and begin to fight each other as they dance together. This representation pushes against the overly aggressive stereotype of Latino men precisely because the two dancers follow a salsa code of movement through a tense, embattled partnership and then disengage. There seems to be no resolution as they fling themselves away from each other to exit opposite sides of the stage. This choreography not only breaks with representations of heteronormative salsa couplings; it also demonstrates the humanity of Latinxs as they engage with a broad range of emotions, including frustration.

In an earlier piece, *Against the Times,* Alvarez choreographed salsa partnerships to show the taut, difficult process of constructing a heterosexual partnership in a patriarchal system. As a man and woman dance together in a nightclub scenario, they try to work out the transitions between each one's leadership and precisely how the maneuvers should be done. They stage a physical battle over leadership—she dips him, he restores order and dips her. By the end of the piece, however, the *salseras* in the piece transform the club's gendered relations. The partnerships are still primarily heterosexual (one pair of women dance together), but the push and pull of gendered tensions are more playful, peaceful, and malleable.

As CONTRA-TIEMPO developed, Alvarez blended salsa with other social dance practices from the African diaspora: samba, rumba, *festejo,* breaking, popping, and house. Alvarez includes practices from her own training in Latinx and Latin American dance practices, including Cuban contemporary and folklorico, Haitian, and tango. The blend is not fusion or appropriation. Instead, the practices she draws from call forth a culturally specific response to oppressive political entanglements.

For example, in the letter-poem "Dearest Hip Hop" (by Walidah Imarisha and Not-4Prophet in *I Dream America,* 2007), spoken word meets with old-school hip-hop moves. The dancers, with slow, nostalgic palpitations, top rock, six step, Zulu spin, freeze, and windmill—all elements of early hip-hop breaking created by Puerto Rican and African American youth in the South Bronx. These old-school moves are in tension with influences of hip hop from the 1990s and what Alvarez calls "Hip Pop," commercial hip-hop choreography that Lopez rejects. Alvarez, however, employs hip pop as a way to convey the tension and disrupt the binary between the old school and the new. The poem's author laments hip hop's transformation over the decades—from "You were our ten-point program, our list of demands, a declaration of existence, our statement of resistance, a shout (out) from those whose tongues had been previously tied by the shitstem, a voice for those who were not supposed to be seen or heard" to "just when you about to bring the noise, it's inevitably drowned out in a bottle of counterfeit Courvesoir and a cup of (jim) crow." In analyzing the choreography alongside the poem, Alvarez deftly brings together the old school and the hip pop, tying a rebellious history to the current racially charged present as #BlackLivesMatter and #SayHerName demand a renewed call for action.

Though Alvarez draws from a number of dance practices, she avoids cultural relativism, avoids representing each dance genre as if its performers somehow existed outside of the networks of power in cultural flows, migration, and travel. Practices such as salsa, capoeira, Afro-Cuban and Haitian folklorico, and postmodern exist together as a repertoire, an arsenal of movement histories that challenges, pushes back against dominant representations of Latinxs and against the violent structures that many Latinxs face in everyday life: police brutality, racial profiling, border walls, immigrant detention centers. Alvarez and

CONTRA-TIEMPO push back by showing the complexity of latinidad. Some understandings of latinidad include only the Spanish and indigenous, but Alvarez represents the Afro-Latinx so often erased from latinidad.[7] Between the movement and the music, CONTRA-TIEMPO's performance summons the histories of the African diaspora, the legacies of European conquest, the cultural practices that developed in the Americas. There is a productive tension between Latinxs as multiple distinctive cultures, Latinxs as drawing from one another's cultural practices, and Latinxs as a unified politicized body that disrupts narratives that flatten latinidad.

Alvarez tells me, "My influences are very rooted in salsa, Afro-Cuban, Dunham technique, Afro-Haitian, the movement of the spine, of the torso and hips. The groundedness, polyrhythm, deep plies, isolations. In college, I also did a lot of contact improv, abstract movement, pedestrian. I work with what I call literal visuals—moments in time or tableaus that represent something really poignant but then disappear back into movement. That's me as a choreographer. But I also really love to respond to who is in the company." Based in Los Angeles, CONTRA-TIEMPO and Futuro have a transnational Los Angeles/Caribbean/Latin American understanding of latinidad that morphs with each body that makes up the company. "My interest in hiring," she says, "has never been who people are and where they come from but their political alignment with the work. I consider the dance styles and techniques they bring, their ability to slide between concert dance and social dance, and to freestyle. They have the ability to learn and grow. No one comes into the company knowing all of it yet (meaning concert, social, various rhythms). People come in with a strong skill set and a desire to make a difference as a dancer, and a mover, and an artist."

Samad Guerra, a longtime African American company member, was adopted by a Mexican woman and considers himself Afro-Latino. He studied Afro-Cuban dance when he went to Cuba in high school and also toured with an Afro-Peruvian dance company. He has a background in salsa and as a percussionist. When he joined the company, he learned modern and floor work. Alvarez says, "We also have a Mexican dancer who does Mexican folklorico, Isis Savalos. We have a piece in *I Dream America:* she does folklorico movement with the skirt even though she is embodying Yemaya. She was in the performance that we restaged for our trip to South America where the audience really appreciated her performance. We have a dancer, Bianca Golden, who grew up dancing and grooving in the clubs of Miami, so she knows how to shake it and move her hips in a deep, and rooted way. She's had that training in social dance, and she's also a skillful contemporary dancer so can slide in between these worlds. Chris is a Filipino street hip-hop dancer from Los Angeles. He brings in this really LA-based popping and locking."

Alvarez makes space for the various cultural backgrounds and histories of migration that each dancer brings. "My experience of latinidad," she explains, "is different than that of someone who migrated from Mexico and swam across the Rio Grande and grew up undocumented in South Texas. That experience of latinidad is legitimate and different than mine. I'm the child of a Cuban immigrant and the child of a white American. My identity is connected to other experiences of latinidad but also in tension with those experiences. Our company is often asked to represent latinidad as if it is one thing, but I'm always working with presenters to see it as an evolving, shifting, multilayered, multidimensional paradigm."

Each member brings multiple dance cultural experiences as well as skills that they have developed through intensive study. Collectively, the members contribute to CONTRA-TIEM-PO's knowledge of Afro-Latinx dance, latinidad, and the African diaspora. Company member Michael Butler, who is African American, was on a stepping team throughout high school and college. Alavarez also did the boot dance from South Africa when she was in an African dance company in North Carolina. Alvarez mixed step and Afro-Cuban rumba in "The Revolution Will Not Be Pasteurized," the last piece of *Full/Still Hungry.* Together, Butler and Alvarez developed a movement vocabulary that connected stepping with rumba. Butler trained the company in stepping and Alvarez trained the company in rumba before presenting dancers with a chore-ography that mixed the two. "We as a company draw on our backgrounds," she adds. "The forms we've been trained in, are rooted in. We bring these forms with the interest of contem-porizing them, creating something that doesn't exist yet. We are always clear about where we are sampling from, what we are connecting to, the history of the forms we are influenced by, inspired by to create. It's always amazing to be able to share the breath of the spaces we are from. That whole idea of this being a living, breathing, responsive palette to work from."

When I speak with Alvarez about the music that influences CONTRA-TIEMPO, she lists clave, Afro-Cuban Orisha dance music, secular dances from Cuba like *comparsa, gaga,* rumba, and *son.* "I've studied in Cuba a lot," she says. "Cuban music is very prominent in my work, informing how I think about rhythm and movement, as well as how hip hop and house connect with Afro-Cuban music." If Afro-Cuban music grounds much of CONTRA-TIEMPO's movement, local musicians have collaborated with the company to create original scores for performances. Cesar Alvarez, Alvarez's brother and the other founding member of CON-TRA-TIEMPO, performed the original sound design of the company's earlier productions such as *Against the Times* and *I Dream America* (2007).

His last project was *Full Still Hungry* (2011), one that examined political relationships between food and consumption. He worked closely with Martha Gonzalez, the lead singer of the Los Angeles Chicano rock band Quetzal, who sang on stage at the Ford Amphitheatre premiere. Gonzalez, whose parents are from Guadalajara, is from East Los Angeles. The col-laboration with Gonzalez brought in her expertise in fandango, a participatory music and dance practice native to Veracruz and now vibrant in Los Angeles, especially Boyle Heights. One of the more famous groups from Veracruz that has influenced Quetzal and the practice of fandango in Los Angeles is the *son jarocho*[8] band Mono Blanco, lead by Gilberto Gutier-rez. Gonzalez says, "This tradition, rooted in Spanish, Indigenous, and African cultural lega-cies, has the dancers central to the music making. There is a wooden platform—the *tarima*—that they dance on and create rhythm, contributing to the sonic experience. The dancers are like the drummers. They react to us as musicians, and we react to them—a call and response. Everybody, from the novice to the experienced, has a role."

In *Full Still Hungry,* Ana Maria asked Gonzalez to sing in dialogue with the dancers, to think about how the dancers were creating rhythms with their feet, as in *son jarocho.* Of the process, Gonzalez says, "*Full Still Hungry* had a composition through Cesar, but in rehearsal we had to refine that to meet the needs of the dancers. The intent of the fandango is to really be in community. That's what I think Ana Maria is doing in her work. They are not forgetting about their responsibility to engage community, to be out in the world, on the street, at a water fountain.[9] They are staying on the ground as much as on the stage."

When Alvarez began working on *Agua Furiosa,* she started working with D. Sabela Grimes, an African American sound archivist. Meeting across cultures but through rhythms, Alvarez and Grimes worked on a section for the second Caliban, a woman on a pedestal, to perform to the underlying beat of Makuta, a celebratory dance-drumming practice. Grimes called his composition "Makuta-Ban," a play on Caliban. In this section, Caliban "signifies the Hottentot Venus, the woman ridiculed and criticized. When she comes down from the pedestal it causes total chaos. The dancers whirl themselves into a celebratory frenzy, a tempest, and into a place where women's hips are no longer restrained. I use Makuta to dislodge the hips from the European construct of womanhood, the fear of moving your hips."

As Alvarez choreographs, she considers the link between gendered, racialized traumas of the past and the present. She brings together diverse bodies and dance knowledges in coalition to push back against disjointed understandings of history. Yet, by bringing together a diverse array of dancers and musicians with varyingly racialized and economic traumatic pasts and presents, Alvarez urges us to make a connection and ask, "What if in the beginning, middle, and end a beat and a beat join together, creating and bearing all songs for us to dream and seek one another?" The dancers of CONTRA-TIEMPO do not start out with a single shared dance practice, but Alvarez opens up space for them to learn from one another in the creation of choreographies that push back against the continued oppression and exploitation of black and brown bodies.

CONCLUSION

I began writing about the performances of Versa-Style and CONTRA-TIEMPO in the summer of 2016 and finished as Donald Trump was about to step into the US presidency. The *Los Angeles Times* reports that black people do not feel safe in Los Angeles in light of the racialized violence supported by Trump and his followers.[10] The critical frameworks of Black Lives Matter and Say Her Name have become even more crucial to the work of these two dance companies. Dances of the African Diaspora have drawn together the bodies in each company, bodies that carry varied histories of trauma and economic exploitation, knowledge and experiences. The coalitional practices that emerge through movement and music on stages throughout Los Angeles continue to drive the way they perform both the past and the present, and imagine new choreographies for the urban future.

NOTES

1. Please see Harney and Moten's work in which they theorize the way that the dislocated, the broken, those whose ancestors were shipped from Africa in the hold of a ship, come to "gather dispossessed feelings in common, to create a new feel in the undercommons" (97). Stefano

Harney and Fred Moten, *The Undercommons: Fugitive Planning & Black Study* (Wivenhoe, New York, Port Watson: Minor Compositions, 2013).

2. Thank you to Ana Maria Alvarez and Miss Funk Jackie Lopez for the number of conversations we had primarily in July 2016 in Los Angeles.

3. Harney and Moten, *The Undercommons,* 98.

4. Ibid.

5. The dances to which I refer have what Brenda Dixon Gottschild has termed the "Africanist Aesthetic," including elements such as bent knees, flexed feet, hip movement, forward-leaning torsos, and undulations. Brenda Dixon Gottschild, *Digging the Africanist Presence in American Performance: Dance and Other Contexts* (Westport, CN: Greenwood, 1996).

6. See Futuro, www.contra-tiempo.org/futuro/#summer-dance-intensive, August 4, 2016.

7. Theater scholar Anita Gonzalez and anthropologist Angela N. Castañeda have addressed this gap. Historically, Afro-Latinos have been left out of the Mexican census, but in 2015, they were included for the first time. Anita Gonzalez, *Afro-Mexico: Dancing between Myth and Reality* (Austin: University of Texas Press, 2010); Angela N. Castañeda, "Performing the African Diaspora in Mexico," in *Comparative Perspectives on Afro-Latin America,* ed. Kwame Dixon and John Burdick (Tallahassee: University of Florida Press, 2012).

8. *Son jarocho* is the traditional rhythm played at fandangos. "La Bamba" is often cited as the best-known *son jarocho.* For more on fandango and *son jarocho,* see Gonzalez.

9. Gonzalez's mention of "water fountains" refers to CONTRA-TIEMPO's Choreographic Laboratories, which were site-specific collaborations that invited local communities to participate in the artistic development of *Agua Furiosa.* The sites with water included the fountain wall at the Annenberg Beach House in Santa Monica, the Royce fountain at UCLA, the Grand Park Splash Pad in downtown Los Angeles, a riverbed in Santa Ana, the Los Angeles River, and Westside Neighborhood Park.

10. See "Trump Presidency Stirs Up Fear among African Americans in L.A.: 'This Election Says There's No Place for Me,'" *Los Angeles Times,* December 5, 2016, www.latimes.com/politics/la-me-blacks-fear-trump-20161129-story.html.

14

BOOMING *BANDAS* OF LOS ÁNGELES

Gender and the Practice of Transnational Zapotec Philharmonic Brass Bands

IN 2013, WHILE CONDUCTING fieldwork in Southern California on Oaxacan brass bands, I drove to a home in Lynwood for a Friday evening rehearsal to meet with Jessica Hernández. She is the first female Oaxacan brass band director in California. The youngest Oaxacan band director on both sides of the border, and the only Oaxacan *banda* musician who holds a degree in music from a university.

After knocking on the front door numerous times and calling the band instructor's cell phone, I began to worry. I did not want to miss the opportunity to meet Jessica and see her directing a second-generation community-based band, La Banda Nueva Dinastia de Zoochila. The intimidating and increasingly aggressive barks of a German shepherd made me think twice about simply walking to the backyard. Rather than take my chances with the dog, I turned to walk away, when suddenly an older woman walked out from the side door of the house, silenced the dog in Spanish, "*quitate chucho!*" and then calmly asked me, "Are you here to see Jessica?" "Yes, Ma'am," I quickly responded. "Come on in. The dog won't bite you. Jessica is in the garage. They are practicing right now—just lift up the garage door."

Relieved that I was given permission to enter, I made my way through the dimly lit driveway and knocked on the white one-car garage door.

As the garage door slowly lifted, a hand emerged and signaled me to come inside. An older man made space for me to stand inside the garage so I could watch the acclaimed twenty-five-year-old Jessica work with the all-male trombone section. In her left hand she held the sheet music while she used her pointer finger on her right hand to seamlessly mark the tempo of the song in the air. After the demonstration, Jessica walked to the front of the band and in a clear yet stern voice she scolded the fifteen-member band, which includes her father, uncles, male cousins, and the bass drummer, her seventeen-year-old sister. "If we are going to play Sinaloense-style music we have to follow the music as it is written. We need to make a choice here. Are we going to play the music the way 'we hear it' as Oaxaqueños or play it as it is composed on the sheet music?" Just as Jessica finished her statement, one of the men signaled that a guest was present. Jessica graciously transitioned from her authoritative band director stance and proceeded to warmly introduce me to the members of this new dynasty of musicians. What ensued was a three-hour group *plática* (talk), with Jessica and the founding male band members recounting the formation of the youth band, in addition to individual testimonies for participating in the band.

What was supposed to be an initial introductory visit quickly turned into a serious *banda* boot camp. That night not only did I gain insight into one community *banda*'s history but also I was initiated into a larger network of Los Angeles Oaxacan community-based brass bands. It was to become an enlightening and musically rich experience, all of which would not have been possible without my alto saxophone and my ability to participate in rehearsals and performances. Being able to sit within the ranks of fellow musicians allowed me to see firsthand the ways in which women participate, peer advise one another, and interact with male colleagues.

TRANSNATIONAL MIGRATION AND CULTURAL PRODUCTION: THE EMERGENCE OF OAXACALIFORNIA

The term "Oaxacalifornia," coined in 1995 by Michael Kearney, refers to a cross-border public space that Zapotec and Mixtec indigenous migrants have continuously traversed in search of employment and economic stability. Since the advent of the Bracero program in the 1940s and again in the 1980s, Indigenous Oaxacan migrants in California have created a vast network across Oaxacalifornia, which also allowed for the reproduction of Zapotec cultural performances, such as the Guelaguetza festival and community-based philharmonic brass bands. It is also a space of "social, civic and cultural engagements" that Oaxaqueño migrants actively shape, bringing "together their lives in the U.S. with their communities of origin."[1] Community-based Oaxacan bands formed in multiple areas of Los Angeles, but especially in the neighborhoods of Koreatown and Midcity. By using vernacular architecture and monthly donations, some bands created a music space for weekly practices in converted cinderblock warehouses, garages, and basements soundproofed with egg cartons.

I showed up at Jessica's garage that day because I am interested in how music—as a production of expressive culture—has helped build and sustain Oaxacalifornia as a binational realm that enables migrants to maintain ties with their *paisanos*. And yet, there has been a lack of scholarly attention paid to Oaxacan community-based brass bands, with virtually no attention paid to the role of women musicians in impacting these stories of performance and transnational migration. Thus, since 2013 I have conducted over thirty oral histories with musicians in Oaxaca and migrant bandleaders in Los Angeles.

My work with Oaxacan communities draws attention to Zapotec women musicians within this traditionally male-dominated musical practice. Although women have become more visible in brass bands, they are usually not revered as equal members of the band, even in cases where women have formal education and training. In most of the bands I interviewed, men continue to assume positions of leadership and provide a mainstream perspective on the bands' origins. Taking seriously Sherrie Tucker's call for "engaged listening" of women musicians,[2] I focus on Zapotec migrant women's experiences as musicians to address the formation of brass bands and the ways they negotiate the challenges they encounter in brass bands. It is through their localized articulations, voiced or played, that women establish a dialogue across the region of Oaxacalifornia.

HISTORY OF OAXACAN BRASS BANDS

The rise of brass bands in Oaxaca began in the 1920s as part of the Institutional Revolutionary Party's (PRI's) nationalist cultural education program, *mestizaje* policy, and *misiones culturales* as part of the nation-building efforts of former President Lázaro Cárdenas. Fiestas and music were utilized to "educate the people" under a unified national identity.[3] Brass bands were also formed at the municipal level as a way to maintain state loyalty. Oaxaca has a vast musical repertoire. Brass bands may play *danzas* (ritual dances), *sones* and *jarabes, chilenas,* and *danzón*. You will also hear the European musical influences in waltzes, marches, and *doble pasos*. These latter musical styles have undergone at least 150 years of transculturation where Mexican composers have created their own distinct sound that has specific meanings for local communities.[4] During the 1930s through the 1950s, community bands were supported through communal donations by residents of the village in order to purchase new instruments. Being part of the village band is a highly respected role and also signifies participation in a civic duty, which exempts musicians from other communal cargo responsibilities (a communal practice that continues today).[5]

Community-based philharmonic bands thrived in the Sierra region until the 1980s. According to Maestro Ismael Mendez, a vast exodus of men left the Sierra villages in search of economic relief, leaving many communities without a band as a result of the devaluation of the Mexican peso in 1982. In Maestro Ismael's words, "a community without a band is a community without a soul." This was a phrase repeatedly declared by villagers and migrant musicians in reference to the importance of their community-based brass bands. In response to this musical downturn, a nearby Zapotec boarding school located in the village of Zoogocho implemented a specialized music program in 1984. Maestro Ismael Mendez was hired as the first music instructor and taught for twenty-five years. Under his tutelage several generations of Zapotec musicians became certified as music instructors in Oaxaca, while others immigrated to Los Angeles, CA, and formed reputable brass bands.

ORIGINS OF *BANDAS* IN LOS ANGELES

In response to ethno-racial discrimination in the harrowing process of immigrating through northern Mexico to California, Oaxacan migrants in Los Angeles formed binational organizations and hometown associations (HTA) based on shared common identities—organized by region of origin, ethnicity, religion, class, and location. One objective of many hometown associations and binational organizations is to raise funds for development projects in their communities of origin.

For example, the HTA of Yatzachi El Bajo formed the first Banda Oaxaqueña in Los Angeles in 1990—as fundraising events became more frequent, so did the need for live music. The initial band members were mostly males, who at some point played in the their pueblo's municipal band before migrating. In order to have a full band, community members were encouraged to become part of it even if they did not have prior experience playing an instrument. What arose from this growing interest in *bandas* was a transnational exchange of musical scores, the purchasing of instruments, and the formalization of a musical pedagogy taught in Zapotec, in Spanish, and, with some concepts, in English.

As more bands began to form, more Oxacan women began to participate. One particularly revealing story belongs to Ofelia Guzman, who is part of the first generation of immigrant band members and among the pioneering women who joined the Oaxacan brass bands of Los Angeles in the early 1990s. Women's initial association with the brass bands was often in a domestic role as the caretakers for male musicians and their children. As we have seen in many studies, the process of immigration causes certain gender norms to shift and ultimately allow space for women to become visible as leaders in their hometown associations and as members of the community bands.

During a lively interview with Ofelia and her husband Esquias Guzman, she eagerly shared how she negotiated the role of wife and mother to become an accomplished alto saxophone player in Banda Yatzachi el bajo LA. In her interview, she recounts proudly how she learned to read music while waiting for her children during solfeggio lessons. Sr. Esquias interjected by saying, "it was because of the lack of musicians in the early formations of the band, wives were 'recruited' to join; in addition they are fulfilling a civic duty for their community" (even awhile abroad). Although his comment spoke to the urgency for musicians, Sra. Ofelia's experience and individual process of asserting that women become part of the band through their husbands remained necessary to tease out more thoroughly. In short, Ofelia's experience illustrates the negotiations women make as mothers and wives for their family in maintaining a community tradition and their continuous confrontation with a historically male-dominated space. After twenty-five years Ofelia continues to actively participate in the *banda* alongside her husband, sons, and grandchildren. Her story also provides a glimpse of how second-generation Oaxaqueño youth were introduced to Bandas

Oaxaqueñas. Despite persisting challenges and patriarchy in the Oaxacan community, today more young women have joined the ranks of their male counterparts as cultural bearers in this musical practice—a reflection of the great strides first-generation women have achieved to diversify the community of traditional musicians.

THE SECOND GENERATION OF BANDAS OAXAQUEÑAS

The first generation of brass bands formed out of a need to contribute to their communities of origin. In contrast, second-generation bands were created as a way to maintain the musical tradition, but also, more importantly, as a way to deter youth from urban street violence. Many musicians also assert that band practice serves as a cathartic and safe space to *desahogarse,* to process their experiences with fellow community members.

By 2001 two second-generation Oaxacan youth brass bands were formed. Maestro Estanislao Maqueos created a band representing the village of San Andres Solaga and together brothers, Maestros Porfirio and Moises Hernández, launched Banda Nueva Dinastia de Zoochila, representing the migrant community of Santiago Zoochila. What distinguishes youth bands in LA from previous generations of brass bands is a more progressive approach to gender; Los Angeles bands tended to incorporate young girls. To form the youth brass bands was no easy feat. Fundraisers were organized in order to acquire instruments, secure stable rehearsal locations, and afford uniforms. To obtain community recognition many of the second-generation groups strive to return to their parent's village of origin and participate in the patron saint day celebration.

This was key to the musical story of Maestra Jessica Hernández. She was born in Los Angeles County and raised during the first generation of Oaxacan brass bands (in the 1990s). Her father, Porifirio, and uncle, Moises, were the founding members of Banda Juarez de Oaxaca. By the age of ten, Jessica began learning music in the public school system. In 2001 she, along with other second-generation youth, began solfeggio (music theory) lessons from her Uncle Moises as the community prepared to debut the youth band, La Banda Nueva Dinastía de Zoochila, the New Dinasty of Zoochila.

Jessica continued to pursue music seriously and earned an undergraduate degree from the department of music at University of California, Riverside, with a specialization in band directing. After her graduation in 2010, the youth band traveled to the village of Santiago Zoochila for the patron saint celebration in the month of July. While there, Maestra Jessica participated in an *audicion de banda,* a friendly battle of the bands, and directed the village band in the song "Nuestra Afición." When the Los Angeles–based band returned to California, they began to work on their next project, recording their first compact disc of Oaxacan music. For this recording, Banda Nueva Dinastía debuted a song specifically composed for their band by the well-known Zapotec composer Gilberto Baltzar titled "Marcha Nueva Dinastía " (March of the New Dynasty). Upon witnessing how second-generation Zapotec youth are maintaining musical traditions in Los Angeles, composer Gilberto Baltzar arranged several handwritten scores for the Nueva Dinastía band. With the circuits of exchange that the Oaxacan immigrant community has established over the years, the musical score for

"Marcha Nueva Dinastía" was hand delivered to the Hernández family. In 2011, Banda Nueva Dinastía, representing the second-generation Zapotec youth brass bands of Los Angeles, released *Zoochila Vive en mi Corazón*.

Some points to highlight: First, the name of the band in and of itself marks a generational distinction as well as its transnational significance because it represents the village of origin but recognizes that the band is based in Los Angeles. Maestra Jessica demonstrates an acute consciousness of identity politics in that "the name 'New Dynasty' acknowledges that we [musicians] were either born or raised in the US. Yes, our parents are from Zoochila, but we [second-generation youth] grew up with Zoochila culture and music while acknowledging that we also are part of the urban Los Angeles landscape. We are the 'New Dynasty of *Zoochileño* in LA.'" Second, participating in this kind of expressive performance illustrates that culture does not only flow in one direction. This is what Juan Flores described as a circular pattern of cultural production—through music LA youth are connecting the "here" of migrant life to the "there" of Mexico.[6] Returning to Oaxaca as a musician representing their community in LA is a great accomplishment and serves as a means to claim their pueblo identity. Likewise, some municipal bands in the Sierra Norte villages began open enrollment for women upon learning how migrant bands were incorporating girls into the youth bands.

Along with Maestra Jessica, another young woman that exemplifies second-generation musical leadership is Yulissa Maqueos of Maqueos Music Academy. Yulissa, born in the village of San Andres Solaga, also grew up in and experienced the daily nuances of Oaxacan community-based bands in Los Angeles. Since the age of thirteen, Yulissa has faithfully assisted her father, Maestro Estanislao Maqueos, in leading band rehearsal for the performance group, presenting music theory lessons, arranging music, and making sure instruments are tuned before performance, among many other duties. Maestras Jessica and Yulissa can independently lead as conductors and musical instructors of their respective community-based bands, yet both have experienced machismo and chauvinism. Both women are the firstborn children of respected founders/directors of community bands and, as a result, they are constantly referred to as "la hija del Maestro … " (daughter of the director …) rather than by their respective names and position as maestras. Now pursuing an undergraduate music degree, Yulissa lamented how she has been overlooked at a community-organized music festival as an upcoming director because she is a woman. She shared that at most community gatherings male musicians tend to receive more recognition for their musical capabilities.

Jessica is quite versatile in several musical styles and also happens to direct a Sinalonese *banda* that performs on a regular basis throughout southern California. At times while playing on the nightclub circuit with the Sinaloa band, her rate of pay often gets cut by $10 to $15 per hour in comparison to her male colleagues, who receive $50 to $65 an hour. For these types of gigs Maestra Jessica instructs her bandmates to list her name as "Jay," a name that is gender-neutral enough, with the hope that club promoters will assume that her band is actually composed of all males and that she will not have to deal with difference in pay.

Lastly, Jessica shared an insightful observation with me about how origin stories of the bands are told. "Men tend to focus solely on themselves and other men," she said. "Many times they neglect to mention the support and labor of their wives and children in the band's history." She continued, "perhaps it's an ingrained form of sexism in us women, but when we are asked to talk about the band the first thing we think about is whether or not we should focus on the men's story. I noticed from our conversations with my mom how women tell their story differently—it's more inclusive and my mother shares what it was like for her and other women who actively provide support to the bands."

Today, that same white-painted one-car garage in Lynwood has been remodeled with a fresh coat of paint, new soundproofed walls, expanded interior space, and an air conditioning unit for those hot summer night rehearsals. Now a third and even a fourth generation of Nueva Dinastía band members practice out of this garage, led by Maestra Jessica Hernández. Across the county of Los Angeles, this new generation of Zapotec musicians includes children of a younger age range and more young women playing what was once considered "masculine instruments of saxophones, tubas, and drums" than previous generations. Impressively, young women musicians have been actively seeking out educational pathways to fulfill their aspirations of becoming music directors and educators. One of the greatest desires voiced by many of the young girls, in particular, is the ability to perform alongside their grandparents, with their *paisanos* (compatriots), in their community festivals in Oaxaca to show how they are carrying on this family tradition and bridging their two cultural identities.

NOTES

1. Jonathan Fox, "Reframing Mexican Migration as Multi-Ethnic Process," *Latino Studies* 4 (2006): 39–61; Michael Kearney, "The Local and the Global: The Anthropology of Globalization and Transnationalism," *Annual Review of Anthropology* 24 (1995): 547–65. J. Grieshop and S. Varese, *Invisible Indians: Mixtec Farmworkers in California,* film (University of California, Davis, Appl. Behavior Science, 1993).

2. Sherri Tucker, *Swing Shift: "All-Girl" Bands of the 1940s* (Durham: Duke University Press, 2000).

3. Charles V. Heath, *The Inevitable Bandstand: The State Band of Oaxaca and the Politics of Sound* (Lincoln: University of Nebraska Press, 2015).

4. Personal conversation with Leonora Saavedra, 2015.

5. Cargo system is a Mesoamerican civil-religious hierarchy used for fiesta or *mayordomia*. This system, used primarily in rural indigenous communities where the head of a household offers service, is a collection of secular or religious positions in a community. During my research visit in 2014 to the Sierra Norte region in Oaxaca, interlocutors between the ages of sixty and ninety-five shared that every male is required to complete a year of community service within the town at various levels, serve as a member in the municipal council, as security, or as an organizer of the patron saint festivities, assist with upkeep of the Catholic church, and so on.

6. Juan Flores, *Divided Borders: Essays on Puerto Rican Identity* (Houston: Arte Publico, 1993).

15

CAMINOS Y CANCIONES EN LOS ANGELES, CA

MEXICAN MUSIC EDUCATION begins in the home. The family is the principal educator around the sonic and lyrical significance of the Mexican musical repertoire, a repertoire that can include but is not limited to *rancheras,* boleros, *son jarocho, huasteco* and the many other *son* traditions that abound in Mexican music. California has generated countless musician families who have contributed to its sonic and cultural landscape.[1] I was born in California to a musical family originally from Guadalajara, Jalisco. In the early 1970s my fathered ushered my brother, siblings, and I into a life of performance via the California Variedad circuit. Although it was enriching on many levels, my father was hard on us. Music was, for the most part, in preparation for the stage. His emphasis on the professionalization of music made it so that music often lost its joyous meaning.

In the late 1990s my father's home teachings and ethics around the staged spectacle were challenged when I came across the East Los Angeles Chicano activists, music, and art scene. It was at the height of Pete Wilson's anti-immigrant policies, Proposition 187, the aftermath of the Los Angeles uprising and neoliberal push that set the community of artists and activists in motion. Most significant was the Mayan Zapatista uprising in 1994, which encouraged new social movement approaches. My values and perceptions of art shifted from *product*-based to *process*-based art interactions. Art as a messaging tool would not suffice and we began to develop participatory modes of art making beyond the confines of capital logic. Inspired by the Zapatista organizing methods of dialogue via *encuentros,* we began to search and develop modes of participatory music and dance practices. The goal was not to create "political art" to sell or disseminate, but rather to engage in creative processes with community to initiate dialogue, dialogue that might lead to critical action. Whether or not there was an outcome, product, or art object at the end of the art practice was not a concern. One of the most important cultural convening methods that we borrowed to supplant community involvement and dialogue, was the participatory music and dance practice native to the state of Veracruz Mexico known as fandango.

In the winter of 2015 my siblings Gabriel and Claudia and I gathered our individual and collective memories to create *Caminos y Canciones of the Gonzalez Family. Caminos y Canciones* was curated by Judy Mitoma and Beto Arcos and produced by Claudia Miranda (my sister) and Quetzal Flores for the Aratani World Music series. I resisted the creation of the show at first. My memories of growing up on stage weren't always pleasant. For me it was more than digging up musical repertoire and childhood memories to tell a story. It was exhuming the memory of my father and the trauma he inflicted. I think my siblings felt the same way and we were in agreement that we would not focus so much on my father but rather tell a story of the City Los Angeles we remembered as children.

The storyline of *Caminos y Canciones* was in stark contrast to the book manuscript I had been working on titled *Chican@ Artivistas: East Los Angeles Trenches Transborder Tactics.*[2] My work as an academic thus far had been about discussing the role of music in community as opposed to music generated on the stage. My book is specifically about the contrast and tensions within these varying spaces along with the ethics and the social and economic parameters that delineate these spheres. *Chican@ Artivistas* quite simply narrates the changing conceptions of music over time. That is to say, along with all the theorizing I perform in the book manuscript, I am quite simply undoing the lessons my father taught us about music and the stage, including his emphasis on the importance of "high professional" in music. After living a lifetime in the East Los Angeles Chican@ music and art movement of the 1990s and experiencing transnational organizing via the fandango movement, my mind was reoriented to other ways in which art and music could be exercised in one's life. These cultural convening methods and experiences had slowly displaced my father's early lessons. Although I tried not to diminish the performative staged spectacle in my book manuscript, "the stage" as a transformative space did take a backseat to the musical work I felt was being done in fandango.

In this essay I am interested in comparing and discussing the possibilities, limitations, tensions, and liberatory exercises in both the fandango and the staged spectacle as I have experienced both within the great city of Los Angeles. The Variedad circuit was by all accounts a business venture. Promoters, theaters, and the vast network of presenters and artists banked on an immigrant people's nostalgia and desire to hold memory as disenfranchised Mexican communities flocked to see the Variedades. Similarly I find that the fandango builds on a people's need to belong to a community and the desire to express oneself within and among them. Both worlds rely on nostalgia and the desire to connect as community. As all things Mexican and immigrant are under fire these days, I ask, which music world is most valuable for Los Angeles? Which one keeps our Mexicano histories and communities intact? Which music world is more inclusive and in this way most transformative for Mexican communities? My deliberation is motivated by my desire to not only articulate the ethical differences between fandango and the stage spectacle but also establish a conversation between them. Ultimately, we are all hailed, in some way or another, into an understanding of music by varying social institutions, be they family or popular media. My hope is that my interrogation of both worlds will highlight how our understanding of music is a social construction and demonstrate how we have the power to change, alter, or, at the very least, acknowledge how music is arranged in our individual and collective lives.

A BRIEF HISTORY OF *SON JAROCHO,* FANDANGO, AND *EL NUEVO MOVIMIENTO JARANERO*

Rooted in a history of colonization, labor exploitation, and resistance, the music, poetry, and dance of fandango–*son jarocho* emerged as a unique cultural mixture of African, Indigenous, and Spanish (Andalusia) influences. Mostly prominent in the region currently known as southern Veracruz, Mexico, fandango is currently exercised as ritual celebration in honor of a town's patron saint or as part of other community celebrations such as weddings, baptisms, and funerals. From fandango emerge the music, dance, and poetry known as the *son jarocho.* The *son jarocho* is manifested and maintained through the everyday practice of the *jaraneros* (musicians who play a small, eight-string, five-course guitar called a *jarana*), *versadores* (poets), and *bailadoras* (dancers). As a point of reference, the best-known *son jarocho* in the fandango repertoire is "La Bamba."

Communities within Veracruz and across the Mexican republic currently practice fandango. This, however, wasn't always the case. In the 1930s and as a result of the grueling Mexican revolution of 1910, Mexico went through a period of codifying its various music, food, and dance from every region in the Mexican republic. With the intent of promoting ideologies around modernity and progress, the national project took shape through the promotion of literature, tourism, and federally funded research of indigenous dances throughout the Mexican republic. The consolidation of cultures and creations of staged spectacles came to be performed in Mexico and abroad through *ballet folklórico* touring groups but mostly popularized through film (*La Época de Oro del Cine Mexicano*) and sound recordings. Indigenous music, culture, and traditions were altered to fit the attention span of theater, film, and radio audiences. This inevitably also reached Los Angeles, and Mexican communities in the US also mirrored the staged spectacles that were being performed by Mexican groups such as Lino Chavez and Andres Huesca.

In the late 1970s Gilberto Gutierrez, a young musician from Tres Zapotes, Veracruz, initiated El Nuevo Movimiento Jaranero with the help of Don Arcadio Hidalgo. This movement consciously strayed from the institutional and commercial canons that had previously represented the state of Veracruz to inform today's global society that the *son* is vibrant and born in fandango and should be valued and practiced by communities at large. El Nuevo Movimiento efforts marked the resurgence of fandango in rural and urban communities. Furthermore, Gilberto, with the help of his *son jarocho* group Mono Blanco, continuously perpetuated a discourse and recognition of the Indigenous, the Spanish, and in particular the African roots in the music and culture.

FANDANGO AESTHETIC AND *CONVIVENCIA* AS RADICAL ACTION AND THOUGHT

Put another way, participatory music and dance is more about the social relations being realized through the performance than about producing art that can somehow be abstracted from those social relations.

—THOMAS TURINO

Convivencia, or the deliberate act of being with each other as community, is a social, moral, and musical aesthetic of fandango practice and a central reason for the gathering. The reconceptualization of music as an activity rooted in *convivencia* is an important disruption in how we think of music in our present age. My use of *convivencia* as a moral and musical aesthetic in community music practice aims to bring focus on relationships and process rather than sounds, outcomes, or product.

After I was introduced to El Nuevo Movimiento Jaranero, I, along with many other Chicano musicians, was determined to share the fandango ethics and practice within our communities in Los Angeles. In 2003 we began to informally call this translocal dialogue *fandango sin fronteras*. In East Los Angeles, early efforts to establish fandango praxis in communities revolved around teaching the basic elements and protocols of the gathering. The goal was to get community acquainted with the practices while we simultaneously planned and fundraised to bring in fandango elders and more experienced practitioners to teach for an extended period of time. Individually and collectively, organizers and musicians such as Marco Amador, Russell Rodríguez, and Carolina Sarmiento, among other Chican@ *artivistas* and East LA bands, artists, poets, and musicians, contributed to the implementation and dialogue around the practice. These efforts, directly or indirectly, began to catch fire. For years to come the fandango practice spread. At present there are communities across the country that practice fandango ritual as important sites of gathering.

FANDANGO COMMUNITIES TO AND FRO

I must note that the musical dialogue, resources, and creative ideas flow in both directions. That is to say, *Jarochos* in Mexican communities have also enthusiastically initiated dialogue and music projects with Chicano communities by drawing on Chicano fandango practitioners from Los Angeles to join them in Veracruz during important holidays or fiesta times, or simply to collaborate on new recordings or performances. From grassroots efforts to state-funded concerts, Mexican and Chicano/Latinos have collaborated and performed extensively. Bay Area regions such as Oakland, Berkeley, and San Francisco have developed relationships with *jarocho* musicians such as Liche Oseguera, Patricio Hidalgo, and Andres Flores, enabling multiple grassroots residencies.

Multiple recording projects have also been significant. Produciones Cimarron, led by Rubi Oseguera, Marco Amador, and Liche Oseguera, produced and recorded the first ever *Encuentro de Leoneros* in Chacalapa Veracruz. Quetzal Flores, Dante Pascuzzo, and I were music producers for Son de Madera's *Las Orquestas del Día* (2003), funded by Xochi Flores. Since then, many Chicano/Latino musicians like La Marisoul from La Santa Cecilia, Jacob Hernandez, Juan Perez, Federico Zuniga, Russell Rodríguez, and myself have participated as core or invited members for touring groups, grassroots community cooperatives, and countless sound recordings.

East LA–based, Guadalupe Custom Strings coowner Gabriel Tenorio produced, arranged, and musically directed *La Conga de Patricio Hidalgo,* which featured many Chicano/Latino artists from Los Angeles. Most recently *Jarocho* transplant Cesar Castro began a *Jarocho* Chicano group, Cambalache, with his wife, Xochi Flores, a Chicana from Los Angeles. They are scheduled to release their second independent album, titled *Constelacion de Sonidos.*

TRANSBORDER MESHWORKS AS SOCIAL MOVEMENT: A METHOD TO THE MADNESS

"Transmigration" and "meshwork" are useful terms to describe *fandango sin fronteras* networks as they disrupt the social science focus on binaries (global/national, local/transnational) and, instead, make visible the material survival strategies within the various communities. Chican@ *artivista* and *Jarocho* community-building methods are reminiscent of transmigrant communities in Oaxaca, California, and Oregon. Socialist Lynn Stephen utilizes the concept of *transborder* to explain how indigenous transmigrant communities have always crossed "racial, ethnic, linguistic, and class boundaries between Mexico and the United States" in both northern and southern directions.[3] Transmigrants can generally be defined as those persons who, "having migrated from one nation-state to another, live their lives across borders, participating simultaneously in social relations that embed them in more than one nation-state."[4] Transborder or transmigrant, along with Arturo Escobar's concept of "meshwork," is generally about understanding the interlinked networks migrant communities are developing as a result of globalization, for both terms emphasize fluid forms and ever-changing strategies of survival. As "meshwork" emphasizes, transmigrant communities are "self-organizing, and grow in unplanned directions; they are made up of diverse elements; and exist in hybridized forms with other hierarchies and *meshworks.*" Furthermore, "they accomplish the articulation of heterogeneous elements without imposing uniformity and they are determined by the degree of connectivity that enables them to become self-sustaining."[5]

The transmigration between Mexican and US fandango communities has been extensive and has grown in unplanned directions. This has made every fandango community unique at present, not only in terms of origin and respective histories but also by the ways in which they organize among themselves and between varying sites. From San Diego to the Bay Area every major city in California is now linked in one way or another to a community or performance group of *fandangueros* in Mexico. Finally, the vast fandango network has been beneficial to both US and Mexican communities. Master practitioners or groups can book entire tours traveling from one city to the next via the informal networks by announcing their engagements on Facebook or via email.

Although Chicana/o *artivista* musicians have historically used the tools of music, art, and other forms of creative expression for political purposes, through fandango we were able to engage with community on a level outside of Western "performance" culture. As a professional musician, I acknowledge the effects a great concert or sound recording can have on an audience, community, or society as a whole. Performance in the most traditional sense can have the ability to incite critical thought, which can eventually lead to social change. However, fandango as a transgenerational, participatory music, poetry, and dance practice enacts individual and communal empowerment in a most exceptional way. The physical and ideological formation democratizes music in a way that disrupts how music functions in capitalist societies. Fandango, in essence, is *the* social change.

Fandango, and particularly the *convivencia* inherent in the practice, incites dialogue in its constituents, which can lead to greater analysis of music in society and one's role in it. It is no coincidence that we see more than one fandango site use the tools of the music (*son jarocho*) and fandango, to build around issues and struggles. Fandango practice and the embodiment of the practice are able to instigate dialogue and critical consciousness among its practitioners. In a small town in Northeast LA we have El Sereno's grassroots community space called the Eastside Café, which holds *son jarocho* classes once a week. In Santa Ana, Son del Centro has utilized *son jarocho* and fandango practice in support of immigrant rights, May Day marches, the Immokalee workers strike, and other related local and international struggles. In Seattle, Washington, the Seattle Fandango Project (SFP) organizes fandangos and workshops in women's shelters, food justice events, preschools, elementary schools, and high schools.

In San Diego the Fandango Fronterizo, or Border Fandango, is a yearly event initiated in 2008 at the US-Mexican border, whereby two *tarimas* are placed on each side of the fence as US and Mexican participants engage in fandango ritual. By managing to hold a fandango at the border, the sociality of sound temporarily wills the border out of existence. Indeed in the case of the Fandango Fronterizo, embodied practices are "an episteme, a praxis, a way of knowing as well as a way of storing and transmitting cultural knowledge and identity that is not adherent to political or nation-state boundaries."[6]

Fandango practice is ever growing in communities and initiating new generations. Through the efforts of El Nuevo Movimiento Jaranero and Chicano/a *artivistas* in East LA, *fandango sin fronteras* continues to thrive. It is through *fandango sin fronteras* efforts that a new generation of fandango practitioners can readily fathom music as more than just another product you buy or sell in our society. Music can also be a pastime, a much needed *convivencia,* and the language of ones community.

CAMINOS Y CANCIONES OF THE FAMILIA GONZALEZ

El Nuevo Movimiento Jaranero, or the New Jarana Movement, strayed from *son jarocho* as solely a staged spectacle in order to remind their communities that music as *convivencia* was what mattered most. As the brief history and origins of the fandango movement in the United States demonstrate, there have been many hands on deck to create the fandango movement. The East LA community trenches have been hailed into fandango practice/ritual. As stated above my first music experience was quite different.

My life in music begins with my brother Gabriel Gonzalez, who as a child was swept up in the Mexican Variedad circuit that frequented the state of California from the late 1970s. The Variedad circuit was an important cultural and economic entity to both artists and their respective Mexican communities, as up-and-coming traveling Mexican artists would perform across cities and hubs delivering a "taste of home" for Mexican migrants. When in Los Angeles the Variedades would often make stops at the historic Million Dollar Theater in Downtown LA. On these tours *Gabrielito Gonzalez y la actuacion infantil* quickly became part of this historic musical moment. As the younger sisters of Gabrielito Gonzalez, my sister and I were expected to accompany my brother. The Variedades hosted up-and-coming as well as established artist such as Juan Gabriel, Aida Cuevas, Mercedes Castro, La Sonora Santanera, Yolanda del Rio, Lucha Villa, Felipe Arriaga, Adalberto "Resortes" Martínez, and David Reynosa, to name a few.

Preparing for *Caminos y Canciones of the Familia Gonzalez* was an exercise in muscle memory. We pulled on selective memory and repertoire to tell our family story. It was corporeal. Revisiting old repertoire, rearranging harmony parts, and rehearsing night after night with my siblings was gratifying but hard work. My vocal range had to improve. Rock music performance had taken me somewhere else and I had to once again sing from that guttural mariachi place. It was a family affair, as we even recruited our children to participate in the show. Most of our children had shown interest in music early on and we thought it might be nice to show the next generation of Gonzalezes. Quickly my father's sense of perfection was mirrored onto our children. Unlike my father's treatment of us, we made sure we did not approach our children in the same way. Although we were demanding of them, we were conscious that they were children and considered the kinds of memory we wanted to instill in them. Our children played together and ran around rehearsal halls and backstage wings just as we had. Watching them interact with us and among one another as cousins backstage and on stage reignited our memories even more vividly.

Throughout the creation of our family story, I could not help but think how every narrative line was challenging my academic book manuscript. As an academic I quickly realized *Caminos y Canciones* was an important historical intervention. The *caminos,* or "roads," we described were paved with songs that held deep histories. In this way, through our families musical repertoire and narration we were documenting yet another Los Angeles immigrant story. Multiple scholars have noted Mexican immigrant people's music repertoire of important cultural, economic, racial, and political significance (Loza, Sanchez, Kun, Lipsitz, Gonzalez, Habell-Pallan, Viesca).[7] Encoding these stories and the musical repertoire, we learned a bit more about the economic and social conditions of immigrant communities in Los Angeles, particularly a Downtown Los Angeles that is slowly disappearing but nevertheless unforgotten. The end of the Variedad circuit was taking place post Pinochet's Chile, the height of Reagonomics, and the neoliberal push. Rampant was the idea that anything could be bought or sold, including dissent, culture, and even rebellion.

My siblings and I delivered a debut, sold-out show on May 28, 2016, in Little Tokyo's Aratani Theater. To my surprise, much like fandango, *Caminos y Canciones* was cathartic for many. Much like in the throes of fandango, we had audience members singing along, crying, and participating from their seats. Audience testimony that was shared with us after the performance was gratifying. According to some, we reignited memories for others and not just our own. By the end of creating and performing *Caminos y Canciones,* my views about the staged spectacle had changed. The process and creation of *Caminos y Canciones* was transformative for my family and the audience that attended the concert. I had somewhat demonized the stage, even as I had built my life around it. In the end and with the creation of *Caminos y Canciones,* I realized that my father's teachings did *teach* me something. My father's apprenticeship style and value system had overshadowed the fundamental beauty and content of music. But as we excavated the history and memories among us as siblings, we realized why my father had believed music was relegated to the stage. He himself was caught in a web of ideology based on nostalgia and belonging. Perhaps he believed that success through the professionalization in music might have brought him economic capital, prestige, and respect. Maybe it was his version of the American Dream and a way of staying connected to the Mexico he missed so much? Perhaps he was vicariously trying to live through us—his children?

Whatever the reason, I am thankful for my East LA rebel artist communities that continued a trajectory of resistance previously established, for they gave me another side of what music and art could be. Music is not the soundtrack to the movement. It *is* the movement and we have a responsibility to create, nurture, and build new music spaces.

CONCLUSION

The fact is music is a social construction and we must recognize the current arrangements under globalized capitalism and how this has had a bearing on our daily existence. Like food, music is transactional and mostly consumed in our society. We buy or we sell music. I believe we must also "grow our own" from time to time. It is a human right and we must build community music spaces and not just consume what the market sells us. We must acknowledge that we have the power to create and direct what we subject our souls to. Through my experience in both worlds I realized that the transformative space that matters most is not the fandango or the stage, but perhaps *the body,* the body in relation to other bodies and how they engage to shape communities. The body is stimulated in varying ways in this great city creating transformative memories in us all and memory never vacates the body. Memory becomes the foundation of the body and how all other human experiences will be received. It can be healthy and generative or it can be divisive and traumatic. Either way we have a responsibility to our humanity and creative selves.

My discussion has been to simply supplant the idea that we must be proactive in our music experiences and understand there are a plethora of musical fronts. I mostly encourage our acknowledgment and active participation in them. Los Angeles will never cease to invite subjects to dream, to remember, to stay, or to flee. The beauty is that whether you are on the stage or in the midst of community, you can experience both right here in LA. I predict that performance-based culture will never cease to be an important cultural and economic venture. To be sure Los Angeles will never cease to be an important site that will generate great musicians and performers. However, Los Angeles is also steadily becoming an important site of participatory music and dance practices that are generating, strengthening, and transforming the city from the entertainment capital of the world to the premier grassroots participatory music and dance trenches in the United States.

NOTES

1. George Sanchez, *Becoming Mexican American: Ethnicity, Culture and Identity in Chicano Los Angeles, 1900–1945* (Oxford: Oxford University Press 1993).

2. Martha Gonzalez, *Chican@ Artivistas: East Los Angeles Trenches Transborder Tactics* (unpublished manuscript).

3. Lynn Stephen, *Transborder Lives: Indigenous Oaxacans in Mexico, California, and Oregon* (Durham: Duke University Press, 2007), xv.

4. Ibid., 19.

5. Ibid.

6. Diana Taylor, *The Archive and the Repertoire: Performing Cultural Memory in the Americas* (Durham: Duke University Press, 2003), xv.

7. Martha Gonzalez, "Zapateado Afro-Chicana Fandango Style: Self Reflective Moments in Zapateado," in *Dancing across Borders: Danzas y Bailes Mexicanos,* ed. Olga Najera-Ramirez, Norma Cantu, and Brenda Romero (Champaign-Urbana: University of Illinois Press, 2008); Sanchez, *Becoming Mexican American;* Victor Viesca, "The Battle of Los Angeles: The Cultural Politics of Chicana/o Music in the Greater Eastside," *American Quarterly* 56, no. 3 (2004): 719–39; Michcelle Habell-Pallán, *Loca Motion: The Travels of Chicana and Latina Popular Culture* (New York: New York University Press, 2005); G. Lipsitz, "Cruising around the Historical Bloc: Postmodernism and Popular Music in East Los Angeles," *Cultural Critique* 5 (1986): 157–77; Josh Kun, "The Aesthetics of Allá: Listening Like a Sonidero," in *Audible Empire: Music Global Politics, Critique,* ed. Ronald Radano and Tejumola Olaniyan (Durham: Duke University Press, 2016).

CONTRIBUTORS

LUIS ALFARO is an associate professor at the USC School of Dramatic Arts. He is a Chicano writer/performer known for his work in poetry, theater, short stories, performance, and journalism. He is the first-ever resident playwright of the Oregon Shakespeare Festival, courtesy of an Andrew W. Mellon Foundation grant, and the recipient of a John D. and Catherine T. MacArthur Foundation fellowship.

BETTO ARCOS is a radio journalist, music critic, and contributor to NPR and PRI-BBC's *The World*. Since 2002, he created a musical component for two courses at Harvard University's Divinity School. Betto has been lecturing on Latin American Music to midlevel career diplomats at the Foreign Service Institute.

XÓCHITL C. CHÁVEZ is an assistant professor at University of California, Riverside, in the Department of Music. She is a scholar of expressive culture and performance, specializing in indigenous communities from southern Mexico and transnational migration, where her current work and ethnographic documentary short titled *Booming Bandas of Los Ángeles* focus on second-generation Zapotec brass bands in Los Angeles County. Dr. Chávez has also collaborated with the Smithsonian Institution as a digital curator and content specialist for the Smithsonian Latino Center Mobile Broadcast Series in creating a digital repository of Latino/a stories since 2014.

WALTER AARON CLARK is a professor of musicology at UC Riverside and the founder and director of the Center for Iberian and Latin American Music there. He is the author or editor of numerous groundbreaking books on Spanish and Latin American music. In 2016, King Felipe VI of Spain awarded him the title of Knight Commander of the Order of Isabel the Catholic.

BRIAN CROSS is a photographer and filmmaker from Limerick, Ireland. He has made several films about Brazilian music, including *Brasilintime: Batucada com Discos.* His first book, *It's Not about a Salary: Rap, Race and Resistance in Los Angeles,* was published by Verso in 1993; his latest photo book, *Ghostnotes: Music of the Unplayed,* will be published by University of Texas Press in 2017. He is currently an assistant professor in Visual Arts at the University of California, San Diego.

CINDY GARCÍA is an associate professor, dance theorist, performance ethnographer, and playwright in the Department of Theatre Arts and Dance at the University of Minnesota. Her book *Salsa Crossings: Dancing Latinidad in Los Angeles* (Duke University Press, 2013) addresses the politics of social performances of Mexican-ness, latinidad, and migration in Los Angeles salsa clubs.

DAVID F. GARCIA is associate professor of Ethnomusicology at the University of North Carolina, Chapel Hill. He is the author of *Listening for Africa: Freedom, Modernity, and the Logic of Black Music's African Origins* (Duke University Press, 2017) and *Arsenio Rodríguez and the Transnational Flows of Latin Popular Music* (Temple University Press, 2006).

MARTHA GONZALEZ is a Chicana *artivista* (artist/activist) musician, feminist music theorist, and assistant professor in the Intercollegiate Department of Chicana/o Latina/o Studies at Scripps/Claremont College. She is a Fulbright fellow (2007–08), Ford fellow (2012–13), and Woodrow Wilson fellow (2016–17), and her academic interest in music has been fueled by her own musicianship as a singer/songwriter and percussionist for Grammy Award–winning band Quetzal.

AGUSTÍN GURZA is an award-winning music journalist (*Los Angeles Times, OC Register*), and writer and editor for the Chicano Studies Research Center at the University of California, Los Angeles. He is the author of *The Arhoolie Foundation's Strachwitz Frontera Collection of Mexican and Mexican American Recordings* (UCLA Chicano Studies Research Center Press, 2012).

CAROL A. HESS teaches at the University of California, Davis. She has received the ASCAP-Deems Taylor Award, the American Musicological Society's Robert M. Stevenson Award for Outstanding Scholarship in Iberian Music, and the Society for American Music's Irving Lowens Award, among other awards. Her most recent book is *Representing the Good Neighbor: Music, Difference, and the Pan-American Dream.*

JOHN KOEGEL, professor of Musicology at California State University, Fullerton, researches musical life in California, Mexican American and Mexican music, and musical theater. His book *Music in German Immigrant Theater: New York City, 1840–1940* received the Irving Lowens Book Award of the Society for American Music (2011) and was a finalist for the Theater Library Association's Freedley Award (2010). Koegel was awarded a NEH Research Fellowship for his in-progress book *Musical Theater in Mexican Los Angeles, 1850–1950,* and his articles and reviews appear in journals, dictionaries, and encyclopedias in the United States, Mexico, Spain, and Britain.

JOSH KUN is professor in the Annenberg School for Communication and the Department of American Studies and Ethnicity at the University of Southern California, where he directs the Popular Music Project of the Norman Lear Center. He is an author and editor of several books, including *Songs in the Key of Los Angeles, To Live and Dine in L.A.,* and the American Book Award–winning *Audiotopia: Music, Race, and America.* As a curator and artist, he has worked with SFMOMA, the Getty Foundation, the California African American Museum, the Grammy Museum, Los Angeles Public Library, Institute of Contemporary Art Los Angeles, Contemporary Jewish Museum, ASU Art Museum, and others. He is a 2016 MacArthur Fellow.

CAROLINA A. MIRANDA is a staff writer for the *Los Angeles Times,* where she covers art, architecture, and culture—from museums to murals and art books to comic books, as well as regular dispatches on Latino and Latin American popular culture. In addition to the *Times,* her stories have appeared in *Time, National Public Radio,* and *ARTnews.*

HANS ULRICH OBRIST (b. 1968, Zurich, Switzerland) is artistic director of the Serpentine Galleries, London. Prior to this, he was the curator of the Musée d'Art Moderne de la Ville de Paris. Since his first show, *World Soup* (*The Kitchen Show*), in 1991, he has curated more than three hundred shows.

GABRIEL REYES-WHITTAKER is an electronic musician, composer, producer, DJ, and musical historian. He is most widely known for his work using the pseudonym GB (Gifted & Blessed). Though his music ranges widely stylistically, he classifies his work under the umbrella term "technoindigenous studies," which is representative of the integration of the technological with the spiritual and ancestral.

ALEXANDRA T. VAZQUEZ is associate professor in the Department of Performance Studies at New York University. Her book *Listening in Detail: Performances of Cuban Music* (Duke University Press, 2013) won the American Studies Association's Lora Romero Book Prize. Vazquez's work has been featured in the journals *American Quarterly, small axe, Social Text, women and performance,* and the *Journal of Popular Music Studies*, and in the edited volumes *Nonstop Metropolis: A New York City Atlas, Reggaeton,* and *Pop When the World Falls Apart.*

INDEX

NOTE: Page numbers in *italics* denote illustrations.